THE MISERY OF INTERNATIONAL LAW

The Misery of International Law

Confrontations with Injustice in the Global Economy

JOHN LINARELLI,
MARGOT E SALOMON,
and
MUTHUCUMARASWAMY SORNARAJAH

OXFORD
UNIVERSITY PRESS

OXFORD
UNIVERSITY PRESS

Great Clarendon Street, Oxford, OX2 6DP,
United Kingdom

Oxford University Press is a department of the University of Oxford.
It furthers the University's objective of excellence in research, scholarship,
and education by publishing worldwide. Oxford is a registered trade mark of
Oxford University Press in the UK and in certain other countries

First Edition published in 2018

Published in the United States of America by Oxford University Press
198 Madison Avenue, New York, NY 10016, United States of America

British Library Cataloguing in Publication Data
Data available

Library of Congress Control Number: 2017947319

ISBN 978–0–19–875395–7

John dedicates this book to his wife Lina, who knows a lot about justice, and to his son John Shih Shin, whose generation will have to deliver it.
Margot dedica questo libro, con amore e gratitudine, al suo marito, alla loro figlia e sua Nonna.
Sorna dedicates this book to Ahila.

John Linarelli is Professor of Commercial Law at Durham University, co-directs the Institute for Commercial and Corporate Law at Durham, and is a member of the Centre for Law and Global Justice at Durham.

Margot E Salomon is Associate Professor in the Department of Law at the London School of Economics and Political Science and directs the interdisciplinary Laboratory for Advanced Research on the Global Economy at LSE Human Rights.

Muthucumaraswamy Sornarajah is CJ Koh Professor of Law at the National University of Singapore.

Preface

This book started as an idea discussed over dinner after a lecture by M Sornarajah ('Sorna') at an event on 31 October 2013 at the LSE Laboratory for Advanced Research on the Global Economy entitled, 'Greed, Humanity and the Neoliberal Retreat in International Law'. Sorna gave the lecture and John and Margot were commentators, the latter also the convener. The dinner conversation after the event was very much in the mold of 'we really do approach the issues in very different ways but usually reach similar conclusions', even if we disagreed on the central point as to whether there was in fact a neoliberal retreat in international law! The conversation moved to how stimulating, albeit challenging, a book co-authored by the three of us would be to write. We agreed to write it anyway and met for many absorbing afternoons to discuss, debate, and rediscover the topics and approaches that have animated our separate scholarship and would be developed in a collective work interrogating the problems of socio-economic injustice found in contemporary international law.

We think our willingness to take a chance has paid off with a book we hope you, dear reader, will find as engaging to read as it was to write. John Linarelli is a legal scholar with longstanding interests in taking the philosophical literature on global justice to the next step of making it more sensitive to institutional design, focusing his work on moral questions relevant to the institutional architecture for the global economy. He also works in the political economy tradition. Margot Salomon is a human rights law scholar focusing on legal dimensions of world poverty and on international law and development. Her work falls within a tradition of applied critical theory, if the concept of 'tradition' suits the varied counter-hegemonic approaches her scholarship takes on. Sorna is a pre-eminent international investment law scholar, having written both textbooks and definitive works on investment law problems facing low and middle-income countries. Sorna was very much present at the earliest days of the New International Economic Order. So, in this book you will find a rich disciplinary mix of international law, economics, history, moral philosophy, political economy, and critical development studies. We have avoided labels such as 'interdisciplinary' or 'multidisciplinary' for this work and will let readers decide if this methodological point requires an answer. What was of interest to us, from our very first conversations in that London restaurant, was how we were going to go about normatively critiquing the regimes of international law relevant to the global economy. It was our conviction, then as now, that international law must be evaluated for the ways in which it fails to respect the lives of persons harmed by the global economic order that it helps constitute. We have sought to expose some tall tales and accepted wisdom, and to make visible and central the disenfranchised of international law. To these ends, we saw our divergent approaches as a challenge to be embraced and not an obstacle to be overcome. We hope our book engages you, calls some settled convictions into question, and even generates disagreements so necessary for scholarly debate eventually to work itself into law and policy.

John, Margot, and Sorna
December 2017

Contents

1

The Legal Rendering of Immiseration

Immiseration: the act of making miserable; especially impoverishment

Merriam-Webster Dictionary

The international economic order is unjust. It continues to reflect the dominance of certain states and to favour their interests while upholding a system of ideas and practices that extends their privileges. The international economic order cannot be justified on grounds of respect for persons, particularly those it harms or for whom life prospects are diminished. This book is preoccupied with the role of international law in advancing this harmful economic order; it is preoccupied with the ways in which international law operates at the service of injustice. International law alone cannot end underdevelopment and eradicate poverty and unjustifiable material inequality, but it is a precondition of achieving those objectives that the means by which law creates wrongs are removed. For all the alleged benefits of the post-war turn to a rules-based system international law is still used as a cloak for pernicious commercial expansion. International economic law's processes are coercive, based on a notion of justice as the will of the stronger and its principal mechanisms and institutions fail to meet the reasonable expectations of those whose lives are regulated by the law. As for outcomes, it enriches the few at the expense of everyone else, it wrongs women with particular efficiency, and it is environmentally destructive and unsustainable. It is one matter to be concerned with violations of international law and another to be concerned with the law itself. This book turns its attention to the latter in an effort to demonstrate how the truth about the role and effects of the law fail adequately to inform it.

The moral disorder of international economic law contradicts what is expected of it, so the place to begin is with the pathologies of international law and why international law is subject to requirements of justice when it operates in the areas of trade, investment, and finance. Chapter 2 ('Confronting the Pathologies of International Law') offers an argument as to why principles of justice apply to contemporary international law. The account of justice for international law set forth in Chapter 2 puts in tension the long history of ostensible claims about justice that have forever animated international law. For too long justice has performed the task of dressing up power to secure its objectives of domination.

The Misery of International Law: Confrontations with Injustice in the Global Economy, John Linarelli, Margot E Salomon, and M Sornarajah. © John Linarelli, Margot E Salomon, and M Sornarajah 2018. Published 2018 by Oxford University Press.

The injustice of the current economic order is reliant on regimes of international law and their instrumental usage. In important ways this has always been the case. The origins of international law were rooted in empire and injustice against distant peoples. Much of that law began in justification of the imperial rule of a European minority over the large majority of the people of Africa, Asia, and Latin America. Successive rationalizations given for colonization and subjugation to imperial rule are constitutive of the genesis and history of international law. The singularly significant modern effort to liberate the Second and Third Worlds from the implications of that history came in the form of the New International Economic Order (NIEO), as Chapter 3 ('The End of Empire and the Search for Justice: NIEO and Beyond') explores. But for all the NIEO's relevance to our understanding of the pursuit of economic justice under international law, the Western world into which those efforts emerged after the ending of imperial rule did not recognize their objectives—objectives that did not even attempt to disrupt a market-oriented international law but merely to expand the range of states that would benefit from it.

The rationalization for the spread of commerce in our age of globalization remains not very different from those given in the days of imperial expansion and colonization just as its beneficiaries remain those states with power and their private corporations. As we see in Chapters 4 ('International Trade'), 5 ('Foreign Investment'), and 6 ('Global Finance'), contemporary international law in the area of trade, but also foreign investment and global finance suffer from various pathologies as a result of the historical rationalities inherited from prior eras. The continued instrumental use of international law is dedicated to capitalist expansion and draws on the unproven claims that trade and investment promote economic development and is a panacea for the ills of poverty. As for the global financial architecture, it is an institutional order to govern the wealth of a community but does so in a way that imposes needless risk and makes the rich richer and the poor poorer. This use of international law provides for 'accumulation by dispossession',[1] a movement of wealth from poor to rich, and from the public to the private, all the while leaving a host of ensuing immiserations in its wake.

Today, international law—from international economic regulation to human rights—is shaped by an economic project premised on the private accumulation of transnational capital, and on its arrogation of the common wealth, social values, and the structures that sustain them. Capitalism as practised reflects a primacy of economic values with its rapacious logic of expansion and uncompromising commitment to profit. In the search for profit, economic growth fails to take inclusivity, fairness, and sustainability into account and the ways in which it may lead to an increase in poverty and other immiserations. In furthering the values of this particular economic project, the regimes of international economic law rely on the fabricated bifurcation, both in theory and institutional practice, of distinct economic and (so-called) non-economic realms.

[1] In the incisive words of David Harvey, *A Brief History of Neoliberalism* (OUP 2005).

International law has always been predicated on private property and commodification and so the social and political values that are constitutive of economies as much as property and contract have been forsaken. The process of fragmentation that has taken place has the economic spheres insulated from other areas of international law such as human rights which—if appositely considered—contain values that may further the interests of society. Today, as always, the global economy is structured around the interests of the rich and the managers of capital, and the easiest way to defend the status quo, as Ha-Joon Chang rightly notes, 'is to say that there is a sacred area called the economy, and then to place within this area everything you want, especially those things you do not want to be changed'.[2] Post-war international institutions were deliberately built upon this bifurcation, and one that decades later any reasonable account of justice is still struggling to see transcended. The separation of the economic and 'non-economic' realms is constantly reinforced through this institutional intermediation. These conceptions reveal a serious flaw about basic market institutions. Human rights and the conditions for justice are not exceptions or worse, breaches of the rules of the market, they are, rather, constitutive of markets, just as rules about contract and property are. The formal modes of reconciling the fragmentation of international law are reflective of this enduring split.[3]

The interests that international economic law was set up to serve have kept social considerations far removed. In so far as the international economic law regimes are concerned,[4] the argument that is still generally vended is that it is their ethos that

[2] H-J Chang in Conversation with J Curtis, 'History, Law and the Myth of Economic Neutrality' Series on Economics and Law in Conversation, Laboratory for Advanced Research on the Global Economy, Centre for the Study of Human Rights, LSE (July 2016) 6, http://www.lse.ac.uk/humanRights/research/projects/theLab/Economics-and-Law-in-Conversation---Interview-with-Ha-Joon-Chang---FINAL.pdf

[3] See, M Koskenniemi et al, Report of the Study Group of the International Law Commission, *Fragmentation of International Law: Difficulties Arising from the Diversification and Expansion of International Law*, International Law Commission, 58th session, General Assembly, A/CN.4/L.682, 13 Apr 2006; cf J Harrison, 'The Case for Investigative Legal Pluralism in the International Economic Law Linkages Debate: A Strategy for Enhancing International Legal Discourse' (2014) 1 London Review of International Law 115 with a plea to avoid an artificial attempt at coherence and instead to expose how legal values may in fact be irreconcilable. See also M Koskenniemi, 'The Politics of International Law—20 Years Later' (2009) 20 EJIL 7, 9: 'Recent debates of global governance and especially international law's fragmentation have well demonstrated the emergence and operation of structural bias. … The point of creating such specialized institutions is precisely to affect the outcomes that are being produced in the international world.'

[4] As for the rules affecting financial globalization at the international level, they are a hodgepodge of norms that cannot always be classified as falling within recognized sources of international law. Be that as it may, the 'club rules' that form a good deal of international financial 'law' have a normative significance similar to that of officially recognized sources of law and deal with matters that are global. They are also subject to a variation of the fragmentation critique familiar to public international law given that global finance has bankers and financial interests as the real makers and beneficiaries of them, with everyone else effectively passive recipients. There are also institutions of international finance that fit within traditional structures and sources of international law, such as the intergovernmental Bretton Woods Institutions, though they play special roles and in some domains are now subordinate to institutions that produce extralegal norms that play an essential role in governing global finance.

When we use the term international economic law herein we are referring to the international law on trade, investment, and finance.

best supports other values, not least the realization of human rights and sustainable development. What we are told, still, is that the remedying of social ills will be served by 'the progressive removal of boundaries of all sorts'[5] and the private accumulation of capital: a neoliberal global economy is touted as coterminous with the aspirations of justice. But the alleged commitments, for example, to higher standards of living and full employment in international trade, to promises of economic development from foreign investment, and to sustainable development generally are among the unmet promises of the global economy. As for financial globalization, whatever overall welfare gains through economic growth are reputed to derive from the rules on banking and capital markets, no robust economic welfare aims are served.

Fragmentation has trade, investment, and finance effectively insulated from the values of international law that we might find in the fields of environment, human rights, the rights of indigenous peoples, and the protection of cultural property. In trade and investment, the movement has been to create distinct regimes with dedicated compliance mechanisms so that the instrumentality of international law could be made to operate in liberalizing trade and protecting investment. Regimes are developed in trade and investment through treaty principles and the expansionary interpretation of such treaty principles that further the objectives of the beneficiaries of neoliberal capitalism. In finance, most of the rules do not even rise to the level of hard international law, but are instead soft law norms created by powerful states that impose the cost of systemic risk on the majority of people in the world who reap few if any benefits from financial globalization. At the same time, there is a subversion of the areas that aspire directly to socio-economic and political security, principally international human rights law. The social conscience of international law—the regime of human rights law—while surely protecting some people from socio-economic harms as well as laying bare damaging structural features of the global economy, is in crucial ways also operating under the predilections of extreme global capitalism. Among the lamentable consequences is that human rights successes are serving to sustain some of capitalism's most destructive tendencies. The insulation provided by the fragmentation of international law facilitates the furthering of neoliberal objectives with little account being taken of other objectives—moral, social, collective, human. All the while, the general ubiquity and dominance of neoliberal capitalism results in it undergirding international human rights in significant ways, serving further to bolster neoliberal values. We introduce this line of inquiry below and address it more fully in Chapter 7 ('Human Rights').

International law has also shown itself to be deeply hypocritical given the nature and scope of the internal economic interventions it allows. Transnational economic regulation penetrates deep within the state—especially within weaker and poorer states South and North—and impacts extensively on social and economic policy, whereas poverty and underdevelopment are all too easily said to arise largely from

[5] W Streeck, *How Will Capitalism End?: Essays on a Failing System* (Verso 2016) 201, 225.

factors endogenous to those states, ignoring the influences of both history and globalization. What we have is the legally sanctioned deep penetration of international commercial intervention that nonetheless allocates matters of justice and remedies for globalization's 'collateral damage' to the internal affairs of the poor state. Even the turn to 'national ownership' in confronting poverty in developing countries is a double-edged sword: it leaves national governments to toil at the domestic level while their possibilities are shaped in many ways by the strictures of global capitalism. This hypocrisy prevails in the area of foreign investment protection, as Chapter 5 demonstrates. Here international law intrudes into an internal process and externalizes it by demanding conformity with imposed standards of treatment, ensuring that the state has to sublimate its essential national interests to the protection of the foreign investment or face the heavy cost of arbitration and the possibility of an even heavier burden by way of an award for damages against it. That the new Sustainable Development Goals (SDGs) situate social protection systems including social protection floors largely within the 'national' domain offers another case in point. 'Policy space' and 'national ownership' properly understood are not meant to leave the solutions to poor (or insolvent) countries while the international structural impediments that delimit those solutions remain firmly in place. As the chapter on human rights contends, in international human rights law the most radical area to confront this double standard—the juridical elaboration of extraterritorial human rights obligations in the area of development—has also been the most politically contentious area and the least operationalized precisely because of the challenge it poses to global capitalism and the interests of influential states.

Both past and present we can find the imposition of two distinct normative orders. Historically there were two core normative principles at work, one justifying force abroad and the other justifying contract. Force was accepted by Europeans as the natural order of things when they encountered non-European peoples, whereas they engaged in treaty-making between themselves—essentially through the contractual notion of *pacta sunt servanda*. Today, duplicitous normative forces are also at work. What is referred to in Chapter 4 as the 'inside–outside distinction' looks at the basic structural problems associated with trade agreements—their use of the contract approach—in which justice is a matter for inside the state only and what happens outside is subject at most to very basic minimum moral demands. The inside–outside distinction also highlights how there are dispossessions and alienations acceptable when undertaken abroad, while these same acts are proscribed at home. The current practice is of two (somewhat) different forms of capitalism, one for compatriots and quite another for foreigners abroad. These two different forms of economic policy can also be seen as between the domestic policies of sovereign creditors and the requirements they impose as lenders on European debtor nations. There is no pan-European compatriotism when it comes to the treatment of debtor nations, as the analysis of the European debt crisis in Chapter 6 demonstrates. Across international legal regimes past and present we see the interests of the powerful applied under the legitimating shelter of law to the detriment of other peoples—laws or their application that would categorically be rejected at home: law for others.

In confronting these and other double standards this book takes a pluralist approach. We deconstruct the present state of affairs with the aim of exposing unconscionable dimensions of the global economic order, the false premises upon which it is built, and the role of international law in constituting and sustaining it. While not prescriptive, this book aims to compel the reader to think beyond existing assumptions and structures. This work has not been written in order to defend a liberal conception of justice or a radical one or anything in between; we are interested in offering a lucid account of the drivers of international law's inequities and the grounds for change. All is fair game: liberal conceptions clarify values and elucidate principles by which to uncover illegitimacy and dysfunction in international society. Radical approaches seek out the roots of exploitation and alienation and treat them as a premise for investing in fundamental transformative purchase. Where as liberalism can help us to challenge the system we have, radicalism reflects a readiness to pass beyond existing society towards a different one.[6] In so far as liberal, radical, or any other traditions shed light on the problems and their possible redress, this book is willing to engage those traditions. This book takes a synthetic approach drawing from different perspectives and methods, but reaches similar conclusions whichever approach is applied. And whichever approach is utilized, the aims remain the same: a sustained realignment of values, interests, and beneficiaries with what justice requires, dramatic improvement in the human condition, and effective change to those ends.[7]

Liberated from the constraints of one theoretical model or another, some parts of this book reflect a dedication to fixing some of the vilest tendencies of the system whereas others veer towards an overhaul of it. On other occasions—such as in Chapter 6—the proposals are relatively modest, but the dysfunction of the financial system by any standard of justice is so fantastic that any improvement would, on one definition, represent radical improvement. In offering a critique, this work points to a new direction of travel if justice, on any reasonable account, is to be served. But any prescriptions provided herein should be taken as a *beginning* to imaging new possibilities under international law, not an end. It may be that in some areas new rules and policies are needed to offer a meaningful alternative, in other areas what is needed are new interpretations of existing rules. In yet other areas we might want to see rejected the present frame altogether and embrace 'postdevelopment' proposals of non-economic possibilities[8] whereby, as JK Gibson-Graham and Arturo Escobar reason 'the domain of the economy is not so seemingly naturally and completely occupied by capitalism'.[9] As such, we do not

[6] This distinction is inspired by André Gorz in his description of the difference between 'subordinate and revolutionary reforms' in *Reclaiming Work: Beyond the Wage-based Society* (Polity 1999) 7.

[7] The approach of this book navigates the perennial tension and intractable dichotomy between the positions of radicals who denounce the legitimation that comes from efforts to improve the current system and those of reformers or pragmatists.

[8] On the parameters of postdevelopment, A Escobar, *Encountering Development: The Making and Unmaking of the Third World* (Princeton UP 1995 with preface to the 2012 edn).

[9] Here Escobar highlights the work of JK Gibson-Graham, *The End of Capitalism (As We Knew It)*, ibid xxxi. There are many models of economies 'not so completely occupied by capitalism'. See generally the work of Wolfgang Streeck.

suggest the broad-minded reader is limited merely to imagining the possibilities of 'globalization with a human face' or 'compassionate capitalism' but also, or perhaps instead, the possibility of reconstituting the brutal world if international law could be made to accommodate that undertaking.[10]

So, this book offers a grand synthesis on liberal and radical perspectives and variations therein, and is richer for that diversity. It also moves among the optimistic and the sceptical, even cynical, proclivities of the various authors on the prospects of international law to serve the cause of justice; the book is pluralist also in that sense. But where there is no pluralism and no diversity of views is on the extent to which the regimes of international law are immiserating and how, with considerable reflection also on the why. On this third dimension, both the history of international law and the pinpointing of current beneficiaries offer clear insights. There is also full consensus among the three authors on the impediments posed by international law and the urgent need for change in our institutional ordering in a manner that foregrounds justice. A relationship of accountability exists between the creators of international law and those affected by it. As Chapter 2 details, international law is subject to the robust demands of justice for reasons having to do with relationships,[11] structural features,[12] domination,[13] and historic wrongdoing.[14] From its role past and present as an institution essential to global endeavours to its effects on whether and how people live their lives, international law must be appraised according to demands of justice. With these aims in mind, we expose international law for what it is and for what it is not.

[10] Even taking care to avoid what Rawlsian-influenced political philosophers call 'unrealistic utopias' and sticking to ideas for change within the realm of human possibilities represents a great challenge still. See Chapter 2 ('Confronting the Pathologies of International Law') 41–43 including the practices that highlight the need for an equality promoting principle (international law should not create or perpetuate inequalities that cannot be morally justified. Instead what we have is the structuring of institutions so that the wealthy accumulate more wealth at the expense of the less well-off, which is an inequality aggravating principle); a freedom from domination principles or anti-alienation principle (international law should develop in a manner that does not challenge self-governance and self-determination of peoples and the autonomy of persons); and an anti-coercion principle (which provides for the moral impermissibility of economic coercion by powerful states against weaker states in the making and interpretation of international law governing the global economy).

[11] International law involves a pervasive and necessary kind of interaction between states, affecting the welfare and conditions for respect of people within states. International economic law is at work in the most fundamental sites of distribution within the state.

[12] The combination of international economic law in its present form and substance along with circumstances created by history, and the choices of governments and other agents historically and in the present, combine to produce a structure vulnerable to the perpetuation of injustice in the global economy.

[13] Domination can be understood as the capacity to interfere on an arbitrary basis in the choices of another. Terrible predations in the form of domination occur as transborder phenomena. Two canonical forms of domination, coercion and manipulation, affect the formation and interpretation of international law, with structural coercion coming from what is essentially mandatory participation in the global economy.

[14] This book has a prospective focus, looking to history not to establish a legal mechanism for reparations but for the normative features of international law in need of critique for revision.

1. Neoliberal Capitalism: Fact, Fiction, Harms, and Alienations

Neoliberalism represents a distinct ideology emphasizing the importance of some of the free market mechanisms of neoclassical economics expressed in policy terms—most particularly private enterprise (expressed in privatization), aggressive liberalized trade, investment, and finance (and the spread of globalization) and property rights and laissez-faire (expressed in so-called deregulation) and was a response to the spread of Keynesian economic intervention policies and socialist economic planning.[15] Its practice is also closely associated with labour market 'flexibility', austerity, and the dismantling of the welfare state.[16] In essence, neoliberal theory sees the market as best in meeting human needs and to those ends we have seen the construction of markets in land, labour, water, health, education, and much else. Neoliberalism treats everything as a commodity based on the view that markets and market signals can best determine all allocative decisions. This commodification, as David Harvey expresses it, 'presumes the existence of property rights over processes, things, and social relations, that a price can be put on them, and that they can be traded subject to legal contract. The market is presumed to work as an appropriate guide—an ethic—for all human action.'[17] Today, as in the height of the European conquest of the New World and its period of what Sven Beckert describes as 'war capitalism',[18] this market primacy requires that capital can roam the globe in search of profit maximization with far too little regard to other values; far-reaching and singularly-focused cross-border trade, investment, and finance are also thus defining features. To this is added a non-mobile, cheap, captive labour force available through restrictions on the free movement of people while extreme capital mobility when used to produce goods and services can move to where labour is cheapest. In the current era, this artificial comparative advantage is a direct result of international trade agreements.[19] Foreign investment law today offers its own particular package of neoliberal edicts that serve corporate interests almost exclusively: privatization policies (and the dismantling of public services), liberal provisions for the entry of foreign investment, definite protection of private property, the sanctity of contract, the equal treatment of local and foreign investment, a market-based compensation standard in the event of expropriation, and a compliance mechanism structured to give foreign investors unilateral access to external arbitration.[20] Dominating the global economic landscape is a neoliberal form of financial globalization. This extreme version of capitalism is reflected in

[15] See ME Salomon and C Arnott, 'Better Development Decision-Making: Applying International Human Rights Law to Neoclassical Economics' (2014) 32 Nordic Journal of Human Rights 44, 46.

[16] For a helpful history of neoliberalism in the context of development economics, see B Akbulut, F Adaman, and YM Madra, 'The Decimation and Displacement of Development Economics' (2015) 46 Development and Change 733, 737ff.

[17] Harvey (n 1) 165.

[18] S Beckert, *Empire of Cotton: A New History of Global Capitalism* (Vintage 2015).

[19] This and other examples of the artificial and detrimental creation of comparative advantages are considered in Chapter 4 ('International Trade').

[20] See Chapter 5 ('Foreign Investment').

liberalized financial flows, a push to securitize all forms of finance,[21] and moves of finance away from investment and development and towards diversification and profit-making on trading,[22] along with risky capital structures for banks and shadow banks. The result is a dangerous cocktail of policies that makes the rich richer while representing a threat of systemic forms of instability that have the potential to do serious damage to the living standards of those who do not participate or at best only marginally benefit from global finance and global banking. As for sovereign debt restructuring, it prioritizes power and creditors over welfare and citizens. As is common knowledge, neoliberal policies informed the Structural Adjustment Programmes of the 1980s as advocated by the International Monetary Fund (IMF) and the World Bank, just as they are being replicated in the conditionalities imposed on the borrowing countries of Europe today as the debt and austerity crisis plays out and more generally as a key aspect of the European Monetary Union.[23] Any suggestion that the days of structural adjustment are long over and that the conditionality attached to IMF loans has been streamlined in recent years to enable policy flexibility in borrowing countries is unsupported by a comprehensive review of the data.[24] The contribution of international law as well as other rules

[21] Onaran provides a clear account: 'The deregulation in the financial markets and the consequent innovations in mortgage backed securities, collateralised debt obligations and credit default swaps facilitated the debt-led growth model. These innovations and the "originate and distribute" model of banking have multiplied the amount of credit that the banks could extend given the limits of their capital. The premiums earned by the bankers, the commissions of the banks, the high CEO incomes thanks to high bank profits, the commissions of the rating agencies all created a perverse mechanism of investments that led to short-termism and ignorance about the risks of this banking model. In the short-run in the sub-prime credit segment, even if the risk of default was known, this was not perceived as a major issue: first, parts of these credits were anyway sold further to other investors, thanks to the generous ratings assigned by the rating agencies. Second, when there is a credit default, the houses, which serve as collateral, could be taken over and as long as house prices kept increasing, this was a profitable business for the creditor. However, this banking model led to a very risky economic model and a time bomb, which was destined to explode eventually. The bad news from the sub-prime markets triggered the explosion eventually, and first the market for collateralised debt obligations (CDOs) and then the interbank market, and finally the whole credit market collapsed at a global scale.' Ö Onaran, 'A Crisis of Distribution' (2009) 44 Economic & Political Weekly 171, 173. See further Chapter 6 ('Global Finance').

[22] Cross-border financial flows today are designed primarily for investors to achieve diversification of assets, in the form of asset swapping by investors in high-income countries. Their purpose is to hedge and share risks among the rich and not for long term finance or to match the supply of savings with the demand for investment among countries. Cross-border financial flows in the contemporary global financial architecture are designed to making the rich richer and result in serious capital deprivation where it is most needed and could be put to more productive uses.

[23] On how neoliberalism was built into the euro, see, for example, W Streeck, *Buying Time: The Delayed Crisis of Democratic Capitalism* (P Camiller tr, Verso 2014) 174: 'In accordance with the neoliberal programme, the euro . . . eliminated a major element of political discretion from the constitution of the common market; member states concerned for the employment, prosperity and social security of their citizens would now have to turn to the instrument of internal devaluation: that is the raising of productivity and competitiveness through more flexible labour markets, lower wages, longer working hours, higher labour market participation, and a welfare state geared to commodification.' See further, Y Varoufakis, *Adults in the Room: My Battle with Europe's Deep Establishment* (Bodley Head 2017).

[24] 'In 2014, IMF Managing Director Christine Lagarde appeared puzzled when a journalist asked about the organization's structural adjustment programs. "Structural adjustments? That was before my time. I have no idea what it is. We do not do that anymore".' Alexander Kentikelenis, Thomas Stubbs, and Lawrence King identified and systematized the 55,465 policy reform conditions mandated in all IMF programmes between 1985 and 2014. They concluded, in short, that 'There is a mismatch

of global normative significance to constituting neoliberal finance is explored in Chapter 6.

The particular dispute settlement mechanisms—or lack thereof—of these international legal regimes bolster their substance: an international trade dispute settlement system with no access for aggrieved individuals or groups, the exclusive competence of investors to sue for damages as part of foreign investment, the virtual impossibility to hold international financial-development institutions such as the World Bank and International Monetary Fund to account for human rights harms. That efforts at advancing obligations and accountability regarding international cooperation for development and socio-economic rights over the past decades—from the NIEO to the right to development to extraterritorial obligations in the area of socio-economic rights—have been stymied reflect how arrangements that serve global capitalism well determine the mechanisms and substance of law.[25] The mechanisms or their absence, from one regime to the next, make possible the substance of neoliberal law. The international law we have is the international law that capitalism has constituted and is an international law that capitalism's ambitions can rely on.

There is little difference today in whether the language used to describe this dominant set of economic and ultimately social rationalities and practices is that of 'neoliberalism' or the 'commodity-form of capitalism'[26] or the 'free market' understood as either the 'free play of market forces'[27] or 'liberalized markets', or 'market capitalism' or just 'the markets' or 'market fundamentalism', or 'global capitalism'.[28] Today, they all turn around many of the same organizing principles and, importantly, represent in theory and practice something far more profound than the resetting of the relation between state and economy;[29] neoliberalism has become the 'governing rationality' allowing it to, in the words of Wendy Brown, 'transmogrif [y] every human domain and endeavour, along with humans themselves, according to a specific image of the economic'.[30] It is a transnational economic project of

between what the IMF says and what the IMF actually does. Available evidence provides little support for the organization's fundamental-transformation rhetoric. Instead, we find that the scale of organizational change was both modest and short-lived ... The return of structural adjustment brings these decades-old criticisms of IMF programs back to the fore. The scale and pace of reforms to the IMF's practices do not match the organization's rhetoric.' A Kentikelenis, T Stubbs, and L King, 'Did the IMF Actually Ease up on Structural Adjustment? Here's What the Data Say' *Washington Post* (2 June 2016). For the full study, see A Kentikelenis, T Stubbs, and L King, 'IMF Conditionality and Development Policy Space 1985–2014' (2016) (23) Review of International Political Economy 1.

25 See Chapter 7 ('Human Rights').

26 EB Pashukanis, *Law and Marxism: A General Theory* (1929 Ink Links tr 1978); EB Pashukanis, 'International Law' in P Beirne and R Sharlet (eds), *Pashukanis: Selected Writings on Marxism and Law* (PB Maggs tr, Academic Press 1980) 168; C Miéville, *Between Equal Rights: A Marxist Theory of International Law* (Brill 2005).

27 W Streeck, 'The Crisis of Democratic Capitalism' (2011) 71 New Left Review 5, 7.

28 See ME Salomon 'You Say You Want a Revolution: Challenges of Market Primacy for the Human Rights Project' in W Vandenhole (ed), *Challenging Territoriality in International Human Rights Law: Building Blocks for a Plural and Diverse Duty-Bearer Regime* (Routledge 2015) 188, 188–89.

29 W Brown, *Undoing the Demos: Neoliberalism's Stealth Revolution* (Zone Books 2015) 9.

30 ibid 9–10.

accumulation aimed at higher rates of profit and control of raw materials, it looks to expand overseas markets for one's own products, and if you have the military clout to deploy it towards neo-imperial ambitions.[31] It is rooted in and reifies commodification.[32] It is a convincing thesis to understand these developments as reflective of a 'new constitutionalism of disciplinary neoliberalism': a project that extends and deepens the power of capital and market civilization.[33]

Of course proponents of the neoliberal project, however named, would argue that it is in fact a project aimed at justice ('market justice as the highest form of social justice')[34] in that material well-being and the social good is maximized by maximizing the reach and frequency of market transactions;[35] that material and human well-being is best satisfied by the market and the role of the state is to guarantee the conditions that best allow markets to function, and of course, that the world has never been richer. The first two arguments—built on the idea that human need will be best addressed as a by-product of individual greed (profit)[36] and that markets structured with no attention to the demands of justice somehow are best for everyone—find no empirical support. The third argument is wholly misleading.

Drawing on a range of studies the International Labour Organization (ILO) presents figures that speak to continual 'widespread poverty and deprivation': 'About 5.1 billion people, 75 per cent of the world population, are not covered by adequate social security (ILO) and 1.4 billion people live on less than US$1.25 a day (World Bank). Thirty-eight per cent of the global population, 2.6 billion people, do not have access to adequate sanitation and 884 million people lack access to adequate sources of drinking water (UN-HABITAT); 925 million suffer from chronic hunger (FAO); nearly 9 million children under the age of five die every year from largely preventable diseases (UNICEF/WHO); 150 million people suffer financial catastrophe annually and 100 million people are pushed below the poverty line when

[31] On this last point: 'US-led imperialism, for which militarisation is not only a domain of accumulation, but the gyroscope that steadies its course of development, stands to benefit from the war and its social, political and financial impact.' A Kadri, *Development under Uncertainty in the Arab World*, SPEAK OUT at The Laboratory for Advanced Research on the Global Economy, Centre for the Study of Human Rights, LSE (June 2016) 1, 2, http://www.lse.ac.uk/humanRights/research/projects/theLab/home.aspx

[32] Cutler defines it in this way: '[Interrelated processes that] involve the continuous transformation of public or common property into private property that is recognized, legitimated and enforced by the state ... The continuous nature of commodification relates to the inherent tendency for capitalism to expand, extensively and intensively, in the drive for new geographic spaces for capital investment and, intensively, in terms of the creation and legitimation of new methods of private appropriation. The geographic expansion of capitalism and its penetration into new modes of human activity are thus integral dimensions of commodification as a continuous process. But equally important is the continuity of the process of transforming or enclosing common or public property into private property.' AC Cutler, 'New Constitutionalism and the Commodity Form of Global Capitalism' in S Gill and AC Cutler (eds), *New Constitutionalism and World* Order (CUP 2014) 45, 49.

[33] S Gill and AC Cutler, 'New Constitutionalism and World Order: General Introduction' in Gill and Cutler (ibid) 6.

[34] Streeck (n 5) 213. [35] Harvey (n 1) 3.

[36] F Magdoff, 'Multiple Crises as Symptoms of an Unsustainable System' (2010) 33 Review: Fernand Braudel Center, Special Issue on Food, Energy, Environment: Crisis of the Modern World System 103, 117.

compelled to pay for health care (WHO).'[37] The recent financial and economic crisis (the result of neoliberalism's penchants for deregulation so-called)[38] pushed an additional 64 million people into extreme poverty already by the end of 2010.[39]

Arguments that globalization has meant that the 'the human race has never had it so good' rely on aggregate findings[40] and in particular the poverty reduction figures since the 1990s in a very small number of populous countries (China and India). Moreover, that familiar soundbite ignores the fact that China's growth strategy was not neoliberal but heterodox; that its policies have been premised on rapid urbanization and state-orchestrated land grabs;[41] that its policies threaten both stability and sustainable development;[42] that the growth in both China and India has been fuelled by a scramble for resources in the South;[43] and that they both retain significant aspects of underdevelopment.[44] The Millennium Development Goals (MDGs) claim that poverty has been cut in half relies on the baseline year starting back in 1990 so that China's gains against poverty during the 1990s could be factored in. Without that backdating, it would not have been possible to contend that the Goal to reduce poverty by half globally had been met.[45] Furthermore, if

[37] *Report of the Social Protection Floor Advisory Group: For a Fair and Inclusive Globalization* (ILO 2011) xxi, http://www.ilo.org/wcmsp5/groups/public/@dgreports/@dcomm/@publ/documents/publication/wcms_150440.pdf

[38] The Governor of the Bank of England refers to 'light touch regulation', while Balakrishnan, Elson, and Patel prefer 'profit-led regulation'. M Carney, 'Inclusive Capitalism: Creating a Sense of the Systemic' Governor of the Bank of England (2014) 5, http://www.inclusivecapitalism.org; R Balakrishnan, D Elson, and R Patel, 'Rethinking Macroeconomic Strategies from a Human Rights Perspective' (2010) 53 Development 27, 35.

[39] ILO (n 37) 19 (drawing on World Bank figures).

[40] 'In aggregate terms, the human race has never had it so good. Life expectancy has risen by more in the past 50 years than in the previous 1,000. When the Berlin Wall fell, two-fifths of humanity lived in extreme poverty. Now it's one-eighth.' S Thompson, 'Globalization for the 99%: Can We Make It Work for All?' *World Economic Forum* (6 July 2016), https://www.weforum.org/agenda/2016/07/globalization-for-the-99-can-we-make-it-work-for-all

[41] This was justified by reference to a general desire for GDP growth and as such claimed to be in the public interest. E Pils, 'Voice, Reflexivity and Say: Governing Access to and Control of Land in China' in O De Schutter and K Pistor (eds), *Governing Access to Essential Resources* (Columbia UP 2015) 127.

[42] China's policy of land acquisition is said to have '(1) been used heavily by local governments to fuel urban development and finance infrastructure provision and (2) has resulted in increasing social tension and injustice that may impose a long-term threat to stability and sustainable development'. C Ding, 'Policy and Praxis of Land Acquisition in China' (2007) 24 Land Use Policy 1.

[43] Magdoff (n 36) 103.

[44] ibid 120. Moreover, 'China's economy has significant weaknesses: an asset bubble has developed and its economy performs more as a platform on which to assemble parts made elsewhere.' (ibid).

[45] J Hickel, 'The True Extent of Global Poverty and Hunger: Questioning the Good News Narrative of the Millennium Development Goals' (2016) 37(5) Third World Quarterly 749, 753. 'If we take China out of the equation, we see that the global poverty headcount at $1.25 actually *increased* during the 1980s and 1990s, while the World Bank was imposing structural adjustment across most of the global South. In 2010 (the final year of the MDGs' real data), the total poverty headcount excluding China was exactly the same as it was in 1981, at just over one billion people. In other words, while the MDGs lead us to believe that poverty has been decreasing around the world, in reality the only place this holds true is in China and East Asia. This is an important point, because China and East Asia are some of the only places in the developing world that were not forcibly liberalised by the World Bank and the IMF. Everywhere else, poverty has been stagnant or getting worse, in aggregate' (ibid). The UN concludes: 'Globally, the number of those living in extreme poverty declined by more than half, falling from 1.9 billion in 1990 to 836 million in 2015, with

poverty figures were based on a higher international poverty line than the deeply contested $1.25 a day,[46] for example closer to $5.00 a day—which would allow for a life expectancy of 74 years and is only half of what many economists conclude is an ethical international poverty line—3.5 billion people globally would be poor.[47] As Jason Hickel points out, 'this is three and a half times what the World Bank and the UN would have us believe, and about half the world's population. Of course, it would be clear that poverty has been getting *worse*, not better, even without excluding China.'[48] According to one account, global GDP is ten times larger than in 1950 in real terms—an increase of 260% per capita;[49] if even nearly accurate it's a tragic figure given the state of deprivation globally. A breakdown by decade, however, demonstrates that over this period neoliberalism has broadly failed to stimulate worldwide growth.[50] It is a convincing thesis that the shifts under neoliberalism, such as the rise of finance, have merely given the appearance of driving a dynamic global economy.[51] For our purposes, the generalized trend is that poverty remains widespread, is now far worse than we've been led to believe, and even if 'the world' has become richer who is the world?

In 1976 the developed market-economy countries, with 20% of the world population, enjoyed 66% of total world income. By the twenty-first century, 20% of the world population is receiving approximately 85% of income, with 6% going to 60% of the population.[52] In absolute terms, 40% of the world population is today living on incomes so low as to preclude fully participating in wealth creation.[53] In

most progress occurring since 2000', http://www.un.org/sustainabledevelopment/blog/2015/12/sustainable-development-goals-kick-off-with-start-of-new-year

[46] In India, a child living just above the $1.25 international poverty line has, according to Wagstaff, a 60% risk of being underweight. In Niger, babies born to families just above the international poverty line face an infant mortality risk more than three times the world average. A Wagstaff, 'Child Health on a Dollar a Day: Some Tentative Cross-country Comparisons' (2003) 57 Social Science and Medicine 1529, as cited in Hickel (n 45). See also TW Pogge and SG Reddy, 'How Not to Count the Poor' (29 Oct 2005), https://ssrn.com/abstract=893159

[47] Hickel (n 45) 755, drawing also on the work of Peter Edwards.

[48] ibid (emphasis in the original). [49] Magdoff (n 36) 120.

[50] As Harvey indicates, aggregate global growth rates were at 3.5% in the 1960s and even at 2.4% during the 'troubled 1970s' but at 1.4% and 1.1% for the neoliberal 1980s and 1990s respectively and a rate that 'barely touches 1% since 2000', with catastrophic losses in countries that submitted to neoliberal shock therapy. Harvey (n 1) 154.

[51] Shifts such as the rise of finance and financial services—including rise in corporate remuneration, the dangerous business of speculation, the creation of financial centres that are 'islands of wealth and privilege' and vast amounts of 'fictitious wealth', along with a burst in information technologies that has most benefited market-driven financialization including speculative activity and short-term market contracts while shifting attention away from investment in physical and social infrastructure (ibid 157–59).

[52] RH Wade and M Wolf [debate], 'Are Global Poverty and Inequality Getting Worse?' in D Held and A McGrew (eds), *The Global Transformations Reader* (2nd edn, Polity 2003) 441. In terms of global *wealth* distribution, 10% of adults account for 85% of the world total of global assets, with half the world's populations—concentrated in developing countries—owning barely 1% of global wealth. J Davies et al, *The World Distribution of Household Wealth*, World Institute for Development Economics (UN University 2006).

[53] *Human Development Report 2005: International Cooperation at a Crossroads: Aid, Trade and Security in an Unequal World* (UNDP 2005) 38.

the opaque world of inequality measurements, some conclusions indicate that the global gap between the richest and the poorest people has been expanding and, moreover, that there is little evidence of actual improvement in the absolute position of the poorest since the 1980s (when the latest wave of globalization began).[54] Others conclude that based on the standards of living of individuals in the global population as a whole inequality, after having risen steadily since the beginning of the nineteenth century, has now begun to fall but due to the performance of emerging countries.[55] As for inequality within countries, it is largely increasing and can be attributed directly and indirectly to globalization.[56] So, in response to the question who is 'the world', the answer can only be that a paradox of *global*ization is that there is not one world.

There is a logic to the harms and alienations that needs also to be introduced at this stage (and that discussions of inequality or even poverty do not nearly capture). While there is a long and violent history of capitalism to account for,[57] in the post-Second World War period the dominant and orthodox understanding of 'development' and 'progress'—(industrialized, western, modern)—along with market capitalism have focused on compelling a shift from non-market to market-based economies. This has been premised on increasing privatization through dispossession and displacement of peasants and indigenous populations, including the

[54] T Lines, *Making Poverty: A History* (Zed Books 2008) 25, 'Progress towards the reduction of absolute poverty is heavily conditioned by inequality. This is true not just for income, but also for wider inequalities in areas such as health, education and politics.' UNDP (n 53) 54.

[55] F Bourguignon, *The Globalization of Inequality* (Princeton UP 2105) 25–26; B Milanovic, *Global Inequality: A New Approach for the Age of Globalization* (Harvard U Press 2016).

[56] 'Directly, because it has lowered the relative compensation for unskilled labor in developed countries which face direct competition from cheap labor costs of emerging economies, and also because it has increased the profits and remuneration of capital and highly skilled labor across the world. Indirectly, through the deep structural changes produced by the heightened competition between and within nations.' Bourguignon (n 55) 117. Branko Milanovic has analysed global inequalities in terms of three concepts: inequality between countries, inequality between countries weighted by population, and income distribution between individuals (or households) in the world, termed 'true world inequality'. B Milanovic, 'Global Income Inequality' in D Ehrenpreis (ed), *The Challenge of Inequality* (UNDP International Poverty Centre 2007) 6. A summary of his 2007 findings on global inequality is that inequality between countries is widening rapidly while inequality between countries weighted by population has shrunk since 1980, however this is due to the fast growth in China and India. In his latest work, former World Bank economist Milanovic concludes similarly that global inequality (income inequality among the citizens of the world) has fallen dramatically among nations, but again due to rising incomes in China and India, while inequality has soared within nations and that there has been a surge of inequality in the west with inequality in both the United States and China 'well-entrenched and self-reproducing'. The beneficiaries of globalization are the people from the emerging Asian economies, predominantly China, but also India, Thailand, Vietnam, and Indonesia as well as the top 1% globally ('global plutocrats')—overwhelmingly from the rich economies—whose real incomes have risen substantially between 1988 and 2008. If the great winners have been the Asian poor and middle classes, the great losers have been the lower middle classes of the rich world. Milanovic (n 55) 19–22.

[57] See Chapters 3 ('The End of Empire and the Search for Justice: NIEO and Beyond'), 4 ('International Trade'), and 5 ('Foreign Investment'). Araghi and Karides capture this trajectory well in their summary of the four historical periods of the process of commodification of land rights: primitive accumulation, colonialism, developmentalism, and globalization. F Araghi and M Karides, 'Land Dispossession and Global Crisis: Introduction to the Special Section on Land Rights in the World-System' (2012) 18 Journal of World-Systems Research 1.

destruction of non-market access to food and self-sustenance.[58] As Henrietta Moore explains in her work on rural households, the framework was one of 'mechanisation, marketisation, proletarianisation and rural migration'.[59] It is not paradoxical that the vast majority of those who are hungry in the world today work as part of the food system; small independent food producers or waged agricultural workers toiling on farms in the formal or informal sector represent over half of the billion who go hungry today,[60] what Farshad Araghi refers to as a living life under a regime of 'forced underconsumption'.[61] Indeed, figures from 2008 show that there was greater profit made by food companies than ever before in history while more people went hungry than ever before in history.[62] The process of 'depeasantization' has land effectively stolen from the poor (or from nature) as its value increases. Market forces see capitalist relations enter rural areas of the developing world with their markets becoming integrated into those of the rest of the world.[63] More than half of humanity now lives in cities, with a third of those (one-sixth of humanity) living in slums.[64] This model of decimation as development is not limited to dispossessing smallhold farmers and fisherpeople, indigenous peoples and peasants in the developing world, its dedication to expanding the reign of the market and enforcing the private over the public (be it enclosures of public space or privatization and commodification) is of course widespread in the industrialized west.[65] The threat posed by the bailout of dangerously leveraged banks at the expense of almost everyone else is a quintessentially modern example of 'accumulation by dispossession'. The model we have, in the words of Harvey, is to redistribute through dispossession.[66] The regimes of international economic law directly facilitate these endeavours.[67] As for

58 See ibid; Harvey (n 1) 159; R Nixon, *Slow Violence and the Environmentalism of the Poor* (Harvard UP 2011).

59 HL Moore, 'Global Prosperity and Sustainable Development Goals' (2015) 27 Journal of International Development 801.

60 O De Schutter, *Report of the United Nations Special Rapporteur on the Right to Food: Agribusiness and the Right to Food* UN Doc A/HRC/13/33, 22 Dec 2009, https://documents-dds-ny.un.org/doc/UNDOC/GEN/G09/177/76/PDF/G0917776.pdf?OpenElement. Women are overrepresented in the informal sector and, for example, constitute 80% of Africa's farmers. UN Millennium Project, *Fast Facts: The Faces of Poverty, UN Millennium Project* (2005), http://www.unmillenniumproject.org/documents/3-MP-PovertyFacts-E.pdf

61 F Araghi, 'Accumulation by Displacement: Global Enclosures, Food Crisis, and the Ecological Contradictions of Capitalism' (2010) 34 Review: Fernand Braudel Center 113.

62 See J Viertel, 'Why Big Ag Won't Feed the World' *Atlantic Monthly* (20 Jan 2010), http://food.theatlantic.com/sustainability/why-big-ag-wont-feed-the-world-l.php. 'And hunger was common and widespread before this period. When supplies are tight "The Market" "decides" the "highest and best use" for products. This means that the wealthy countries and the wealthy within even poor countries are advantaged while poor people suffer.' Magdoff (n 36) 110–11.

63 Magdoff (n 36) 107. Magdoff's use of the term 'depeasantization' is taken from Araghi (n 61).

64 ibid 106.

65 See, among other accounts, D Stuckler and S Basu, *The Body Economic: Eight Experiments in Economic Recovery from Iceland to Greece* (Penguin 2013).

66 Harvey (n 1) 159.

67 For a selection of (by now familiar) examples: 'Some of this displacement from rural areas to slums has been directly caused by neoliberal trade policies promoted by the United States and the World Trade Organization … [T]he drive to enhance U.S. exports of food through reduction of import tariffs in poor countries has had a very detrimental outcome, because local farmers couldn't compete with the relatively low price of imported foods.' Magdoff (n 36) 106. The literature on land

international human rights law, while its elaboration and interpretation have been effective in protecting certain people from some socio-economic harms, as we argue herein, in significant ways international human rights law has been reinforcing the contemporary enterprise of global capitalism.

Fred Magdoff's depiction of capitalism today aptly refers to the 'attitudes and mores needed for the smooth functioning of the system—greed, individualism, competitiveness, exploitation of others, and consumerism',[68] characteristics that arise because they are 'built into the inner nature and logic of our present system of production'. In industrialized countries, those who can afford it consume far beyond any reasonable conception of human need or indeed indulgence, using up natural resources and contributing to environmental destruction.[69] Indeed, from the pollution of air, water, and soil to greenhouse gas emissions we destroy the support systems upon which we depend, and then turn to the global commodification of pollution rights for their contested market-based solution.[70] The destructive cycle continues through our model of development that equates it with modernity premised primarily on the ability of more and more people to join the consuming classes all the while closing off routes that foster alternative values and systems.

Not only has global neoliberalism been accompanied by particular forms of dispossession, violence, and immiseration, it has failed on its own terms. Moore's work mirrors that of many others when she concludes that countries in the global South that adopted trade liberalization, privatization, and fiscal discipline through the 1990s saw their economic growth rates turn out to be low not only in absolute terms but also relative to other countries that did not follow such reforms or only partially.[71] In countries that underwent neoliberal shock therapy from the countries of the former Soviet Union in the 1990s to Greece from 2010, there have been

grabs—foreign corporate land takeovers in developing countries to produce crops for export—is extensive (see ibid). 'Another distortion has resulted from the patenting of life and individual genes so they become the property of a corporation ... The top four firms now control over 40% of the global seed market and it is estimated that in the United States over 80% of the corn and the over 90% of the soybeans planted use traits developed by Monsanto' (ibid 109). 'In poor countries, the opening of markets to competition and the cessation of government support for agriculture under pressure of international organizations, such as the IMF and the World Bank, have had devastating results, as imports and lack of government support have driven farmers out of business. The neoliberal ("Washington Consensus") dogma holds that by dropping government supports and import taxes or restrictions, each nation will produce items for which it has a "comparative advantage" and all will prosper as "free trade" governs economic relations among nations' (ibid 109–10).

68 ibid 123.

69 See ibid 122, and F Magdoff and J Bellamy Foster, 'What Every Environmentalist Needs to Know about Capitalism' (2010) 61 Monthly Review, http://monthlyreview.org/2010/03/01/what-every-environmentalist-needs-to-know-about-capitalism. If unsustainable consumption by the middle class in industrialized countries is necessary for economic growth, then there is a problem not least with the absence of policies to prevent or mitigate that need.

70 See further, L Lohmann, 'Marketing and Making Carbon Dumps: Commodification, Calculation and Counterfactuals in Climate Change Mitigation' (2005) 14 Science as Culture 203; F Araghi, 'The End of "Cheap Ecology" and the Crisis of "Long Keynesianism"' (2010) 45 Economic & Political Weekly 39.

71 Moore (n 59) 807–08. Harvey (n 1) 154, and see generally the work of Ha-Joon Chang.

catastrophic losses. It is trite to suggest that globalization was oversold, in many cases its disinclined customers never bought it but were saddled with it nonetheless. In other cases it was galvanized by the end of communism and the unhindered thrust towards global market capitalism.

The reader may be familiar with the figures and trends offered in this section, as they have been repeated in various forms for decades. Still there are a number of points to draw out even from this brief statistical review and the wider insights offered: one, that any debates over trends do not mask the persistence and magnitude of both poverty and inequality on a global scale. Two, the consequences are not merely those of persistent and very considerable poverty and an explosion in material inequality, but that poverty and inequality are accompanied by systemic dispossession, alienation, and immiseration. Three, the dominant narrative and practices have 'development' and human betterment rely upon this grossly disempowering system that has both failed to benefit most people and created a huge alienated transnational class in the process. This alienated class is not an unfortunate side effect of a largely benevolent and successful economic model as we are often told—it is part of the sacrificial logic of its functioning;[72] it is a dispensable necessity. The fourth point, for our purposes, is that the drivers of this systemic alienation and these unforgiving trends persist with the support of international law as international law licenses 'the raw avarice of the market'.[73]

There have been responses to this model of globalization of course—see the work of the Via Campesina movement supporting small-scale sustainable agriculture since 1993 as a way to promote social justice and dignity; alternatives highlighted at the annual World Social Forum that seek to rethink the singular dominant model of the economy that has underpinned rural development policies and to work with local communities;[74] there is agroecology in Latin America and the Caribbean;[75] the articulation of rights against global capitalism captured in the process around a UN draft Declaration on the Rights of Peasants, and many more examples. It is a point of significant note that these efforts are known to incur violent responses by vested interests: the 2016 cases in Honduras where indigenous opponents of large-scale land deals and hydroelectric projects that threatened the food and water supplies of local communities were murdered for challenging powerful corporations and their compradors is just one recent, egregious example.[76]

[72] See S Marks, 'Human Rights and the Bottom Billion' (2009) 1 European Human Rights Law Review 37; S Marks, 'Exploitation as an International Legal Concept' in S Marks (ed), *International Law on the Left: Re-examining Marxist Legacies* (CUP 2008) 281, 301–02.

[73] BJ Stark, 'What's Left? A Review of *International Law on the Left* by Susan Marks' (2010) 42 George Washington International Law Review 191, 211, referring to the chapter by A Claire Cutler and her consideration of the normalizing function of international trade law.

[74] Alternatives include in-kind labour remuneration, reciprocal labour exchanges, local currencies, neighbourhood care networks and ritual practices—that Moore explains are well documented and well understood. Moore (n 59) 808.

[75] ibid.

[76] According to Global Witness, figures available for 2014 suggest 40% of global killings of land and environmental defenders are people from indigenous communities, https://www.globalwitness.org/en/press-releases/global-witness-releases-new-data-murder-rate-environmental-and-land-activists-honduras-highest-world

But bottom-up efforts do not change the fact that top-down efforts continue to shape our economic, political, and social models. It is a convincing thesis that the wrong questions are being asked and the wrong results are being measured: 'All too often privatization, liberalization, and even macro stabilization have been treated as objectives of reform … But all too often no scorecard was kept on the number of individuals who were pushed into poverty, or the number of jobs destroyed versus those created, or on the increase in violence, or on the increase in the sense of insecurity or the feeling of powerlessness.'[77] The dominant approach too often measures the wrong things, telling us that we are all better off, and selling the current world system not merely as the best there is but as all there really is. International law plays an integral role in this charade; it is not merely reflective of it and complicit in it, but constitutive of it.

2. The Determinacy of International Law

There are important accounts of international law that foreground its malleability and its indeterminacy—in that it can be deployed to support any outcome;[78] 'what gets read into it (or out of it) is a matter of subtle interpretative strategy'.[79] In so far as the interpretation of international rules can, in principle, be helpfully indeterminate, that is able to bend towards justice (or retain the prospect that they will), it is not hard to see the ways in which it is dangerously determinate (with human rights law not being immune as Chapter 7 demonstrates).[80] That

[77] JE Stiglitz, 'Foreword' in K Polanyi (ed), *The Great Transformation: The Political and Economic Origins of our Time* (Beacon Press 2001 edn) xv–xvi.

[78] M Koskenniemi, *From Apology to Utopia: The Structure of International Legal Argument* (Finnish Lawyers' Publication Co 1989). 'The structuralism of FATU was designed to destabilize the sense that the immediate aspects of international law were true and fixed and action-determining. They were produced, instead, by techniques and arguments that were quite contested and even contradictory.' The official rules and policies that an institution claims to follow are indeterminate and 'there are always many alternatives for such an interpretation – many ways to choose': M Koskenniemi, 'What is Critical Research in International Law: Celebrating Structuralism' (2016) 29 LJIL 727, 729 and 732. See generally N Purvis, 'Critical Legal Studies in International Law' (1991) 32 Harvard International Law Journal 81, 109.

[79] Koskenniemi (n 3, 'Politics of International Law') 9.

[80] Our position is not as far from Martti Koskenniemi's as it might at first seem. He writes in the 2005 Epilogue of *From Apology to Utopia*: 'My intuition was—and remains—that the most serious problems of the international world are related to its sharp division into a relatively prosperous and peaceful North and an impoverished and conflict-ridden South (it is not necessary to take these descriptions in their original geographical sense) and that our practices, institutions and conceptual frameworks somehow help to sustain it. Undoubtedly international law may be used for valuable purposes for challenging aspects of the international political or economic system, for instance. In practice, however, it is constantly directing attention away from important problems by defining them as "political" or "economic" or "technical" and thus allegedly beyond the law's grasp … [There is] an astonishing insensitivity to the permissive role of legal rules—the way they liberate powerful actors and reproduce day by day key aspects of the world that, although they are contingent and contestable, have begun to seem natural or unavoidable. Why is it that concepts and structures that are themselves indeterminate nonetheless still end up always on the side of the status quo? These intuitions lead me to what I now think is the main political point of From Apology to Utopia. For the "weak" indeterminacy thesis to turn into a "strong" one, it needs to be supplemented by an empirical argument, namely that irrespective of indeterminacy, *the system still de facto prefers some*

international legal rules offer the basis for contradictory positions, a platform for diverse interpretations, and reflect varying political perspectives is so only once we account for how categorical the assumptions and premises of neoliberal capitalism are in international law—from the density of trade and investment treaties to trade law's 'obligation-exception/defence structure'[81] to the dominant approach in trade and investment circles that their subject matter is largely distinct from the social contract that states have with their people (with those 'domestic' issues to be addressed by international organizations specializing in development or perhaps by human rights). In the realms of international economic law, we are presented with an understanding of property that defines it as individually owned and commercially exploitable. Norms related to private property (and its protection) as well as to the sanctity of contract (and the insinuation that these international 'contracts' govern purely private global matters) have been presented as essential to economic development as well as, in the latter case, to the functioning of the financial order.[82] 'Non-market' values—such as the protection of human health and the environment—are conceptualized as intrusions into the market and allowable only as exceptions to free trade, which is 'the necessary ideal'.[83] Alongside these 'exceptions and flexibilities' there has been a huge and needless loss of life over the past decades, prime examples being the unaffordability of patented antiretroviral drugs under the WTO's Intellectual Property Agreement[84] and trade commitment restrictions on national food security strategies.[85] International treaties in trade and

outcomes or distributive choices to other outcomes or choices ... Some of my later writings have sought to show how biases emerge and operate in the law ... They seek to show that out of any number of equally "possible" choices, some choices—typically conservative or *status quo* oriented choices are *methodologically privileged* in the relevant institutions', *From Apology to Utopia: The Structure of International Legal Argument* (CUP 2005) 606–10, references removed, emphasis in the original.

[81] General Agreement on Tariffs and Trade (GATT), 30 Oct 1947, 55 UNTS 194, Art XX; General Agreement on Trade in Services (GATS), 15 Apr 1994, 1869 UNTS 183, Art XIV. This is also a feature of some international investment agreements but general exceptions are still found in only a minority of the 3,500-plus agreements concluded. For a critique of the obligation–exception/defence structure, see Chapter 4: these exceptions show us not only the way in which so-called 'non-trade values' are dealt with in trade agreements, but conceptualizing treaties in the economic language of contracts constrains our thinking about trade treaties as involving primarily issues associated with the institutions of transacting and not much else. The general exceptions provisions illustrate problems in the contract approach.

[82] See Chapters 4 ('International Trade'), 5 ('Foreign Investment'), and 6 ('Global Finance').

[83] See Fakhri on the position of the former WTO Director-General Pascal Lamy, M Fakhri, 'Food as a Matter of Global Governance' (2015) 11 Journal of International Law and International Relations 68, 70.

[84] On 23 January 2017 the first amendment to WTO rules since the organization was established back in 1995 entered into force. The Protocol Amending the Agreement on Trade-Related Aspects of Intellectually Property Rights provides a legal pathway to ease access to affordable medicines in developing countries that mostly rely on imports for their medicinal needs. Unlike earlier efforts in the WTO to address this issue, the amendment gives legal certainty that generic versions of patent-protected medicines can be produced under compulsory licensing specifically for export to countries with limited or no pharmaceutical production capacity. It has taken over a decade for the amendment to enter into force. Its effective use remains an open question.

[85] Still no resolution found at the latest WTO Ministerial Conference. *Public Stockholding for Food Security Purposes*, WTO Ministerial Decision of 19 Dec 2015, WT/MIN(15)/44, 21 Dec 2015, Nairobi Ministerial Conference.

investment combine in a way that provides many benefits to capital but none to labour: capital is mobile and protected, but labour is immobile and unprotected. It is in the nature of international law that treaties are open to interpretation and that ambiguities in treaties will be exploited and may reflect shifts over time.[86] But in so far as the interpretation of economic rules might contribute to the welfare of the subaltern classes,[87] it is a partial and profoundly unsatisfying project that does not change the terms of the debate nor open up space for shaping real alternatives to the global economy.[88] Nor does it invite consideration of the role of international law in constituting and licensing the power of capital, driving the demise of democratic governance, and marshalling the immiseration of many a people.

The neoliberal ideal conceptualizes principles of justice (including human rights) as alien intrusions which work against international law's liberating (and liberalizing) potential. But rules that seek to promote justice should be constitutive of markets, not alien to them. As Robert Knox points out, this circumscription of international law's potential is seen in so far as legal argument deals with effects—'violations' and 'disputes'—while it does not do well at examining 'the general structural causes that lurk beneath them'.[89] Where causes are exposed, as at

If the aim of international trade rules was to see the world well fed there would be a move to limit states' excessive reliance on international trade in the pursuit of food security and in increasing small-scale food production, particularly among women, and by pursuing economic policies that increase, rather than decrease employment and livelihoods. See TA Wise, 'Feeding the World: The Ultimate First World Conceit' *Triple Crisis* (18 July 2015), http://triplecrisis.com/feeding-the-world-the-ultimate-first-world-conceit; D James, 'Investing in Agriculture in Developing Countries: The World Says Yes, But the WTO Says No' *Alternet* (31 Mar 2015), http://www.alternet.org/world/investing-agriculture-developing-countries-whole-world-says-yes-wto-says-no; O De Schutter, *The World Trade Organization and the Post-Global Food Crisis Agenda: Putting Food Security First in the International Trade System*, Briefing Note 04 (Nov 2011), http://www.ohchr.org/Documents/Issues/Food/BN4_SRRTF_WTO_EN.pdf

86 See A Lang, *World Trade Law After Neoliberalism: Re-imagining the Global Economic Order* (OUP 2011) 164–69 on the indeterminacy of WTO law. There are creative proposals on how to interpret WTO law towards progressive ends, see R Howse, *Climate Mitigation Subsidies and the WTO Legal Framework: A Policy Analysis*, International Institute for Sustainable Development (May 2010) and R Howse and J Langille, 'Permitting Pluralism: The *Seal Products* Dispute and Why the WTO Should Accept Trade Restrictions Justified by Noninstrumental Moral Values' (2012) 37 Yale Journal of International Law 367, 401–02. The law on foreign investment offers its own (tenuous) solutions—see M Sornarajah, *Resistance and Change in the International Law of Foreign Investment* (CUP 2015) ch 6.

87 One of the features of Chimni's critical Marxist international law scholarship, BS Chimni, 'An Outline of a Marxist Course on Public International Law' in Marks (n 72, *International Law on the Left*) 53, 56–57.

88 As Orford points out on the conditioned response of 'progressives' to Europe's farm subsidies: '[T]he idea that Europe should abandon its support for agriculture, that industrialised subsidies for farmers are the cause of food insecurity, and that agricultural policy is not social policy, is now becoming something of a mantra even amongst progressive critics. There is little consideration of the possibility that what is needed is precisely *more* social policy in the form of agricultural policy—a recognition that how land and food is organised goes to the heart of every polity. In my view, this is not the time to demand that the European countryside begin to be managed in the same way that the countryside of Asia, Africa and Latin America has been, but rather this is a moment to revisit the alternatives to the management of agriculture and rural life that might yet be available.' A Orford, 'Food Security, Free Trade, and the Battle for the State' (2015) 11 Journal of International Law and International Relations 1, 67.

89 Knox suggests that international law is 'incapable' of dealing with causes ('this is where legal argument proves too specific. Legal argument resolves specific 'violations', 'disputes', or 'instances', but

times is the case in international human rights law, the approach adopted in human rights law is largely hortatory, since the form of its international legal mechanisms still offer few ways of redressing those structural impediments.[90] Structural and causal accounts are increasingly considered in international human rights law, even if there is still too little it can do about it.

International law was developed to facilitate economic relations;[91] it codified laws of property and contract built on the cardinal principle of capitalism—that the state must respect the will of private parties—legitimating and enforcing private ownership of means of production and exchange.[92] China Miéville convincingly reasons, since private ownership implies the exclusion of others it builds in disputation and contestation, with coercive force implied in the defence of what is mine; this coercion (that something is mine and thus not yours and I can assert my claim) is at the heart of commodity-form and the coercion that underpins it.[93] As the Soviet jurist Evgeny B Pashukanis exposed in his seminal work of the 1920s and 1930s, it is competition among capitalist states that underpins international law.[94] In short, international law has always reflected the fight for greater coercive force among (unequal) participants in economic relations.[95]

it never questions the general structural logics that lurk beneath them, and so cannot fully eradicate the problems it addresses'). R Knox, 'Marxism, International Law, and Political Strategy' (2009) 22 LJIL 413, 430.

[90] CESCR, Statement on the World Food Crisis, E/C 12/2008/1, 20 May 2008, where the UN Committee on Economic, Social and Cultural Rights demonstrates a clear concern for causal factors precipitating and exacerbating the food crisis even if the remedies are only at the level of broad-based recommendation. On the (creative) application of the Optional Protocol to the International Covenant on Economic, Social and Cultural Rights to multiple states causing indivisible harm, see ME Salomon, 'Deprivation, Causation and the Law of International Cooperation' in M Langford, M Scheinin, W van Genugten, and W Vandenhole (eds), *Global Justice, State Duties: The Extra-Territorial Scope of Economic, Social and Cultural Rights in International Law* (CUP 2013) 259.

[91] The foundations of international law for the modern state offered justifications for the use of force in support of European commercial interests to compel non-European peoples to trade and in the conquest of the land and resources of non-European peoples. It was frequently based on the unrestrained actions of private individuals (Beckert) and multinational companies had the right to conclude treaties with foreign powers, to wage war, and to levy taxes. For an elaboration, see Chapter 3 ('The End of Empire and the Search for Justice: NIEO and Beyond') and especially Chapter 4 ('International Trade'). See also, C Miéville, 'The Commodity-Form Theory of International Law' in Marks (n 72, *International Law on the Left*) 92, 109, including his coverage of Pashukanis: 'The development of law as a system was evoked not by the requirements of the state, but they necessary conditions for commercial relations ... Commercial relations ... ushered in the ius gentium' (ibid 115); 'The spread and development of international law occurred on the basis of the spread and development of the capitalist mode of production.' Pashukanis (n 26, 'International Law') 168, 171–72.

[92] D Kennedy, 'The Role of Law in Economic Thought: Essays on the Fetishism of Commodities' (1985) 34 American University Law Review 939, 956; Cutler (n 32) 48.

[93] Miéville (n 91) 112–13, 115ff.

[94] Pashukanis (n 26, 'International Law') 168, 172; and see Miéville (n 91) 118–20.

[95] The argument that international law is a consent-based system and as such coercion is justified, flowing as it does from the consent of states, is wholly unconvincing. The independence formally afforded states as sovereign equals under international law does not endow them with functional equality in the shaping or enforcement of the rules. On this implied voluntarism see further ME Salomon,

The DNA of international law as a capitalist, commercial, coercive enterprise was set up to facilitate the political–economic interests of the day and continues to give authoritative expression to dominant interests. As such, the widespread immiseration we know today is in good part a result of the pivotal role played by the international legal system. There is a compelling argument that suggests in order to address the social and international problems of immiseration change would be required not only or initially of the dominant capitalist schematic, but of the eradication of the forms of capitalist law that have been established to support it and which give it expression.[96] On this account, anything less 'can only ever tinker with the surface level of institutions'.[97] It may, however, have to be enough merely to tinker—merely to qualify the law of neoliberal capitalism—but while any meaningful improvement to the current dysfunctions that immiserate would constitute a certain kind of success, it would come at a cost of legitimating and sustaining the international legal system that gives rise to immiseration in the first place.[98]

3. International Law to the Ends of Justice: NIEO and Human Rights?

Perhaps the two most significant post-war examples of deploying international law to the ends of economic justice have come in the form of the drive for a New International Economic Order and the advance of international human rights law, in particular in the area of development and socio-economic rights. In important ways, the demands by Third World developing countries for an NIEO in the wake of decolonization continues to represent the high-water mark of challenging the precepts of international law, even if it didn't achieve its aims of a different form of global economic integration based on equality between states whereby the South could catch up with the North. It is a convincing thesis that the NIEO was never going to be transformative given the ways it sustained the deleterious logic of the capitalist world economy.[99] But, as explored in Chapter 3, it was the first time a set of concrete economic principles were prescribed in international law, for the whole world, articulating a form of justice based not on domination of one people

'Poverty, Privilege and International Law: The Millennium Development Goals and the Guise of Humanitarianism' (2008–09) German Yearbook of International Law 39, 41–43.

96 That is, as Miéville frames it, the fundamental reformulation of the political economic system. A fundamental impediment to radical change through law 'or even the systematic amelioration of social and international problems' through law comes also from the juridical system: 'Law is a relation between subjects abstracted of social context, facing each other in a relationship predicated on private property, intrinsically depending on coercion.' Miéville (n 91) 131.

97 ibid 130.

98 Knox (n 89) 431–32. Knox's solution to this dilemma is one of 'principled pragmatism' whereby international law is never used 'because it "is law", but only insofar as its content can advance the aims of progressive constituencies' (ibid 433).

99 See H Addo (ed), *Transforming the World Economy: Nine Critical Essays on the New International Economic Order* (United Nations University 1984).

over another. Despite its significance however, the NIEO effort was ultimately not successful.

The NIEO initiative failed on a number of counts: in so far as it was the aim, it failed to displace the power and advantage held by influential states, it failed to modify the rules of international law that served and continue to serve the economic interests of capital-exporting states,[100] and, most pointedly, it reflected the acceptance of the Third World to the economic ideology of the advanced capitalist world, bolstering the commitment to universally recognized value of foreign capital including exploitation of local labour in 'periphery' countries.[101] The one normative success which is often said to have emerged from the efforts by developing states to shape the evolving rules of international economic law under the NIEO initiative—the general acceptance by the international community of the principle of permanent sovereignty over natural resources (PSNR)—did not go far enough in entrenching any transformative or redistributive agenda.[102] Moreover, the claim of developing states to their natural resources aimed at domestic use and benefit still served to reinforce the contested terms upon which the world economy operates—of the primacy of private property and the exploitation of nature. As one commentator put it, PSNR represented 'a continuation of, rather than a break with, the colonial interpretation of the earth and what it contains'.[103] Far from posing a challenge to the terms of the global economy, the NIEO can be said to have done its share in reinforcing it. If, as Herb Addo and others suggested, we are interested in transformation not reformation, then we need to judge the newness of the new order 'on the extent to which the newness amounts to a radical departure from the world capitalist historic theme of capital accumulation in pursuit of the world capitalist historic motives ... and the conflicts they engender, both at the national and international levels: the movement from an exploitative and therefore dehumanizing world-system to a non-exploitative and therefore

[100] See, for example, ME Salomon, 'From NIEO to Now and the Unfinishable Story of Economic Justice' (2013) 62 ICLQ 31; DP Fidler, 'Revolt Against or from Within the West: TWAIL, the Developing World, and the Future Direction of International Law' (2003) 2 Chinese Journal of International Law 41; S Pahuja, *Decolonising International Law: Development, Economic Growth and the Politics of Universality* (CUP 2011), as well as; JT Gathii, 'Third World Approaches to International Economic Governance' in R Falk, B Rajagopal, and J Stevens (eds), *International Law and the Third World: Reshaping Justice* (Routledge 2008) 255.

[101] BS Chimni, 'The Principle of Permanent Sovereignty over Natural Resources: Toward a Radical Interpretation' (1998) 38 Indian Journal of International Law 208; AG Frank, 'Rhetoric and Reality of the New International Economic Order' in Addo (n 99) 165.

[102] See Salomon (n 100). But in highlighting some of the results of the struggle for PSNR, see Chapter 3 which explains that, 'permanent sovereignty over natural resources' did pass into the constitutional provisions of the major resource exporting nations of the developing world, with these constitutional formulations vesting natural resources in the people of the state, not in the state itself.

[103] Pahuja (n 100) 125; G Abi-Saab, 'Permanent Sovereignty over Natural Resources' in M Bedjaoui (ed), *International Law: Achievements and Prospects* (UNESCO/Martinus Nijhoff 1991) 600.

humanizing world-system'.[104] It is a perfectly reasonable proposition that had the NIEO been successful, it would have in any case served to reinforce the contested terms upon which the world economy was operating.

If the ideas and practice of NIEO did not take the world and its disenfranchised where many hoped it would, it did take us somewhere notable. The NIEO was a rejection of colonialism (even if not of an imperialist international law);[105] it represented an effort to assert the sovereign autonomy of the non-western world; and it was an attempt to redirect international economic governance towards distributional equity and fairness.[106] It also exemplified precisely why different legal regimes cannot exist in isolation, presaging the subsequent focus on linking human rights and development and the importance of duties of international cooperation to those ends.[107] If the NIEO initiative can be criticized for being 'reformist and capitalist',[108] it could also be said to have represented a form of 'socialism among states';[109] certainly the vision and efforts by lead UN economists of the day were directed at a socialist form of globalization.[110] As is well known, the Second and Third World internationalism of the time faced active resistance by the United States and other colonial powers. And while imperialism had been deeply contested by jurists from across the globe, powerful interests continued to work against transformation, as did wider developments in global capitalism that saw the steep rise of neoliberalism in the 1980s and early 1990s. Although there were challenges that worked against radical change both from within the movement and from outside of it, the call for a New International Economic Order was, as Samir Amin points out, rebellion just the same.[111]

[104] H Addo, 'Introduction: Pertinent Questions about the NIEO' in Addo (n 99) 1, 4.

[105] For a detailed exploration of the imperialist roots of international law, see A Anghie, *Imperialism, Sovereignty and the Making of International Law* (CUP 2004).

[106] For a consideration of the way in which ideas of the NIEO serve to animate the positions of developing states today, see Chapter 3 ('The End of Empire and the Search for Justice: The NIEO and Beyond'). For example, the push for control of multinational corporations through hard law, a project that has now been revived by Ecuador and South Africa within the UN Human Rights Council.

[107] Salomon (n 100) 49.

[108] See J Bockman, 'Socialist Globalization against Capitalist Neocolonialism: The Economic Ideas behind the New International Economic Order' *Humanity* (Spring 2015) 109, 118ff.

[109] N Gilman, 'The New International Economic Order: A Reintroduction' *Humanity* (Spring 2015) 1, 4.

[110] Bockman on Raúl Prebisch as the head of UNCTAD and Jan Tinbergen, a lead economist at the UN. Bockman (n 108) 119ff. Bockman writes that, 'UNCTAD assumed a normative or anticipatory socialism within a truly interconnected global economy of free markets, the endless flow of trade, finance, and people, universal trade laws that apply to all, as well as universal participation, the end of corporations, and so on. It was not clear how to get to this new world: through a social planner, through a revolutionary like Che, or through diplomatic agreement on multilateral laws? In any case, UNCTAD's vision of a truly global economy required a social restructuring of the existing neo-colonial world system' (ibid 121).

[111] Addo (n 104) 11; S Amin, 'Self-Reliance and the New International Economic Order' in Addo (n 99) 204. Addo draws an interesting distinction between '*anti-regime forces* that may contribute to the transformation of the system but are not necessarily *anti-systemic forces*'. Addo (n 104) 15, emphasis in the original. Gathii drawing on Chimni offers a global justice lens through which to consider the contribution of the NIEO and suggests that looking at the principle of permanent sovereignty over natural resources from a material, rather than a formal or statist perspective, 'would acknowledge

To be sure, to acknowledge the failures of the NIEO is not the same as disregarding its contributions. As BS Chimni rightly points out in his own critical account of international law and institutions, we need to be alive to the different historical and political contexts within which attempts at renewal take place, and their differential social impacts, lest we 'privilege form over content and conflate different historical and political conjectures'.[112] To query whether NIEO was transformative is not to question the drive of Second and Third World internationalists behind NIEO who sought to challenge the unfair rules of international economic governance to meet their development needs following the retreat of formal colonialism.[113] That they hitched their claims to the vehicle of international law that had served them so badly over centuries was a result not least of protecting their hard won sovereignty, even if it was a central concept of European international law that had long worked against them. Historical critique is always imbued with the extravagance of distance and the arrogance of detachment; the NIEO was surely radical for its time and, indeed, there has hardly been a more notable undertaking aimed at international solidarity since.

Any search for norms of justice today may not involve the revival of the norms of the NIEO but may well draw inspiration from them. Be that as it may, if we are to care also about consequences, which is essential if the *realization* of justice is really to matter, then judging the impact of international law on peasants, the poor and other subaltern people is a telling exercise, as is whether it provides accountability to the people who are wrongly affected by its rules, interpretations, and effects.[114] Through this empirical lens, it is easy to conclude that much of international law in the area of economic governance can only be defined as an ongoing project of immiseration, tethered as it continues to be to economic globalization.

The picture painted so far is one of the subordination of peoples to the economy with a snapshot of international law's role in that endeavour and the NIEO's efforts at overcoming that subordination. The place to begin a study of international human rights law and immiseration is merely to recognize that it is under the terms of global capitalism that human rights operate. Before we probe how human rights can create more just societies, we must first expose the ways in which they are a reflection of those societies and, crucially, how they assist in reproducing the underlying terms of immiseration that will ensure human rights protection

its original motivation in addressing the inequities of resource exploitation between alien colonial rulers and formerly colonised peoples'. Gathii (n 100) 261.

[112] BS Chimni, 'International Institutions Today: An Imperial Global State in the Making' (2004) 15 EJIL 1, 30.

[113] For a concise and thoughtful overview of Second and Third World efforts to challenge international economic governance, see Gathii (n 100); Salomon (n 100).

[114] The lower middle classes of the rich world are also bearing the brunt of economic globalization, but one might take a different approach to the consideration of victims in rich and powerful countries in that those countries play a significant role in shaping globalization and have the domestic resources to mitigate its worst effects at home.

is forever necessary. While international human rights law has played a role in addressing socio-economic harms and increasingly it has sought to confront the immiserating structural features of the global economy, there are still important questions to be asked as to the ways in which human rights work against a transformative or radical agenda, to the detriment of their own aims and objectives. We are interested herein not only in how human rights are being circumscribed by the logic and force of contemporary capitalism, nor how their terms are challenged and misappropriated to those ends, but also how they are co-opted in sustaining capitalism through their perceived *successes*. As explored in Chapter 7, a far greater awareness is required as to how the interpretation of international human rights law within an era of global neoliberalism sees growth fetishized as an essential precondition of human betterment and how distributional and ecological violence prefigure seemingly progressive social policies. The interpretation and application of international human rights law has a foremost function under conditions of economic globalization: to ensure that its terms do not help to reproduce the violent appropriations that sustain globalization. This would offer an important first step in the 'neutral' application of socio-economic rights, as has long been their claim.[115] The subversion of human rights to the predilections of capitalism invites in Chapter 7 a consideration of the place of economic growth in human rights law, the reproduction of harms under the social protection floors initiative, as well as the fate of human rights most cosmopolitan effort—obligations of international cooperation. When it comes to advancing extraterritorial human rights obligations, including obligations of international cooperation in the area of socio-economic rights and earlier as part of the right to development, this subversion is clearly at work. Three decades ago, the seminal doctrine of international cooperation under the right to development drew attention to the complementary duties of the international community to right-holders generally, given the emerging implications of economic interdependence. But, as has become evident, it is precisely its demands of international cooperation for structural change that have left the right to development as the most contentious and least operationalized of all human rights. The doctrinal and operational underdevelopment of these obligations are not to be excused merely as part of the *evolving* promise of international human rights law; more accurately, it is a reflection of the past and current limits of international politics to transform the 'deep global structures' of the international political economy in favour of new beneficiaries. Obligations of international cooperation aimed at people-centred development and socio-economic rights is a radical idea and, as the human rights chapter submits, it is precisely its radical prospect that has undermined its potential. Put differently, the threat we face today is that while international human rights lawyering is far from silent about the structural obstacles to justice, those efforts are hardly recognized outside of their own epistemic community.

115 CESCR, General Comment No 3, The Nature of States Parties' Obligations, Art 2(1) UN Doc E/1991/23 (1990), annex III, para 8.

There may be a combination of factors that contribute to this state of affairs, not least the revival of the TINA doctrine—the idea that 'there is no alternative' to neoliberalism.[116] The prevailing view is that the current system serves us all best and the recent economic and financial crisis has not dramatically altered that perspective nor its central practices.[117] One of the many distortions to come from TINA's disregard for alternatives is that what has come to be referred to as 'radical' today tends really to be very elementary: calls for a dignified existence whereby joined up institutions and policies would ensure that no one would starve to death in a world in which there is an abundance of food, or die for lack of medicine where a sufficient supply is available or be denied a life of possibility. It is indicative of how very far we have strayed from a humane global society that bringing economic forces under rational control[118] is reasoned to be irrational.[119]

4. The Stories We Like to Tell

This book unites a grave disaffection with the state of the world and the inescapable conclusion that international law is negatively implicated. That international law has offered a platform for the vindication of human rights, that at times it serves the underdog, and that it might demonstrate shifts towards resisting its extreme capitalist proclivities, does not weaken that central critique. In fact, the recent backlash

[116] The very language of neoliberalism supports the TINA doctrine: the 'free market' is 'a term that suggests a natural, non-political ordering process that operates independently of human will. Thus, standards appropriate to the exercise of public power are made to appear inapplicable.' BR Roth, 'Marxian Insights for the Human Rights Project' in Marks (n 72, *International Law on the Left*) 220, 235–36. Similarly, the risks associated with the current global financial architecture are accepted as a fait accompli, a danger we have to live with, as if capital markets were inevitable, when they are really just legal constructions—see Chapter 6 ('Global Finance'). An aspect of the TINA doctrine is also explored in Chapter 2, 71–73, in its consideration of exploitation. For example, if the caloric intake of a slave is increased, she is still a slave. Another example is sweatshop labour and other substandard labour conditions—one could argue people are 'better off' making low wages in bad working conditions—but it is still taking advantage of their situation which is exploitative.

[117] Wade remarks that this is contrary to the pattern in earlier bouts of hard times. RH Wade, 'Capitalism and Democracy at Cross-Purposes' (2013) 28 New Zealand Sociology 208, 211. Note, for example, the widespread adoption of fiscal contraction (austerity) in much of the western world as well as in the developing world; the capture by the wealthiest 1% in the United States of 95% of post-financial crisis growth since 2009, while the bottom 90% became poorer. The World Top Incomes Database, http://topincomes.g-mond.parisschoolofeconomics.eu and http://www.oxfam.org/sites/www.oxfam.org/files/bp-working-for-few-political-capture-economic-inequality-200114-summ-en.pdf. See, generally, C Crouch, *The Strange Non-death of Neoliberalism* (Polity 2011) as well as (the excellent piece on fascism and neoliberalism by) AS Chaudhary and R Chappe, 'The Supermanagerial Reich' *Los Angeles Review of Books* (7 Nov 2016): 'Neoliberalism has now clearly outlasted the 2008 financial crisis, and further consolidated and entrenched both its forms of governance and the concentration of wealth and income for the top 0.1 percent.'

[118] Roth (n 116) 249 provides (in a somewhat different context) this idea of 'bringing economic forces under rational control' as a feature of a socialist society.

[119] Gill drawing on Gramsci speaks of the terms that make up the 'neo-liberal common sense' to be contrasted with 'good sense'. S Gill, 'Market Civilization, New Constitutionalism and World Order' in Gill and Cutler (n 32) 29, 30.

against bilateral investment treaties by some capital-importing states (besides the fact these challenges to instruments of neoliberal orthodoxy can be reversed with a change of government)[120] and attempts in the past years by European debtor states to resist neoliberal conditionality at the hands of public international lenders, demonstrate the power and influence of 'disciplinary neoliberalism'[121] as much as anything else. Stephen Gill is right to define the constitutive features of the contemporary civilization as 'the institutionalization of a hierarchical, disciplinary, and materially unequal world order increasingly dominated by capital'.[122]

Arguments that we have moved from a reified state-centric world view to one in which 'individuals are the hub around which international law revolves'[123] and towards global governance based on accountability standards such as a transparency, participation, and reasoned decisions point to that which we might aspire rather than what practice tends to demonstrate. In the international realm, state action fails quite systematically to provide evidence of the actual wishes of most people and certainly not the people most affected by those decisions.[124] There is neither the appearance of fairness nor is there fair practice when it comes to the social consequences of economic globalization's processes and outcomes. The principles of best practice in global governance—if they can be said here and there meaningfully to be exercised—are simply bypassed when edicts of neoliberalism require it,[125] or are directed by those edicts in subtle ways that mask the methods by which power is retained and reinforced.[126] A more accurate description of the defining feature of global governance under international law today is the *absence* of accountability not least of international institutions, their member states, as well as their staff for the impact of decisions.[127]

120 D Schneiderman, 'How to Govern Differently: Neo-liberalism, New Constitutionalism and International Investment Law' in Gill and Cutler (n 32) 165, 175–78 ('Rolling back new constitutionalism').

121 '[T]he power and discipline of capital in social relations.' Gill (n 119) 29.

122 ibid 30.

123 Dunoff and Trachtman on the 'Constitutionalization of International Law' thesis. J Dunoff and JP Trachtman, 'The Lotus Eaters' (Debate) in J Klabbers, A Peters, and G Ulfstein, *The Constitutionalization of International Law* (OUP 2011) 369, 370.

124 In contrast here to the point made by Dunoff and Trachtman that '[T]he best evidence of individuals' actual wishes today is still derived inductively from state action' (ibid 372).

125 For coverage of a recent and egregious example, see 'The IMF and the Crisis in Greece, Ireland, and Portugal: An Evaluation by the Independent Evaluation Office' (8 July 2016); and further Chapter 6 ('Global Finance').

126 See the rich literature on indicators and global governance, for example: SE Merry, 'Measuring the World: Indicators, Human Rights and Global Governance' (2011) 52(S3) Current Anthropology 83; K Davis, A Fisher, B Kingsbury, and SE Merry (eds), *Governance by Indicators: Global Power through Classification and Ranking* (OUP 2012).

127 Chimni's critiques in 2004 of international financial and development institutions could have equally been written today, thirteen years later, without having changed a word: 'II's [international institutions] are [. . .] not accountable to the people who are *affected* by their decisions . . . It is said that states establish IIs and therefore remain responsible for their acts of omission and commission . . . There is, in addition, the problem that IIs are modern bureaucracies that exclude the possibility of ascribing individual responsibility for acts of omission and commission . . . A myriad small decisions are taken and advanced for which no one in particular is responsible . . . Structural adjustment policies can have devastating consequences for the peoples of the country on which they are imposed, yet no one state or individual or set of individuals can be assigned the authorship of these programmes making IIs the

The possibility that we have entered an era defined by a process of constitutionalization at the international level that would offer 'a protected public realm', that is, it would 'put a fence around the public, and protect it as well as it can' is but a welcome dream.[128] It is no exaggeration to say that what we have today is the economization of all aspects of life where no realm is left untouched by neoliberal reasoning;[129] globalization is creating pressures towards common 'constitutional' norms such as the right to property and its protection in international investment and international trade and a contract model for international economic law that does not require that the interests of the other party or wider public interests are taken into account. Instead, the aim of such contracting parties is to extract as much from the bargain as possible for themselves.[130] Governance principles have been subverted such that what constitutes 'good governance' is ensuring the sanctity of private property whereas 'the rule of law' is meant to provide stability for foreign investors. These are among the dominant global values today. The rise of norms and practices meant to shore up private gain, more than any other development, explains much of the world today. To recognize constitutionalism as 'the philosophy of striving towards some form of political legitimacy typified by

perfect vehicle for the exploitation and dominance of subaltern states and peoples.' Chimni (n 112) esp 19 and 21–22, emphasis in the original. For a recent account of many of the same legal obstacles, see ME Salomon and O De Schutter, 'Economic Policy Conditionality, Socio-Economic Rights and International Legal Responsibility: The Case of Greece 2010–2015' legal brief prepared for the Special Committee of the Hellenic Parliament on the Audit of the Greek Debt (15 June 2015), http://www.lse.ac.uk/humanRights/documents/2015/SalomonDeSchutterGreekDebtTruth.pdf

[128] J Klabbers, 'Setting the Scene' in J Klabbers, A Peters, and G Ulfstein (eds), *The Constitutionalization of International Law* (OUP 2011) 1, 19. In pointing to these ripostes that constitutionalization offers, that book works from the assumption that constitutionalization 'is indeed taking place, however much in fits and starts perhaps' while the author acknowledges that 'no miracles should be expected' (ibid 4 and 19). As Susan Marks warns us, we need to be aware of 'the temptation we all face to analyse events as stories of progress', 'Naming Global Administrative Law' (2005) 37 New York University Journal of International Law and Politics 995, 997. At the level of the European Union, the debt, austerity, and social rights crisis, the vociferous efforts by civil society to make transparent the Transatlantic Trade and Partnership (TTIP) negotiations and to challenge its core terms, along with the Brexit referendum decision suggests, at a minimum, that Europe is equally engaged in an exercise of 'disciplinary neoliberalism' while necessarily failing to represent the will of the people.

[129] See notably Wendy Brown's recent work on the ubiquity of neoliberal reasoning. Brown (n 29) 17.

[130] As addressed in Chapter 4 on the trade treaty as contract: parties to a contract bargain for the best result they can obtain. They are free to be self-interested; it is entirely permissible and expected that they be so. They are not required to be impartial or to take the interests of the other parties into account. They do not have to comply with the moral conditions of reasonable acceptance by all parties or justify their position to others. Contracting parties, moreover, are free to take full advantage of disparities in bargaining power or inequalities between the parties. The aim of such contracting parties is to extract as much rent as possible from the bargain for themselves. As addressed in Chapter 6, in the area of sovereign debt, the legal system governs seemingly private activities as if those activities are purely a matter of contract and exchange despite their enormous public significance. In global finance more generally, the risk is not only between the parties to a transaction. It is not simply risk between the buyers and sellers of financial products. It is systemic risk. Systemic financial risk imposes 'negative externalities' on persons who have nothing to do with the financial practices causing the risk and who often have no stake in any potential gains accumulating from these practices.

respect for . . . a constitution'[131] is to recognize how far we are from that noble ideal in international law.[132]

5. We're Not Falling for That Old Trick: Eschewing False Dichotomies (or What This Work Isn't About)

At the heart of this book is the basic premise that international law is too market-oriented; for a whole host of historical and political reasons, it is a construction biased in favour of a 'highly aggressive' capitalism.[133] Arguably that would not be a problem if the result was that the world these days was remotely just, but it is not. As noted above, we reject the bifurcation of the economic and non-economic realms which forms the central premise of mainstream economics and is the basis upon which the modern international legal and institutional architecture was built.[134] Following the Second World War, in starts and bursts, we have seen attempts at reconciling this artificial split, but with very few positive results. The expositions provided in the chapters of this book are a testament to that gross deficiency, to the false premise that there is a 'sacrosanct domain that we call the economy, in which market logic should reign supreme, and then there are some other fields around it

[131] Klabbers (n 128) 10.

[132] In Gill's words: '[L]aw is not simply understood as "superstructure" or indeed as a set of constraints on the exercise of authority of government; rather, law is seen as an active governing technique that is productive of political authority: it is seen as central to the constitution of the power of capital as well as neo-liberal forms of state, or political and civil society, in the emerging world order' Gill (n 119) 29.

[133] Beckert (n 18) xvi.

[134] The linkages between economic and so-called non-economic areas and institutions were anticipated. For example, the UN Charter saw a role for the relevant UN specialized agencies in social and economic affairs of the UN (UN Charter Arts 63, 64, and 70) and they were brought into the UN family through relationship agreements with ECOSOC (UN Charter Art 57). But the IMF still asserts its independence as an international organization for the purposes of rejecting that it would have obligations in the area of socio-economic rights, for example. See, quintessentially, the article by the then IMF Counsel, F Gianviti, 'Economic, Social and Cultural Rights and the International Monetary Fund' in Philip Alston (ed), *Non-state Actors and Human Rights* (OUP 2005) 113, http://www.imf.org/external/np/leg/sem/2002/cdmfl/eng/gianv3.pdf; and the recent Evaluation Report by the IMF's Independent Evaluation Office on the IMF and Social Protection (2017) which does not consider the question of human rights and the IMF at all, whether duties, accountability, or anything else, http://www.ieo-imf.org/ieo/files/completedevaluations/SP%20-%202017EvalReport.pdf. The elaboration of an international trading system was undertaken as a separate endeavour outside of the UN 'family', with the role of UNCTAD providing the link and as Quinn Slobodian insightfully provides: '[O]ne can say plainly that the world economic imaginary of the developing world—represented by UNCTAD and the G-77—was the Other against which the neoliberal field of IEL was defined', 'Ordoglobalism: The Invention of International Economic Law', Scales of Economy Conference, University of Sydney, (July 2016), https://www.academia.edu/28283843/Ordoglobalism_The_Invention_of_International_Economic_Law. Notably, the Second and Third World internationalism of the time faced active resistance by the United States and other colonial powers and the key UN institutions of change, such as UNCTAD, were said to have been 'normalized' at the behest of the US opposition to their agenda. Chimni (n 112) 2; Bockman (n 108), referring also to the UN Environmental Programme (UNEP) and the UN Educational, Social and Cultural Organization (UNESCO) and the US efforts to limit their support of Third World causes.

where you can implement social ideals'.[135] In this work we eschew the false premise that the economy is something that is separate from the political and social realms and naturally operates outside of them only perhaps (and depending on your view) to be united at some later point in the form of redistribution (which in any case globalization works against[136] and international law disregards).

Another false dichotomy that this work eschews is that if one challenges liberalization, one is in favour of protectionism—we reject the familiar trope that one is either in favour of protectionism or in favour of liberalization and that essentially all commentators must come down on the side of one or the other (and that this work endorses the former position). For one, protectionism is but a response to globalization. It is a defensive strategy. It may be an important tool of deterrence that states must keep at hand, but it is not itself a source of prosperity.[137] Second, the free trade–protectionist dichotomy ignores the rise of social welfare democracies, a positive law of socio-economic human rights, and the role of the regulatory state. Framing the debate as between those two options serves to narrow our field of vision and thus our sense of possibility.

There is, of course, no such thing as the 'free market'. As many have pointed out, the term suggests that it somehow operates outside of politics and human will as if the rights and obligations that make it possible have appeared spontaneously and naturally.[138] This masks the fact that the global economy is highly regulated but in such a way as to protect some interests and not others. Contrary to the platitude that neoliberals govern as little as possible, they can be accused of 'govern[ing]

[135] Chang (n 2) 6.

[136] '[E]conomists learn at school that ... markets and prices must be left to do their work, by having as few distortions as possible (this is the famous "free and undistorted competition"), even if that means redistribution later, "in the second instance" ... Over the past thirty years, trade in goods and services has been profoundly liberalized, mostly in the name of this logic. But the "second instance"—greater redistribution—never came ... [t]rade liberalization and tax dumping work hand in glove'. T Piketty, *Chronicles on Our Troubled Times (Protectionism: A Useful Weapon ... For Lack of Anything Better, 20 Dec 2011)* (S Ackerman tr, Viking 2016, 91, 91–92.

[137] ibid 93. On Trump's narrow and ultimately unworkable vision for US protectionism, Ha-Joon Chang offers the following: 'The point is that, the hollowing out of American manufacturing industry has progressed in the contexts of (US-led) globalization of production and restructuring of the international trade system and cannot be reversed with simple protectionist measures ... Even at the domestic level, American economic revival will require far more radical measures than what the Trump administration is contemplating. It will require a systematic industrial policy that rebuilds the depleted productive capabilities of the US economy, ranging from worker skills, managerial competences, industrial research base and modernised infrastructure. To be successful, such industrial policy will have to be backed up by a radical redesigning of the financial system, so that more "patient capital" is made available for long-term-oriented investments and more talented people come to work in the industrial sector, rather than going into investment banking or foreign exchange trading.' CJ Polychroniou, 'Exposing the Myths of Neoliberal Capitalism: An Interview with Ha-Joon Chang', *Truthout* (8 Feb 2017), http://www.truth-out.org/opinion/item/39393-exposing-the-myths-of-neoliberal-capitalism-an-interview-with-ha-joon-chang.

[138] See BS Chimni, 'Third World Approaches to International Law: A Manifesto' in A Anghie, BS Chimni, K Mickelson, and O Okafor (eds), *The Third World and International Order: Law, Politics and Globalization* (Brill 2003) 47; D Kennedy, 'Introduction: International Symposium on the International Legal Order' (2003) 16 LJIL 839; Marks (n 72, 'International Legal Concept'); Marks (n 72, 'Human Rights and the Bottom Billion'); Salomon (n 95) 6.

everything down to the last detail' and far from producing 'freedom', they continually limit it.[139] As unpacked in Chapter 4, the very notion of liberalized markets and free trade is deceptive, most notably because they are not actually about free trade at all, they are about the distribution of advantages through a coercively structured legal order. Nonetheless, so pervasive is the myth of the consummately constructive free market today that it tends to be invoked as a matter of course, irrespective of its implications for the many people across the globe who are subordinated by its machinations, including by the concentration of market power within the private sector and the direct and indirect government subsidies in aid of those concentrations.[140] The strongest claim of those who defend the current system and push for ever greater opening of markets is to point to how rich the world has become under this model of global capitalism. As addressed above and elsewhere in this book, this blunt argument has limited purchase: it misleads us with the offer of an aggregate figure only and fails to account for the fact that gains from trade and other forms of liberalization are not the only phenomenon at work; we also see a distribution of immiseration.

Yet, to challenge the canon and current practice of the so-called free market is automatically to be labelled and derided as 'protectionist' and put on the defensive. This book dismisses the argument of being pro-protectionism if one is not pro-liberalization because it dismisses the idea that all we have are these two (misleading) options—reducing or erecting barriers to transnational capital. The deceit of this dualism leads us to ignore propositions that reject the commodified global economy altogether or systems that reimagine markets; the centrality of these false options blunt our ability to recall that the global economy is subordinate to society and not the other way around. Reflecting on a programme of 'definancialization' for example, Amin proposes markets that are 'for the first time truly transparent and regulated by democratic negotiation among social partners (for the first time they are no longer adversaries as they are necessarily under capitalism). It is the financial "market"—opaque by nature and subjected to the requirements of management for the benefit of monopolies—that is abolished.'[141] The assertion that limits options to being between a celebrated open system or a perilous closed global system is

[139] M Lazzarato, *Governing by Debt* (JD Jordan tr, semiotext(e) 2013) 11; Chaudhary and Chappe (n 117).

[140] Roth (n 116) 236.

[141] S Amin, *The Implosion of Capitalism* (Pluto 2014) 142–43. 'I use here the term "de-linking" that I proposed half a century ago, a term that contemporary discourse appears to have replaced with "de-globalization". I have never conceptualized de-linking as an autarkic retreat, but rather as a strategic reversal in the face of both internal and external forces in response to the unavoidable requirements of self-determined development. De-linking promotes the reconstruction of a globalization based on negotiation, rather than a submission to the exclusive interests of the imperialist monopolies. It also makes possible the reduction of international inequalities' (ibid 143). Piketty, for his part, writes about how trade could be an 'indispensable weapon' '[t]o force the tax havens' hands and, more generally, to institute the financial, social, and environmental regulations we need to take control of a globalized capitalism gone mad'. Piketty (n 136) 93. 'There is a huge difference in saying that trade is essential for economic development and saying that free trade is best.' H-J Chang, 'Protecting the Global Poor' *Prospect Magazine* issue 136 (2007).

conditioned by history. It is also the language of many an orthodox economist that underprops international law today, but it is an exercise in narrowing our sense of possibilities for a just future through a tacit endorsement of the idea that 'there is no alternative' to capitalist globalization.

Third, we eschew the false dichotomy that one is either for the market or for the state. As a first order principle, we reject the fictitious neoliberal construction that pits the state against the market. That position flows from the view that the market is a natural entity while the state is an artificial one and that the private sector is a connate resource to be freed from the injuries of state regulation.[142] As Bengi Akbulut et al remind us, there are social and ecological tolls of both private and statist variants of capitalist processes.[143] The democratic state (where this can be said still truly to exist) has a particular role to play in that its actions (may) have to be justified in terms of societal values, in a manner that the actions of private firms do not,[144] and, as we have already pointed out, the market is always regulated by the state, it is a question of how and in whose interests. The false dichotomy between state and market also sees peddled the alleged consequences as to the negative impact of greater state regulation on economic activity and GDP growth[145] and overstates the role of the private sector. There are ample examples that show how the state can be a bold and valuable innovator.[146] That said, as Marxists have long warned, 'the capitalist state is unlikely ever to become an active agent of popular empowerment and social transformation, and the left should therefore always guard against tendencies to prioritize the state as the primary site of struggle'.[147] By presenting the choice as between the market and the state a defence of one or the other is invited; and to question the centrality of the market has the state vended largely as a benevolent and rights protecting entity, thereby shielding its failures. In short, the polarizing allusions of the market or state dichotomy rob us of nuance in how we approach the role of both of those entities.

Through this false dichotomy the myriad ideas around alternative visions are obscured, including alternative visions of exchange economies.[148] So one final

[142] Wade (n 117) 230. [143] Akbulut, Adaman, and Madra (n 16) 742.

[144] 'For all its faults, the democratic state has an advantage over the private sector in that state actions do have to be justified in terms of societal values, as the actions of private firms do not; and the leaders of the state can be replaced (and their remuneration set) as a result of citizen preferences expressed in public forums—which is not the case for leaders of firms. The state can also exercise comprehensive foresight about the economy's future growth, in a way that private firms typically do not.' Wade (n 117) 230.

[145] 'Pro-regulatory arguments are more often than not simply ignored because they do not serve the short term self-interests of the powerful. But where the arguments cannot be avoided, corporations reflexively respond to calls for greater regulation by warning that this will depress economic activity and GDP growth, which will have the effect of lowering state revenues that can be spent on social goods. Here it must be noted that it is not theoretically true that more regulation will result in less economic activity and GDP growth. But more importantly, there is no evidence that this is the case.' Chang (n 2) 11.

[146] M Mazzucato, *The Entrepreneurial State: Debunking Public v Private Sector Myths* (Anthem 2015).

[147] J Roos, 'Towards a New Anti-Capitalist Politics' issue 0 *Roar Magazine*, https://roarmag.org/magazine/anti-capitalist-politics-21st-century

[148] See, for example, Bockman (n 108), 115 and 119–20 on Raúl Prebisch and market socialism whereby 'such market socialism would not lead to capitalism but was rather "a quest for a new modus

reason we eschew this false dichotomy is to leave open the space for imagining more radical futures than between the capitalist state and the capitalist market, futures that may not involve the state or the transnational market at all, as we currently understand them.

6. What This Work Is About

The issues and ideas that animate this book indicate that we are unapologetically concerned with what Arturo Escobar refers to as a 'naturalized hegemony of the economic conception of the world'[149] and with the poverty, inequality, dispossessions, alienations, and concomitant immiseration that accompany the dominant choice of economic rationale. In particular, we are interested in how international law and its regimes of trade, investment, finance, and human rights are implicated in the construction of this misery; how international law is producing, reproducing, and embedding these ills and narrowing the frame of alternatives that might really serve humanity. In the pursuit of this endeavour we seek to avoid falling into traps that presuppose one can only hold views from among a series of predetermined options (eg: trade or protectionism) and that assume life under some form of transnational capitalism with its defining features of commodification and profit.

While we reject being labelled—as if there was one that would capture the views of all three authors—we are committed to the legitimate aspirations of the free development and self-realization of all people on terms that honour the same for others. We are committed to a logic whereby collective, social, economic, political, and ecological interests matter. This commitment makes demands on international law. International law is subject to the demands of justice because of its role as an institution essential to global cooperation, because it intrudes far into the distributional issues linked closely to how people live their lives, because of its historic and ongoing role in perpetuating and legitimizing moral wrongs, and because it can, and indeed does, lead to domination and the deprivation of freedom if states and international organizations do not get matters right: international law is subject to the demands of justice because it is constitutive of the current economic order.[150]

Far greater accountability is required in order for international law to make any legitimate appeal to respect it by those dictated to by it.[151] A just international law would not treat people as passive recipients or supplicants to rules that benefit those in stronger positions. The economic model that international law supports

operandi compatible with the collective ownership of the means of production"'. Bockman, citing Gustav Castell (ibid 119). See also Amin (n 141).

[149] Escobar (n 8) xii.

[150] See Chapter 2 ('Confronting the Pathologies of International Law').

[151] For example, on three interrelated features of the global financial architecture—the production of insecurity, perverse redistribution that flows from poor to rich, and real concerns about domination—that make it susceptible to reasonable rejection by those who bear its burdens, see Chapter 6 ('Global Finance').

at any given time must comply with moral requirements of equal concern for each person, and so humans must ensure the institutions of their making comport with that which is just. If one is said to have adopted the position of 'radical critique' by suggesting that international law institutionalizes domination by some states over others, and domination by transnational corporations over poorer or weaker states and their citizens and that 'the current institutions of global governance can be seen as "imperial" institutions, furthering the goals and stabilizing the dominance of Northern industrialized countries at the expense of the South, and of the dominant capitalist classes at the expense of subaltern peoples' then we are to be labelled radicals.[152] Except so-called 'radicals' abound today.

It is the case that some consider the current system to be just or our best hope at justice for the disenfranchised, but that would be at odds with the 'lived experience' and empirical reality of the majority of people.[153] We know too much to accept that the current system represents a universal good, rather than particular interests, motives, and mandates driven by the morally problematic manoeuvrings of the powerful that do not align with any reasonable conception of justice. If those who defend the current system were sure it was just, they could begin by evaluating their rules, policies, decisions, and institutions against a number of important variables relating to fair processes, including having those stakeholders at the table who will bear the social costs of the form and rules of international law.[154] Whether the system is likely to meet the demands of justice will depend on whether it meets a plural set of principles relating to egalitarian justice but also anti-domination principles relevant to different contexts, as explored in Chapter 2.

7. Predistribution Not Just Redistribution

An argument that runs through this book is that redistribution alone does not satisfy the problems highlighted, and does not meaningfully exist at the global level nor as part of the general international legal system.[155] Redistribution is also

[152] B Kingsbury, N Krisch, RB Stewart, 'The Emergence of Global Administrative Law' (2005) 68 Law and Contemporary Problems 15, 52. 'In order to address the central problems of accountability, global administrative law might have to devise ways to empower and include people and their representatives from the South. From this perspective, a more effective participation of the developing world in global administrative structures might be more urgent than implementing yet another path of influence for the affluent parts of the world' (ibid).

[153] As poignantly expressed by BS Chimni, 'The Past, Present and Future of International Law: A Critical Third World Approach' (2007) 8 Melbourne Journal of International Law 499, 500.

[154] On effective equality of power in social decision as 'the essence of democracy' measured by 'the extent to which the interests and the views of the bottom half of the socioeconomic ladder have commensurate weight in political decision-making', see Roth (n 116) 244.

[155] See, for example, Chapter 4 including the coverage of special and differential treatment which fails on at least four grounds, including that of redistribution through assistance. A better approach is to turn away from non-reciprocity exceptions and towards more basic restructuring of what constitutes an obligation in an international trade agreement as a matter of the basic structure of those agreements. As Joel Trachtman quips in his critique of the WTO on redistribution: '[T]his concept [of Special and Differential Treatment] seems to mask the fact that the international trade system has done little

often inhibited by the workings of globalization at the domestic level.[156] What is called for herein is a robust awareness of the importance of reconfiguring the current model of *predistribution*: priorities, rules and their application, systems and structures, the failures of which are demonstrated not least by the fact that the need for subsequent redistribution is required; redistribution which in any case may not come.

If the idea of redistribution is reflective of *ex post* initiative, then predistribution is dedicated to *ex ante* action—making international law just in a structural sense.[157] Redistribution alone masks the far deeper problem and the far less scrutinized phenomenon whereby laws—including international law—allow for 'sluicing market incomes upwards'[158] and fails to address the relationships—past and present—between capitalism and international law. At best, redistribution addresses the symptoms not the causes of immiseration. Distributive justice and policies of redistribution are also conventionally associated with the internal affairs of states. This conventional account expects redistribution to be a national responsibility so international economic law is assumed to have nothing or little to do with it. But there is a broad consensus on this, explicit in political theory, and recognized in critical and creative thinking about international law: Justice also has to occur at the site of international law. This work is not prepared to defend an arrangement that is content with rules, systems, and structures that fail to mitigate losses and share gains and then with very uncertain dedication seek, or do not disallow, for redistribution in order (allegedly) to support vast number of alienated people. Instead, any rules and their institutions must themselves be fair.

Despite its partial function, redistribution still faces a number of practical difficulties. On the one hand, we have unconcealed impediments: domestic efforts at policies of redistribution where desperately needed are prohibited by forces outside of the state: the austerity imposed by international lenders and the 'trade-distorting' subsidies by governments seeking to buy and distribute food where needed offer but two examples. On the other hand, there are the concealed impediments. The widespread turn to social protection—also supported in the Sustainable Development

specifically intended to alleviate poverty: it is not special and differential enough.' 'Legal Aspects of a Poverty Agenda at the WTO: Trade Law and "Global Apartheid"' (2003) 6 JIEL 3, 10–11.

[156] As above, see for example Piketty on how globalization fails in the 'second instance' to facilitate redistribution through international tax competition and 'the hammering of progressive levies'. 'The richest benefited from sharp cuts in taxes, even though they were already the main beneficiaries of trade liberalization and globalization ... Instead of a more equitable sharing of gains from liberalization, tax redistribution has, on the contrary, tended to worsen its egalitarian effects'. Piketty (n 136) 92. For another example of the ways in which redistribution is inhibited at the national level by international actors, see the case study on the injustices of sovereign debt in Chapter 6 ('Global Finance').

[157] As addressed in Chapter 2 ('Confronting the Pathologies of International Law'), this is so that the elements of international law relevant to the global economy are designed to make it structurally impossible for injustice to exist in the global economy in any material sense. For example, if the focus is on domination in the global economy, the aim would be for international law to be structured to eliminate or, given the limitations of the law as an instrument to effectuate change, to make it exceedingly difficult for powerful actors to dominate in the global economy.

[158] See, generally, Wade (n 117) 229.

Goals and by the United Nations Committee on Economic, Social and Cultural Rights—might see cushioned the worst effects of domestic policies that engender poverty and inequality, all the while entrenching the capitalist growth economy that made possible the poverty and inequality in the first place, a topic explored in Chapter 7 on human rights. The paradox is that the social protection floor celebrated in the SDGs tells us not that we have won an important battle in protecting fundamental socio-economic well-being, but that we have lost. We have lost because it demonstrates that we are prepared to settle for preventing or mitigating suffering but not to changing the terms under which that suffering is made possible and reproduced. The social protection floor is redistributive but not predistributive, which are the terms required for a transformative enterprise to take hold. It would seem then, that the allotment of advantages and disadvantages under a coercively structured legal order is the most successful example of global 'redistribution' that there is.

8. Concluding Remarks

The various chapters in this book cover the legal regimes of international trade, foreign investment, global finance, and human rights and demonstrate that there are serious pathologies at work in international law. The construction that is international law has been shaped by the past quests for capitalist expansion of dominant powers and continues on that trajectory today. That international law is both constituted by capitalism and constitutive of it seems clear, but it is an open question whether international law is path-dependent. The arguments herein for a different type of international law, one that better accords with demands of justice, implies that there may still be hope, but if there is it is faint. This book is a contribution to the uphill battle to recover international law so that, 'ordinary life' might become 'the focus of the entire discipline'.[159]

[159] Chimni (n 153) 515.

2

Confronting the Pathologies of International Law

From Neoliberalism to Justice

In his dialogue with Socrates in Plato's Republic, Thrasymachus argues, 'justice is nothing other than the advantage of the stronger'.[1] He elaborates that the various kinds of rulers for the city states of ancient Greece, regardless of the form of government, tyrannical, democratic, or other, make laws to their own advantage. 'Democracy makes democratic laws, tyranny makes tyrannical laws, and so on with the others. And they declare what they have made—what is to their own advantage—to be just for their subjects, and to punish anyone who goes against this as lawless and unjust.'[2] So too the Athenians argued to the Melians during the Peloponnesian War about relationships between city states, to persuade the Melians to accede to Athenian domination.[3] From Thucydides' Melian Dialogue in his *History of the Peloponnesian War* comes '[t]he strong do what they can and the weak suffer what they must'.[4]

The Thrasymachian idea of justice found its way into the work of one of the most important philosophers writing at the beginning of the modern state, Thomas Hobbes. John Rawls tells us that '[i]t is useful to think of modern moral and political philosophy as beginning with Hobbes, and the reaction to Hobbes'.[5] A broad consensus in political philosophy, however, rejects the Hobbesian power-based understanding of justice, as does human rights theory and practice. The rhetoric if not the practice of 'real world' politics rejects it as well. With the rise of Kantian-influenced theories, political philosophy has moved away from accounts of justice based in power and interest toward accounts based in principles of right and the good, with the power of the state transforming from a force to be imposed to a

[1] Plato, 'The Republic' in JM Cooper (ed), *Plato, Complete Works* (Hackett 1997) 338c2–338c3.

[2] ibid 338e.

[3] Thucydides, *The History of the Peloponnesian War*, ch XVII, the so-called 'Melian Dialogue'. For a creative application of the Melian Dialogue to the Greek financial crisis in 2015, see R Zaretsky, 'What Would Thucydides Say About the Crisis in Greece?' *New York Times* (1 July 2015). Y Varoufakis made the phrase from Thucydides the title of his book on Greece and the eurozone Crisis, *And The Weak Suffer What They Must?: Europe, Austerity and the Threat to Global Stability* (Vintage 2017).

[4] Thucydides (n 3); see J Crawford, *Chance, Order, Change: The Course of International Law* (Hague Academy of International Law 2014) 27.

[5] J Rawls, *Lectures on the History of Political Philosophy* (Harvard UP 2007) 24.

politics to be justified to each person, regardless of power. Hobbes wrote in the historical context in which order, not justice, was the primary subject of justification, when states were in early stages of evolution, when peace was confronted by fundamental religious disagreement, and when religion was central to official authority in Europe. A Kantian-influenced justification of state power now flourishes, which censors power through the constraints of impartiality and respect for each person. In the past several decades, a considerable body of philosophical work has proliferated on global justice in this tradition.[6]

These moves in philosophy have made few inroads into the practices of states as reflected in international law. International law is in what could be characterized as a Thrasymachian trap. It is structured to serve power and interest. Throughout its history, international law has privileged the power of Europe and the West. Start with Hugo Grotius, credited rightly or wrongly with bringing the idea of an international society governed by rules to modern states.[7] Consider, for example, his principle of natural right that in the absence of a state, any private individual has the right to punish. This principle was a justification to permit the Dutch to wage offensive wars to open trade routes in South East Asia and elsewhere.[8] Grotius claimed this principle could be logically deduced but it is difficult not to see it actually as a piece of advocacy to support Dutch power at the time. When international law made its positivist turn in the nineteenth century, it distinguished between civilized and uncivilized nations, with only the former forming a 'family of nations' deserving to be governed by international law.[9]

The result is that international law suffers from serious moral disorder. As Andrew Hurrell explains, the aspirations of international society 'remain deeply contaminated by the interests and values of powerful states and of the private actors that they may represent'.[10] International law is a normative order perpetuated by powerful states to serve as an instrument of their power rather than as a restraint upon it.[11] In a legal order structured around neoliberal ideologies rather than principles of justice, every state can and does grab what it can in the economic sphere on the basis of power and interest, legally so and under colour of law. International law cannot

[6] On the state of theories of global justice, see, eg, G Brock, 'Theories of Global Justice' in J Linarelli (ed), *Research Handbook on Global Justice and International Economic Law* (Edward Elgar 2013) 1.

[7] See H Bull, 'The Importance of Grotius in the Study of International Relations' in H Bull, B Kingsbury, and A Roberts (eds), *Hugo Grotius and International Relations* (OUP 1992) 65.

[8] R Tuck, *The Rights of War and Peace: Political Thought and the International Order from Grotius to Kant* (OUP 2001) 82.

[9] See Chapter 3 ('The End of Empire and the Search for Justice: NIEO and Beyond'), and for a discussion of these theories, see A Anghie, *Imperialism, Sovereignty and the Making of International Law* (CUP 2004) 35.

[10] A Hurrell, 'International Law and the Changing Constitution of International Society' in M Byers (ed), *The Role of Law in International Politics: Essays in International Relations and International Law* (OUP 2001) 327, 334–36.

[11] M Sornarajah, 'Power and Justice in International Law' (1997) 1 Singapore Journal of International and Comparative Law 28; see also T Franck, *The Power of Legitimacy Among Nations* (OUP 1990); R Steinberg and JM Zasloff, 'Power and International Law' (2006) 100 AJIL 64.

meet a basic standard of justification to humans as moral deliberators—of justification to each person for whom international law has consequences.

Markets serve important roles. But markets require institutions. Institutions are human-created social practices. They are not natural entities like comets or trees. They do not exist in a state of nature. Their structure is not inevitable, existing outside the reach of law. They require law to exist. Injustice that comes from markets is within our control. A market is determined by a set of human-constructed rules about who owns what and on what conditions, what is a public versus a private function, and how to pay for things. So, a 'free market' is not something the government intrudes upon with regulation. Rather, it is government regulation, in the form of law that makes markets of any sufficient scale possible.[12] How we design markets is up to us, based on what we value in whatever community is doing the valuing and depending on what values get voiced. Both market and justice norms are constitutive of rules of the game. The moral disorder in international law comes from its failure to internalize these basic features of just law.

The moral disorder of international law contradicts what we expect from international law. The Thrasymachian structure of international law would be rejected by an overwhelming majority of international lawyers if they were asked to consider what principles of justice would be acceptable as a normative foundation for international law. Let us engage very briefly in the sort of thought experiment common in both law and philosophy and ask hypothetically about what values international lawyers would expect international law to uphold.[13] What would we learn if we were to survey international lawyers on the normative standards supporting international law's claim to our fidelity? The international lawyers in our survey would be those in practice representing their governments, lawyers who work for intergovernmental organizations, those who work for nongovernmental organizations, those who represent private interests and multinational companies, and international legal scholars in academia. We would, of course, not limit our survey only to international lawyers situated in the West or in rich countries. We would likely find that most of these international lawyers hold some basic shared conception about the role of justice in international law, though, given value pluralism, they may differ on the particulars. Even if we accept the existence of value pluralism across the world,[14] it would be difficult for international law even to

[12] Much has been written on markets and institutions. For a compelling and recent explanation, see R Reich, *Saving Capitalism: For the Many, Not the Few* (Icon 2016) ch 1, 'The Prevailing View'.

[13] Hypothetical thinking to develop normative standards is common in both law and philosophy. For examples in law, one only has to look to the substantial work on default rules. See, eg, I Ayres and R Gertner, 'Filling Gaps in Incomplete Contracts: An Economic Theory of Default Rules' (1989) 99 Yale Law Journal 87. In philosophy, hypothetical arguments are used in social contract theory, with a recent prominent example being Rawls' use of the concept of the original position behind a veil of ignorance. J Rawls, *A Theory of Justice* (rev edn, Harvard UP 1999); J Rawls, *The Law of Peoples* (Harvard UP 2001) (international original position).

[14] When this pluralism is understood as claims about relativity and ethnocentricity, there is some reason to doubt its soundness. See J Griffin, *On Human Rights* (OUP 2008) ch 7.

exist if states, intergovernmental organizations, and their officials were to accept that international law fails to achieve some basic threshold of approximate or 'real-world' justice that most people could agree about.[15] Why would those actors justify their actions on international law grounds if they could not claim that international law treats its subjects fairly, justly, with respect, or according to some principle of right or common good? Justification of state action has been one of international law's primary purposes throughout the ages. International law is the main avenue by which states and their lawyers argue that they are not engaging in power play. It is difficult for an international lawyer to be a realist as that idea is employed in international relations theory, seeing international law only as an argument about power and as epiphenomenal when push comes to shove.[16] It is a contradiction that no government could reasonably maintain that international law has powers to direct us or states on our behalf to do particular things, yet we do not expect it to conform in its main applications to basic principles of justice. A basic claim to justice is one that the authors of international law must make to each person subject to international law if they are to reasonably expect these persons to accept international law's authority. It is well accepted, now axiomatic, that power fails to offer the right kind of reasons for action for law.[17]

The aim of this chapter is to offer a philosophically influenced argument on why the international law on trade, investment, and finance is subject to the demands of justice and on how those demands are greater than the basic minimums often suggested as applicable outside the state. Though international law remains trapped in a power-based notion of justice, political philosophy has done little to remedy the moral disorder. Theories about what is known in the literature as global justice bloomed mainly in response to Rawls' *Law of Peoples*.[18] Many consider Rawls' *Law of Peoples* to be deeply flawed, offering only a limited humanitarianism and basic human rights for international relations among liberal and decent peoples, but no duties of justice among these peoples at the global level. Opposing Rawls, cosmopolitans have argued that membership in a people or some form of political community like a state is not morally relevant but being human is, and therefore the full panoply of principles of justice apply across the globe and to each person regardless of nationality. These two camps—the liberal nationalists and the cosmopolitans—form major schools of contemporary philosophical thought about justice beyond state borders. Neither have had much influence in the actual making and

[15] 'Approximate justice' is a phrase that philosopher George Sher has used to distinguish accounts of ideals about justice from accounts addressing problems of justice in non-ideal conditions of actual societies. G Sher, *Approximate Justice: Studies in Ideal Theory* (Rowman & Littlefield 1997).

[16] Though the constructivist approach to international relations is less hostile to international law. See SD Krasner, 'International Law and International Relations: Together, Apart, Together?' (2000) 1 Chicago Journal of International Law, Article 10.

[17] This proposition is reflected in the significant change in legal positivism from Austin's sanction theory to Hart's union of primary and secondary rules. See GJ Postema, *Legal Philosophy in the Twentieth Century: The Common Law World*, vol 11 (Springer 2011).

[18] Rawls (n 13, *Law of Peoples*).

application of international law.[19] In too many theories about justice, international law is mysterious, a 'black box'. Charles Mills's lamentation on the relevance of theories about justice within state borders holds for theories of justice for beyond state borders as well:

> [W]e need to ask how it came about, and has come to seem normal, that 'social justice' as a philosophical concept has become so detached from the concerns of actual social justice movements. Certainly it's not the case that if people in the civil rights community were planning a conference on racial justice next month that they would be heatedly debating which philosophers to invite! Rather, mainstream political philosophy is seen as irrelevant to such forums because of the bizarre way it has developed since Rawls (a bizarreness not recognized as such by its practitioners because of the ... norms of disciplinary socialization). Social justice theory should be reconnected with its real-world roots, the correction of injustices, which means that rectificatory justice in non-ideal societies should be the theoretical priority, not distributive justice in ideal societies. Political philosophy needs to exit Rawlsland—a fantasy world in the same extraterrestrial league as Wonderland, Oz and Middle-earth (if not as much fun)—and return to planet Earth.[20]

This chapter takes a step towards a correction. It argues that international law is subject to the demands of justice in a way that is sensitive to how international law operates. The argument might be understood in some respects as falling within what political philosophers call the 'non-ideal' but no claims are made that it fits neatly in what appears to be a subject of some contestability and ongoing attention in philosophy.[21]

[19] This is so even though some cosmopolitans have sought to develop institutionally sensitive accounts. For more institutionally sensitive approaches, see C Barry and TW Pogge (eds), *Global Institutions and Responsibilities* (Blackwell 2005).

[20] G Yancy and C Mills, 'Lost in Rawlsland' *New York Times* (16 Nov 2014). Stanley Fish similarly argues:

> But philosophy is not the name of, or the site of, thought generally; it is a special, insular form of thought and its propositions have weight and value only in the precincts of its game. Points are awarded in that game to the player who has the best argument going ('best' is a disciplinary judgment) for moral relativism or its opposite or some other position considered 'major.' When it's not the game of philosophy that is being played, but some other—energy policy, trade policy, debt reduction, military strategy, domestic life—grand philosophical theses like 'there are no moral absolutes' or 'yes there are' will at best be rhetorical flourishes; they will not be genuine currency or do any decisive work.
>
> In short, the conclusions reached in philosophical disquisitions do not travel. They do not travel into contexts that are not explicitly philosophical (as seminars, academic journals, and conferences are), and they do not even make their way into the non-philosophical lives of those who hold them.

S Fish, 'Does Philosophy Matter?' *New York Times* (1 Aug 2011).

[21] Rawls first made the ideal–non-ideal distinction in *The Law of Peoples*. Amartya Sen's *The Idea of Justice* (Penguin 2010) is a substantial critique of ideal theory. See also J Tomasi, *Free Market Fairness* (Princeton UP 2012); D Estlund, 'Just and Juster' in D Sobel, P Vallentyne, and S Wall (eds), *Oxford Studies in Political Philosophy Vol 2* (OUP 2016) 9; B Hendrix, 'Where Should We Expect Social Change in Non-Ideal Theory?' (2013) 41 Political Theory 116; P Gilabert, 'Comparative Assessments of Justice, Political Feasibility, and Ideal Theory' (2012) 15 Ethical Theory and Moral Practice 39; R Jubb, 'Tragedies of Non-Ideal Theory' (2012) 11 European Journal of Political Theory 229; D Wiens, 'Prescribing Institutions without Ideal Theory' (2012) 20 Journal of Political Philosophy 45; AJ Simmons, 'Ideal and Nonideal Theory' (2010) 38 Philosophy and Public Affairs 5; A Hamlin and Z Stemplowska, 'Theory, Ideal Theory, and the Theory of Ideals' (2012) 10 Political Studies Review

It is essential that the connection of international law to theories of justice be established, otherwise lawyers and government officials will continue to consider these theories to be unrealistically utopian exercises serving only to engage the minds of philosophers. A suggestion to the global economic policy elite in any major capital that trade and investment agreements, or the regulation of global finance, should be governed by a principle of justice would likely might be met with a platitude about how the world should be fair, that the agreements under their purview are indeed fair, or worse, a blank stare. Walk into a mainstream conference on international law and the global economy, and the unexamined assumptions for any evaluation of the law or recommendations for its reform are progressive liberalization for international trade, open and minimally regulated borders for foreign direct investment, and the free flow of capital for international finance. When these assumptions are challenged, the challenger is often seen as engaging in fanciful and 'unrealistic' argument or essentially tolerated then ignored. To help make these challenges stick, a place to start is with an institutionally sensitive account of justice for international law.

1. The Thrasymachian Trap

International law is trapped in a notion of justice as the will of the stronger for two reasons. These reasons relate to the traditional division of responsibilities between international and domestic law. They are identified in this chapter as the 'practical association' and the 'domain of politics' arguments. These arguments are related, with 'practical association' referring to the features of a state's external relations with other states and 'domain of politics' referring to the features of a state's internal relations with its citizens. They support differentiated approaches to justice for international and domestic law, with practical association requiring only moral minimums outside the state and the domain of politics requiring full-blown justice inside the state. In the practical association argument, international law is primarily a set of norms for the coexistence of states with diverse and often conflicting ends. So, the argument goes, international law lacks something undergirding municipal law, a political community, whose purposes serve the ends of states grounded in

48; WA Galston, 'Realism in Political Theory' (2010) 9 European Journal of Political Theory 385; L Ypi, 'On the Confusion between Ideal and Non-ideal in Recent Debates in Global Justice' (2010) 58 Political Studies 536; L Valentini, 'On the Apparent Paradox of Ideal Theory' (2009) 17 Journal of Political Philosophy 332; P Gilabert, 'Global Justice and Poverty Relief in Nonideal Circumstances' (2008) 34 Social Theory and Practice 411; I Robeyns, 'Ideal Theory in Theory and Practice' (2008) 34 Social Theory and Practice 341; Z Stemplowska, 'What's Ideal about Ideal Theory?' (2008) 34 Social Theory and Practice 319; A Swift, 'The Value of Philosophy in Nonideal Circumstances' (2008) 34 Social Theory and Practice 363; CW Mills, '"Ideal Theory" as Ideology' (2005) 20 Hyapatia 165; R Goodin, 'Political Ideals and Political Practice' (1995) 25 British Journal of Political Science 37; J Raikka, 'The Feasibility Condition in Political Theory' (1998) 6 Journal of Political Philosophy 27; O O'Neill, 'Abstraction, Idealization and Ideology in Ethics' (1987) 20 Royal Institute of Philosophy Series 55; M Phillips, 'Reflections on the Transition from Ideal to Non-Ideal Theory' (1985) 19 Nous 551.

politics, with a shared conception of justice. The domain of politics tells us what justice is for states and their 'internal' law.

The consequences of the practical association and domain of politics arguments are significant. Together, they inform us that it is morally permissible, indeed, even morally required, that states and their representatives wield whatever power they possess to the advantage of their citizens, regardless of the consequences to other states and vulnerable persons in those other states. International law relevant to the global economy can be designed around whatever agendas powerful states may have with little concern for the moral legitimacy of the resulting rules and institutional structure governing the global economy. We should have few moral qualms, save those relating to the very limited moral considerations of humanitarianism and extraterritorial obligations of international cooperation based on human rights principles, in cutting short the life expectancies and causing the death of persons in poor countries through the force of power relations in structuring markets to support powerful states.[22]

If international law could be said to exist, says Martti Koskenniemi, it is a 'practical association' with no common end other than to coordinate the diverse ends of political communities known as states.[23] As Koskenniemi explains:

> In accordance with the founding myth of the system, the Peace of Westphalia in 1648 laid the basis for an agnostic, procedural international law whose merit consisted in its refraining from imposing any external normative ideal on the international society. The objectives of that society would now arise from itself and not from any religious, moral or political notions of the good given externally to it. If there is an 'international community', it is a practical association not designed to realize ultimate ends but to coordinate action to further the objectives of existing communities. Sovereign equality builds on this: because there are no natural ends, every member of the international society is free to decide on its own ends, and to that extent, they are all equal. The law that governs them is not natural but artificial, created by the sovereigns through the processes that are acceptable because neutral (see, eg, Nardin, 1983). To say international law is for 'peace', 'security', and 'justice' is to say that it is for peace, security, and justice as agreed and understood between the members of the system.[24]

Koskenniemi makes an analytical and not a normative claim about international law as practical association.

Antonio Cassese similarly argues in his textbook, *International Law*. After explaining that most states have written constitutions setting forth 'fundamental principles regulating social intercourse' constituting 'the pinnacle of the [domestic] legal system and are intended to serve as basic guidelines for the life of the whole community',[25] Cassese goes on to explain as follows for international law:

[22] As explored in Chapter 7 ('Human Rights'), obligations of international cooperation to the ends of socio-economic rights and people-centred development is a radical idea but it is precisely its radical prospects that have undermined its potential.

[23] M Koskenniemi, *The Politics of International Law* (Hart 2011) 209; see also 'What Is International Law For?' in MD Evans (ed), *International Law* (3rd edn, OUP 2010) 32–57, 33.

[24] Koskenniemi (n 23) *Politics of International Law*, 243 (fn omitted).

[25] A Cassese, *International Law* (OUP 2005) 46.

The situation is different in the world community. When this community came into existence, no State or other authority set forth any fundamental principles for regulating international dealings: no State had enough power to impose standards of behaviour on all members. A body of law gradually evolved under the impulse of convergent interests and exigencies of States, but no general, overarching principle was agreed upon.[26]

Cassese goes on to say that a few principles to govern international relations between states evolved, based on what he calls postulates of freedom of states, including a formal notion of sovereign equality. These underlie what he characterizes as the 'laissez faire approach' of classic international law.[27]

These descriptions reflect the historical path of international law grounded in a Westphalian conception of international law as a law only to support the coexistence of states, with states as the only agents to be recognized in an appeal to the authority of international law and with the highest level norms of sovereign equality and *pacta sunt servanda* blocking any possibility of these appeals going beyond a stripped down notion of international law as in substance a law of contract for formally equal entities. The conception of international law as practical association requires a strong version of formal sovereign equality,[28] leading to rationales for the non-application or irrelevance of justice based on a notion of non-intervention in the internal affairs of states.[29] The post 1945 international order was built on claims of international cooperation in the areas of peace and security, human rights, and development. But these ideals are underpinned by the animating principles of international law as practical association.

In explicating the practical association argument, Koskenniemi cites from Terry Nardin's 1983 book, *Law, Morality and the Relations of States*.[30] Legal and political theory have worked in tandem in this analytical project. As we shall learn, Rawls also relied on Nardin for the domain of politics argument.

Nardin distinguished between a practical association and a purposive association. A practical association, according to Nardin, is based on an 'authoritative practice', in which the actors within the association 'are related in terms of constraints they are all expected to observe whatever their individual purposes may be'.[31] Often in a practical association 'there is no shared purpose uniting those whose conduct is governed by an authoritative practice such as a morality or system of laws, and in such cases there is no basis of association other than these common constraints'.[32] Practical association is a relationship among those who are engaged in the pursuit of different and possibly incompatible purposes, and who are associated with one another, if at all, only in respecting certain restrictions on how each may pursue his own purpose. It is not a common goal but the authority of the common constraints

[26] ibid. [27] ibid.

[28] See R Dworkin, 'A New Philosophy for International Law' (2013) 41 Philosophy and Public Affairs 2, 3–10.

[29] See B Kingsbury, 'Sovereignty and Inequality' (1998) 9 EJIL 599.

[30] T Nardin, *Law, Morality and the Relations of States* (Princeton UP 1983); see also SR Ratner, *The Thin Justice of International Law: A Moral Reckoning of the Law of Nations* (OUP 2015) 31.

[31] Nardin (n 30) 9. [32] ibid.

that bind members of a practical association. According to Nardin, for a practical association, the common good 'is not a set of aims to be achieved through cooperation' but 'a set of values defined by common laws'.[33]

To be distinguished from practical association in Nardin's account is a purposive association. In a purposive association, 'the authority of the rules governing the relations among the associates is derived from the shared purposes that the association exists to promote'.[34] Association members pursue a common end in a purposive association, and the rules of the purposive association have authority only because they are instrumental to realizing the shared common ends of the members. Nardin does say that some international law reflects purposive association, and he states but does not elaborate that states engage in cooperation through purposive associations in trade and mutual defence, a contention that fails once the substance of contemporary trade agreements are explored, as in Chapter 4 ('International Trade').[35]

Nardin at least partially connects the practical–purposive distinction to differing kinds of moral theorizing relevant to each type of association. According to Nardin, a purposive association is consequentialist in aims. A purposive association gets its authority from the consequences or outcomes the rules of the association produces in achieving some purpose. In contrast, the authority of the rules of the practical association derives from conformity to the rules of the practical association. Says Nardin, '[w]hereas purposive theories hold that activities should be judged in relation to the contribution they make to producing the greatest happiness or some other end, the practical perspective postulates no such ends. On the contrary, it assumes the existence of individuals or groups pursuing ends of their own, and judges their actions according to the rules of conduct that constitute the normative order within which they are related.'[36]

Nardin denies distributive justice a role in the international order. For Nardin, justice in international law is formal justice: conformity of conduct to authoritative practices comprising the common rules of international society. Nardin uses the practice–purpose distinction to deal with the question 'whether a just international order is one in which the conduct of states conforms to the common rules of an international society, or one in which wealth and power are more evenly distributed'.[37] He concludes: 'The concept of distributive justice is tied to a purposive conception of society and government and has no place in discourse concerning practical association.'[38] Nardin argues that distributive justice can enter into the realm of formal justice only indirectly, as when formal justice requires policies to benefit particular members of society not to serve egalitarian ends but to assist persons who are unable to participate in society from the standpoint of formal equality.

In 1979, four years before Nardin's *Law, Morality and the Relations of States* was published, Charles Beitz, in his book *Political Theory and International Relations* offered a cosmopolitan account, arguing that duties of distributive justice apply globally, regardless of state borders. Beitz's work was published eight years after

[33] ibid. [34] ibid 10. [35] ibid.

[36] T Nardin, 'International Ethics and International Law' (1992) 18 Review of International Studies 19.

[37] Nardin (n 30) 256. [38] Nardin (n 36).

the unrevised edition of Rawls' *A Theory of Justice* was published in 1971. Beitz's work comes squarely within the Rawlsian tradition, though he rejected Rawlsian limits on distributive justice as applicable only to domestic societies and argued for a global basic structure of an international society to which the moral demands of distributive justice have full force. Says Beitz:

> [I]f evidence of global economic and political interdependence shows the existence of a global scheme of social cooperation, we should not view national boundaries as having fundamental moral significance. Since boundaries are not coextensive with the scope of social cooperation, they do not mark the limits of social obligation. Thus the parties to the original position cannot be assumed to know that they are members of a particular national society, choosing principles of justice primarily for that society. The veil of ignorance must extend to all matters of national citizenship, and the principles chosen will therefore apply globally.[39]

Rawls' *Law of Peoples*, published in 1999, at least implicitly rejected Beitz's argument of twenty years earlier that a global basic structure existed which required the application of Rawls' principles of justice at the global level. Rawls instead accepted Nardin's practical association argument. This is not the place for a full exegetical account of Rawls' *Law of Peoples* but a summary is in order because it reflects the domain of the political and practical association arguments in the fullest manifestation. Rawls argued that at the international level, liberal and decent peoples should pursue a foreign policy based on principles familiar for the most part to international lawyers. These included principles respecting the independence of peoples, *pact sunt servanda*-type principles, a duty of non-intervention, a right of self-defence, laws of war, respect for human rights, and a duty to assist peoples living in unfavourable conditions preventing them from having 'a just or decent political and social regime'.[40] Rawls' list of human rights, moreover, was very basic and truncated. In addition, Rawls' duty to assist is a minimal form of humanitarianism or beneficence distinct from justice. So, unlike Beitz, Rawls specified an international basic structure but not a global one. And he relied on Nardin's *Law, Morality and the Relations of States* for the above principles, characterizing them as 'familiar and traditional principles of justice among free and democratic peoples'.[41] He also relied on JL Brierly's traditional international law text for these principles.[42] Rawls' *Law of Peoples* made an influential but controversial step in political philosophy in the twentieth century. It maintained a link between contemporary political philosophy and traditional Westphalian notions of international law, at a time when those Westphalian notions were under considerable attack. Many have argued this was a move in the wrong direction.[43]

[39] CR Beitz, *Political Theory and International Relations* (Princeton UP 1979) 151.

[40] Rawls (n 13, *Law of Peoples*) 37.

[41] ibid.

[42] ibid. Frank Garcia draws our attention to this as well. FJ Garcia, *Global Justice and International Economic Law: Three Takes* (CUP 2013) 62. Ratner argues that Rawls 'cited and endorses an outdated restatement of international law that, most glaringly, does not reflect the developments in human rights law that limit a state's freedom to govern itself however it chooses (as well as its immunity from external, non-military interference)' (n 30) 33. Ratner cites A Buchanan, 'Rawls's Law of Peoples: Rules for a Vanished Westphalian World' (2000) 111 Ethics 697.

[43] See, eg, Buchanan (n 42); TW Pogge, *World Poverty and Human Rights* (2nd edn, Polity 2008).

For Rawls, his two principles of justice, including his difference and equality of opportunity principles, form part of a political conception of justice applicable only to what he calls a 'closed' or 'self-contained' society in the form of a modern constitutional democracy.[44] At some point, this closed society must deal with relationships between peoples, but that is a different matter entirely for Rawls, one in which, as explained above, no robust principles of justice will apply. With this division between the domestic and the international clear in Rawls' work, the concept of the political entails a number of limiting principles for Rawls. First, though liberal democratic societies are likely required to comply with Rawls' principles of justice, it is not necessarily the case that all societies must do so. There will be 'decent peoples' and other forms of social organization that may have different conceptions of justice, particularly conceptions that are located in some comprehensive doctrine of the good, which would have to be respected by other peoples according to a just law of peoples, so long as the human rights in Rawls's basic list of human rights are not violated. Second, no people (effectively a state) is required to seek or even promote distributive justice at the international level. Third, it is entirely proper and legitimate for states to use their power to promote their interests to the detriment of other states, so long as they do not violate Rawls's basic list of minimum principles. Fourth, and most fundamentally, the very concept of the political itself is something that applies only within state borders. States are organized politically. The world is not. And so, we have the domains of the domestic or political and the international clearly separated. Equality, says Thomas Nagel, as a demand of justice 'is a specifically political demand, which applies to the basic structure of the nation-state'.[45] This is politics with a capital P, with a particular philosophical meaning.

The demarcation of the political in this way has become fundamental in normative political theory. It marks the divisions between cosmopolitans on one side and liberal nationalists and communitarians on the other.[46] It is among the most

[44] J Rawls, *Political Liberalism* (2nd edn, Columbia UP 2005) 10–11.

[45] T Nagel, 'The Problem of Global Justice' (2005) 33 Philosophy and Public Affairs 113, 114.

[46] A stark example of the divide can be found in the work of Michael Walzer. He has argued that political theory must be grounded in the traditions and culture of particular societies and egalitarian forms of justice are morally relevant only within states. For Walzer:

> The only plausible alternative to the political community is humanity itself, the society of nations, the entire globe. But were we able to take the globe as our setting, we would have to imagine what does not yet exist: a community that included all men and women everywhere. We would have to invent a set of common meanings for these people, avoiding if we could the stipulation of our own values. And we would have to ask the members of this hypothetical community (or their hypothetical representatives) to agree among themselves on what distributive arrangements and patterns of conversion are to count as just ... But whatever the hypothetical agreement, it could not be enforced without breaking the political monopolies of existing states and centralizing power at the global level. Hence the agreement (or the enforcement) would make not for complex but for simple equality—if power was dominant and widely shared—or simply for tyranny—if power was seized, as it probably would be, by a set of international bureaucrats.

M Walzer, *Spheres of Justice: A Defense of Pluralism and Equality* (Basic 1984) 29–30. He continues:

important insights in political theory in the post-Rawlsian age. And, as shown, it shares a connection to the demarcation between domestic and international in law.

Thomas Nagel's Storrs lecture represents a somewhat more recent and influential argument for the practical association and domain of the political arguments. At the centre of the discussion is the application of principles of justice, in the form of distributive or egalitarian justice, beyond state borders. Nagel, argues: '[e]galitarian justice is a requirement of the internal political, economic, and social structure of nation-states and cannot be extrapolated to different contexts, which require different standards'.[47] For Nagel, egalitarian justice has no role without a sovereign. Nagel distinguishes between two conceptions of justice, the political and cosmopolitan.[48] In Nagel's political conception of justice, the existence of sovereign states 'is precisely what gives the value of justice its application, by putting the fellow citizens of a sovereign state into a relation they do not have with the rest of humanity, an institutional relation which must then be evaluated by the special standards of fairness and equality that fill out the content of justice'.[49] Nagel tells us no justice without sovereignty, so we really cannot have justice in international law until we either divorce notions of justice from sovereignty in a way that has widespread acceptance, move sovereignty elsewhere, beyond the state, or eliminate sovereignty as a relevant concept altogether.

Though Nagel does not explicitly argue that international law is a practical association, to be distinguished from the political association of the state, he argues:

> Current rules and international institutions … lack something that according to the political conception is crucial for the application and implementation of standards of justice: They are not collectively enacted and coercively imposed in the name of all individuals whose lives they affect; and they do not ask for the kind of authorization by individuals that carries with it a responsibility to treat all those individuals in some sense equally.[50]

> The idea of distributive justice presupposes a bounded world within which distribution takes place: a group of people committed to dividing, exchanging, and sharing social goods, first of all among themselves. That world … is a political community, whose members distribute power to one another and avoid, if they possibly can, sharing it with anyone else. When we think about distributive justice, we think about independent cities or countries capable of arranging their own patterns of division and exchange, justly or unjustly.

ibid 31. Walzer's theory of complex equality provides that egalitarian justice cannot be determined by a single criterion or set of primary goods, but rather it demands that each good be distributed according to its social meaning. For Walzer, equality in political communities is complex, which means that it is about a diversity of social goods distributed through a number of different distributive procedures and that no good (like money or political power) should distort the distribution of goods in other spheres. See also C Kukathas, 'The Mirage of Global Justice' in E Frankel Paul, FD Miller, and J Paul (eds), *Justice and Global Politics* (CUP 2006).

[47] Nagel (n 45) 115. [48] ibid 120.

[49] ibid. Nagel quotes Dworkin: 'A political community that exercises dominion over its own citizens, and demands from them allegiance and obedience to its laws, must take up an impartial, objective attitude toward them all, and each of its citizens enact laws and for governmental policies, with that responsibility in mind. Equal concern … is the special and indispensable virtue of sovereigns.' R Dworkin, *Sovereign Virtue: The Theory and Practice of Equality* (Harvard UP 2000) 120–21.

[50] Nagel (n 45) 138.

Rather, 'they are set up by bargaining among mutually self-interested sovereign parties'.[51] They act 'not in the name of individuals, but in the name of the states or state instruments or agencies that have created them' and their responsibility to individuals 'is filtered through states that represent and bear primary responsibility for those individuals'.[52] So Nagel concludes:

> The absence of sovereign authority over participant states and their members not only makes it practically infeasible for such institutions to pursue justice but also makes them, under the political conception, an inappropriate site for claims of justice. For such claims to become applicable it is not enough that a number of individuals or groups be engaged in a collective activity that serves their mutual advantage. Mere economic interaction does not trigger the heightened standards of socioeconomic justice.[53]

In Nagel's conception, states come to agreement on international law and institutions with their own ends, representing their own citizens, to reach practical accommodation to further the ends of their own governments and the interest of their own citizens. This is international law as practical association.

The practical association and domain of politics arguments are about order as the normative foundation for international law, not justice. These arguments combine to tell us that order and not justice is what gives international law its legitimacy or practical authority. In the opening paragraph of *A Theory of Justice*, which concerns closed political societies formed by states, Rawls says: 'justice is the first virtue of social institutions, as truth is of systems of thought'.[54] Though not writing about the international, Bernard Williams captures the spirit of what seems to be at play in what he called global political theory: 'I identify the "first" political question in Hobbesian terms as the securing of order, protection, safety, trust, and the conditions of cooperation. It is "first" because solving it is the condition of solving, indeed posing, any others.'[55] Going back to Hobbes once more is instructive. Hobbes argued that political rights and duties come not from nature but from sovereigns. We thus have the origins of the modern state set forth by Hobbes as cooperation in the form of a state, with social practices forming a social contract. Hobbes torn asunder predecessor scholastic philosophy on the natural sociability of persons and argued that the law of nature comes down to a single natural right: 'The Right of nature, which Writers commonly call the *jus naturale* is the Liberty each man hath, to use his own power, as he will himself, for the preservation of his own Nature; that is to say, of his own Life, and consequently of doing anything, which in his own Judgement and Reason, he shall conceive to be the aptest means thereunto.'[56] States, to both Hobbes and Grotius writing in the seventeenth century, were no different from individuals. For Hobbes, people form states because of self-interest. They determine that they are better off being ruled by a sovereign than having constantly to deal with the conflict that will be inevitable as each person exercises his right of self-preservation. But

[51] ibid. [52] ibid. [53] ibid 137–38. [54] Rawls (n 13, *Theory of Justice*) 3.

[55] B Williams, *In the Beginning Was the Deed: Realism and Moralism in Political Argument* (Princeton UP 2005) 3.

[56] T Hobbes, *Leviathan* (CB McPherson ed, Penguin 1968) 189.

what about relations between states? The state of nature persists, with no sovereign to bring order to interstate relations. As for relations between states, for Hobbes, 'In all times' states are 'in continual jealousies, and in the state and postures of Gladiators'.[57] In the stripped-down version of natural law that Hobbes offered, the right of self-preservation becomes ever more important in relations between states. Grotius, more well known to international lawyers, argues similarly.[58] Certainly, order is a natural focus in a world of substantial value pluralism, in which it is difficult to agree on a theory of justice of a global scale. Hobbes, Grotius, and others were writing at a time when that pluralism was making itself known to Europeans, in their early interactions with non-westerners and European attempts to justify the conquest of the New World. The persistence of thinking about international law as a system of order, not justice, despite some superficial claims to the contrary, prevails still today.

2. A Way Out

The practical association and domain of politics arguments fail. This section elucidates at least four reasons why, which should be considered in combination as a set of plausible balance of reasons for holding international law accountable to the demands of justice. The significance of international law to normative ordering of the economic sphere across the globe means there may be additional reasons. Section 3 addresses what it means to hold international law accountable to the demands of justice. It also articulates principles of justice that international law should comply with if it is going to meet these demands. For now, let us move on to the reasons in support this exercise.

First, the reasons for holding international law unaccountable to the demands of justice rely on a version of liberalism which in turn relies on an approach to associative duties and membership that is both unrealistic and lacking in relevance to the way social and economic arrangements operate today. Relationships exist of sufficient kind and intensity to put in serious doubt the notion that international law is a practical association concerned only with order or coexistence. The description of international law as a practical association and no more, divorced from some artificial realm of politics, cannot hold, with international law forming essential roles of complex regulation in the realm of what are typically understood as the domestic affairs of states. International law now intrudes into what once was the domestic sphere even of the most powerful states. International law involves a pervasive and necessary kind of interaction between states, affecting the welfare and conditions for respect of people within states, which no state can ignore or abrogate away. International economic law affects human flourishing within states in profound ways, sometimes in substantially more profound ways than domestic law. International economic law is at work in the most fundamental sites of distribution within the state.

[57] ibid 187. [58] Tuck (n 8).

Second, the structural features of international law are compelling in their normative consequences.[59] The combination of international economic law in its present form and substance along with circumstances created by history, and the choices of governments and other agents historically and in the present, combine to produce a structure vulnerable to the perpetuation of injustice in the global economy. The result can be systematic injustice, requiring the corrective of an international law conforming to principles of justice.

Third, the worst predations, in the form of domination, occur as transborder phenomena. Domination can be understood along republican lines as the capacity to interfere on an arbitrary basis in the choices of another. This chapter does not make a case for a republican approach to evaluating international law but the lessons from republicanism seem apt when it comes to understanding the circumstances for creating the conditions for obligations of justice to be required for international law.[60] Domination comes in two main forms, coercion and manipulation. Internationally, states and multinational enterprises apply power in unaccountable ways with far fewer constraints than they can domestically. It is well understood that multinational enterprises, for example, operate with legal impunity in foreign countries in ways that would be intolerable and plainly illegal in their home countries.[61] Liberal political theorists rely on the 'black letter law' coercion of formal legal systems to argue for full-blown duties of justice at the domestic but not the international level. That literature usually proceeds by looking either for relationships, with common nationality or humanity serving as a basis for finding duties of justice, or by looking for coercion in the form that has traditionally taken place within a state, such as in its legal system, in the finding that 'shared liability in a coercive state' has moral relevance.[62] A compelling case exists for application of the demands of justice in a global context, however, precisely because coercion at the international level does *not* occur as part of a domestic legal system. At the international level, coercion is disordered and has in many cases evolved from historically unjust practices.

Finally, historic wrongdoing has played a substantial part in giving international law the structure that it has today. Turning to history, much of the international law governing the global economy was formed in conditions of what Sven Beckert calls war capitalism: the use of the force of the state, either directly or outsourced to the multinational enterprises of their time, to acquire economic gains in the form of violent reorganizations of markets, confiscation of resources, and involuntary exchange to benefit the aggressor with superior weaponry at the expense of the vulnerable who lacked such force of arms.[63] There was no ideal just starting point for

[59] IM Young, *Responsibility for Justice* (OUP 2011) 123.

[60] For republican-centred accounts about international law, see the contributions in section C on republican international law in S Besson and JL Martí (eds), *Legal Republicanism: National and International Perspectives* (OUP 2009).

[61] L Wenar, *Blood Oil: Tyrants, Violence, and the Rules that Run the World* (OUP 2016) offers a recent account of these practices.

[62] See M Blake, 'Coercion and Egalitarian Justice' (2011) 94 The Monist 555.

[63] See S Beckert, *Empire of Cotton: A Global History* (Vintage 2015). For further discussion, see Chapter 4 ('International Trade') at 110–121.

international law. Historic wrongdoing relates to structural injustice but merits a distinct ground to capture features of injustice that might go missing if the focus is only in the present.

2.1 The ties that bind

At bottom, the domain of politics and practical association arguments articulate a zone for an associative obligation owed by citizens of a state to each other through a set of shared institutions.[64] It is one kind of special obligation tied to group membership, in this case the group being the state. This membership argument is too narrow. It makes mysterious a significant set of rules that states share and that intrude deeply into the domestic legal systems and social and economic structures of states. The necessary move must be either to discard the notion of associative duty when it comes to working out which institutions are subject to the demands of justice or to relax it to refer broadly to relationships and the domain of cooperation rather than narrowly to membership. This section argues for the latter. The argument to follow connects to how international law operates in practice in substantial respects. We need not go as far as the cosmopolitans and simply deny association has any role. But, as we shall see, membership cannot do the work that needs to be done to understand how justice ought to operate within the state because too much happens from an institutional context outside of the state that affects the conditions for justice both inside and outside the state. The creators or authors of international law must be accountable to persons whose lives they affect, often very substantially and negatively, through international law. The inside–outside or member–not member distinction cannot do the work of informing us about justice inside the state because institutions that play a large part in bringing justice to one state's citizens and the citizens of other states alike are simply no longer inside the state.

International law should be understood as a necessary institution within the panoply of institutions that are needed for states and their peoples to flourish. Associative theory makes what can be characterized as the 'no plausible alternative' mistake: it mistakenly relies on an unrealistic distinction between community in the form of an institutionally ordered state versus all of humanity outside of any community. This reflects the classic distinction between liberal nationalism and cosmopolitanism. Michael Walzer, for example, argues that 'the only plausible alternative to the political community is humanity itself, the society of nations, the entire globe'.[65] Walzer conflates 'humanity itself' with the 'society of nations' and 'the entire globe'. These arguments are unconvincing because they ignore the existence of international law or treat it as epiphenomenal. They are stuck in an outdated empirical understanding of a world comprised of Hobbesian gladiators.

International law is a shared institution constitutive of important parts of the legal systems of states. Its contemporary manifestations are in the form of a

[64] See Nagel (n 45) 121. [65] Walzer (n 46) 29–30.

pervasive public law of regulation. This may seem uncontroversial for states with legal traditions that have tended to classify international law as a category of public law,[66] but what we want to deal with here is not with international law's formal categorization as law but with how it actually operates. The regulatory character of international law has more to do with the basic structure of a domestic society than even some core areas of domestic law and regulation. It forms a fundamental part of the contemporary regulatory state. The state, according to Saskia Sassen, is denationalizing.[67] The law of the WTO, with its substantial beyond the border reach in areas of environmental law, health and safety law, intellectual property law, and in the setting of standards for product quality, intrudes far into the basic structure of a domestic society.[68] So too does international investment law, with its focus almost wholly on how foreign investors are treated within the state as a matter of property, tax, regulation, dispute resolution, and the like. International financial law is substantially intrusive into the core into basic redistributive institutions in domestic society. The International Monetary Fund (IMF), for example, imposes conditions on countries that go to the centre of domestic economic policy, requiring countries to transfer public funds destined for their citizens to external creditors in rich countries.[69] We can see this phenomenon in action by looking at the lawyers who are expert in the fields that are subject to the areas of regulatory international law, for example, the experts on TRIPs will not be international lawyers of the conventional sort. Rather, they will be intellectual property lawyers. In sum, much of international law of any importance is regulatory, law of the kind traditionally reserved for state agencies or substantially determining the law these agencies apply or produce. Its subject is about the governing of a domestic society, not, or at least not only, the association between states external to domestic society.

Aaron James characterizes the global economy as 'organised by a distinctive kind of international social practice, a social practice in which countries mutually rely on common markets'.[70] According to James, the burdens and benefits of the global

[66] M Koskenniemi, *The Gentle Civilizer of Nations: The Rise and Fall of International Law 1870–1960* (CUP 2001) 209–10.

[67] S Sassen, *Territory, Authority, Rights: From Medieval to Global Assemblages* (Princeton UP 2006) 230–71.

[68] J Cohen and C Sabel, 'Extra Rempublicam Nulla Justitia? (2006) 34 Philosophy and Public Affairs 147, 171 ('But in fact the WTO anticipates that trade rules will frequently conflict with, and need to be modified to accommodate, a wide range of normative concerns embodied in the domestic laws and regulations of those trading in world markets').

[69] See ME Salomon, 'Of Austerity, Human Rights and International Institutions' (2015) 21 European Law Journal 521; CD Zimmerman, *A Contemporary Concept of Monetary Sovereignty* (OUP 2013); CD Zimmerman, 'The Concept of Monetary Sovereignty Revisited' (2013) 24 EJIL 797; RP Buckley, 'The Direct Contribution of the International Financial System to Global Poverty' in KN Schefer (ed), *Poverty in the International Economic Legal System* (CUP 2013) 278; AF Lowenfeld, 'The International Monetary System and the Erosion of Sovereignty: Essay in Honor of Cynthia Lichtenstein' (2002) 25 Boston College International and Comparative Law Review 257.

[70] A James, *Fairness in Practice: A Social Contract for a Global Economy* (OUP 2012) 17; cf S Loriaux and A Herwig, 'International Trade, Fairness, and Labour Migration' (2014) 1 Moral Philosophy and Politics 1.

economy come from a distinctive and pervasive form of social cooperation, a 'joint product of the social practice of mutual market reliance'.[71] Following on James's lead, with such a pervasive form of cooperation linking states and communities, rules are needed to constitute this shared market practice. These are the rules of international law. States cannot do what they do for domestic constituencies without international law. There is a shared agency of states in areas that were once typically reserved for domestic law only. Moreover, international law allocates and distributes. It deals with fundamental legal issues of property and entitlements. But as we describe below, international law deals with these issues in fragmented and differentiated ways to produce moral quandaries.

Wolfgang Friedmann, in his 1964 book, *The Changing Structure of International Law*, was prescient in his coverage of these issues in his distinction between a classical international law of coexistence and a new international law of cooperation. His often-quoted passage:

> In international law it is today of both theoretical and practical importance to distinguish between the international law of 'coexistence', governing essentially diplomatic inter-state relations, and the international law of cooperation, expressed in the growing structure of international organisation and the pursuit of common human interests.[72]

Of course, these distinctions do not tell us whether international law achieves justice. But from a descriptive standpoint, the relationships formed in an international law of cooperation are representative of relationships that go beyond the practical association limitations discussed earlier. In *The Future of International Law*, Joel Trachtman builds on Friedmann and describes the function of international law as a 'system of transnational political linkage'.[73] Trachtman writes:

> The future of international law is a set of functional, nuanced, differentiated, and organic links between the political systems of different states. As these links grow in terms of their mandatory character, specificity, and institutional support, they will increasingly ascend the scale from a more contractual type of international law to mechanisms that appear to have more of the characteristics of government.[74]

The normative consequences of these linkages are that the practical association and domain of politics arguments dissolve away. The international legal system is directly constitutive of both domestic and international communities.

That international law ought to be understood as a law of cooperation does not mean that it functions well as a law of cooperation in its current form and substance. The argument here is that because international law governs cooperation and regulates inside the state it must comply with normative principles for such a

[71] James (n 70).

[72] W Friedmann, *The Changing Structure of International Law* (Columbia UP 1964) vii. Joel Trachtman brings Friedmann into the twenty-first century in *The Future of International Law*, examining areas of regulation that will need a denser, thicker international law of regulation to deal with complex problems demanding interstate cooperation. JP Trachtman, *The Future of International Law: Global Government* (CUP 2013).

[73] Trachtman (n 72) 107. [74] ibid 41.

law and that means it must meet the demands of justice. Pathologies in a relationship do not call into question that the relationship exists or its normative significance, but directs us to how those pathologies need to be addressed in line with what the relationship requires.

International law might be serving cooperative ends only for some states (or their successors) that formulated the classical international law of coexistence, with some new additions of states whose significance to the global economy cannot be ignored.[75] Friedmann argued that the 'active agents and participants' in formulating classic international law were a 'small club of European nations, joined in the nineteenth century by the newly emerging nations of the American Continent'.[76] It appears that a similar division of states continues, with a possible change in membership and configuration with the rise of BRICS, even as international law has transformed to a much denser form of governance of the global economy. Anne-Marie Slaughter identifies the 'ineradicability' of power and asks whether the trans-governmental networks she examines 'either replicate or even magnify asymmetries of power in the existing international system'.[77]

A distinction may be possible between 'rule takers', a phrased offered by Andrew Hurrell, and 'rule makers'. Hurrell explains: '[t]here is deformity … in terms of who sets the rules of international society. Institutions are not, as liberal theory often suggests, neutral arenas for the solution of common problems but rather sites of power and dominance. The clear majority of weaker actors are increasingly "rule takers" over a whole range of issues that affect all aspects of social, economic, and political life.'[78] Similarly, Rainer Forst argues that the global poor are not 'agents' in the global order but mere 'passive recipients' of its dictates.[79]

It is widely understood that some states and persons continue in central instances of international lawmaking to be mere recipients but not active agents in the making

[75] An example with potentially significant consequences for internal regulation within both the United States and the European Union is the proposed Transatlantic Trade and Investment Partnership. See SI Akhtar and VC Jones, *Proposed Transatlantic Trade and Investment Partnership (TTIP): In Brief* (Congressional Research Service 2014). The authors state:

> Regulatory issues are widely regarded by many stakeholders as the core of the T-TIP negotiations, potentially 'making or breaking' the agreement. Key sectors of interest include automobiles, chemicals, cosmetics, information communication technologies, medical devices, pesticides, and pharmaceuticals. Economic gains from greater regulatory coherence and compatibility could be significant. At the same time, there is debate about whether a comprehensive agreement on regulatory issues can be reached. First, the United States and EU have been communicating on various regulatory differences for some time, and although many have been resolved, a number of seemingly intractable issues remain. Second, some of the regulatory differences relate to divergent public preferences and values. (p 7)

See also European Commission, Detailed Explanation on the EU Proposal for a Chapter on Regulatory Cooperation (6 May 2015). The EU's Textual Proposal was tabled in negotiations with the United States on 2–6 Feb 2015. See generally D Vogel and JFM Swinnen, *Transatlantic Regulatory Cooperation: The Shifting Roles of the EU, the US and California* (Edward Elgar 2011).

[76] Friedmann (n 72) 4–5.

[77] AM Slaughter, *A New World Order* (Princeton UP 2004) 227.

[78] Hurrell (n 10) 11.

[79] R Forst, *The Right to Justification: Elements of a Constructivist Theory of Justice* (Columbia UP 2007).

of international law. The rule takers or passive recipients of international law often are in a position of domination by the rule makers or agents of international law. Passive recipient states often ratify international economic agreements on a take it or leave it basis, entering these agreements based on pressure from powerful states to set the rules for markets not in a principled way to promote a normative goal of economic efficiency towards shared benefits, but to carve up markets to benefit the constituents of these rich states, which are often multinational enterprises. The mandatory multilateral structure of global economic arrangements such as the WTO makes opting out impossible.[80] Many international economic arrangements make it practically impossible for states not to participate. The leaders of weaker states may uncritically assume that economic agreements are beneficial (an increasingly less likely occurrence), often because they have no or inadequate capacity for evaluating the evidence.[81] Or, they enter into trade and investment agreements in the hope of benefiting from the reputational signals of being 'open for business' based on advice they receive from or conditionalities imposed by international financial institutions or aid agencies as to what is needed to reap the benefits of the global economy.[82] Good evidence exists of what is known as international policy diffusion, where policy decisions by a state are 'systematically conditioned' by prior policy decisions of other states.[83] Finally, in some cases elites in weaker states profit both in political power and in enriching themselves materially from continuing the status quo.[84]

Interaction among states which may have normative significance for imposing duties of justice on states may sometimes come in two forms: *de jure* and de facto. *De jure* cooperation refers to explicit policy decisions by states to engage in particular forms of cooperation that take on legal form, such as in a binding trade or investment agreement, or in soft law that results in domestic law in compliance with that soft law. Cooperation on financial regulation sometimes comes in the latter soft law form.[85] De facto cooperation is a looser form of policy coordination,

[80] See Cohen and Sabel (n 68) 168 ('opting out is not a real option' because 'the WTO is a "take it or leave it" arrangement').

[81] M Sornarajah, *Resistance and Change in the International Law on Foreign Investment* (CUP 2015) 13–14 ('Developing states signed BITs and other investment treaties but 'seldom understood the nuances of the treaties they adopted'); see also LN Skovegaard Poulsen, *Bounded Rationality and Economic Diplomacy: The Politics of Investment Treaties in Developing Countries* (CUP 2015).

[82] To the extent that the literature on signalling is in political economy and law and economics, it focuses mainly on treaty 'compliance' but this literature does not make a clear distinction between complying with a treaty and entering one. See AT Guzman, 'Reputation and International Law' (2006) 34 Georgia Journal of International and Comparative Law 379; AT Guzman, 'A Compliance Based Theory of International Law' (2002) 90 California Law Review 1823; GW Downs and MA Jones, 'Reputation, Compliance, and International Law' (2002) 31 Journal of Legal Studies S94. For relevant work not in political economy or law and economics, see G Van Harten, 'Five Justifications for Investment Treaties: A Critical Discussion' (2010) 2 Trade Law and Development 19.

[83] B Simmons, F Dobbin, and G Garrett (eds), *The Global Diffusion of Markets and Democracy* (CUP 2007).

[84] See AH Amsdan, A Di Caprio, and JA Robinson (eds), *The Role of Elites in Economic Development* (OUP 2012).

[85] C Brummer, *Soft Law and the Global Financial System: Rule Making in the 21st Century* (2nd edn, CUP 2015).

which may not rise to the level of binding international law, but which is important for distributing resources or welfare among states, and for which substantial levels of compliance are evident.[86] This is not, of course, to imply that this 'cooperation' is among equals, but it reflects a level of interaction that gives rise to legitimate demands of justice.

International lawyers well understand *de jure* cooperation. A substantial and multilayered formal regulatory system has emerged mainly among powerful states.[87] The United States and the European Union engage in perhaps more regulatory cooperation than any other ensemble of states and international organizations. Discussions about regulatory cooperation between the United States and the European Union as part of the Transatlantic Trade and Investment Partnership (TTIP) negotiations have indicated a substantial ramping up of already significant regulatory cooperation,[88] though the future of these negotiations is uncertain with the change of administration in the United States. The European Union itself is a form of regulatory cooperation among states. Slaughter argues that the European Union 'has emerged as a regulatory state, exercising power through rulemaking rather than taxing and spending'.[89] The global financial architecture (Chapter 6 ('Global Finance')) is an example of shared institutions. International soft law and domestic law operate together to on a common purpose of financial stability.

An example of de facto cooperation is found in the cuddly versus cut-throat capitalism research conducted by Daron Acemoglu and colleagues.[90] This research examines the effects of technological interdependence of states with differing varieties of capitalist economies. The research takes into account that encouraging technological innovation requires incentives for workers and entrepreneurs and that this results in greater inequality and poverty. But the global economy is characterized by technological interdependence, and when a small number of states contribute disproportionately to technological advancement, the incentives for other states to contribute will be weaker. So, some economies will produce more growth by advancing technology, while others will benefit from higher incomes from the technology innovation, and hence be able to invest that income in welfare for its population. For such a state of affairs to occur, the technologically leading states have to opt for so-called 'cut-throat' capitalist institutions with more powerful incentives for its populace to innovate, relatively less social insurance and higher income inequality, while states benefiting from the innovation opt for 'cuddly' capitalist institutions as a best response to the technology leader's innovations and are therefore able to provide better social insurance to their population and greater

[86] ibid. [87] Slaughter (n 77) 43.

[88] See 'The Transatlantic Trade and Investment Partnership (TTIP)—State of Play' (27 Apr 2016), http://trade.ec.europa.eu/doclib/docs/2016/april/tradoc_154477.pdf.

[89] Slaughter (n 77) 43.

[90] D Acemoglu, JA Robinson, and T Verdier, 'Can't We All Be More Like Scandinavians? Asymmetric Growth and Institutions in an Interdependent World' National Bureau of Economic Research Working Paper No 18441 (Oct 2012), Massachusetts Institute of Technology Department of Economics Working Paper No 12–22 (Aug 2012). For a summary of some of the controversial issues this paper raises, see TB Edsall, 'Why Can't America Be Sweden?' *New York Times* (29 May 2013).

equality. The result comes out that the cutthroat capitalist country is richer but the cuddly capitalist country, while poorer, is able to provide more welfare to its people. This research might explain how, for example, the Scandinavian countries and the United States engage in a form of de facto cooperation. De facto cooperation may not tell us much directly about international law but it does tell us that it may be implausible to try to neatly differentiate the domestic from the international. It supports the relational argument made here.

Another way to understand the relational argument is from the perspective of sovereignty. Sovereignty is purportedly about the power states have over their territories and to govern within their borders. Moreover, sovereign equality is a kind of formal as opposed to material or substantive equality. Sovereign equality tells us that each state is equal to any other state based on a single characteristic: statehood. No other investigations into material conditions are warranted to determine if states are in fact equal along other variables. Sovereign equality has features similar to the individualism of classical liberal thought or in libertarianism. In associative accounts, sovereignty and sovereign equality form an impenetrable barrier for norms of justice. As Friedmann explains, classical international law 'did not purport to penetrate beyond the shell of diplomatic intercourse into the economic and social aspects of the polities that dealt with each other as units' and 'had little concern with matters of welfare, of economic conditions of nations whose sovereigns entered into mutual diplomatic and legal relations'.[91] Norms of justice therefore applied within states but not beyond or across them.

But contemporary international law does in fact 'penetrate beyond the shell of diplomatic intercourse' and into the 'economic and social aspects' of states, and has substantial relevance to 'matters of welfare, of economic conditions of nations'. To the extent that it fails to perform these functions fairly it is subject to critique on the grounds of justice. If we overlook the sharing of international law by states and their peoples, we will mistakenly accept the moral disorder that sovereignty arguments are prone to produce.

Behind the veneer of sovereignty as formal equality of states is a substantial substantive *inequality*. Poor and weak states have very little of sovereignty while rich and powerful ones have plenty. Sovereignty can be understood along two lines—durable or permeable. Poor states tend to have permeable sovereignty. Rich states tend to have durable sovereignty. States with permeable sovereignty are takers and not makers of international law. They are not the authors of international law, but passive recipients of it. The permeable condition of their sovereignty often has an imperial or colonial legacy.[92] The makers and real agents in the international legal system are states with durable sovereignty. The relational argument for justice may require that we discard the notion of sovereignty in some important respects to the

[91] Friedmann (n 72) 5–6.
[92] Anghie (n 9); Koskenniemi (n 66) 90–187.

extent that it is a euphemism for state power that masks rather than clarifies how international law operates and what is required from the standpoint of justice.

2.2 Structural vulnerabilities

International law is accountable to the demands of justice because its structure has been prone to exploitative and dominating conditions in the global economy. To rely on Aaron James's framing of the issue, international law fails to achieve 'structural equity' to the extent that it would be reasonable for some state or class of persons to reject the way it affects it or them, in favour of some feasible alternative set of rules.[93] For Iris Marion Young, structural injustice exists 'when social processes put large categories of persons under a systematic threat of domination or deprivation of the means to develop and exercise their capacities, at the same time as these processes enable others to dominate or have a wide range of opportunities for developing and exercising their capacities'.[94] If international law has the potential to produce such injustice, it is subject to the demands of justice.

A separate ground of justice dealing with the global structure is necessary to cover all the potential sources of injustice that may be operating in the global economy. A structural argument allows for the distinction between three sources of injustice: (1) moral wrongs attributable to the choices or actions of states or persons, acting individually or in combination; (2) moral wrongs attributable to particular laws and other institutions; and (3) choices or actions by many states, persons, and entities pursuing their self-interest, within the limits of law and other socially produced rules, but which when taken together produce circumstances that bring about substantial harm. Market norms formed around neoliberal ideology can form a central part of this structure. To use a metaphor developed by Charles Lindblom, they operate like a prison. They form a 'change repressing system' and individual attempts to deviate trigger something like a punishment.[95] International law is unjust to the extent that it produces or contributes to producing such wrongs, if it could feasibly prevent wrongs associated with structure from occurring, or if it fails to rectify such wrongs if and when they occur.

A potentially serious form of structural vulnerability may arise from what we characterize as the disorder in international law. This disorder results from its fragmented structure. It is morally disordered by design.[96] Add to this the related

[93] James (n 70) 131.

[94] IM Young, 'Responsibility and Global Justice: A Social Connection Model' (2006) 23 Social Philosophy and Policy 102, 114. Young is perhaps the most influential source for theories of structural injustice. See IM Young (n 59).

[95] CE Lindblom, 'The Market as Prison' (1982) 44 Journal of Politics 324.

[96] See M Koskenniem et al, Report of the Study Group of the International Law Commission, *Fragmentation of International Law: Difficulties Arising from the Diversification and Expansion of International Law*, International Law Commission, 58th session, General Assembly, A/CN.4/L.682, 13 Apr 2006. As Chin Lim and Bryan Mercurio explain:

> As international economic lawyers know, this Bretton Woods 'system' evolved over several decades during the second half of the twentieth century, and in many ways is unrecognisable today from what had been envisaged during the post-war years. *These changes, and others, have given rise to what we* see *now as a fragmented discipline of international economic law*— a system whereby trade, investment, monetary and exchange rate cooperation, financial

linkage problem,[97] which identifies vertical disconnections between international law and a state's regulatory architecture. These features of the global legal order are prone to producing legal rules privileging economic considerations to the exclusion or detriment of other more pressing values that should be either overriding or at least taken into account in the content of international law or in dispute settlement.

2.3 Domination

Someone dominates another when: (1) they have the capacity to interfere in (2) choices of the other and (3) they can exercise that capacity arbitrarily.[98] This is the standard understanding of domination as found in the republican literature but domination might be unreasonable for persons to accept from the standpoint of liberal political theory as well.[99] Domination is a moral wrong because it deprives us of freedom.[100] For international law to be morally legitimate, it must comply with moral principles that prevent or eliminate domination in the domains in which it applies.[101]

Two canonical forms of domination, coercion and manipulation, affect the formation and interpretation of international law.[102] Coercion can be understood as

> regulation, intellectual property (IP) protection, the regulation of trade in goods and the trade in services, and international development law have evolved away from an initially coherent Bretton Woods design. This, in turn, *produced a multiplicity of norms which are not always easy bedfellows, a plurality of international institutions,* and in some cases global norms of a different kind altogether—namely, certain norms which are characterised by the total absence of formal institutional anchorage.

CL Lim and B Mercurio, 'The Fragmented Disciplines of International Economic Law After the Global Financial and Economic Crisis: An Introduction' in CL Lim and B Mercurio (eds), *International Economic Law After the Global Crisis: A Tale of Fragmented Disciplines* (CUP 2015) 5.

[97] Lim and Mercurio (n 96) 2; see C Barry and SG Reddy, *International Trade and Labor Standards: A Proposal for Linkage* (Columbia UP 2008).

[98] P Pettit, *Republicanism* (OUP 1997) 52.

[99] C Saenz, 'Republicanism: An Unattractive Version of Liberalism' (2008) 7 Ethics 267.

[100] Pettit (n 98).

[101] Because we do not provide a full-blown republican account, no position is taken on whether domination is a moral wrong in a deontological or consequentialist sense. The most prominent proponents of republicanism offer a consequentialist version and hence seek to minimize domination. See ibid. What should be apparent is that the approach of this chapter is contractualist.

Frank Garcia refers to domination in the form of a lack of real consent to economic treaties by vulnerable states as 'transactional' as opposed to 'relational' and this characterization nicely distinguishes this ground for justice from the prior ground of shared practices and institutions. Garcia (n 42) 265–66.

[102] As covered briefly in section 1, some political philosophers have argued no duties of justice can exist only in the presence of a coercive legal system. They argue that domestic law is either more coercive than international law or that domestic law is coercive and international law is not. Nagel (n 45); Blake (n 62); M Blake, *Justice and Foreign Policy* (OUP 2013); M Blake, 'Distributive Justice, State Coercion, and Autonomy' (2001) 30 Philosophy and Public Affairs 257. They argue that the 'shared liability' of a system of coercive laws with courts of compulsory jurisdiction makes for the application of robust demands for distributive justice within states. Blake (n 102, *Justice and Foreign Policy*) 97; M Blake, 'International Law and Global Justice' in A Marmor (ed), *The Routledge Companion to Philosophy of Law* (Routledge 2012) 335. In effect, equality is the 'price' paid for the coercive features of domestic law, or in the language of philosophy, a justification of that coercion. Put simply, the coercive effects of domestic law either result in or contribute to socially produced inequalities or make worse natural inequalities, and these inequalities must be neutralized if society is to be just.

credible threats to which a person succumbs[103] or from the context of power: '*A* has power over *B* to the extent that he can get *B* to do something that *B* would not otherwise do'.[104] Coercion can be 'of the will' and need not be as a result of the use of physical force or the threat of it.[105] Coercion can be understood as a threat by someone who indicates that if his demand is rejected, he will make the recipient worse off, usually in the form of some abrogation of the recipient's rights.[106] The republican literature includes an explicit 'arbitrary' component: when someone is in a position to choose or not choose at their pleasure; they can choose or reject without reference to the interests or opinions of those affected.[107] Power is used arbitrarily if, in republican theory, 'not externally constrained by effective rules, procedures, or goals that are common knowledge to all persons or groups concerned'.[108] Power exercised through law is arbitrary if it supports factions or interests and not overall 'welfare or world view'.[109] Domination can occur as a result of dependency, such as where substantial exit costs are a barrier.[110] Manipulation usually threatens choice in covert and indirect ways, such as in deception or, common

They also argue that international law does not have these qualities. Rebutting these arguments is unnecessary in this chapter because more compelling grounds are present than looking to the formal coercive elements of a legal system. These arguments are, however, wrong. International law is coercive from a legal point of view. A mistake in analytical legal philosophy seems to have made its way into normative political philosophy. The argument seems to be that because international law lacks the particular institutional features of domestic law, it is somehow deficient or even lacks standing as law. J Waldron, 'International Law: A "Relatively Small and Unimportant" Part of Jurisprudence?' in L Duarte D'Almeida, J Edwards, and A Dolcetti (eds), *Reading HLA Hart's 'The Concept of Law'* (Hart 2013) 209. These arguments look only to international law in the form of an old-fashioned classical international law of coexistence. Their focus is on the positive law features of coercion from the standpoint of a judicial process, the paradigmatic case of a domestic court with compulsory jurisdiction. It is an incomplete approach to understanding the law.

While international tribunals might not resemble domestic courts in many respects they certainly have evolved beyond the primitive stages when international law was primarily about coexistence and diplomacy was the order of the day. ICSID awards in international investment law are directly coercive. They can be enforced by domestic courts and grounds to overturn are extremely limited. Article 54(1) of the ICSID Convention requires contracting states to recognize an ICSID award 'as binding and enforce the pecuniary obligations imposed by that award within its territories *as if it were a final judgment of a court in that State*'. Convention on the Settlement of Investment Disputes Between States and Nationals of Other States, 17 UST 1270, TIAS 6090, 575 UNTS 159 (1965) (emphasis added). What was new in the Uruguay Round is now old news: the rules governing international trade, including those on dispute settlement, have moved from the norms of diplomats to the rules of lawyers, to what is known as 'trade legalism'. GR Shell, 'Trade Legalism and International Relations Theory' (1995) 44 Duke Law Journal 829. The ultimate remedy in WTO dispute settlement, undertaken when the parties cannot agree compensation or other arrangement is suspension of concessions, which are put in place against the will of the respondent (and which poorer countries cannot avail themselves of). International tribunals both have and claim coercive authority in a way that matters for justice.

[103] See R Nozick, 'Coercion' in S Morganbesser, P Suppes, and M White (eds), *Philosophy, Science, and Method: Essays in Honour of Ernst Nagel* (St Martin's Press 1969) 440.

[104] RA Dahl, 'The Concept of Power' (1957) 2 Behavioral Science 201, 202–03.

[105] Pettit (n 98) 53.

[106] A Wertheimer, *Coercion* (Princeton UP 2014).

[107] Pettit (n 98) 55.

[108] F Lovett, *A General Theory of Domination and Justice* (OUP 2010) 96.

[109] Pettit (n 98) 56; see also F Lovett, 'What Counts as Arbitrary Power?' (2012) 5 Journal of Political Power 137.

[110] Pettit (n 98) 49–54.

in institutional contexts, the fixing of agendas to lock in agents to particular courses of action that are against their interests.[111]

In the context of international relations between states and the diffusion of neoliberal policies, '[i]nternational coercion occurs when powerful actors influence the policy choices of governments directly or when such actors alter the outcome of a domestic policy struggle by favouring the domestic coalition supporting a given policy'.[112] Harold Lasswell and Abraham Kaplan similarly argue that coercion involves a 'high degree of constraint and/or inducement'.[113] Moreover, for participation in the international law of the global economy, no possibility of exit exists. There is simply no exit at all.

In far too many instances, powerful actors dominate to get what they want into international law.[114] The concern is with the morally problematic exercise of power to produce legal rules that institutionalize or make legally permissible domination by high-income states over low-income states, or domination by transnational corporations over low-income states and their citizens. The reasons for states to commit to neoliberal policies in international treaties can fall into several categories and the categories are not mutually exclusive.[115] Subtle forms of coercion need to be identified and understood. Poor states might accede to treaties that promote neoliberalism because they have limited or no real options and are desperate for capital.[116] Ratifying BITs, for example, may be a strategy by a poor state to defect as an individual prisoner in a prisoners dilemma game from the common positions taken by similarly situated states about the New International Economic Order (NIEO) but with no intention to undermine the NIEO agenda.[117] States (through their officials) may fear exclusion and loss of opportunity to join a legal regime at a time more appropriate for their economic conditions, a problem that Greece may have faced in the most recent eurozone crisis. The power disparities between the active agents of international treaty making and the mere passive recipients likely means a substantial bias in the content of the treaties in favour of the agents.[118] Once a state commits to neoliberal policies, and other states reinforce these choices, neoliberal market norms repress change and attempts to alter the norms trigger negative consequences.[119]

[111] Manipulation is 'usually covert and may take the form of agenda fixing, the deceptive or nonrational shaping of people's beliefs or desires, or the rigging of the consequences of people's actions'. Pettit (n 98) 53.

[112] WJ Henisz, BA Zelner, and MF Guillén, 'International Coercion, Emulation and Policy Diffusion: Market-Oriented Infrastructure Reforms' (2005) 70 American Sociological Review 871.

[113] HD Lasswell and A Kaplan, *Power and Society: A Framework for Political Inquiry* (Yale UP 1950) 97–98.

[114] These issues have also been discussed in section 2.1 in the context of makers versus takers or agents versus recipients.

[115] See P Nel, 'The Rise and Fall of BITs', www.otago.ac.nz/politics/otago061036.pdf, 7.

[116] L Gruber, *Ruling the World: Power Politics and the Rise of Supranational Institutions* (Princeton UP 2000); AT Guzman, 'Why LDCs Sign Treaties That Hurt Them: Explaining the Popularity of Bilateral Investment Treaties' (1998) 38 Virginia Journal of International Law 639.

[117] Guzman (n 116).

[118] Gruber (n 116); Nel (n 115).

[119] Lindblom (n 95).

Once it is established that coercion may in some instances occur in the making of international economic agreements, we would then be in a position to critique the effects of that coercion on particular states. It was something of a common critique in earlier waves of legal scholarship about the Uruguay Round that the WTO and its agreements placed considerable constraints on the ability of states to regulate the environment, health and safety, and consumer protection in accordance with the widely held moral convictions of the citizens of the affected states.[120] Before the Uruguay Round, the GATT primarily regulated border measures such as tariffs. The Uruguay Round brought non-tariff barriers into the WTO's fullest purview, striking at the core of the regulatory state. Similar arguments can be made about intrusions by BITs. And, the global financial order as it is presently constructed likewise could be said to make substantial incursions into deciding national economic policy, the regulation of banks, and the distribution of burdens and benefits in the regulation of the banking and financial sectors. Neoliberal international arrangements have a way of replacing democratic deliberation. All of this forms part of the structural coercion coming from what is essentially mandatory participation in the global economy. It is doubtful that many weaker states really have a choice in whether to conform to the neoliberal agenda that has been at work in international law.

Some irony is in order when we see how coercion did not make it into the Vienna Convention on the Law of Treaties as a ground to void a treaty. Article 52 of the Vienna Convention provides that '[a] treaty is void if its conclusion has been procured by the threat or use of force in violation of the principles of international law embodied in the Charter of the United Nations'.[121] In the Vienna Convention negotiations of the late 1960s, there was considerable debate on whether Article 52 included economic and political forms of coercion.[122] A proposal to include 'economic and political pressure' in Article 52 was introduced by former colonies that had recently acquired statehood at the time. The amendment could well have carried if put to a formal vote. As the American representatives record of the negotiations:

> The course of the debate had made it clear that if the amendment were put to the vote it would carry by quite a substantial majority. On the other hand, in private discussions it had been made quite clear to the proponents that adoption could wreck the conference because states concerned with the stability of treaties found the proposal intolerable.[123]

[120] See JP Trachtman, *The International Economic Law Revolution and the Right to Regulate* (Cameron May 2005); RH Wade, 'What Strategies Are Viable for Developing Countries Today: The World Trade Organization and the Shrinking of "Development Space"' (2003) 10 Review of International Political Economy 621; R Howse, 'Democracy, Science, and Free Trade: Risk Regulation on Trial at the World Trade Organization' (2000) 98 Michigan Law Review 2329.

[121] Vienna Convention on the Law of Treaties, Art 52, 1155 United Nations Treaty Series 331, entered into force 27 Jan 1980.

[122] See O Corten and P Klein (eds), *The Vienna Conventions on the Law of Treaties: A Commentary* (OUP 2011).

[123] RD Kearney and RE Dalton 'The Treaty on Treaties' (1970) 64 AJIL 495, 533–35 (citations omitted).

Olivier Corten explains in his commentary on Article 52 that 'after several particularly powerful states had insinuated that the adoption of this amendment would jeopardize their signature of the Convention, the amendment was removed before being put to a vote'.[124] The result was that the amendment has been characterized as 'defeated'[125] and the alternative was a non-binding 'Declaration on the Prohibition of Military, Political or Economic Coercion' condemning the threat or use of economic and political pressure.[126] The position of powerful states to walk away from the Convention negotiations if they did not get their way on Article 52 is an example of coercion actually practised by states.

Finally, the moral disorder in international law identified in section 2.2 makes the coercion brought out in international treaty making ever more problematic. Unlike the coercive features of domestic law, international law takes on a far more arbitrary constellation of coercive features with no or insufficient connections to democratic deliberation, legislative processes in which legislators have an opportunity to balance competing interests, and in which the give and take of political accountability plays a role in mediating those interests. In short, power and coercion are much rawer and more immediate when exercised in international law.[127]

2.4 Historic wrongdoing

History has moral significance.[128] We should not ignore the 'violence, ruthlessness, and arrogance' accompanying the disseminating of a European vision of international law, which effectively destroyed other forms of law and norms in the process.[129] If we are to critique or justify principles of international law from a moral point of view, then we need to account for the wrongdoing that international law and its predecessors has justified for several centuries in the form of colonialism and imperialism or in what historian Sven Beckert calls 'war capitalism'—international law's historic wrongdoing—particularly when these wrongs do appear to continue to be reflected in international law. The focus is not only on the disadvantages that may or may not have resulted but also on the way international law has been on the wrong side of what is right, for the most part, and that international economic law continues to reflect that moral failure. To ignore the history of international law is to overlook how the past is reflected in present day international law. Ignoring history would put us at risk of masking deep-rooted problems that stubbornly persist into the present time, lead us to promoting a guise of neutrality

124 Corten and Klein (n 122) 1206 (citations omitted).

125 JE Alvarez, 'A Bit on Custom' (2009) 42 NYU Journal of International Law and Politics 17, 38 n 79.

126 Corten and Klein (n 122) 1205–06.

127 See discussion (n 102).

128 D Butt, *Rectifying International Injustice: Principles of Compensation and Restitution Between Nations* (OUP 2009).

129 B Fassbender and A Peters, 'Introduction: Towards a Global History of International Law' in B Fassbender and A Peters (eds), *The Oxford Handbook of the History of International Law* (OUP 2012) 2.

in the face of histories that have given peoples impaired starting points, and putting too much focus on simple fixes without an accounting for the past.

It is well accepted that historic wrongdoing is at least a contributing cause to global poverty and inequality and to difficulties that some states have in developing societies that give their citizens opportunities to realize their potential. Historic wrongdoing has detrimentally affected the qualities of institutions in a society, which in turn affects wealth, resources, opportunities, and life chances in a society.[130] This is an argument that goes beyond endowment arguments in economics. Rather, it is that states may have differing endowments because of historic wrongdoing and that historic wrongdoing has been supported and facilitated by international law and its predecessors. As the chapters to follow show, international law continues to place undue priorities on the commercial interests of the powerful, carving up the world to their greater advantage, and feigning mutual gain as it did in the past.

As elaborated in section 2.1, historic wrongdoing has also contributed to an agency problem in international law. Some peoples have not been represented at the table in the formative stages of international law. Some of these were former colonies, who, with independence in post-war twentieth century, began to pursue the development of alternative legal principles, but these principles were rejected. This development is discussed in Chapter 3 ('The End of Empire and the Search for Justice: NIEO and Beyond').

There are two ways to understand historic wrongdoing, prospectively or retrospectively. To focus retrospectively is to focus on redress and rectification. Historic wrongdoing has brought about claims for redress, though these have had low levels of success in domestic societies and very limited success at the international level. Some of the principal difficulties in dealing with redress are causal and empirical and have to do with the allocations of moral and legal responsibilities on current generations for wrongs committed by or inflicted upon prior generations.[131] To focus prospectively is to focus on the relationship of historic wrongdoing to international law today and to seek to change the law, so that its historical effects no longer maintain their normative force. These two ways of understanding the effects of historic wrongdoing are related in so far as a causal relationship exists between the development of international law and wealth and poverty through the ages. But that causal link aside, international law is implicated in a morally problematic history of gain by the powerful of the day and indeed, as studies have ably shown, has been shaped by past interventions. In significant ways, we have not shaken off that history. This book has a prospective focus, looking to history not to establish a legal mechanism for reparations but to critique international law for what it continues to be and for possible future reform.

[130] These findings can be found in the law and development literature and in the literature on the role of institutions in development. See, eg, MJ Trebilcock and M Mota Prado, *Advanced Introduction to Law and Development* (Edward Elgar 2014); D Acemoglu and J Robinson, *Why Nations Fail: The Origins of Power, Prosperity, and Poverty* (Profile 2013).

[131] See Butt (n 128); J Waldron, 'Superseding Historic Injustice' (1992) 103 Ethics 4.

3. The Way Forward

The prior section offered reasons why international law is subject to the demands of justice. International law has no 'out' based on a claim that because it is not domestic law or governs what goes on inside national communities, it is excused from the requirements of justice. These claims have been shown to be untenable on both empirical and conceptual grounds. No sound reasons for a differentiated structure or an 'inside–outside distinction' requiring states to mandate justice only for its citizens and permitting the infliction of misery for everyone else outside its borders. This section will deal with the way forward: what the demands of justice require of international law. It moves justification of international law from one of interest and expedience based on order and power to one of morality based in justice. Rejected are the morally minimalist approaches the practical association conception entails for international law, effectively exempting state conduct from moral evaluation when it comes to markets and economics.

This section offers a brief sketch on how states have duties to improve the moral legitimacy of international law, originating in a right of justification that persons affected by international law hold. Agents to whom international law applies (usually and predominantly states) have what philosopher Stephen Darwall calls a second personal obligation to recognize and respect each person as a participant in the making, application, and enforcement of international law.[132] 'Second personal' refers to a basic moral idea that legal rules must comply with moral duties owed between moral agents if they are to be morally legitimate. This right of justification exists because of the above relational, structural, dominating, and historic wrongdoing features of international law. These obligations lead to a set of moral principles, grounded in notions of impartiality and reasonable rejection, obligating states to improve the moral legitimacy of international law.

3.1 International law and 'justification to'

International law as it currently stands is a moral failure. By its own structure and content, international law creates and maintains relationships with significant moral consequences. It is a shared institution affecting the life prospects of many, creating rights and liabilities, benefits, and burdens. It is no less consequential in doing these things than domestic law and in some cases more so. But as Forst, Hurrell, and Slaughter help us understand, there are in fact both makers and takers, agents and passive recipients of international law. These facts cast doubt on international law's moral authority as it is made and practised. They infuse moral inequality into the structure of international law. The result is a failure of accountability of international law, a moral failure.

[132] S Darwall, *The Second Person Standpoint* (Harvard UP 2006).

These facts on the ground are the conditions we need to work with. The remedy is to get clear on how to make normative claims about these facts, in the form of moral claims relating to justice. Section 2 leads to the conclusion that persons affected by international law have a *right of justification* for the rights, liabilities, burdens, and benefits it allocates. These persons affected by international law therefore stand in an authority or accountability relation to the makers of international law. 'Justification to' is necessary to ensure that persons receive respect as agents in the international legal system, and not merely passive recipients of international law. Let us dissect the core claims at work here: right of justification, to each person, requiring respect as agents in the international legal system.

As for the right to justification, states have what is known in moral theory as a second personal obligation, resulting in a right of justification held by others.[133] This move is necessary to understand international law as a system of governance supported by a right to govern. The right of justification requires that states justify the international legal rules they create and apply to persons affected by them. States are not in a position to reject the claim that the grounds elaborated in the previous section (relation, structure, domination, historical wrong) create the conditions for accountability between the creators of international law and those affected by international law. Those with substantial powers to generate social practices affecting and sometimes harming numerous others must justify these social practices to those affected or harmed. This is not about accountability in a domestic constitutional order within a state as in, for example, democratic accountability of government to citizens, but about moral accountability of the makers of international law to persons who are the subjects of regulation or affected by international law.

What is meant by second personal? Think of it as the circumstances in which a state is bound to accept a claim or demand for it to conduct its affairs in a certain way, based on an authority or accountability relationship between the state and the claimant. The state as addressee must accept the authority of the person making the claim or demand for second person obligations to work. An addressee who accepts that the addresser can make these second personal demands must also accept that the addresser has grounds to complain or to engage in some other accountability seeking action if the addressee fails to accept the demands. The addresser–addressee relationship is not limited to state and citizen. And it would be too simple to limit moral claims to state-to-state interaction, though our focus here is on the accountability of states, and indirectly, intergovernmental organizations, which are effectively agents of states. A proper addresser of moral claims might be a vulnerable population, group of persons, or community within a state, or the state itself, such

[133] See Forst (n 79); Darwall (n 132). Darwall's discussion of a second personal obligation does not address its relevance to law. It is meta-ethics; it is about the form of moral argument. This is what makes it important for us, because it informs us about how the basic structure of moral obligation operates. Darwall has himself developed some domestic legal applications. S Darwall, *Morality, Authority, and Law: Essays in Second-Personal Ethics* (OUP 2013). Moreover, Darwall claims the second personal is a foundation for contractualism and there are forms of contractualism that deal with law and institutions.

as in the case of a poor state suffering injustice because of predations by a former colonizing state.[134]

The second personal features of moral responsibility mean that each person is an agent deserving of respect. Duties are owed first and foremost to individual persons. All moral theory of whatever kind starts with the conception of the person and how persons are conceived determines the aims and methods of a moral theory. This is a feature that makes a theory a moral one. By 'each person' we refer to a standard moral understanding of a person not motivated only by their own concerns, but who as moral agents exercise capacities to be reasonable and not only capacities associated with means–ends rationality. An important feature of moral argument is that of impartiality, the notion that morally motivated persons, when engaged in moral reasoning, must necessarily do so from an impartial standpoint.[135] To promote moral equality, this justification runs to each person affected by international law; it respects a basic 'separateness of persons' requirement common to contractualist and deontological forms of moral reasoning.[136] It mandates no unreasonable burdens that persons should be required to accept when international law promotes economic globalization.

The separateness of persons requirements means that persons cannot be treated as means to ends that deviate from supporting their humanity. Each person is an end and are not to be treated as a means to some broader end or to serve the interests of the whole or a larger community. In moral theory, this means that aggregation is impermissible except in rare cases. This chapter does not offer a welfare-based account such as that found in normative welfare economics, but a contractualist account in which principles of justice might bar placing great burdens on a few to benefit the many. Aggregation is at the core of approaches to economic growth that can cause or contributed to the moral failures condemned in this book.

These requirements are not as demanding as they might seem at first blush. The 'each person' feature of moral deliberation must be brought to its logical conclusion. It also requires that persons not make unreasonable demands on states and other international actors. Properly articulated demands for justice, however, are not unreasonable. When the move is made to the non-ideal or legal context, in many cases the impacts of legal arrangements on classes or groups of similarly situated persons, such as farmers, steelworkers, debtors, households, and local communities, can be evaluated.

[134] Examining the issues from a positive law standpoint, international human rights law remains extremely limited in its ability to apply to issues of poverty, inequality, and immiseration when the source of the violation is a state other than the right-holders own. See ME Salomon, 'Deprivation, Causation and the Law of International Cooperation' in M Langford, M Scheinin, W van Genugten, and W Vandenhole (eds), *Global Justice, State Duties: The Extra-Territorial Scope of Economic, Social and Cultural Rights in International Law* (CUP 2013) 259, 288–95 and A Khalfan, 'Accountability Mechanisms' ibid 391. As for the human rights accountability of international organizations, it is inchoate, as it has been for decades.

[135] For discussions of the role of impartiality in moral reasoning, see B Barry, *Justice as Impartiality* (OUP 1995); MD Adler, *Well-Being and Fair Distribution: Beyond Cost Benefit Analysis* (OUP 2012) ch 1.

[136] Rawls (n 13, *Theory of Justice*) 24–30.

Think of the respect owed to persons affected by international law along the lines of a categorical or master principle found in contractualism about the structure of moral argument.[137] International law should reflect general principles for the regulation of the behaviour of states and others who are subject to international law's reach that no one could reasonably reject.[138] If some person could reasonably reject an international legal rule or set of rules intended to regulate trade, investment, or finance, then that rule or set of rules is unreasonable and should not be put in place or implemented. This standard gives primacy to impartiality, which becomes a standard also for the evaluation and development of law. As Mathew Adler explains, '[m]oral evaluation gives a central role (it not necessarily an exclusive role) to the interests of *persons*, more specifically human persons. Moral evaluation tries to achieve some kind of *impartiality* between persons.'[139]

How should states implement their responsibilities in meeting this basic right of justification? States with the requisite capacity have a duty to improve the moral legitimacy of international law. They need to deliver an international law which meets standards of moral justification, responsive to the grounds we have identified as generating claims of justice at the international level.

Various formulations of this basic duty of states have been developed. Dworkin offers a duty of states to improve the moral legitimacy of international law, to mitigate the moral defects in a system built around sovereign states, coupled with what he calls a principle of salience. Dworkin explains:

> Coercive government (I include not just traditional 'sovereign' states but also any institution or organization claiming coercive authority) has a standing duty to improve its own legitimacy. Each traditional state therefore has a duty to pursue available means to mitigate the failures and risks of the sovereign-state system. That duty of mitigation provides the most general structural principle and interpretive background of international law.[140]

Dworkin's principle of salience provides that if a number of states covering a significant population has reached agreement on some aspect of international law, other states have 'at least a *prima facie* duty' to agree to the development, subject to an 'important proviso' that the duty holds only if the development would improve the moral legitimacy of the subscribing state and the international order.[141] Of course, Dworkin's account presupposes a Westphalian system of sovereign states and as discussed in section 2, sovereignty can often mask serious moral problems for international law.

A potential problem with Dworkin's account is that it may be too lax on demands on states. It is only a duty that specifies a procedure and not substantive rights or duties, and we are dealing with injustices of a very stark kind when it comes to international law. It tells us nothing about duties states and other international

[137] TM Scanlon, *What We Owe to Each Other* (Harvard UP 1998).

[138] This is a well-understood contractualist form of moral argument, adapted to evaluate legal principles on moral grounds. See Darwall (n 133); TM Scanlon, *The Difficulty of Tolerance: Essays in Political Philosophy* (CUP 2009).

[139] Adler (n 135) 3. For the application of these principles in the explicit context of within states, see Dworkin (n 49).

[140] Dworkin (n 28) 19.

[141] ibid.

actors may or may not have. It simply claims that states must pursue moral legitimacy in the development of international law.

Dworkin exempts the WTO and the European Union from these requirements, as he sees these institutions similar to 'clubs' with states expressly admitted to membership and 'institutional procedures that cannot sensibly be used outside that club'.[142] In other words, membership in these economic 'clubs' is voluntary. Dworkin's exemptions are easily rejected. As argued throughout this book, the WTO and organizations like it are structurally coercive, offering a 'take it or leave it' structure for the basic international law of the global economy, which states cannot exempt themselves from without serious risk of being left out of the global economy. The mandatory features of membership, coupled with the substance of international economic agreements determined by the exercise of state power, require justification to those affected by these institutional features.

An example of second personal obligations at work can be found in Richard Miller's account of advantage taking in the global economy. Miller has argued that governments, firms, and individuals in rich states take advantage of people in poor states in the processes of production, exchange, and finance and in the institutional framework regulating these processes. This advantage taking, says Miller, results in a duty of the rich to 'give up consequent benefits'.[143] To Miller, advantage taking occurs when the more well off derive benefits in advancing their own interests from the difficulties the less well-off encounter in interactions in which both participate, in a process showing inadequate regard for the equal moral importance of the other's interests and their capacity for choice. According to Miller, in globalization contexts advantage taking arises in the presence of 'bargaining weaknesses due to desperate neediness'.[144] The concern here is in using another person's weakness to get one's way. Miller argues that these interactions requires justification but more than that the weaker party is simply better off. To bring this latter point home, consider a standard example of exploitation: A slave is better off if you increase her calorie count or provide better sleeping quarters, but she is still a slave. To deal with these moral failures, Miller offers a solution something like Dworkin's though he makes no claims about the character of international law: the more well-off states should 'support new measures that reasonable deliberations would yield'.[145] For Miller, reasonable deliberations encompass 'international responsibilities of good faith and domestic responsibility'.[146] Good faith involves two kinds of reciprocity. First, 'each must seek an arrangement that all can responsibly willingly accept,

[142] ibid.

[143] RW Miller, *Globalizing Justice: The Ethics of Poverty and Power* (OUP 2010) 59.

[144] ibid 60. [145] ibid 4.

[146] ibid. Miller's moral concept of good faith differs from the narrower legal concept application to treaty interpretation found in Arts 26 and 31 of the Vienna Convention on the Law of Treaties.

In addition to their international responsibilities, states have domestic responsibilities. Says Miller: 'the representatives have to fulfil their responsibilities to those they represent. They can only accept outcomes that they can justify to their own people in terms that those people can accept while regarding their interests and autonomy as no less important than others' (ibid 72). There are two parallel sets of obligations at work—one of the state to its citizens and the other to agents outside of the state. This parallelism means that states have to take their domestic obligations into account when

provided that all of the others have corresponding commitments'.[147] Second, 'the representatives must observe reciprocity in their reasoning, backing their own proposals with morally relevant reason and giving weight, in proportion to seriousness, to relevantly similar reasons offered by others, so that the importance of a consideration is assessed by its strength rather than the identity of those affected by it'.[148]

The structure of both Dworkin's salience and mitigation principles and Miller's good faith reasonable deliberation principles are second personal, requiring those responsible for the making and enforcing of international law to treat all those affected by international law as agents.[149] They and other similar accounts offer a framework in which to assess the conformity of international law to the moral requirements of 'justification to'. They go to the reasons why international law may or may not have authority from a moral point of view to regulate the global economy.

3.2 Principles

What precisely are the demands of justice? Michael Walzer and Matthias Risse are right to argue that concepts of justice are pluralistic.[150] Different principles of justice will apply in different contexts as they are presented in trade, investment, and finance contexts. That principles are pluralistic means that there might be different

deliberating on their international obligations. They cannot, for example, impose unreasonable burdens on their own citizens in discharging their international obligations.

[147] ibid. [148] ibid.

[149] We are beginning to see strategies for a moralized conception of international law at work, though we are in early stages, and it is up to governments to take the initiative. An example of how to get out of the Thrasymachian trap can be found in Lim's recent work on global trade and monetary cooperation. Writing on the context of China's currency manipulation and the range of responses the United States could take, Lim explains:

> International economic lawyers have ... tended to focus their writings on what the rules say. To the extent that they find the rules uncertain, these writings underscore the apparent permissibility of the PBC's [People's Bank of China's] policies and also the fact that unilateral action by China's trading partners may be permissible where such action doesn't contravene the rules. International lawyers routinely 'tolerate' unilateral, sovereign action in such a manner where, as here, our fragmented legal regimes—the WTO and the IMF—are incapable of providing practical guidance. 'Tolerance' may not be the exact word. I use it here only to denote professional acceptance of the limits of legal rules, and—as I shall argue further below—acceptance that there are 'gaps' in the law where specific issues fall through the cracks between the fragmented, yet sometimes overlapping, regimes which characterize the discipline of international economic law.

CL Lim, '"The Law Works Itself Pure": The Fragmented Disciplines of Global Trade and Monetary Cooperation, and the Chinese Currency Problem' in Lim and Mercurio (n 96) 134, 137. Lim argues that these gaps have to be filled using moral judgment. He says: '[F]ragmentation and the absence of adequate global rules do not mean a regulatory free-for-all' (ibid 136). So, no Hobbesian gladiators but rather something in the character of a *jus gentium,* or perhaps more accurately a combination of moral judgment and positive law: 'In this sense, the debate is as old as that between the natural lawyers who would not *confine* all that we would call "law" to that which may be traced to the voluntary consent of sovereigns to international rules, and so-called legal positivists, who would' (ibid 137–38).

[150] Walzer (n 46) (justice is 'complex'); M Risse, *On Global Justice* (Princeton UP 2015).

principles at work in different contexts, not that no principles are at work at all or even anything as dogmatic that each situation requires a different principle. Some grouping of like contexts can be accomplished. Principles of justice can very generally be elucidated along lines consistent with the grounds for justice set forth in section 2, though applications should use those grounds as starting points and not as strict constraints.

In this book, there has been discussion of the misery that international law can and does inflict. Misery is a central organizing principle for the book. From the perspective of this chapter, an anti-misery principle could reflect a moral minimum. It is reasonable for a person to reject any legal arrangement for the global economy that would impose or perpetuate misery in her economic and social situation. What is misery? Our convictions might tell us that the concept might refer to impoverishment, great distress, discomfort, hardship, or suffering. An anti-misery principle would make morally objectionable any institutional arrangement that causes or contributes to these ills. To make an anti-misery principle sensible as a moral principle requires two restrictions. First, it would be too weak as a principle if it were the only moral principle relevant to the global economic order. Go back to the slave example. We can make a slave less miserable by increasing calorie intake or providing better sleeping quarters. These life improvements certainly do not eliminate misery or the moral wrong of slavery. Second, misery should be constrained by our master principle of reasonable rejection. Suppose a legal ordering causes hardship because it rectifies injustice, say of ill-gotten gains. Changes in the global financial architecture, for example, such as in the banning of particular kinds of speculation or leveraging in financial markets, might make people who have spent their lives as traders in capital markets suffer losses, or from their perspective make them miserable. But here we might argue that it is unreasonable to expect to profit from imposing misery on others and these traders have alternatives to making a good living in productive matters outside of these dangerous activities. In other words, it is unreasonable for these traders to believe they have been subjected to a form of misery in such cases.

Another basic principle of justice is Thomas Pogge's negative duty not to harm principle.[151] The basic idea behind Pogge's anti-harm principle is that rich countries violate a negative duty not to harm by imposing a coercive institutional arrangement that systematically disadvantages poor countries and deprives persons in poor countries of security in access to the objects of their human rights.

Principles of justice that reflect relational or anti-domination rationales might reflect moral principles such as an equality promoting principle: international law should not create or perpetuate inequalities that cannot be morally justified. This principle could require a difference principle to apply to the making and interpretation of international agreements relating to the global economy.

What seems to be pervasively at work in the extreme version of capitalism operating in the global economy is a reverse difference principle. In practical politics, this has been referred to as a reverse Robin Hood principle.[152] The reverse

[151] Pogge (n 43). [152] Chapter 6 ('Global Finance') at 198–200.

difference principle in operation produces something like an accumulation by dispossession. David Harvey has argued that the international order has adhered to a neoliberal economic principle, which he calls accumulation by dispossession, the structuring of institutions so that the wealthy accumulate more wealth at the expense of the less well off.[153] The result is a norm that is the opposite of a difference principle: a priority for the better off. It is an inequality aggravating principle. Trade agreements carve up markets; one of their primary features is that of distribution. They open markets for products for which powerful constituencies in powerful states have a comparative advantage, create comparative advantages for powerful constituencies, and protect markets in rich states from competition from producers in poor states. Investment agreements promote liberal investment protection regimes that alter the distribution of resources from poor host states to investors from rich states. Global finance offers examples of all sorts of accumulations by dispossession, with a global financial architecture that produces insecurity for millions yet producing few benefits. Human rights seek to protect people from the negative impacts of these regimes and the ideology that underpins them, but it is up against a ubiquitous foe.

Staggering inequalities in basic life chances are evident across and within countries. It is morally arbitrary that a person's life chances are determined by the luck of being born in a particular country. To the extent that international law creates, exacerbates, or maintains such gross inequalities, it will need to be subject to an equality of opportunity principle. Such a principle might, for example, require that international law should neutralize bad brute luck, if that bad luck is best neutralized at the international and not the domestic level. For example, Chapter 4 describes a situation in which there are winners and losers in trade agreements. Trade agreements are good at compensating winners but bad at compensating losers. Their basic structure needs to change.

A freedom from domination or anti-alienation principle could be at work to evaluate international law from the standpoint of justice: international law should develop in a manner that does not challenge self-governance and self-determination of peoples and the autonomy of persons. Freedom from domination can serve as a complement to principles of equality, where persons can govern themselves based on principles and values they can reasonably endorse upon due reflection.[154] The recent Greek referendum of 5 July 2015 is an example of a breach of this principle. In the referendum, Greek citizens overwhelmingly voted against economic austerity required by the bailout conditions proposed by the European Commission, the European Central Bank, and the IMF, yet these institutions insisted on them nevertheless, and the Greek government was left with little choice but to relent.[155]

[153] D Harvey, *The New Imperialism* (OUP 2005) 137–82.
[154] See E Anderson, *Value in Ethics and Economics* (Harvard UP 1993) 142.
[155] See Chapter 6 ('Global Finance') at 211–224.

Closely related to a freedom from domination principle is an anti-coercion principle, which provides for the moral impermissibility of economic coercion by powerful states against weaker states in the making and interpretation of the international law governing the global economy. Coercion is a pervasive phenomenon that is core to the very structure of the international law governing the global economy.

The Introduction to this chapter quote's Charles Mill's argument that justice needs to be focused more on rectification in actual societies than on justice in ideal societies. Daniel Butt sets forth just such an argument, linking current generations in political communities to past wrongdoing by prior generations.[156] Butt argues that three forms of connection are morally relevant for establishing a duty of rectification, running from developed to developing countries. The first connection is one of benefit: when a political community continues to benefit and another is burdened by historic injustice. The second connection is entitlement: when a community possesses property to which another is morally entitled. The third connection is responsibility, the case in which a political community is responsible for ongoing injustice that relates to a failure to comply with a duty of rectification over time. The history of trade and investment law show us that historic injustice is indeed at work in the global economy. And when we add the dire effects that historic injustices can have on the life chances of people, then it seems clear that international law must take rectification of historic injustice into account if it is to reflect basic precepts of moral accountability.

Ultimately the requirements for the moral acceptability of international law rests on the notion of whether international law supports the positive freedom of persons, which means a focus on whether international law contributes to or works toward eliminating poverty, alienation, exploitation, poor economic opportunities, deprivation, and other ills that are obstacles to human flourishing.[157] It also requires that international human rights law play its role to prevent and redress harm and support civil and political participation.[158] These matters require a focus not on economic growth, or at least not on economic growth alone, but on how economic growth is accomplished.

This book offers a critique of the structure and institutions of the global economy. Moving from critique to reform would lead to a focus on getting the law right in the first place rather than on leaving it in some morally unacceptable extreme capitalist form and attempting to redistribute through some sort of compensatory process, for which no adequate legal mechanisms in international sphere exist in any event. Critique of structure and institutions naturally lead to think about predistribution.[159] The aim of predistribution is to make international law just in a structural sense, *ex ante*, so that the elements of international law relevant to the

156 See Butt (n 128).

157 While Amartya Sen does not deal with international law his work deals with these issues. A Sen, *Development as Freedom* (Anchor 1999).

158 See Chapter 7 ('Human Rights').

159 For what is probably the first book-length treatment of predistribution, see A Thomas, *Republic of Equals: Predistribution and Property-Owning Democracy* (OUP 2017). The origin of the concept has

global economy are designed to make it structurally impossible in a practical sense for injustice to exist in the global economy in any material sense. For example, if the focus is on domination in the global economy, the aim would be for international law to be structured to eliminate or, given the limitations of the law as an instrument to effectuate change, to make it exceedingly difficult for powerful actors to dominate in the global economy.[160] The advantages of a predistribution approach are several. It supports a normative approach in which states and other global actors have duties to improve the moral legitimacy of international law. It deters agenda setting at the formative stage for international law, when powerful interests may attempt to grab whatever rents they can in the formulation of unjust international law. It eliminates the need for states to set up complex redistribution mechanisms. Tax and transfer mechanisms simply do not exist at the international level and they often work poorly even within states. It avoids the loss aversion problem, where people prefer to avoid losses than to acquire equivalent gains. Loss aversion reflects the insight that once something is given it is very difficult to take it away.[161] Leaving in place an extreme version of capitalism and hoping for the best in some future redistribution is unrealistic at best. The bottom line is that dealing with justice at the level of international law naturally leads us to predistribution as the only feasible mode of change.

4. Concluding Remarks

This chapter sets forth a special kind of normative argument, a moral one, for why international law is subject to principles of justice when it operates in the areas of trade, investment, and finance. International law is subject to the demands of justice because of its role as an institution essential to global cooperation, because it intrudes far into the distributional issues linking closely to how people live their lives, because of its historic role in perpetuating and legitimizing moral wrongs, and because it can lead to domination and the deprivation of freedom if states and international organizations do not get it right. After elaborating these grounds, this chapter proceeds to a theory of justice for international law, based largely on the idea that these grounds produce moral accountability for international actors with the power and capacity to take corrective action and that this moral accountability must transpose into legal accountability for international law to make any legitimate appeal to those dictated by it to respect it. International law must meet

been credited to Jacob Hacker. See JS Hacker, *Winner Take All Politics* (Simon & Schuster 2011); JS Hacker, 'The Institutional Foundations of Middle-Class Democracy' (Progressive Governance conference, May 2011, Oslo).

160 Thomas (n 159) 6, 19, 23, 80, 86, 374, 397.

161 See D Kahneman and A Tversky, 'Choices, Values, and Frames' (1984) 34 American Psychologist 341.

a standard of respect and 'justification to' each person, particularly those in weaker positions. International law cannot treat any person as only a passive recipient or supplicant to rules that benefit those in power or stronger positions. Justice is complex and different principles of justice apply in different contexts in the global economy. But as the following chapters will show, international law fails to comply with the demands of justice when it comes to international trade, foreign investment, and global finance, while the efforts of the human rights regime are bound up with this extreme capitalism, with grave consequences. Immiseration follows.

3

The End of Empire and the Search for Justice

NIEO and Beyond

It is difficult to evaluate the claim of justice in international law without some historical inquiry into the justifications given for empire.[1] European states justified empire for its moral rightness or in altruistic or paternalistic terms of bringing benefits to colonized peoples. Though the Westphalian peace ending the Thirty Years War (1648) is taken as the origin for modern international law, it is more appropriate to regard the successive rationalizations given for colonization and subjugation to imperial rule of the peoples of America, Asia, and Africa as constituting the true origins of international law. These rationalizations for colonization and subjugation were attempts to support a global normative order, iniquitous though it be, rather than the purely European order that the Treaty of Westphalia brought about.[2] Conquering European states first offered justifications for the rapacious plunder of the Aztecs and the Incas and then for the building of empires in Africa and Asia. A succession of the great international lawyers devoted their work to the project. Often described as the fathers of international law, they largely devoted their writings to the purported legitimacy of European control of far off lands. These were early attempts to justify imperialism as morally right action, at a time when legal thought mixed moral reasoning with description of social practices.[3] Imperialism supported trade and investment. These justifications continue. It befuddles the search for justice in contemporary times. There was a great divergence between the reality of oppression and its justification. In contemporary times, this divergence remains visible through arguments that trade and investment promote economic development and end poverty, which have come to be stated with greater finesse in the language of economic well-being and normative welfare economics. Justification for the spread of commerce in the contemporary age of globalization does not differ materially from those given in the past ages of imperial expansion and colonization. Conflicting views of what justice requires, however conceptualized, will continue between the opposites of its use as a cloak for commercial and

[1] Many modern studies are based on this fact. A Pagden, *The Burdens of Empire: 1539 to the Present* (CUP 2015); A Anghie, *Imperialism, Sovereignty and the Making of International Law* (CUP 2005).

[2] R Hernandez, 'The Internationalization of Francisco de Vitoria and Domingo de Soto' (1991) 15 Fordham International Law Journal 1031.

[3] Pagden (n 1); SC Neff, *Justice Among Nations: A History of International Law* (Harvard UP 2014).

The Misery of International Law: Confrontations with Injustice in the Global Economy, John Linarelli, Margot E Salomon, and M Sornarajah. Published 2018 by Oxford University Press.

political expansion and its use as a cosmopolitan imperative that supports normative prescriptions for ensuring an end to global poverty, an end to unjustifiable inequalities, and various forms of immiseration, and to address related pressing issues of humanity such as human rights and climate change.

Empire was the precedent fact, which caused inequalities among the people of the world along with various forms of immiseration. Inequality between the rulers and ruled was the basis of the imperial system which international law made possible and maintained. As a range of international legal scholars have ably exposed,[4] the end of colonialism did not lead to the dismantling of techniques and rules of a system that maintains unequal relationships, a divide between active participants making international law and those who can only passively be subject to it. The continuation of the seeds of empire within international law ensures the maintenance of the historical divisions that had been created at earlier periods of history. Justice as it is understood in Chapter 2 ('Confronting the Pathologies of International Law') and elsewhere in this book, cannot come about unless these path dependencies in international law are identified and the techniques and rules associated with the maintenance of the imperial system are rooted out. Inequality, poverty, and underdevelopment do not come about because of inherent cosmic imbalances or (only a) lack of efficiency in governance among some peoples but because of the continuation or imposition of rules and ideologies ensuring that affluent states maintain their dominance over others. International law alone cannot provide for the realization of objectives such as the ending of underdevelopment or the eradication of poverty but it is a precondition of achieving these objectives that its forms and substance creating inequalities and other moral wrongs are removed.

The political and legal struggles throughout the 1960s and 1970s of former colonized peoples seeking to bring about a new world order have resonance today with peoples across the world who find themselves oppressed by rules that are too oriented towards large economic actors in a global marketplace but which do not account for how they affect the poor and maintain injustice. The aims of the former colonized peoples were ambitious but not high; they were radical for their time even if many would say not nearly radical enough. They were the aims of ensuring that the resources found in their lands are not exploited to the benefit of other people and to the detriment of their own, that just prices be paid for them and for the finished products manufactured with them, that multinational corporations should not be able to control exploitation of resources or the marketing of manufactured goods, and that there should be access to the markets of the world for their manufactured goods. That the world into which they emerged after the ending of imperial rule did not recognize even these low-end objectives—objectives that did not even attempt to disrupt a market-oriented international law but merely to expand the range of states that would benefit from it—is an indictment of the situation

[4] Anghie (n 1); S Pahuja, *Decolonising International Law: Development, Growth, and the Politics of Universality* (CUP 2011); IM Porras, 'Constructing Sovereignty in the East Indian Seas: Property, Sovereignty, Commerce and War' (2006) 31 Brooklyn Journal of International Law 741.

that existed in the days of imperialism, in the postcolonial period and in important ways continues to exist to this day. The continuation of the system into the present world through structures perpetuating dominance is an indictment of modern international law. Justice requires the identification and removal of institutions that perpetuate unjustifiable coercion and the dominance of one group of states or market actors over others along with the maintenance of ideologies that ensure such coercion and dominance. The New International Economic Order (NIEO) may not have been transformative for international law but it rested on a conception of justice that if implemented would reflect the associative duties at work in the international sphere as they are explicated in Chapter 2 ('Confronting the Pathologies of International Law'). The NIEO required that international law not be used to serve ideologies that would perpetuate immiseration and that in its best usage would effectuate real justice, something that has so far eluded us.

The effects of international law on inequality, poverty, and various forms of immiseration are not confined to the peoples of low-income or developing countries. A noted political scientist argued in 1999 that the Third World is present within the First World because of the prevalence of increasing income disparities that the same ideologies have brought about within the societies of the developed world.[5] The disparities in most developed countries have become wider in recent years with global disparities at exceptional levels unless income inequality among citizens of the world is considered along with the recent performance of some emerging economies.[6] Oxfam has used Credit Suisse data to show that the top 1% of people in developed societies control more wealth than the rest of the world combined.[7] The Credit Suisse Global Wealth Report 2016 concludes that the top 10% of the world population owns 89% of global wealth compared to 1% for the bottom half of all

[5] C Thomas 'Where Is the Third World Now?' (1999) 25 Review of International Studies 225. Thomas argues that globalization is replicating Third World problems in the developed states. She attributes the phenomenon to the legitimation and mainstreaming of the neoliberal policies. For a recent example that highlights how the IMF and European creditors are imposing structural adjustment policies on Greece, increasing poverty and inequality, and undermining the exercise of a range of human rights, see ME Salomon, 'Of Austerity, Human Rights and International Institutions' (2015) 21 European Law Journal 521.

[6] F Bourguignon, *The Globalization of Inequality* (Princeton UP 2015) 25–26; B Milanovic, *Global Inequality: A New Approach for the Age of Globalization* (Harvard U Press 2016). Branko Milanovic has analysed global inequalities in terms of three concepts: inequality between states, inequality between countries weighted by population, and income distribution between individuals (or households) in the world, termed 'true world inequality'. B Milanovic, 'Global Income Inequality' in D Ehrenpreis (ed), *The Challenge of Inequality* (UNDP International Poverty Centre 2007) 6. A summary of his 2006 findings on global inequality is that inequality between states is widening rapidly while inequality between countries weighted by population has shrunk since 1980; however, this is due to the fast growth in China and India. In his 2016 work, former World Bank economist Milanovic concludes similarly that global inequality (income inequality among the citizens of the world) has fallen dramatically among nations, but again due to rising incomes in China and India, while inequality has soared within nations and that there has been a surge of inequality in the West with inequality in both the United States and China 'well-entrenched and self-reproducing'. Milanovic, *Global Inequality*.

[7] 'Oxfam Says Wealth of Richest 1% Equal to Other 99%' (18 Jan 2016), http://www.bbc.co.uk/news/business-35339475

adults.[8] Substantial inequality in the United States is increasingly well understood.[9] The adoption of uniform policies and globalization through an international law fashioned to perpetuate the dominance of the ruling elite from imperial times plays a substantial part in accounting for the disparity in wealth among people within states as well as the widening gap between states and between peoples of different states (inequality globally can be considered to be decreasing only when rising incomes in China and India are factored in and in any case inequality in China for example is 'well-entrenched and self-reproducing').[10] When it comes to poverty, arguments that globalization has meant that the 'we have never had it so good' rely on aggregate findings and in particular the poverty reduction figures since the 1990s in a very small number of populous countries (ie: China and India).[11] Empire, imperial dominance, and the current normative order associated with it provide at least partial explanations for the immiserations that continue to exist today. Decolonization and its consequences, and the perpetuation of elite supremacy through international law based on a problematic normative framework, must be revealed and understood to be able to address the problems of justice that afflict the peoples of the world today. The context of empire, the instrumental law devised to support it, the continuation of those doctrines in the post-imperial age, and the globalization of those doctrines play a substantial part in the immiserations that continue in the world.[12] The ending of such inequities requires an understanding of the events that led to the dissolution of empire but not the dismantling of the global network of political and economic control. Power is still in the hands of the former imperial states and the multinational corporations located within them. Public power still operates in tandem with private power to preserve the imperial system. The role of private power within the system has been widely studied.[13] Its historical role in founding colonialism illustrates its power to maintain imperialism.

[8] Credit Suisse Global Wealth Report 2016, https://www.credit-suisse.com/us/en/about-us/research/research-institute/news-and-videos/articles/news-and-expertise/2016/11/en/the-global-wealth-report-2016.html

[9] JE Stiglitz, *The Great Divide* (Allen Lane 2015). Pope Francis has described the situation in the following terms:

> [S]ome people continue to defend trickle-down theories which assume that economic growth, encouraged by a free market, will inevitably succeed in bringing greater justice and inclusiveness in the world. This opinion, which has never been confirmed by the facts, expresses a crude and naive trust in the goodness of those wielding economic power and in the sacralised workings of the prevailing economic system. Meanwhile, the excluded are still waiting.

As reported in M Hiltzik, 'Today's Most Incisive Critic of Capitalism: Pope Francis' *Los Angeles Times* (26 Nov 2013).

[10] Milanovic (n 6, *Global Inequality*).

[11] For a fuller consideration of poverty, inequality under conditions of globalization, and the logic of harms and dislocations beyond poverty and inequality, see Chapter 1 ('Legal Rendering of Immiseration').

[12] See Anghie (n 1); Pahuja (n 4); Porras (n 4).

[13] D Rothkop, *Power Inc.: The Epic Rivalry between Government and Big Business* (Farrar 2013) arguing that the power of multinational corporations has outstripped those of states due to the adoption of neoliberal policies. Susan Sell has examined the power of global pharmaceutical companies in devising international intellectual protection. SK Sell, *Private Power, Public Law: The Globalization of Intellectual*

Decolonization and the end of empire came about through the assertion of justice-based principles relating to self-determination. These principles, first formulated to redraw the map of Europe to reflect the ethnic composition of the European states after the First World War, were not intended to be applied outside Europe, least of all to the colonies. There was as it was said a pigmentational factor in self-determination.[14] Self-determination as applied after the First World War was confined to European peoples. In the period after decolonization, the newly independent developing countries addressed the fact that though they were politically independent, the economic structure of the world did not permit them to emerge from centuries of colonial domination or to restructure their economies that continued to be dependent on the metropolitan powers. They responded by articulating a set of principles that came to be known as the New International Economic Order (NIEO). States without power articulated these principles. For the first time, the non-European world was articulating a set of normative prescriptions for the whole world. These new principles were not based on the old altruistic or paternalistic justifications for colonialism, which were in truth justifications for exploitation and dominance. Rather, they could only be addressed in terms of justice by people of the many states lacking in power. The NIEO principles must therefore be taken as the first time a prescription was made for justice in a global context not based on domination of one people over another. For this reason alone, there is value in taking NIEO seriously in the formulation of any prescription relating to justice on a global scale.

This chapter is a study of the themes of the NIEO as a prelude to the search for the prescriptions of justice. For the first time, a substantial portion—indeed the larger section of humanity—had put forward a set of principles as alternative prescriptions based on ideas of justice or more generally on moral imperatives. They are contained in General Assembly Resolutions of the United Nations that were hard fought for: the Declaration on Permanent Sovereignty over Natural Resources, the Declaration on the Establishment of a New International Economic Order and Programme of Action, and the Charter on the Economic Rights and Duties of States. Competing principles are contained in instruments of international law with some taking the form of customary international law: international law has generally not favoured NIEO aims.[15] The NIEO aims and principles are a uniquely

Property (CUP 2003); see also RB Hall and TJ Biersteker, *The Emergence of Private Authority in Global Governance* (CUP 2002); S Gill and C Cutler (eds), *New Constitutionalism and World Order* (CUP 2014).

[14] The term 'pigmentational' was widely used to denote that self-determination was intended to end European colonialism and not internal colonialism-domination of black people by other black people within newly independent states. So, in the situation of Biafra, self-determination was denied to the Ibo people. The fear was that self-determination would lead to the break-up of African and Asian states if applied out of the pigmentational context. Logically, there is no reason why it should not be so applied as these states were constructs of the European colonial powers.

[15] The treatment standards that the capital-exporting states have advanced are as sources of customary law. For a recent discussion, see P Dumberry, *The Formation and Identification of Rules of Customary International Law in International Investment Law* (CUP 2016). They were contested by the Latin American states at the time of their development and later by states of Africa and Asia. The NIEO marks a significant moment of that contestation. It must be seen as that and in that context, as a reflective still of the contestation between two sets of norms.

important part of legal and political history and the pursuit of justice in economic affairs. Their study is the focus of this chapter. The chapter begins, in section 1, with a statement of the notion of a justice that had been constructed in imperial law, and should be read in conjunction with other chapters in this text, particularly the prior two chapters. Unlike other chapters, this chapter focuses more extensively on empire. This chapter traces the history of empire from its origins through the articulation of justifications for it in terms of a global concept of moral rightness by a succession of jurists who are regarded as the major founders and makers of international law. Section 2 moves on to discuss the reasons for the origins of the NIEO. Section 3 describes the principles of the NIEO and the extent to which they came into conflict with dominant international law as accepted by the United States and European states. In describing tussles that arose, the outcomes of the tussles are also described. Section 4 deals with the rise of the neoliberal ideology that led to the displacement of the NIEO. Section 5 examines the issue of whether the NIEO and its ideals are passé or whether they continue to be or should be influential on international law. Section 6 examines the ideas of the NIEO alongside new efforts at promoting a fuller account of justice by which to justify and evaluate international law. It sets forth the argument, as do other chapters, that history matters. Contending visions—those of global neoliberalism, the NEIO, human rights, and justice—in important ways shape the conflicts that continue to exist in international law.

1. Prevailing Conceptions of Justice in an Age of Empire

Empire has in every period of history shaped a vision of right and justice for its needs. It was in the context of empire that international law truly emerged for empire required contact by the European hegemon with peoples in the other parts of the world. The rules of the relations between European states, famously supplied by the Treaty of Westphalia of 1648,[16] were but rules of a regional system. The justification of global hegemony through empire required conceptions of right and justice to be advanced to demonstrate that the dominance of distant peoples that attended empire could be justified in altruistic and cosmopolitan terms when in fact the effects of empire led to the destruction of pre-existing customs and cultural practices in these lands and the despoliation of the natural and other wealth of the peoples. It is in the rationalization of empire and hegemony that the origin of the principles of justice that were contained in international law are to be found. It may

[16] The treaty, which brought an end to the religious war between Catholic and Protestant states, consisted of two treaties, the Treaty of Munster and the Treaty of Innsbruck. The Holy Roman Empire, Spain, France, Holland, Sweden, and the princes of the Holy Roman Empire were the principal signatories. Its twin principles of equality between states and non-interference in the domestic affairs of states continue to be cornerstones of the present system of international law even though the first is a fiction and the second considerably eroded by the rise of the human rights movement. It would be difficult to find the origins of international law in the treaty when its principles were not universally applicable and confined to Europe.

be disconcerting to international lawyers that their discipline's origin and its early animating principles were associated with conceptions that sought to hide the callousness involved in the subservience of a vast part of humanity so that a small part of it could despoil their wealth. The condonation of the violence involved in the dominance, the destruction of the existing structures of governance of these alien peoples, the imposition on them of new rules of governance, and the despoliation of their wealth were covered through the formulation of ostensibly altruistic or paternalistic views of justice that continue to animate present day international law. Not least for understanding the immiseration in international law today, it is necessary to understand the nature of the early justifications provided for the imperial order that was imposed on the world.

Though imperial control was traced through Roman law notions of the *jus gentium* which was used to deal with Roman relationships with non-Roman citizens, the fuller considerations of the subject begin with the Spanish invasions of Latin America. The destruction of the Inca and Aztec civilizations, the transfer of their immense wealth to Spain, and the spreading of Christianity among the natives required consideration of the legitimacy of what was being done. Vitoria, a leading Jesuit theologian of the time, sought to rationalize the conquest in terms of what we would now call international law, demonstrating a trend of justification in moral terms of the colossal atrocities that were being committed in the name of the Spanish state.[17]

The works of Vitoria are essentially about the right of the Spanish ruler to conquer the peoples of Latin America. The issue faced was whether the newly discovered peoples should be regarded as the same as European states. If they were, their conquest would become difficult to justify. It would be incorrect to regard Vitoria as treating the Indian peoples of Latin America as having equal sovereignty with European states. Vitoria regarded them as living in different cultural systems.[18] While his philosophy argued a form of natural equality, it certainly did not offer what we understand as moral equality today, as that concept is examined in Chapter 2 on principles of justice for contemporary international law. For Vitoria, native peoples really could not be equal in that the ability of subjugation of one by the other required that they not be equal. Power would have to be denied for this result to be achieved. The early law failed to treat non-Christian people as equal. The Pope divided the New World between Portugal and Spain, demonstrating the role of religion in the exercise of power. Vitoria secularized this justification by removing from it the authority of the Church. It is based on a universal natural law that Vitoria asserted the right of the Spanish to travel to the land of the native Indians and sojourn there for purposes of trade. Trade becomes the central feature of the relationship which Vitoria argues is an equal relationship in that Spanish are exercising their 'right' to trade in their wares and in return

[17] See also the works of Suarez, Gentili, and Grotius. Pagden (n 1); Neff (n 3); R Tuck, *The Rights of War and Peace* (OUP 1999).

[18] Anghie (n 1) 15.

take gold from the natives.[19] The relationship was alleged to be reciprocal as there was no formal hindrance on the Indians to travel to Spain and trade there.

Chapter 4 ('International Trade') deals with these issues in the international trade context. That chapter relies on historian Sven Beckert's characterization of the early stages of modern capitalism as 'war capitalism' because of the use of organized violence by European sovereigns and the multinational enterprises of the day to force the creation and structure of a global order to benefit themselves at the expense of the subjugated.[20] The relevance of this argument to the bilateral investment treaty of today founded on reciprocity also seems clear. What was the law on what we would now call 'investment', then as now, protected reciprocity of flows of investment except that the developing state party (or in that time the tribes in far off lands) was not in any real position to 'invest' into a Western nation and to protect their interests against those of the 'investors' in their lands. Moreover, as explained in Chapter 4 on international trade, the Europeans used legal and moral arguments to claim that Indians committed acts of war when they sought to exclude Europeans from establishing trade relations. Chapter 4 offers complementary historical and current examples. The retaliation is through force. What results is a claim of defensive aggression against an offence committed by the Indians. Power is accommodated in this system of natural law which is a subterfuge for the conquest of the Indians because it is their fault for resisting trade. The victim was at fault and the use of force was a retaliation against the violation of the freedom of trade.[21]

Vitoria asserts a second justification that ostensibly accepts the equality of the Spanish and the Indians but which is a justification for Spanish conquest. He idealizes the Spanish culture as the one that accords with the universal norms of natural law. According to Vitoria, the Indian aberrations from such practices need to be corrected. The Spanish correction of such internal practices of the Indians permits Spanish intervention in Indian territories. It is the victim's non-conformity with the ideal elements of universal law which the Spanish comply with which justifies unlimited Spanish intervention in Latin America. Both arguments seemingly appeal to natural law, considered the embodiment of reason and hence the font of justice, along with some mixture of human sources in the form of a purported universal or at least European consensus, but are naked cloaks for the exercise of power by the Spaniards to conquer the New World. Though a secular theory is attempted, Christianity remains the repository of the universal values that must be

[19] See Chapter 4 ('International Trade') at 137–138.

[20] See also Chapter 5 ('Foreign Investment') at 147, 154–157.

[21] As Porras cogently argues:

> Vitoria (writing in the context of the Spanish conquest of the New World) and Grotius (writing in the context of the incipient Dutch challenge to Iberian control over the trade routes to the East Indies) both positioned the right of hospitality within a just war equation. Simply put, both men, albeit in slightly different ways, discovered a right, whose inevitable violation provided a cause for just war. Thus, while the right of hospitality was identified as a precondition for the possibility of trade and inter-national friendship, in practice it served to justify war.

IM Porras, 'European Origins, the Doctrine of Provident Function of Commerce, and International Law's Embrace of Economic Growth' (2013) 107 ASIL Proceedings 374, 377.

aspired to by the Indians. Refusal to accept Christianity becomes a cause for war as the rejection of the civilizing mission requires its imposition by force. There is no reciprocity in applying this second justification. Only Christians can fight a just war. Only Christians can conquer and subjugate other peoples as the imposition of universal values contained within Christianity is a civilizing mission. Since the condition of not possessing the requisite values is perpetual, the subjugation of the people could also be perpetual or at least until they can absorb the necessary values. The Indian is perennially at fault for it is the Indian who denies the right of commerce and does not measure up to universal values. Those people are therefore subject to unlimited intrusions. 'Against the unbeliever', Vitoria declared, 'it is useless ever to hope for a just peace on any terms. The only remedy is to destroy all of them who can bear arms against us, provided they have already been at fault.'[22] The proviso is meaningless for under the construct it is inevitable that the Indian is in a permanent condition of fault. Yet, based on inconsistent statements, there is a spectrum of opinions that has come to be possible about Vitoria that range from a cosmopolitan natural law protective of Indians to one that facilitates their conquest based on a denial of the right to trade and humanitarian interventions. Later events that took place are consistent with the interpretation that Vitoria enabled Spanish dominance of Latin America.

The formulation of the justifications for the conquest of Indians on the twin basis that refusal of commerce justifies force and that imposition of superior values requires force cloaks the power of the Spanish to impose their rule in Latin America through a natural law that appeals to reason and justice. The reasoning and justice, of course, are biased towards the assertion of the principles that favour power though the reasoning is couched in terms of justice that centralizes the fault of the victims of the subjugation. If not for their refusal of trade or the non-conformity to the higher values, the need for forcible subjugation would not have arisen. Justice performs the task of dressing up the use of power to secure its objectives of domination.

In later periods, the justifications advanced for colonialism could be understood as variants of Vitoria's arguments. The twin justifications of the need for trade and the requirement that the lesser breed in Africa and Asia should be brought up to the standard of civilization enjoyed by the Europeans feature in all the justifications that are provided to shore up the iniquitous system of imperial control of the peoples of Africa and Asia by the Europeans.

The stage had been set for the formulation of rules relating to acquisition of property from the people of the colonies, ostensibly on the ground of trade. What was plunder was dressed up as trade. It has also been suggested that a secondary system of private law had been developed to provide for private transactions relating to transfers of property involved in commerce the breach of which was sanctioned by war.[23]

[22] F de Vitoria, *De Indis* (1532).
[23] See Chapter 4 ('International Trade') for further discussion of these points.

A century later, Grotius's essays offer justifications which track the patterns drawn by Vitoria but with greater sophistication because the markers had already been developed in the earlier writings of Vitoria and other jurists who followed him. Some writers have seen Vitoria as the progenitor of the western strategy of domination of other peoples through the fashioning of international law in an instrumental manner that permitted colonialism and the advancement of the interests of the West at the cost of other peoples.[24] There is a cosmopolitan recognition of the rights of the native peoples but the result achieved accords with the realist vision that enables conquest and acquisition of the wealth of the Indians.[25] The discussions relating to trade are reminiscent of the later Ricardian ideas that a state must seek out other states which have plenty of a commodity and exchange that commodity for the commodity it has an abundance of. The Incas and the Aztecs had an abundance of gold, land, and slave labour. They were under a duty to part with them.

Grotius, often described as the father or founder of international law, wrote his early work *De Jure Praedae* as a servant of the Dutch East India Company, justifying its claim to the Portuguese vessel that sank off the coast of the Straits of Malacca based on the Dutch right to freedom of commerce in South East Asia and the freedom of the high seas, enabling the newly emerging Dutch naval power the ability to traverse the oceans of the world for trade and conquest. These ideas were supported by natural law, which once more became a servant of power, giving a veneer of respectability to the rules that ensured the spread of the power of the Dutch East India Company. The idea of right more overtly became the handmaiden of power. Though apologists for Grotius tend to pick out his emphasis on an international society and references to the equality of some Asian sovereigns, principally the Dutch ally, the Sultan of Johore, many read his work sceptically, as using arguments about *jus gentium* to formulate a theory that gives a semblance of justice to the Dutch pursuit of power. As in the case of the Salamancan writers, Grotius's work contains many references to the brotherhood of man and the equality of people but, in the context of the extensive cruelties that the Dutch practised to the knowledge of Grotius, what was justified as right action in Grotius's work was a surface phenomenon hiding the aggrandizement of Dutch power.

In the period of British hegemony with its heyday from the eighteenth century, the non-conferment of personality on the peoples of Africa and Asia was continued.

[24] Anghie (n 1); RA Williams, *The American Indian in Western Legal Thought. The Discourses of Conquest* (OUP 1990) 6–8, 106. Anghie has stated similar views (n 1) as has B Bowden, 'The Colonial Origins of International Law: European Expansion and the Classical Standard of Civilization' (2005) 7 Journal of the History of International Law 1, 3, 13, 23; B Bowden, 'Civilization and Savagery in the Crucible of War' (2007) 19 Global Change, Peace & Security 3; see also P Keal, ' "Just Backward Children:" International Law and the Conquest of Non-European Peoples' (1995) 49 Australian Journal of International Affairs 191, 192.

[25] There are kinder treatments of Vitoria. See G Cavallar, 'Vitoria, Grotius, Pufendorf, Wolff and Vattel: Accomplices of European Colonialism and Exploitation or True Cosmopolitans?' (2008) 10 Journal of the History of International Law 181. Vitoria made many inconsistent statements such that both detractors and admirers could construct their own visions as to what he wanted to establish. But events turned out in a manner that accorded with the negative interpretation of Vitoria.

The continuance of empire was facilitated through the law. The myth that was maintained was that these peoples still did not possess the standard of civilization that had been attained by the Europeans. The sacred trust was to ensure that through their domination they could be brought to such a standard and could be liberated. Until then, the Europeans could hold them in control. The thesis facilitated the plunder of the resources from the lands of the people and their wealth. Cheap sources of labour and markets for finished products were the result. Freedom of the high seas was maintained. The Opium War was based on the idea that denial of entry to even dangerous substances like opium was a violation of international law that entitled the forcible submission of China to opening its borders to trade and to the establishment of treaty ports in which European law could be administered based on extraterritoriality.

English international lawyers maintained an earlier system of international law that favoured such imperial control ostensibly on the basis of the satisfaction of the 'white man's burden' of carrying the natives of Asia and Africa on their able shoulders until they are sufficiently civilized to rule themselves.[26] English international lawyers eventually shifted the theory of maintaining suzerainty over native peoples of Asia and Africa from a natural law (or mixed natural law-positive law) justification to a more purely positivist justification of such control. The justification came to accord with reality and moved away from the fiction of the brotherhood of man to the reality that a subject people were firmly ruled by the imperial power. Equality could not have been the basis of the imperial order. Such order was based on the presence of superiors controlling inferiors. English international lawyers recognized this inequality and created an international order that explained this inequality. The Westphalian order had recognized the equality of states. That was clearly not applicable to the African and Asian peoples as they were ruled from above and were therefore inferior. The situation required the exclusion of these peoples from the order that had been created. They were nomadic people who did not possess lands,[27] though the lands provided them sustenance both in terms of food chains and in a spiritual sense. The exclusion was achieved based on a standard of civilization and the conferment of international personality only to those

[26] In Amitav Ghosh's historical trilogy on the Opium Wars (*Sea of Poppies*), Mr Burnham, a pompous and moralizing fictional character, states prior to a battle: 'On shoulders such as these will fall the task ofbestowing on the people of China the gift of liberty that the British Empire has already conferred on all those parts of the globe that it has conquered and subjugated.' A Ghosh, *Flood of Fire* (John Murray 2015).

[27] These lands were regarded as *terra nullius*. A near total genocide of the Tasmanian aboriginals took place in the early nineteenth century when Tasmania was ethnically cleansed with many aboriginals killed and the remaining taken to a camp on Flinders Island. The policy was rationalized on the ground of development of Tasmania, which was resisted by its native peoples. So, they had to be eliminated. The rationale was like the ones that the Spanish used in Latin America. See also the discussion of Dutch genocide on the Banda Islands in what is now present-day Indonesia in Chapter 4 ('International Trade') and the discussion of war capitalism more generally in that chapter. For a current application of international law's Eurocentric assumptions, see JT Gathii, 'Geographical Hegelianism in Territorial Disputes Involving Non-European Land Relations: An Analysis of the Case Concerning Kasikili/Sedudu Island (Botswana/Namibia)' (2002) 15 LJIL 581.

who had achieved such a standard. Recognition of personality came to play a role in determining whether a people had a right to form a state that could be regarded as an equal to that of the European states. European states formed a club so that membership of that club was open only to those who were recognized as capable of satisfying the membership requirements of the club. Colonial people were never capable of doing so. The sun was not to set on the empire. Freedom was never to be granted by the imperial states. It had to be wrested from them. What was wrested was an external and ostensible political freedom, the structural domination of the political and economic order hardly passed from the hands of the hegemonic powers.

Early modern approaches to international law, as reflected in the works of Vitoria, Grotius, and others, place the law in a moral frame. Though human sources of law can be found in the work of Grotius and others, this was in the main a pre-positivist period for international law when reason could be used to deduce legal principles. These jurists cloaked the ignominy of imperialism. As explained above and in Chapter 4, they justified it largely in terms of freedom of trade, the giving of finer standards of governance to the native peoples, lifting the standard of civilization and the spread of Christianity. The real reason for imperialism was the subjugation of the peoples, the transfer of the resources of their lands or the settlement of these lands and provision of markets for finished products of the imperial state. The justifications advance based on a prior conception of a global justice that underlay international law of the imperial age was a facade for maintaining an iniquitous system based on military control of subject peoples of other lands.

Independence and the ostensible end of imperialism came after the Second World War. Though the struggles for independence of the peoples of Africa and Asia resulted in their freedom from colonialism, the fact that the imperial powers were weakened by the Second World War and were too depleted to quell the freedom movements, some non-violent, others violent, had a part to play in the success of those freedom movements. Political freedom was achieved largely by resorting to the injustice involved in imperialism but the economic control of the erstwhile imperial powers and its corporations remained. The NIEO was a set of normative prescriptions, expressed through various UN instruments in the 1960s and 1970s, designed to bring about a change in this situation. The next section describes these prescriptions, the effects it had on the existing order, the nature of the opposition to their acceptance and the eventual backlash against the NIEO through the norms of neoliberalism that served to supplant the NIEO prescriptions.

As Chapter 2 explains, contemporary philosophical investigations centring around global poverty and inequality have often not taken the international law context into account, though this is not invariably so. This chapter explains that the NIEO was one of the principal events, and possibly the only substantial case in which states argued for a package of principles to change international law to reflect a concept of justice in the trade, investment, and financial global order. The importance of the NIEO is enhanced in that it, for the first time, articulated a body of principles for the implementation of prescriptions that would return control over resources and the economy to the newly independent people of the Third World. The NIEO assumes importance because of this historical role.[28]

2. The NIEO and Its Course

The former colonial states struggled for independence through the extension of the principle of self-determination. In its earlier form, political self-determination had been confined to Europe to redraw its boundaries so that ethnic groups were not caught up in different states and subjected to discrimination as minorities. It was a dangerous doctrine for Europe as the colonies of Europe could clamour, as they did, for the application of the same principle so that imperial power over distant people could be ended. The acceptance that it should be ended came about with the conclusion of the Second World War. With the independence of India in 1947, other colonies progressively achieved independence. Its culmination was the acceptance of colonialism as contrary to international law in the form of the General Assembly Resolution on the Granting of Independence to Colonial Peoples.[29] This Resolution affirmed that the process of independence is irresistible and irreversible. It declared self-determination to be a fundamental human right of all peoples. The principle, in certain contexts, is now considered a *jus cogens* norm of international law.

Quite early in its movement to establish the principle of self-determination, the newly independent states which had become independent recognized that political independence would be meaningless without economic independence. Their economies were still controlled by the multinational companies established during imperial times. The imperial powers, through the agency of their multinational corporations, had developed sectors of the economy on which the peoples of the colonies had become dependent. Their traditional economies had been altered so that the new sectors created by the colonial powers now provided the bases of the economies of these states. Tea in Sri Lanka and oil in Nigeria are examples. It was realized early that the situation should be changed if independence was to become meaningful. New doctrines of international law would have to be formulated to end this situation of economic dominance and privilege.

The context in which these principles had to be articulated is also important. As the new states were forming due to decolonization, the cold war between the United States and the USSR was intensifying. Both parties to the cold war were courting the newly independent states. The leaders of the newly independent states, however, saw their interests being best conserved through the formation of a non-aligned movement, in the context of which they could bargain for their special

[28] Moreover, there is hardly any reference to the NIEO in the philosophical literature. This, again, is a reason why the NIEO should be brought to the forefront of discussions relating to justice in matters of the global economy. It constitutes a corrective not only to the historical subterfuge of using moral concepts to camouflage gross inequities of imperialism but it enables definite prescriptions to be considered in ideal philosophical considerations of justice.

[29] General Assembly Resolution 1514 (XV), 14 Dec 1960.

interests. Their unity was forged during the Bandung Conference. This Conference was held in Bandung, Indonesia from 18 to 24 April 1955 and was attended by most of the first-generation leaders of the newly independent states of Africa and Asia. The principal leaders of these states, Jawaharlal Nehru of India, Julius Nyerere of Tanzania, Sukarno of Indonesia, Tunku Abdul Rahman of Malaysia, and Chou En Lai of China, played major roles in articulating the aims of the conference. It was a stepping stone in the setting up of a Group of Non-Aligned Nations which reflected neutrality in the cold war. The Group functions still.[30]

The Bandung Conference, in its declaration, articulated a ten-point formula to be followed in international relations. The ten-point programme, on analysis, is not materially different from the Westphalian prescriptions in that they assert sovereignty and equality as the organizing principles of the desired order, except that they want these prescriptions to be more meaningfully applied. International law was not to be displaced. It was to be changed from within.

The leaders of what was known then as the Third World were educated in the West. They did not seek to displace the models with which they were familiar. Most importantly, they did not want the state boundaries that they inherited to be redrawn, even though they had been artificially drawn by the colonial powers, without heed to the ethnic and religious composition of the states that they had created. Adherence to the *uti possidetis* principle remained paramount.[31] Internally, the inability to provide a balance in the constitutional systems of these artificially created states that put together disparate ethnic, tribal, and religious groups was to impair these states to the present and hinder their progress. But this internal issue had to be sorted out in every independent country through a long and painful process. For the moment, hard-won sovereignty, a central concept of European international law and its organization, had to be protected. Commitments to justice in any legitimate sense were lacking in imperial international law so economic justice became imperative as the hard-won political independence was meaningless unless there could be the right to control the economies of the states that had been established. Justice was the basis of the cry for changes to the international economic order that the instruments of this period sought to advance.

[30] There is a literature published in the 1970s and 1980s that deals with the NIEO, which provides insights of participants in the debates at the time. We can only cite a small sampling of this literature. See, eg, J Hart, *The New International Economic Order: Conflict and Cooperation in North–South Relations, 1974–77* (Palgrave 1983); PN Agarwala, *The New International Economic Order: An Overview* (Pergamon 1982); E Laszlo and J Kurtzman (eds), *Political and Institutional Issues of the New International Economic Order* (Pergamon 1981); T Nawaz, *New International Economic Order: A Bibliography* (Greenwood Press 1980); K Hossain (ed), *Legal Aspects of the New International Economic Order* (Francis Pinter 1980); K Hasenpflug and KP Sauvant (eds), *The New International Economic Order: Confrontation or Cooperation Between North and South?* (Wilton House 1977); A Akinsanya and A Davies, 'Third World Quest for a New International Economic Order' (1984) 33 ICLQ 208.

[31] The principle is said to have come down from the Berlin Conference at which states decided to respect colonial borders they had drawn. See M Craven, 'Between Law and History: The Berlin Conference of 1884–1885 and the Logic of Free Trade' (2015) 3 London Review of International Law 31.

This concern began early. The Bandung Declaration spoke of the need for economic cooperation among the newly independent states. The genesis of a larger economic programme based on economic justice can be seen in this early conference. The notion of economic self-determination in the form of a peoples' right to use their natural resources and to control their economic wealth appears early in the General Assembly Resolutions from 1952 onwards. They get fleshed out progressively. The culmination was the Resolution on Permanent Sovereignty over Natural Resources.[32] As with political self-determination, the right of control over natural resources are claimed as peoples' rights, which reflected a Third World influence on human rights framed as they were according to western precepts as the rights of individuals. Indeed, western states have long shown hostility towards the recognition of peoples' rights and in important ways continue to do so to date as the protracted negotiations on the United Nations Declaration on the Rights of Indigenous Peoples demonstrated.[33]

It is the affirmation of the rights of peoples that characterizes the call for a NIEO. Self-determination, which is the animating principle of freedom, was born out of peoples' movements and, in some cases, through violent struggles. The idea is strong in the language of the NIEO. Its principal documents contain references to claims made on behalf of peoples. The most evident instance of this appears in the Declaration on the Permanent Sovereignty Over Natural Resources where the state is seen as holding natural resources as a trustee for the people.[34] The freedom of the large numbers of the peoples of the world and the idea that resources of the lands they inhabit should be used for their betterment is an increasingly significant aspect of human rights in modern times. Indeed, the idea of peoples' rights sees the moral authority of human rights harnessed precisely to advance these collective ends.[35] It is a significant idea. It is in the subversion of that idea that the dominant international law has invested much effort. The characterization of international law in terms of the rights of peoples frees it from embedded public

[32] GA Resolution 1803 (XVII) 14 Dec 1962. And also common Art 1(2) of the International Covenant on Civil and Political Rights (1966) and the International Covenant on Economic, Social and Cultural Rights (1966).

[33] See P Alston, 'Making Space for New Human Rights: The Case of the Right to Development' (1988) 1 Harvard Human Rights Year Book 3; J Donnelly, 'In Search of the Unicorn: The Jurisprudence and Politics of the Right to Development' (1985) 15 California Western Journal of International Law 473; J Crawford (ed), *The Rights of Peoples* (OUP 1988); M Weller and J Hohmann (eds), *The UN Declaration on the Rights of Indigenous Peoples: A Commentary* (OUP 2017).

[34] The NIEO Declaration and the Declaration on Permanent Sovereignty Over Natural Resources are replete with references to peoples. The NIEO Resolution, after stating in its first article that 'the greatest and most significant achievement during the last decades has been the independence from colonial and alien domination of a large number of peoples and nations which has enabled them to become members of the community of free peoples' spoke of the need to provide a 'solid potential for improving the well-being of all peoples'. The Declaration of Permanent Sovereignty Over Natural Resources envisaged such sovereignty as involving the state's trusteeship of resources on behalf of people. The first article of the Declaration reads: 'The right of peoples and nations to permanent sovereignty over their natural wealth and resources must be exercised in the interest of their national development and of the well-being of the people of the State concerned.'

[35] ME Salomon, 'From NIEO to Now and the Unfinishable Story of Economic Justice' (2013) 62 ICLQ 31, 51.

power of hegemonic states and private power of multinational companies, which had hitherto dictated its terms. That characterization also freed it from the analytical and formalistic shrouds. These shrouds cloaked dominant international law so that the manipulation of international law by power became transparent and open to resistance by people.

The NIEO was the assertion of the recently freed peoples of the world for an economic structure that would be based on fairness, ensuring the right of a people to their natural resources, their right to control the economies of their states, the right of access to markets for their finished products and the right to be freed from existing unfair obligations on the payment of adequate compensation to foreign companies.[36] Its proclamations are replete with recourses to justice and the redressing of inequalities and injustices of the past. Its basis is proclaimed to be 'the united determination to work urgently for an Order based on equity, sovereign equality, interdependence, common interest and cooperation among all States ... which shall correct inequalities and redress existing injustices and eliminate the widening gap between developed and developing countries'.[37] Its principles noted that the gap between the developed and developing worlds was great and should be reduced.[38] NIEO principles called for the addressing of the 'disequilibrium' between states.[39] The NIEO was formed around a belief that the economic order could only work within a secure political order which it identified as 'sovereign equality of states, self-determination of all peoples, inadmissibility of acquisition of territories by force, territorial integrity and non-interference in the internal affairs of other states'.[40]

It is this package of rights that constituted the NIEO and are spelled out in the associated document, the Charter of Economic Rights and Duties of States.[41] The NIEO aimed to provide significant changes that would incorporate notions of justice through a redistributive agenda so that centuries of deprivation during the period of colonialism could be remedied. Ideas in it recognized the granting of aid by the rich nations as a matter of obligation so that poverty in the Third World might be eradicated. The new norms also required preferential access to manufactured goods from developing countries and demanded the payment of just prices for natural resources and manufactured goods exported from developing countries. The NIEO principles also addressed the role of multinational corporations in the international economy, 'requiring the regulation and supervision of the activities of transnational corporations' to ensure that they operate based on the sovereignty of the host states.[42] Consequently, the United Nations established a Centre on Transnational Corporations (UNCTC), which was later effectively disbanded.[43]

[36] The Resolution on the Establishment of a New International Economic Order was passed at the Sixth Special Session of the General Assembly on 1 May 1974. Declaration on the Establishment of a New International Economic Order, A/Res/5-6/3201, 1 May 1974.

[37] ibid Preamble. [38] ibid. [39] ibid Art 3. [40] ibid Art 4.

[41] General Assembly Resolution 3281 (XXIX), A/Res/29/3281, 12 Dec 1974.

[42] Declaration on the Establishment of a New International Economic Order, Art 4 (n 36).

[43] The UNCTC was abolished in 1993 and its work in modified form was merged into the UN Conference on Trade and Development (UNCTAD). L Emmerij and R Jolly, UN Intellectual History Project, Briefing Note No 17, July 2009.

The history of the Centre and the tussle to bring about the aim of regulation of transnational corporations itself encapsulates a story of the clash between power and justice in this area. The NIEO required transfer of technology to developing countries and the elimination of 'waste of natural resources, including food products'. As noted, an important feature of the NIEO was that it reaffirmed the principle of permanent sovereignty over natural resources—a doctrine that has been consistently asserted by developing countries containing a self-evident idea based on territorial sovereignty that there is complete sovereignty over natural resources existing within a state.[44] It asserts full control over such resources included the right to nationalize such resources (without mentioning any obligation on compensation). It refers to the doctrine as involving an 'inalienable right'.

The NIEO presented a comprehensive set of principles based on what the newly independent states of the Third World regarded as essential to justice and international solidarity. These were principles that motivated the international lawyers who were the prime movers of the NIEO.[45] The vision is to see a system that embraces the whole field of international economic activity set within a system of political order respecting values such as self-determination, international solidarity, non-interferences, and respect for sovereignty. Today, human rights and the obligation that states must secure them at home have strengthened the objectives of the NIEO claims with a contemporary articulation also often expressed through demand for 'policy space'.[46]

The Charter of Economic Rights and Duties of States fleshed out these principles in more concrete terms. Its first provision states the political context in which economic rights should operate, thus evincing a desire to adopt an unfragmented approach to the identification of a comprehensive international order. Chapter One of the Charter articulates the political order within which the economic rights should function. It states more than the twin principles of the Westphalian system in that it identifies also other general norms such as peaceful coexistence (taken out of the Bandung Declaration), equal rights and self-determination of peoples (taking a people-centred approach), remedying of past injustices brought about by force (requiring distributive justice in the light of colonial exploitation), respect for human rights (insisting that economic and political interstate relations are governed by human rights), exclusion of hegemonic power and influence, promotion of international justice, cooperation for development and access to

[44] ibid. Self-evident in so far as one accepts as a right of states that natural resources are to be possessed and exploited. See G Abi-Saab, 'Permanent Sovereignty over Natural Resources' in M Bedjaoui (ed), *International Law: Achievements and Prospects* (UNESCO/Martinus Nijhoff 1991) 600; Pahuja (n 4) 125.

[45] There are now studies on the thinking of these lawyers. On Mohammed Bedjaoui, see U Özsu, 'In the Interests of Mankind as a Whole: Mohammed Bedjaoui's New International Economic Order' (2015) Humanity 129. On Kamal Hossein, see M Sornarajah, 'The Return of the NIEO and the Retreat of Neoliberalism in International Law' in S Bhuiyan, P Sands, and N Schrijver (eds), *International Law and Developing Countries: Essays in Honour of Kamal Hossein* (Brill 2013) 32.

[46] See eg SA Sparks, 'The Quest for Policy Space in a New Generation of International Investment Agreements' (2010) 13 JIEL 1037.

the sea for landlocked countries. The principles identified include ideas developed by the non-aligned states in their successive meetings and show also other developments that had taken place within the international political order, such as the refusal of the developing states to accept consideration of investment issues within the WTO. The Charter—while itself a resolution—spelled out in terms of definite rights and duties the norms identified in the resolution establishing the NIEO.

The feature of the NIEO and the Charter, which had attracted most attention and scholarly comment, is their statement of the doctrine of permanent sovereignty over natural resources.[47] Neither instrument requires compensation in the event of the nationalization of resource projects owned by foreign investors. Western international law had mandated the payment of prompt, adequate, and effective compensation in the event of such nationalization. On this, the developed states had taken a stance and made it the beachhead through which they launched their principal attack on the NIEO principles. The doctrine was important from the point of view of multinational corporations as it was their investments in natural resources that was to be most affected by the doctrine. Private power and public power combined to thwart the acceptance of the doctrine and through it undermine the project towards the acceptance of the NIEO.

It is nonetheless the case that the NIEO should have continuing value for international law for it is the first time that an alternative construct in international law had been articulated since Westphalia. It represents the consciously stated aspirations of states representing over one-quarter of humankind, states which had been released from the thraldom imposed on them through power and justified through means of international law. The NIEO principles draw validity also from their renunciation of power, which sought to underlay the development of international law, with an appeal to a new understanding of justice.

The developed world attacked these principles directly from the outset, for their formulation both on the political and legal fronts. The fact that the principles were contained in General Assembly resolutions and that such resolutions are not binding instruments was the first line of attack. The NIEO resolutions were dismissed as *lex ferenda*, as mere aspirations without any binding content. The second line of attack was to argue that some of its principles, particularly the doctrine on permanent sovereignty over natural resources, competed with already established rules elevating foreign investment contracts almost to the status of treaties, especially if they contained stabilization clauses secured through a compliance mechanism involving external arbitration.[48] The backlash was virulent as powerful states had much to retain in the existing system.

[47] For a valuable contribution, see N Schrijver, *Sovereignty over Natural Resources: Balancing Rights and Duties* (CUP 1997).

[48] The theory of internationalization of foreign investment contracts maintains that the introduction of appropriate clauses in the contract removes the contract from the jurisdiction of the host state and subjects it to an international regime. M Sornarajah, *International Law on Foreign Investment* (4th edn, CUP 2017) 289–305.

But the NIEO principles had their own staying power. The most important of them, the permanent sovereignty over natural resources, passed into the constitutional provisions of the major resource-exporting nations of the developing world.[49] These constitutional formulations are in the precise terms of the international law doctrine vesting natural resources in the people of the state, not in the state itself. State entities were created through public law instruments vesting the power to deal with sectors of the economy that are vital to the public. At the micro level, contracts assume a change in that they become instruments of state control of the operation of the sector, with the state always having ultimate powers of control of the sector or ownership of the resources until transfer. As explained below, the change from the concession agreement in the oil sector with power in the hands of the foreign petroleum company to the production-sharing agreement with property in the hands of the state oil company until it is put on board a tanker is emblematic of this change. Despite these trends, powerful states continued to push the international law on foreign investment towards a different result, one which benefits investors at the expense of local interests.

The next section describes the onslaught against NIEO principles but perhaps assumptions as to the demise of NIEO are premature. It is valuable to consider the changes that were brought about by the NIEO. Nationalizations had been effected without the payment of compensation. The developing states did not have money in their coffers to pay full compensation as the developed states' rules required. They articulated the alternative form of appropriate compensation in the resolutions on the NIEO and permanent sovereignty over natural resources. That standard of compensation remains an important contestation to the standard of full compensation to this day, even if practice has forsaken it.[50] Some writers, prominent western writers included, thought that the doctrine of permanent sovereignty over natural resources constituted a *jus cogens* norm.[51]

So, is the demise of the NIEO exaggerated?[52] Advances set forth in NIEO principles are conserved to this day and perform certain necessary safeguards to the interests of the developing states, though implementation of NIEO principles is incomplete at best. The entrustment of sectors to state owned companies accelerated

[49] See M Sornarajah, *Resistance and Change in the International Law on Foreign Investment* (CUP 2015) 35–37 for a discussion of these points.

[50] See Chapter 5 ('Foreign Investment'). Treaties still continue to use the formula of appropriate compensation. Though awards are high in cases that foreign investors win, in more recent times the number of cases won by foreign investors has declined. So, the scope for high compensation has diminished. In some cases where the expropriation is found to be a regulatory taking, no compensation is awarded. The new balanced treaties increase the scope for such a result, though the introduction of a rule on proportionality somewhat detracts from this trend. When the proportionality rule is used, the resulting damages can never be high as the initial justification for the taking is accepted. The advancement of the arguments on regulatory expropriation are closely parallel to the ideas of sovereignty inherent in the NIEO.

[51] On the doctrine of permanent sovereignty over natural resources, see, eg, Schrijver (n 47); K Hossain and SR Chowdhury (eds), *Permanent Sovereignty Over Natural Recourses in International Law* (St Martin's Press 1995).

[52] On the 'demise' of the NIEO, see G Sacerdoti, 'New International Economic Order (NIEO)', *Max Planck Encyclopaedia of Public International Law* (June 2014).

during the period of the ascendency of the NIEO and despite neoliberal privatization drives, those state sectors have continued. There were new contracts that the NIEO principles were influential in developing, the best example of which is the production-sharing contract, which the Indonesian state oil company Pertamina initially developed, and which nicely captures the idea of permanent sovereignty over natural resources.[53] Variants of that form of contract are currently in use in the petroleum industry throughout the world. They ensure risk sharing, transfer of technology, and optimal delivery of production. The terms of such contracts ensure that property in the resource passed only at the time of loading the oil onto a vessel. That contract form was adopted universally in almost all developing countries. Laws screening entry of foreign investment so that they could be harnessed to the developmental goals of the host state became a feature of the period. They enable states to restrict jurisdiction of arbitration tribunals on the basis that the investor had not satisfied the requirements for entry to justify protection under the treaty. The performance requirements, which were again an implied feature of investment control under the NIEO, continue to be a feature of investment policy despite efforts of the developed states to dismantle them.[54] The control of multinational corporations through hard laws was an offshoot of the NIEO pursued by the UNCTC. It may have taken some time, but those aims are still being fought for—most recently the project has been revived by Ecuador within the UN Human Rights Council.[55] The drive towards such control continues. One could go on in this manner. The point to be made is that there is a parallel system inspired by NIEO and very much alive, even if less effective than one would hope, challenging the entrenched global tenets of neoliberalism. The NIEO has its detractors and depending on one's level of ambition it may or may not be viewed as transformative.[56] But its merits should not be overlooked. It was an expression of the aspirations of the large majority of the people of the world. Its principles were articulated not as rights of states but as rights of peoples. The NIEO was also a rejection of colonialism (even if not of imperialist international law); it represented an effort to assert the sovereign autonomy of the non-western world, and it was an attempt to redirect international economic governance towards distributional equity and fairness.

[53] K Hossain, *Law and Policy in Petroleum Development: Changing Relations Between Transnationals and States* (Nichols Publishing 1979). See also R Fabrikant, 'Production Sharing Contracts in the Indonesian Petroleum Industry' (1975) 16 Harvard International Law Journal 303; EF Smith, 'From Concessions to Service Contracts' (1992) 27 Tulsa Law Journal 493; TW Walde, 'Transnational Investment in the Natural Resources Industries' (1979) 11 Law and Policy in International Business 691.

[54] US Model Investment Treaties (2004 and 2012) uniformly forbid performance requirements on foreign investment. Yet, they continue to be used by developing states through provision of tax benefits or through other incentives for export of production or reinvestment of profits. See US Department of State, 2012 US Model Bilateral Investment Treaty, https://www.state.gov/documents/organization/188371.pdf; US Department of State, 2004 US Model Bilateral Investment Treaty, https://www.state.gov/documents/organization/117601.pdf

[55] See JG Ruggie, 'The Past as Prologue? A Moment of Truth for UN Business and Human Rights Treaty' IHBR Commentary, July 2014, 8 (Kennedy School of Government, Harvard University).

[56] For a set of excellent critical essays written at the time, see H Addo (ed), *Transforming the World Economy: Nine Critical Essays on the New International Economic Order* (United Nations University 1984).

NIEO concepts have also been absorbed into other fields, principally human rights. While the NIEO was being formulated, human rights were complementing its concern with individual rights as well as collective rights. Among the most important of these rights at the time was the right to development which encapsulated the central animating features of the NIEO.[57] The influence of the NIEO on human rights also helped foreground the links between human rights and development:[58] a holistic, human-centred view of development whereby economic aspects of development cannot be disassociated from social, political, environmental, and cultural aspects.[59] Finally, with its focus on the duty of international cooperation the aspirations of the NIEO, like the objectives of the Declaration on the Right to Development, underpin the current focus of international human rights law in its application to globalization.[60] Yet while collective rights have survived and the right to development may well make a distinctive normative contribution to international human rights law, it is also yet to fulfil its programme of international economic justice. What it can be said to reflect is that the NIEO in a different guise has continued in international law.

3. The Backlash against the NIEO

The decision to thwart the proposals of the newly independent states had been made no sooner than they came to be known. As explained above, western states began to point out that the NIEO prescriptions were couched in non-binding resolutions of the General Assembly. Moreover, the general realist, power-based view was that 'what happens in the South is of no importance'.[61] At the Rambouillet meeting of the G7 states in 1975, the leaders targeted the Third World project regarding the NIEO as one of the three problems to be attacked, the other two being the socialist agenda and the communist agenda.[62] The notable success of the oil cartel aroused

[57] General Assembly Resolution 41/128, annex, UN GAOR, 41st session, Supp No 53, at 186 UN Doc A/41/53 (1986). Under the terms of the Declaration on the Right to Development, it is each person, and not the state per se, that is the central subject of development, and as such the person should be the active participant and beneficiary of the right to development. While the focus shifted to the person, this human right in international law represents a set of claims born of the NIEO.

[58] Salomon (n 35) 51.

[59] See DD Bradlow, 'Development Decision-Making and the Content of International Development Law' (2004) 27 Boston College International and Comparative Law Review 205, 207.

[60] ME Salomon, *Global Responsibility for Human Rights: World Poverty and the Development of International Law* (OUP 2007); *Maastricht Principles on Extraterritorial Obligations of States in the Area of Economic, Social and Cultural Rights* 2011, www.maastrichtuniversity.nl/web/Institutes/MaastrichtCentreForHumanRights/MaastrichtETOPrinciples.htm; O De Schutter, A Eide, A Khalfan, M Orellana, ME Salomon, and I Seiderman, 'Commentary to the Maastricht Principles on Extraterritorial Obligations of States in the area of Economic, Social and Cultural Rights' (2012) 34 HRQ 1084.

[61] Statement attributed to Henry Kissinger made in 1969. S Hersch, *The Price of Power: Kissinger in the White House* (Summit Books 1983) 263; V Prashad, *The Poorer Nations: A Possible History of the Global South* (Verso 2014) 4.

[62] Memorandum of Conversation Rambouillet, France, 16 Nov 1975, 10:45 am, Trade and Monetary Issues 16 Nov 1975:

anxiety in the developed states and its association with the NIEO was not lost.[63] The developed states were bent on ensuring that the NIEO principles did not take hold; their economic interests as capital-exporting states depended on it.

A succession of events ensured that the NIEO went into eclipse. A sovereign debt crisis occurred in the 1980s because of defaults on petrodollar loans. With the rise to power of neoliberal governments in the United States (Reagan), the United Kingdom (Thatcher), and Germany (Kohl), foreign aid decreased. The fall of the Soviet Union ended communism and new states in Eastern Europe announced that they would espouse neoliberal policies to show their movement away from communism. The developing states had primarily multinational corporations as a source for foreign capital. In that environment, they could not hold onto a programme which furthered the NIEO principles. Power-based norms then became ascendant. As is evident in these changes, norms espoused in one period when international circumstances are favourable to them—such as in the decolonization period, lose fervour under the weight of the law of realpolitik and can be replaced by pre-existing norms in different guises. Norms relating to property protection and contractual sanctity came back with vigour dressed up in neoliberal garbs as a package of legal institutions essential for economic development. This does not mean that the earlier norms are destroyed. They can go into abeyance, lurk around in interstitial spaces, and come into prominence once more when circumstances are propitious for their return. They may do so in different guises but the cyclical pattern can eventuate, indicating that, as in human life, in the life of the international community as well, there is a struggle between power and justice and between realism and the struggle for moral foundations. The events leading to the eclipse of the justice-based norms of the NIEO need first to be described. The ideological underpinnings of the change to power-based norms are then discussed. Finally, the types of norms associated with the change are detailed showing that they reflect the preferences of actors with private power, the multinational corporations and the actors with public power, the developed states of the world.

> Although the confrontation between the developed and developing nations was never of our making, we in the industrialized world have played a full part in replacing it by the present armistice. At the Seventh Special Session, the UK's proposals at Kingston, the united approach by the EC and the wide-ranging US proposals led to the final resolution of the session. For the resolution adopted unanimously by the UN General Assembly on September 16, at the close of the Seventh Special Session, see Yearbook of the United Nations, 1975, pp. 348–354. This would have been unthinkable a year earlier. We must demonstrate in the future the same unity that we then achieved or the Group of 77 will divide us. (Prime Minister Wilson of the UK).

KB Rasmussen, *Foreign Economic Policy 1973–1976* (US GPO 2009) 424, https://history.state.gov/historicaldocuments/frus1969-76v31/d123

[63] The oil-producing states created OPEC in 1960. It is based on the notion of sovereign control of oil. Its relationship to the notion of permanent sovereignty over natural resources is clear. The link is drawn in K Hossein (ed), *Legal Aspects of the New International Economic Order* (Francis Pinter 1980). US courts recognized the antitrust immunity of the cartel on the basis that the cartel was the act of sovereign states, thereby conceding such sovereignty. *International Association of Machinists v OPEC*, 477 F Supp 553 (CD Cal 1979).

4. Events Leading to the Eclipse of the NIEO

The NIEO was held together by a group of first-generation leaders of the newly independent states of Africa and Asia, who had themselves participated in the freedom struggles of their nations or changed policy radically to free their nations from the stranglehold of foreign powers. When the Bandung Conference took place, these leaders came together and initiated a common plan of action for the non-aligned nations and thereafter the Group of 77. By the 1970s, this group of first-generation leaders were no longer on the scene and the essential personal cohesion needed to sustain fervour for a common programme began to lapse with new leaders who did not share in the same vision of common progress.

A chain of events occurred leading to the loosening of the cohesion of states supporting the NIEO. These events may briefly be repeated. The petrodollar crisis of the 1980s was one such event. The crisis came about because of the accumulation of huge amounts of capital in the petroleum-producing states of the Middle East and the establishment of the OPEC cartel in 1972. The increase in the price of oil meant huge profits for these states. They had no internal need or means for the investment of these monies which they began to keep in banks in the United States and Europe. The banks lent the money to developing states at higher interest rates because these countries were considered to be less creditworthy than borrowers in developed states. The developing states were unable to service the loans leading to a sovereign lending crisis in the 1980s and the rise of so-called Brady bonds, which pushed sovereign debt into the bond market. As a result of difficulties associated with sovereign debt, developing states looked toward foreign direct investment. The principal way to ensure inflows of capital into developing states was through the courting of multinational corporations in the hope that they would invest in the developing countries and this model had been sold to those countries by western states. There was a scramble among the developing countries to attract multinational corporations and their investment. In that context, many of the brave propositions of the NIEO had to be given up. There were tax incentives, guarantees against expropriation and other incentives given to multinational corporations in the hope that they would enter the different developing countries which had begun competing for such investments under rules fashioned by western states that would advantage their companies looking to invest abroad. The NIEO became an impediment under the circumstances. Though domestic laws based on the NIEO were never changed, the policies on issues of foreign investment and capital access were changed. There was a compulsion to go soft on the NIEO and to go hard on global capitalism.

The key event that changed the cycle against the NIEO was the fall of the Soviet Union in 1989. Then, the competing philosophy of communism, became displaced and understood as a failure. The triumphant announcement was made that the free market and democracy were the twin pillars for the organization of the state and the international community. The espousal of the free market by the newly released states of the former Soviet Union meant that there was a new rush in courting foreign investment, the competition for which increased, thereby creating a legal climate conducive to the creation of new rules favourable to investment both in the domestic and international arenas. The United States emerged as the sole hegemonic power in the world. There was a drive towards globalization, facilitated by a feature in world history: a push towards globalization whenever a new hegemon supported by superior technology and armed power emerges.

In the context of these changing circumstances, the twin philosophy of market capitalism and democracy advocated by the United States took hold. Market capitalism became the dominant philosophy that came to be advanced by the two international financial institutions, the World Bank and the International Monetary Fund, leading to the view that a Washington Consensus[64] had emerged during the period to drive liberal ideas as the central themes to organize the international economy. International law was instrumental in driving this ideology onto the international scene in that institutions and laws were fashioned based on it. International law did not accommodate democratic principles or principles of justice but it did accommodate market principles, and this is how the developed states wanted it to be. The process marked another occasion in history of sanctifying domination and coercion under the guise of legal authority.[65]

Significant among these institutions was the World Trade Organization (WTO).[66] It went much further than any other trade agreement. It sought not only to liberalize trade in goods but contained a strict set of intellectual property rules designed to protect intellectual property-exporting states, and attacked features of the regulatory state that were seen to impede international trade.[67] Because the most effective dispute settlement system so far devised in international law is an integral part of the WTO system, the rules fashioned by the WTO had an effective compliance system. The initial prescriptions of the WTO system were intended to give effect to neoliberal prescriptions in international trade.

In international investment, similar trends took place.[68] The amount of bilateral investment treaties that stood at around 800 had a sudden spurt during the last decade of the twentieth century so that when that decade ended there were nearly 3,000 treaties. Unlike previously, the treaties contained effective standards of investment protection. Since the award in *AAPL v Sri Lanka*,[69] where it was held that a dispute settlement provision could create compulsory jurisdiction in the nominated arbitral tribunal, there came about an effective system for the

[64] This was taken as including a package of norms and an economic philosophy of market supremacy. The legal prescriptions included liberalization of flows of assets and investment, free trade, protection of contracts and property, and compliance with standards of treatment of investment and trade through dispute settlement processes. The term apparently was coined by John Williamson. For a discussion of the origin of the phrase, see J Williamson 'A Short History of the Washington Consensus 1' in N Serra and JE Stiglitz (eds), *The Washington Consensus Reconsidered* (OUP 2008) 14.

[65] See Chapter 4 ('International Trade').

[66] For a discussion of these issues generally, see Sornarajah (n 49) 10–16.

[67] Chapter 4 ('International Trade') covers these and other issues in more detail.

[68] ibid. [69] (1990) 4 ICSID Rpts 245.

maintenance of these treaty standards. The decade and the following years witnessed a dramatic rise in the number of arbitrations. These arbitral awards, largely made by a handful of arbitrators who were inclined towards neoliberal views, ensured that the treaties were expansively interpreted to build up effective robust standards of investor protection. The World Bank and the International Monetary Fund—with power wielded there by the United States and other western states—were willing allies and advanced the cause of liberalization, privatization, and market-friendly policies in borrowing countries with little consideration for the range of negative impacts, including on the exercise of socio-economic rights.

As these developments took place, justice-based ideas were shunted to the back and power-based notions favoured by the multinational corporations and the developed states took hold. Commentators have pointed out that the private power of large multinational corporations working in tandem with the public power of the dominant state drove developments in the law giving protection to the corporations.[70] The large multinational pharmaceutical companies were intent on the global protection of patents. Equally, the large multinational publishing companies promoted protection of copyright, with proprietary rights excluding multitudes from access to educational materials, by way of merely two examples. The interests, and indeed human rights, of people affected by such protection did not come into the picture in the formulation of the norms of protection of such intellectual property rights. International human rights standard-setting and implementation were flourishing, but largely on a discrete track spearheaded internationally through the UN. Indeed, then as now, the strategy of developed countries was precisely to keep human rights dealt with in the UN with international economic law and policy in institutions where they hold the balance of power. There was the triumph of power over justice in an absolute sense at least during the period of the initial formulation of the norms. The developing countries have tried to secure NIEO-type objectives through mechanisms in the WTO framework such as special and differential treatment and the Doha Development Round but these efforts were either not sufficient or were outright failures.[71] Reactions against these trends did take place later—including through attempts to have human rights influence international economic institutions—but they took time to arise and in any case have had varying degrees of effectiveness. Immediately after the WTO was set up, the triumph of neoliberalism in driving the law towards the formulation of international law based on its tenets was complete.

In international investment, similar trends were taking place. Neoliberal prescriptions were based on the idea that the flows of foreign investment were for the betterment of economic development in poorer states. Not only does immediate capital transfer and formation take place because of the inflow, it would, it was said, lead to greater production in a new market, transfer of technology to local

[70] AC Cutler, *Private Power and Global Authority: Transnational Merchant Law in the Global Political Economy* (CUP 2003); Sell (n 13).

[71] See JP Trachtman, 'Developing Countries, the Doha Round, Preferences, and the Right to Regulate' in C Thomas and JP Trachtman (eds), *Developing Countries in the WTO Legal System* (OUP 2009).

employees, creation of jobs, upgrading of infrastructure, and the earning of foreign exchange through exports. This was a part of the neoliberal argument which helped to fuel the increase in the number of bilateral investment treaties and lay the foundation for the expansive interpretation of their standards by arbitral tribunals.

It is necessary here briefly to set down the course of events in the international law on foreign investment, an important area on which NIEO principles such as the doctrine of permanent sovereignty over natural resources were enunciated. Throughout the 'naughty nineties' and the first few years of the twenty-first century, efforts were made to shore up and build on the law of investment protection on the ground that such law was essential for the promotion of flows of foreign investment.[72] The law on expropriation expanded so that any measure by a government leading to the depreciation in the value of property could be regarded as an expropriation, which carried an obligation of full compensation.[73] The amorphous and hitherto unused phrase 'fair and equitable treatment' developed new meanings never contemplated by the states' parties to the treaties. The principal meaning that was given was that the violation of the legitimate expectations of the foreign investor at the time of the investment will result in an obligation to pay compensation. The case law on this phrase expanded justifying the writing of several books and theses. 'Highly qualified publicists' found a profitable occupation in this expansionary law simply because of aspirations of acting as arbitrators or experts in such litigation.[74] They joined the bandwagon of greed rather than act as an 'invisible college of international lawyers',[75] standing as a bulwark in favour of justice.

The epitome of these developments is exemplified in terms of the Argentine arbitrations that began in the early years of the new century.[76] Argentina, the home of the Calvo doctrine which required investment disputes to be settled by domestic tribunals applying domestic law, the long-preferred position of developing countries, joined the neoliberal push and signed many investment treaties guaranteeing investment arbitration at the instance of the foreign investor. It signed an investment treaty with the United States in 1992 and investment treaties with many European states. The Argentine government agreed these treaties with the intention of attracting investments. The Argentine government also promised to keep the Argentine peso pegged to the US dollar and that commodity prices

[72] These expansionary developments are dealt with in Sornarajah (n 49).

[73] In *Ethyl v Canada* (1999) 38 ILM 708, it was argued that a ministerial statement that the manufacture of a suspected carcinogenic substance could be banned was an expropriation. The Canadian government settled the case by paying compensation.

[74] 'Highly qualified publicists' became abject servants of neoliberalism as there were personal profits in it for them. Many became arbitrators who reinforced the neoliberal prescriptions to the detriment of justice-based notions.

[75] O Schachter, 'The Invisible College of International Lawyers' (1977) 72 Northwestern Law Review 217. Schachter wrote on the permanent sovereignty over natural resources with approval and had asserted the basis of the doctrine in terms of justice. Schachter was against the fragmentation of international law.

[76] For further discussions of the Argentinian arbitrations, see Sornarajah (n 49) 13, 196, 354, 388, 399–415.

in Argentina would be pegged to the US consumer price index. Consistent with neoliberal programmes and on the advice of the IMF, Argentina also embarked on a privatization programme. The IMF had advised Argentina throughout the reform measures and up to the time of the crisis. Large numbers of US investors bought the divested shares of public utilities in Argentina. There was an initial spurt of economic development but a crisis set in when the economy went into depression in 1998. An economic crisis set in with depositors moving money out of Argentinian banks. Amidst widespread food riots brought about by the crisis and frequent changes in government, the new government in 2002 devalued the Argentinian currency as a measure to curb the crisis and removed the promise to peg the prices of commodities in Argentina to the US price index. Both measures affected foreign investors. They challenged the measures before arbitration tribunals as violating treaty standards and as expropriation. There were fifty-two arbitrations brought against Argentina by various foreign investors based on the investment treaties.

The early arbitrations went against Argentina despite the creative defences that Argentina put up. The first award did agree that there could not be any expropriations on the facts as there had been no dispossession of foreign investors. But it held, relying on the fair and equitable treatment provision, for the first time in any investment arbitration, that the failure to abide by the promise to keep the parity between the US dollar and the Argentine peso and to maintain the price of commodities in accordance with the US price index were violations of the legitimate expectations that arose from promises given to the investors at the time of entry. The defence of necessity was denied on the ground that necessity required there to be an absence of an alternative course of action whereas here there was the alternative of borrowing from the IMF to ensure that promises were kept. The view taken in this award was approved in the others which followed it. Argentina, however, vigorously resisted the law in it and contrary awards began to emerge.

For one thing, the law on necessity as stated in the first award was regarded as in error, the later awards indicating that the presence of an alternative by itself will not lead to the denial of the defence. In some later awards, the plea of necessity was upheld for the period of the crisis. Besides, the application of the notion of legitimate expectation itself came to be doubted, some tribunals raising queries as to the legitimacy of any expectations in a foreign investor who invests in a risky country like Argentina with its history of political and economic failures.

The decisions of the tribunals considering the interpretation of the fair and equitable standard became so diverse that no certainty resulted as to the application of the standard. The schisms that opened in the views of tribunals as to other aspects of international investment law around 2004–13 led to the questioning of the legitimacy of the system. There was a build-up of resentment against the system not least due to large sums being awarded based on theories of interpretation of the fair and equitable treatment standard that states had never contemplated. The allegation became commonplace that a handful of arbitrators, who shared a common interest in bolstering the system of investment arbitration, continuously expanded the bases of such arbitration through increasing the jurisdiction of tribunals and the applicable substantive law.[77] At the same time, critical academic studies and NGO activism on human rights and investment were highlighting the injustices of the investment system.[78] Add to the mix that states were still continuing to push forward with a system of investor-state arbitration.[79] Challenges led to the start of rethinking of the system of investment arbitration.

From 2013, we can see a trend towards states adopting different measures to deal with the deleterious situation.[80] Some states withdrew their consent to arbitral institutions. Others announced that they would not sign any more bilateral investment treaties. Australia adopted for a time the position that it would not sign investment treaties with investor-state arbitration. Many developed states took to draft treaties, which provided for a wide array of defences to liability for breach of the treaty standards. Expropriation was not considered compensable under the so-called balanced treaties if it had a regulatory purpose. These changes were adopted both by developing countries and by developed countries. Developed countries themselves became cautious as they were becoming targets of investment arbitrations. Since they were recipients of foreign investments, the boot was now on the other foot. Hence, in anticipation of future problems created through arbitration, they redesigned their treaties so that there would be sufficient escape routes in the event of claims being brought against them. There was also questioning of whether the investment treaties did in fact promote flows of foreign investment. The claim that they did came to be dented with an increase in studies which came to an opposite conclusion.

The extent of the flux indicates the nature of the changes that take place in an area of international law in response to changing circumstances. It demonstrates the extent of change when the norms of power and the norms of justice clash. The clash is represented in the schism in the awards of different arbitrators, the academic writings on the subject, the attitudes of states and the many NGOs that have entered the fray. The entry of these NGOs lent considerable countervailing strength to the combination of multinational corporations and the developed states which supported the norms of power. The jury is out on whether these changes reflect challenges to the deep structures of neoliberalism or merely a qualified neoliberalism

[77] S Puig, 'Social Capital in the Arbitration Market' (2014) 25 EJIL 387 (listing the few arbitrators commanding investment arbitration).

[78] Book-length studies began to emerge of the failure to accommodate human rights and environmental rights in foreign investment arbitration. See eg J Vinuales, *Foreign Investment and the Environment in International Law* (CUP 2012).

[79] See further Chapter 5 ('Foreign Investment').

[80] Sornarajah (n 49) 382–407. Changes have been effected at least at the fringes in that new treaties seek a balance between the rights of foreign investors and the right of a state to regulate. These new treaties are dealt with in Sornarajah (n 49). They provide defences to states where measures are regulatory and in the public interest. Some states have relinquished the system altogether (eg South Africa). Others have been ambivalent towards investor-state dispute settlement (eg Australia). The European Union has advocated a permanent court for investment disputes. There is evident discontent with the existing system. Developed states like Germany, Spain, the United Kingdom, United States, and Canada have been respondents in investment arbitration. They have also responded negatively to the system by participating in changes.

and, moreover, after imparting great harms on many and great gains on the few. There may be successes, but they require that one is an optimist or pragmatist to feel able to celebrate these 'tinkerings'.[81]

During the period of the unqualified triumph of neoliberalism, there were significant techniques that were employed. The law was fragmented with the development of international investment law in isolation so that the cardinal objective of it could be the promotion of the norms that gave absolute protection to foreign investment in isolation from competing norms that could be drawn from other areas of international law like human rights and the protection of the environment. Power favoured such fragmentation so that its resources could be concentrated in an undiluted fashion on developing isolated sectors of international law in accordance with desired goals by concentrating its immense resources in knowledge and research in those insulated areas. Perhaps this insulation can be broken by insistence of consideration of other competing norms from related areas that may have relevance to the whole of the international community. These trends were at work when the global economic crisis of 2008 occurred. The chances are, however, that neoliberalism's tenacity is such that it was only dimmed by this crisis.

5. Concluding Remarks

As argued throughout this text, the global economic order remains tightly designed around neoliberal norms. Neoliberalism should have suffered a setback with the global economic crisis in 2008 but it did not.[82] Some slight signs of the restoration of the state function may be viewed as a decline of neoliberalism but not convincingly so. It would be wildly optimistic to announce the total displacement of neoliberalism; it just is not the case. Vestiges of it, or rather large chunks of the law that had been instituted in this period would remain to compete with any new norms that could arise. In that sense, the tenacity of neoliberal norms would ensure its survival with the help of the bases of power and its displacement will not take place.

NIEO principles can be of value to the prescriptions of economists writing on alternatives to neoliberalism. Some economists have frequently argued against the rigid uniformity of neoliberalism as the answer to the problems in the global economy. They have long advocated, for example, for the existence of a multiplicity of models that suit the particular circumstances of each country rather than the one-size-fits-all prescriptions of the Washington Consensus model—or some variation thereof—based on neoliberalism.[83] The rejection of global governance rules and

[81] See C Miéville, 'The Commodity-Form Theory of International Law' in S Marks (ed), *International Law on the Left: Re-examining Marxist Legacies* (CUP 2008) 92, 130.

[82] See, eg, C Crouch, *The Strange Non-death of Neoliberalism* (Polity 2011); RH Wade, 'Capitalism and Democracy at Cross-Purposes' (2013) 28 New Zealand Sociology 208.

[83] D Rodrik, *The Globalization Paradox* (OUP 2012); D Rodrik, 'The Globalization Dilemma and the Way Out' (2012) 47 Indian Journal of Industrial Economics 393; JE Stiglitz (n 9).

the stressing of each state's right based on sovereignty to choose its own economic policies is being reasserted as a panacea to the problems of neoliberal globalization that advocated standards of governance through treaties. And this right of economic self-determination is now a demand of the 'South in North' as European countries have themselves become borrowers with economic policy conditionality imposed on them by international creditors.

The set of propositions, which some have been put up as a counter to the Washington Consensus and have come to be known as the Beijing Consensus asserts norms in opposition to the norms of the Washington Consensus.[84] Though its contours are assessed differently by commentators since the idea is not contained in any official document, the principal aim of the Beijing Consensus is to offer a different development model to that conventionally endorsed by the West. The principal feature of the Beijing Consensus is to stress the economic sovereignty of every state and its right to experiment with different solutions as to its political and economic system. The assertion of domestic sovereignty, the control of domestic resources, the notion of sovereignty adopting heterogeneous solutions rather than uniform ones, and the existence of a diversity of systems resonates with the model that was inherent in the NIEO, even if China's assertion of a right to choose its own political and economic systems seems especially convenient in a country without democracy. The search for new norms of justice globally may not necessarily involve the revival of NIEO principles but may well draw inspiration from them.

There are other areas which have aroused concern with power in the immediate postcolonial era which were shunted to the back of the queue during the new liberal era. There is the concern with the private power of multinational corporations, which became apparent when studies of the role of multinational corporations became the focus of attention of the United Nations Conference on Trade and Development (UNCTAD) and other institutions concerned with economic development. Although the rights of multinational corporations came to be recognized, there were few efforts to recognize the obligations of these corporations towards the peoples of the host states. The harm that they caused to such people remains largely unaddressed. Despite several efforts, the United Nations has only ever come out with soft law prescriptions on curtailing the misconduct of these corporations. Here, too, the NIEO principles required stricter rules, although without much success. The United Nations Centre on Transnational Corporations, which had been established to complement the activities of the NIEO, sought a binding code relating to the behaviour of multinational corporations, though the results have been mixed at best.[85] The strong preferences of western states (and their multinational

[84] Much has been written on the Beijing Consensus. See S Halper, *The Beijing Consensus: Legitimising Authoritarianism in Our Time* (repr edn, Basic 2012).

[85] K Hamdani and L Ruffing, *United Nations Centre on Transnational Corporations: Corporate Conduct and the Public Interest* (Routledge 2015); T Sagafi-Nejad, *The United Nations and Transnational Corporations: From Code of Conduct to Global Compact* (Indiana UP 2008). KP Sauvant, 'Negotiations of the United Nations Code of Conduct on Transnational Corporations: Experiences and Lessons Learned' (2015) 16 Journal of World Investment and Trade 11.

corporations) for only non-binding codes, found expression more recently in the effort by the United Nations Special Representative on Business and Human Rights who again advocated soft prescriptions, despite acknowledging the need for control.[86] On 26 June 2014, at the behest of developing states, the UN Human Rights Council voted to begin fresh negotiations on the elaboration of an internationally legally binding instrument on transnational corporations and other business enterprises with respect to human rights.[87] Ecuador, with its experience of frequent violations of indigenous rights by oil corporations, is playing a leading role in arguing for the bringing about of such an instrument.[88] Another facet of this direction of travel is that investment treaties now include provisions on the liability of multinational corporations operating in the host state for any damages they cause. Here, again, the system is undergoing a change towards notions that were articulated in the NIEO. These are a consequence of the disquiet with neoliberal policies. They may be overdue, and they may not be enough, but there is change.

A problem with the assertion of sovereignty that followed decolonization has been the perpetuation of the model of sovereign states based on European international law. Within such sovereign states, political elites form alliances with foreign multinational corporations. Such alliances could keep themselves in power through manipulations of the democratic process and ensure that the profits of the business associations are siphoned off to the domestic elite and to foreign investors. The breaking up of such models has become important for the progress of developing countries but there are a range of challenges. There have been moves towards making corruption unlawful which may prevent the worst excesses associated with such alliances.[89]

The origins of international law were shrouded in empire and injustice against distant people. Much of that law began in justification of the imperial rule of a European minority over the large majority of the people of Africa, Asia, and Latin America. Despite the ending of official or explicit versions of imperialism through the movement towards decolonization, the imperial system fought for dominance. The system that the developed states wanted both in the political and economic spheres was facilitated when the cold war ended. In the context of the emerging triumph of the capitalist ideology it was possible to ram through legal prescriptions that supported liberalization of trade and investment and there was no regime and no country immune. The change toward greater justice may well eventuate but there are competing narratives and an extreme global capitalism that has failed the

[86] Special Representative of the Secretary-General, Guiding Principles on Business and Human Rights: Implementing the United Nations 'Protect, Respect and Remedy' Framework, UN Human Rights Council (A/HRC/17/31) (2011).

[87] UN Human Rights Council, Elaboration of an international legally binding instrument on transnational corporations and other business enterprises with respect to human rights, A/HRC/RES/26/9.

[88] Co-sponsors of the resolution were: Bolivia (Plurinational State of), Cuba, Ecuador, South Africa, and Venezuela.

[89] See, eg, General Assembly Resolution 58/4 of 31 Oct 2003 United Nations Convention against Corruption.

cause of justice but is yet to be dislodged from its place of power, not least given its support by international law. A movement towards justice is visible but so is an entrenched transnational commercialization. In the interest of real justice, this book seeks first and foremost to expose international law's facilitation of immiseration and economic violence in the hope that they might be dismantled.

4

International Trade

From War Capitalism to Contracts of Distribution

The idea that international law of the global economy should comply with principles of justice received substantial attention after the creation of the World Trade Organization.[1] Once governments shifted the aims of trade regulation from tariffs at the border, limited in scope only to international trade, to regulation inside states, covering more broadly matters of the social contract within the state, justice became a more salient issue for the global trade order. Despite significant attention, the law of international trade has been remarkably resilient in steering clear of compliance with the demands of justice. Clarity is needed on what is taking place and to deconstruct to reconstruct—to think beyond the constraints imposed by existing institutions about international trade so that alternative architectures can be seen as realistic possibilities.

States have constructed the law on international trade around three path dependencies, which have contributed to moral failure in trade relations between states and peoples. First, the law on international trade has its foundations in what Sven Beckert calls the 'war capitalism' of European conquest of the New World.[2] The history of trade and commerce is rooted in forms of coercion and violence designed to promote the interests of powerful states and their multinational enterprises. Second, this troubled history led governments to promote the wrong values in international trade relations between states. Governments wrongly prioritize contract, if not in a legal sense then in an economic sense, and an erroneous notion of market over right, and they do so in a manner in which a pathological form of politics tends to promote the interests of multinational enterprises over all else. The term 'right' as opposed to 'rights' refers to moral principles such as those relating to distributive justice or to freedom from domination and exploitation.[3] The concept of 'right' includes human rights that are meant to promote justice in economic

[1] This work is summarized in Chapter 1 ('Legal Rendering of Immiseration').

[2] S Beckert, *Empire of Cotton: A Global History* (Vintage 2015).

[3] Just to be clear for readers who wish to explore the philosophical issues more deeply, we go beyond a strictly Kantian principle of right as freedom from constraints from another's choice, though a Kantian separateness of persons requirement does figure into the discussion in that a person might have a reasonable complaint against a trade policy that causes her undue burdens regardless of any net aggregate welfare benefits of the trade policy. This is an often-used strategy in contemporary political philosophy. Chapter 2 ('Confronting the Pathologies of International Law') recounts some of these lines of inquiry.

contexts and to protect against domination and exploitation.[4] These principles are explored in Chapters 1 ('Legal Rendering of Immiseration'), 2 ('Confronting the Pathologies of International Law'), and 3 ('The End of Empire and the Search for Justice: NIEO and Beyond'). The term 'market' refers in a limited sense to markets that are poorly designed because the institutions that make them possible fail to comply with the demands of justice.[5] Trade agreements should be designed around a set of priorities in which right trumps contract, market, and politics. In the actual affairs of states, however, right is a weak norm in international affairs, particularly when it comes to trade. International human rights law, for example, has only very partially reigned in the worst tendencies of 'liberalized' trade. The politics of the global trade architecture is not the principled kind in which the public interest matters and shapes policy, but the bad, pathological kind in which powerful interest groups wield influence in the negotiation of trade agreements, leading not to open markets and certainly not to justice but to a constructed set of bargains of selective liberalization and protectionism in support of influential interests and powerful states. Trade agreements are not about free markets. They are about distribution.[6] They distribute resources and as institutions whose main purpose is distribution, are subject to the demands of justice.

The sections below proceed as follows. Section 1 explicates what was the first norm of international trade law of the modern state: the principle of freedom to trade as something akin to a natural right. Europeans used this principle to practise what Sven Becket calls war capitalism[7]—to commit atrocities, even genocide, so that Europeans could enjoy their natural freedom to trade. Section 2 examines the international trade order put in place when treaties and positive law became more important and industrial forms of capitalism became ascendant. This was a time in the eighteenth and nineteenth centuries when bilateral trade treaties between western states took on more prominence. These treaties are prototypes for contemporary trade agreements though of course they differed in substantial ways from current models. This treaty framework is structured around a concept of contract, or in the language of international law, *pacta sunt servanda*. Thinking of trade relations through a contract paradigm informs us how states can permissibly ignore notions of justice, disparities in bargaining power, global inequality, and other values. Power is permissibly exercised via a transactional model between states. In this model, trade treaties are all about bargaining. Economic justice of the kind we are concerned with here has almost nothing to do with bargains. In this institutional context, a national or mercantilist conception of market took absolute priority, a conception in which markets are divided up according to power imposed in bargaining. Section 3 examines how the contemporary trade treaty suffers from various

[4] ME Salomon, 'Why Should It Matter That Others Have More: Poverty, Inequality and the Potential of International Human Rights Law' (2011) 5 Review of International Studies 2137.

[5] The necessity of institutions for markets, well understood in economics, is discussed in Chapter 2 ('Confronting the Pathologies of International Law').

[6] See M Somers in Conversation with J Curtis 'Socially Embedding the Market and the Role of Law' Series on Economics and Law in Conversation, Laboratory for Advanced Research on the Global Economy, Centre for the Study of Human Rights, LSE (Mar 2016) 12, http:// www.lse.ac.uk/humanRights/research/projects/theLab/Economics-and-Law-in-Conversation---Interview-with-Margaret-Somers-FINAL.pdf.

[7] Beckert (n 2).

pathologies as a result of the historical rationalities imposed on it from these prior eras. The result is a failure of contemporary trade agreements to respect pluralism of non-trade values among states and to privilege trade over non-trade values. Contemporary trade agreements also disadvantage labour rights but are extremely generous to the interests of capital, and suffer from interest group capture that leads to morally problematic distributions of the costs and benefits—of gains and losses—of trade agreements.

1. The Very Strange Doctrine

The foundations of international law of the modern state are in justifications for the use of force in support of European commercial interests to compel non-European peoples to trade and in the conquest of the land and resources of non-European peoples.[8] International lawyers often underappreciate this point because international law took a positivist turn in the nineteenth century and international trade law became treaty based and so has at least the formal characteristics of consent and voluntary exchange associated with it. As well, linking to Wolfgang Friedmann's and Joel Trachtman's insights explored in Chapter 2,[9] international law is now understood to be increasingly regulatory in structure and therefore must be understood as an international law of cooperation and not merely as a law of coexistence. Trade law's origins, are, however, in a law of nations forming the groundwork for the early conception of international law as a law of coexistence. Trade law principles, founded in a law of nations grounded in what at the time was considered to be the universal laws of nature, formed around the only natural law duty left by the time Hobbes and Grotius stripped natural law down to minimum notions of sociability: a duty of self-preservation, serving as a master norm by which to judge actions beyond the state by everyone, including chartered companies, individuals, states, and princes.

Two ways to tell the history of international trade predominate the historical narrative. One is the Whiggish approach of economic historians, as 'progress' from the discredited notions of mercantilism to the 'right' approach, that of free trade. The standard economic narrative tells us that the Europeans adhering to mercantilist approaches in prior ages made themselves worse off because they failed to grasp the notion of gains from trade and that it took until 1817 when David Ricardo first wrote about comparative advantage for the notions of free trade to begin to take hold in European capitals. But this is an unrealistically utopian narrative, a fiction. States still employed what economists characterized as a mercantilist worldview but more fundamentally, the notion of mercantilism masks what was truly happening in the history of international trade.

[8] Other ways of constructing the origin story for international law are certainly possible but the dominant story is western and Eurocentric. See U Baxi, 'India–Europe' in B Fassbender and A Peters (eds), *The Oxford Handbook of the History of International Law* (OUP 2012) 744.

[9] Chapter 2 ('Confronting the Pathologies of International Law') at 55–59.

Another approach to the history of international trade is to investigate the violence and coercion the West was willing to perpetuate to enrich itself at the expense of others. In his influential book, *Empire of Cotton*, Sven Beckert characterizes the early period of capitalism as 'war capitalism'. Beckert distinguishes industrial capitalism, associated with contract and markets, with an earlier stage of capitalism 'based often as not on violence and bodily coercion'.[10] Beckert continues:

> Modern capitalism privileges property rights, but this earlier moment was characterised just as much by massive expropriations as by secure ownership. Latter day capitalism rests upon the rule of law and powerful institutions backed by the state, but capitalism's early phase, although ultimately requiring state power to create world-spanning empires, was frequently based on the unrestrained actions of private individuals—the domination of master over slaves and of frontier capitalists over indigenous inhabitants.[11]

Beckert shows that the result of this 'highly aggressive' capitalism was European domination and a restructuring of exchange to benefit European interests at the expense of others.[12] This is classic accumulation by dispossession as described in earlier chapters. In the nineteenth century Marx explained war capitalism this way: 'The discovery of gold and silver in America, the extirpation, enslavement, and entombment in mines of the aboriginal population, the beginning of conquest and looting of the East Indies, the turning of Africa into a warren for the commercial hunting of black skins, signalled the rosy dawn of the era of capitalist production.'[13]

There were a set of principles in the law of nations that the founders of international law used to justify war capitalism. These principles applied to trade. Vitoria was discussed in Chapter 3 on the NIEO and that discussion is continued here. He is worth a revisit because he states what might be the very first, or at least an early statement of what might be the first legal principle on the regulation of international trade. None of his work was published in his lifetime but in 1557, ten years after his death, his students published a set of special lectures he gave annually as part of his duties as professor of theology at Salamanca.[14] One of his lectures, *De Indis*, given in 1539, was of special relevance to the development of international trade and investment law. As its title tells us, this was a lecture on the American Indians. In very quick summary and only as it is relevant to our focus on international trade law, Vitoria's argument proceeded as follows:[15] Indians are humans with the capacity to reason and are bound by natural law. They are therefore bound by *jus gentium*, a form of natural law administered by sovereigns. Because they are so bound, they cannot interfere with the right of the Spanish under the *jus gentium* to travel on Indian lands and trade with the Indians. The Indians have the same right to do these things in Spain. It is an act of war to keep the Spaniards out or to

[10] Beckert (n 2) xvi. Section 2 informs us that the contract model for trade treaties still produces morally problematic outcomes.

[11] ibid. [12] ibid xvi. [13] K Marx, *Capital Vol 1* (new edn, Penguin 1990) 915.

[14] P Bobbitt, *The Shield of Achilles: War, Peace, and the Course of History* (Knopf 2002) 490.

[15] See ibid 489–91; A Anghie, *Imperialism, Sovereignty and the Making of International Law* (CUP 2007) 13–31; A Fitzmaurice, *Sovereignty, Property and Empire, 1500–2000* (CUP 2014).

limit their activities and Spanish retaliation is permissible in such cases. Moreover, Indian social and cultural practices violate the *jus gentium* and they can remedy these violations by adopting Spanish social and cultural practices. The Spaniards can use force to achieve the transformation. Consent by the Indians is irrelevant and resistance is an act of war, a violation of the law of nations. The Indians lack sovereignty as a nation because of their violations and only Christians can wage just war against them to transform their practices. The rules of just war do not apply to the Indians. The Spaniards can kill or enslave their women and children if they fail to comply.

Other founders of international law, Gentili and Grotius, argued similarly. Grotius's *De Indis,* an apology for Dutch aggression in what is now known as south-east Asia, articulates what Locke will later call the 'very strange doctrine' that in the absence of the law of the state as it is found within the state, each person in nature is morally identical to the state and has the power to punish for violations of the law of nations.[16] So, for example, the Dutch East India Company, the Vereenigde Oost-Indische Compagnie (VOC) was justified, at least according to Grotius, in enforcing natural rights of trade and occupation through use of force. The VOC, probably the second multinational company after that of the British East India Company (EIC),[17] had the right to conclude treaties with foreign powers, to wage war, and to levy taxes.[18] The EIC maintained its own armed forces of about 200,000, more than most European states of the time, and could call on the Royal Navy and Army for support if needed.[19] These chartered companies were the first companies permitted to organize on a limited liability basis. The EIC sold shares on the Royal Exchange.[20]

[16] J Locke, *Second Treatise of Government* (Hackett 1980) §9, 10; H Grotius, *De jure praedae commentaries,* ed and intro by M Julia van Ittersum (Liberty Fund 2006) ch 1; H Grotius, *De jure belli ac pacis,* ed and intro by R Tuck (Liberty Fund 2005) ch II.

[17] The British East India Company was the first joint stock company and the VOC the second. D Acemoglu and JA Robinson, *Why Nations Fail: The Origins of Power, Prosperity & Poverty* (Profile 2013) 247.

[18] FS Gaastra, *The Dutch East India Company: Expansion and Decline* (Walburg Pers 2003).

[19] Beckert explains:

> [P]rivate capitalists, often organised in chartered companies (such as the British East India Company) asserted sovereignty over land and people, and structured connections to local rulers. Heavily armed privateering capitalists became the symbol of this new world of European domination, as their cannon-filled boats and their soldier-traders, armed private militias, and settlers captured land and labour and blew competitors, quite literally, out of the water. Privatised violence was one of their core competencies. While European states had envisioned, encouraged, and enabled the creation of vast colonial empires, they remained weak and thin on the ground, providing private actors the space and leeway to forge new modes of trade and production. Not secure property rights but a wave of expropriation of labor and land characterised this moment, testifying to capitalism's illiberal origins.

Beckert (n 2) 37.

[20] N Robins, *The Corporation That Changed the World: How the East India Company Shaped the Modern Multinational* (2nd edn, Pluto 2012); HV Bowen, *The Business of Empire: The East India Company* (CUP 2009); J Keay, *The Honourable Company: A History of the English East India Company* (HarperCollins 1993); P Lawson, *The East India Company: A History, 1600–1857* (Routledge 1993); W Dalrymple, 'The East India Company: The Original Corporate Raiders' *The Guardian* (London,

Adam Smith was a critic of his day of the EIC and war capitalism generally, declaring these chartered companies to be 'bloodstained monopolies', 'useless', and 'burdensome', responsible for grotesque massacres.[21] Smith, however, did not write on the law of nations. Of course, the right to trade in war capitalism had, it is assumed, little to do with the sort of voluntary exchange about which Smith articulated as an ideal form of commerce. In the way that market transactions are idealized around Smithian notions of voluntary exchange, any person can refuse to enter a transaction if she does not believe it will make her better off. This ideal exchange model certainly was not at work for many in the period under investigation.

Refusal of non-European peoples to engage in trade with Europeans was considered to be contrary to the laws of nature or nations and apt for punishment. Of course, these legal arguments were pretence for European conquest, just as the notions of consent, contract, and voluntary exchange today mask the imposition of the interests of the powerful. Grotius wrote as an advocate for Dutch actions in the East, Vitoria for the Spaniards in the Americas, and Gentili against Spain and for England.

The very strange doctrine and the right to trade are the first principles of international trade law in an era of war capitalism. War capitalism could be said to still manifest itself today. Shadrack Gutto remarks that 'the whole institution of imperialism is an expression of the union between so called "private" corporations along with state power to expand outside the territorial boundaries for purposes of exploiting social and economic advantages in other societies'.[22]

In the era when war capitalism became ascendant, western states began the practice of maintaining stark distinctions between law-governed institutions regulating voluntary exchange inside the state and force-governed practices to get what they wanted outside the state. In the era of war capitalism that Beckert describes, Europeans divided the world into an 'inside' and 'outside'.[23] 'Inside' refers to within the European state, where established laws, institutions, and customs governed.

4 Mar 2015); 'The East India Company: The Company That Rules the Waves' *The Economist* (17 Dec 2011).

[21] 'The East India Company: The Company That Rules the Waves' *The Economist* (17 Dec 2011); GM Anderson and RD Tollison, 'Adam Smith's Analysis of Joint-Stock Companies' (1982) 90 Journal of Political Economy 1237.

[22] SBO Gutto, 'Violation of Human Rights in the Third World: Responsibility of States and TNCs' in FE Snyder and S Sathirathai (eds), *Third World Attitudes Toward International Law: An Introduction* (Martinus Nijhoff 1987) 275, 283.

[23] Says Beckert:

> War capitalism relied on the capacity of rich and powerful Europeans to divide the world into an 'inside' and an 'outside'. The 'inside' encompassed the laws, institutions, and customs of the mother country, where state-enforced order ruled. The 'outside', by contrast, was characterised by imperial domination, the expropriation of vast territories, decimation of indigenous peoples, theft of their resources, enslavement, and the domination of vast tracts of land by private capitalists with little effective oversight by distant European states. In these imperial dependencies, the rules of the inside did not apply. There, masters trumped states, violence defied the law, and bold physical coercion by private actors remade markets.

Beckert (n 2) 38.

The 'outside' was exempt from these laws and institutions, the province of 'imperial domination, the expropriation of vast territories, decimation of indigenous peoples, theft of their resources, enslavement, and the domination of vast tracts of land by private capitalists with little effective oversight by distant European states'.[24] Outside, 'masters trumped states, violence defied the law, and bold physical coercion by private actors remade markets'.[25] These distinctions conformed to the stripped-down version of natural law propagated by Grotius, one of the founding figures of international law.

The inside–outside distinction maintains today. For example, in oil and mining, whoever seizes control of the resource by whatever means has the right to dispose of it.[26] In important ways not much has changed: the values exported need not be the values deployed at home in industrialized countries, that is, states can organize their societies under (some version of) socialism at home and imperialism abroad.[27]

When war capitalism appeared on the world stage, the common law of England of the time distinguished between settlement by Europeans on unoccupied land versus land taken by military conquest. For settled colonies, English law applied, but in the case of conquest, English law did not apply but conquered territories were under Crown and parliamentary control.[28] British law up until the early nineteenth century was designed to support slavery and the plantation economies in British colonies and treated slaves as property under the law. Slavery was an essential aspect of the global economy of the time. Two sets of laws were in play, one for British subjects and the other for those outside of direct British rule. Blackstone states that these distinctions were 'founded on the law of nature, or at least upon that of nations'.[29] Lord Mansfield's judgment in *Somerset v Stewart* plainly confirms the inside–outside distinction in its dicta in which Lord Mansfield stated that slavery was prohibited in England but not in its colonies.[30] The narrow holding in *Somerset* also confirms the distinction. Mansfield himself later construed the holding in that *habeas corpus* case as going 'no further than that the master cannot by force compel him [the slave] to go out of the kingdom'.[31] In his iconic work, historian Eric Williams wrote in the 1940s that praise for Mansfield's *Somerset* judgment 'is merely poetic sentimentality translated into modern history'.[32] The inside–outside distinction assists in understanding contemporary forms of structural or institutional racism. We really cannot understand structural and institutional forms of

[24] ibid. [25] ibid.

[26] L Wenar, *Blood Oil: Tyrants, Violence, and the Rules That Run the World* (OUP 2016).

[27] Our thanks to Ali Kadri for this particular language that captures the idea so well. See A Kadri, 'Development Under Uncertainty in the Arab World' SPEAK OUT at the Laboratory for Advanced Research on the Global Economy, Centre for the Study of Human Rights, LSE (June 2016), http://www.lse.ac.uk/humanRights/research/projects/theLab/home.aspx

[28] See W Blackstone, *Commentaries on the Laws of England*, vol 1 (University of Chicago Press 2008) 104–05.

[29] ibid. [30] *Somerset v Stewart* (1772) 98 ER 499.

[31] *Rex v Inhabitants of Thomas Ditton*, 4 Doug 300, 301 (1785). See J Oldham, *English Common Law in the Age of Mansfield* (University of North Carolina Press 2004) 314.

[32] E Williams, *Capitalism and Slavery* (André Deutsch 1944) 45. See also J Oldham, 'New Light on Mansfield and Slavery' (1988) 27 Journal of British Studies 45.

racism only by looking inside the borders of developed states in the West because these borders were used in a long history to maintain slavery and exploitation in the New World and 'civilization' in the Old World.[33]

The division between inside and outside the state can still be seen in differences in thinking about the economic development issues facing low-income countries today. Economists tend to look for solutions to economic development puzzles in domestic institutions, in the institutions in the state governing property, contract, capital markets, credit, and so on. International trade policy supports an approach that has any redistributive necessities of trade benefits understood solely as the responsibility of domestic policymaking. As Patrick Macklem points out, a consequence of international law's foundational commitment to the formal equality of states is that substantive equality of states plays a marginal role in the normative architecture of the international legal order.[34] A long-standing debate in political philosophy is between those who see states as the site for egalitarian justice and those who argue for cosmopolitan approaches to a more globalized idea of justice.[35] Progressive human rights lawyers working in the area of socio-economic rights seek to see complemented the obligations of (low-income) states acting at home with those of influential states acting extraterritorially, including under the auspices of international organizations.[36]

The inside–outside distinction finds support in the stripped-down version of natural law of Grotius and Hobbes, based on an overriding duty of self-preservation outside the state and substantial civil duties to comply with positive law within the state. For Hobbes in particular it is civil justice in the state, imposed by a strong sovereign, but outside of the state is perpetual war. The result is two very different forms of capitalism, one for compatriots and quite another for foreigners.

War capitalism produced predictable results. The Molucca Islands are part of modern-day Indonesia. In the early seventeenth century, they were at the centre of global production of spices and were known as the Spice Islands to Europeans. The

[33] See Chapter 3 ('The End of Empire and the Search for Justice: NIEO and Beyond') at 85–92.

[34] P Macklem, 'Human Rights in International Law: Three Generations or One?' (2015) 3 London Review of International Law 1, 61, 91. Macklem goes on to draw the further implication: 'However valuable international law's commitment to the formal equality of states, its banishment of substantive equality to the domestic realm further implicates the structure of the international legal order in the natural, geographical and social contingencies that contribute to global poverty' (ibid).

[35] See Chapter 2 ('Confronting the Pathologies of International Law'); J Linarelli, 'Law Rights and Development' in J Linarelli (ed), *Research Handbook on Global Justice and International Economic Law* (Edward Elgar 2013) 301.

[36] See Chapter 7 ('Human Rights'). The Committee on Economic, Social and Cultural Rights (CESCR) recently emphasized the extraterritorial obligations of states, including as members of intergovernmental organizations, to ensure compliance with their existing socio-economic obligations:

> States parties to the Covenant would be acting in violation of their obligations if they were to delegate powers to the IMF or to other agencies and to allow such powers to be exercised without ensuring that they do not infringe on human rights. Similarly, they would be acting in breach of their obligations if they were to exercise their voting rights within such agencies without taking such rights into account. The same duties apply to States that are not parties to the Covenant, under human rights law as part of general international law. Their responsibility would not be absolved even where a State party, in its capacity as a member State of an international organisation, would be acting fully in accordance with the rules of the organisation.

CESCR Statement on Public Debt, Austerity Measures and the International Covenant on Economic, Social and Cultural Rights UN Doc E/C.12/2016/1, 24 June 2016, para 9.

Banda Islands in the middle Moluccas was the only producers of mace and nutmeg in the world at the time and they traded mace and nutmeg in the region and also with China, India, and Arabia for other goods. The Dutch wanted to take over the supply of nutmeg and mace from the Bandanese. The Bandanese lacked a unified central authority, so the Dutch could not make a political deal with any single ruler to control the supply of nutmeg and mace or take over a pre-existing local system of tribute. The Dutch governor of what was then Batavia, Jan Pieterszoon Coen sailed to Banda with a fleet and killed almost the entire population of the Banda Islands. The Dutch executed all of the Bandanese leaders. The Dutch spared the lives of just enough Bandanese to transfer the know-how necessary for mace and nutmeg production. With the extermination of the Bandanese complete, the Dutch then put a plantation society in place on the Banda Islands. They divided the islands into sixty-eight parcels and gave the parcels to Dutchmen, mostly former and current VOC employees. The few Bandanese that the Dutch spared taught the Dutch how to produce the spices. The new Dutch owners bought slaves from the VOC to populate the islands they emptied and to produce spices. The arrangement was for spices to be produced and sold at fixed prices to the VOC.[37] By the end of the seventeenth century, the Dutch had reduced the world supply of mace and nutmeg by about 60%, causing the price of nutmeg to double.[38]

The Dutch spread this genocidal strategy[39] to the entire region. Some societies abandoned trade and crop production in the hopes of keeping the Dutch out, leading to poverty and population declines. The Burmese moved their capital very far inland up the Irrawaddy River to keep away from the Dutch.[40]

Similar depredations still occur. An example is the operation of Texaco (now Chevron) for twenty-three years in Ecuador, from 1964 to 1990.[41] Texaco discovered oil in Ecuador's Amazon rainforest, in an area known as Lago Agrio, or, as the Ecuadorians call the region, the Oriente. The area was pristine forest and the consortium, which included the national petroleum company, initially had to bring in equipment by helicopter, but eventually built roads and an airport. In 1993, a group of Ecuadorian citizens, many of whom are members of indigenous communities in the area, began litigation in Ecuador to hold Texaco liable for what they have described as extreme environmental devastation, along with the serious health effects on the local population, brought on by operations that would not have been permitted in the United States. Chevron as Texaco's successor in interest very aggressively

[37] The above is summarized from D Acemoglu and JA Robinson, *Why Nations Fail: The Origins of Power, Prosperity & Poverty* (Profile 2013) 248–49.

[38] ibid.

[39] While Dutch actions towards the Bandanese occurred well before the Genocide Convention came into force, it seems clear that their actions meet the definition of the crime of genocide found in the Convention. Convention on the Prevention and Punishment of the Crime of Genocide, adopted by Resolution 260 (III) A of the United Nations General Assembly on 9 Dec 1948, 78 UNTS 277, entered into force 12 Jan 1951.

[40] Acemoglu and Robinson (n 37) 248–50.

[41] What follows is primarily from PR Keefe, 'Reversal of Fortune' *New Yorker* (9 Jan 2012). Much has been written about the Chevron–Ecuador litigation. An entire issue of the first volume of the *Stanford Journal of Complex Litigation* is dedicated to it. See 'Lessons from Chevron', Volume 1, Issue 2 (Spring 2013) of the Stanford Journal of Complex Litigation.

fought this litigation and it became extremely complex, with litigation in Ecuador, the United States, Canada, Brazil, Argentina, and three arbitrations before international tribunals. The litigation is in its twenty-fourth year and is still ongoing.[42] A Chevron lobbyist in 2008 said that 'we can't let little countries screw around with big companies like this'.[43] At the time of this writing, Chevron is the fourth largest company headquartered in the United States, operating in over one hundred countries, with gross revenues twice that of Ecuador's GDP. When Texaco began operations in Ecuador in 1964, the country was unstable and extremely poor, with bananas as its main export. One lawyer who works for Oxfam has argued that 'Texaco ran the country for twenty years. They had the U.S. Embassy in their pocket. They had the military. Politically, there was no way that Texaco was going to be held accountable in Ecuador.'[44] At the time, Ecuador needed Texaco's expertise and technology if it was to extract the oil. The lawsuit alleged that Texaco dumped 18 billion gallons of toxic waste into the water system in the region, along with 17 billion gallons of crude oil, and left 916 clearly visible unlined toxic waste pits full of black sludge throughout the region. At the time, Texaco's operations did not violate Ecuadorian law; Ecuador had no real environmental law at the time. While Chevron vigorously contests the facts, the evidence shows that Texaco failed to use environmentally sustainable technologies in its operations in Ecuador. Texaco ignored American Petroleum Institute minimum standards for oil operations in place when it started its operations in Ecuador. As the former Ecuador Ambassador to the United States Nathalie Cely has put it: 'When Texaco left Ecuador, significant profits in hand, it left unprecedented damage to the environment and no compensation to those affected in its wake.'[45] Similar examples can be provided.[46]

Returning to the historical discussion, war capitalism produced some interesting effects in the labour market. Slavery is an ancient institution but what made it different in the conquest of the Americas was that it was intricately linked to international trade. This very close connection between New World slavery and trade differentiates it from the general form of slavery of the ancient world or more recent forms.[47] Beckert summarises: 'three moves—imperial expansion, expropriation and slavery—became central to the forging of a new global economic order and eventually the emergence of capitalism' and '[t]he beating heart of this new system was slavery'.[48]

Between 1600 and 1800 and extending well into the nineteenth century, slave-produced goods dominated world trade.[49] Between 1600 and 1800, slaves in the Americas accounted for less than one-fifth of the population of the western

[42] P Barrett, 'Chevron Slams Canadian Backdoor in $9.5 Billion Pollution Fight' *Bloomberg Business Week* (23 Jan 2017).

[43] Keefe (n 41). [44] ibid.

[45] N Cely, 'Balancing Profit and Environmental Sustainability in Ecuador: Lessons Learned from the Chevron Case' (2014) 24 Duke Environmental Law and Policy Forum 353, 355.

[46] See Wenar (n 26).

[47] See RW Fogel, *Without Consent or Contract: The Rise and Fall of American Slavery* (Norton 1989) 22.

[48] Beckert (n 2) 37. [49] What follows is from Fogel (n 47) 17–40.

hemisphere and less than 1% of the world's population but during this period and well into the nineteenth century, commodities produced by slaves 'dominated the channels of world trade'.[50] Sugar was the single most important commodity in this period, accounting for one-fifth of British imports at the time of American Independence. Adding other slave-produced commodities to the mix, slaves produced about 30% of British imports in the mid-eighteenth century and over half of Britain's exports went to its slave colonies. Britain's shipping was primarily engaged in either transporting imports or exports of slave produced commodities, or slaves themselves. Between 60 and 70% of Africans who survived the transatlantic voyage ended up on sugar plantations. Similar findings can be offered for France, Spain, Portugal, Holland, and Denmark. The sugar plantations in the Caribbean were large-scale operations, the substantial equivalent of a modern multinational enterprise.

We can see in the international market for cotton a forced restructuring of a global industry to enrich British and eventually American interests at the expense of both Indian weavers and African slaves.[51] In the seventeenth century, the East India Company (EIC) depended on Indian trading networks for cotton cloth. The (EIC) maintained warehouses of cotton cloth it bought from local traders who served as middlemen to obtain cloth from inland weavers in India. The Indian weavers profited from this set of relationships, trading not only with the British but also with Indian and Arab traders. The cotton industry ran this way for about two centuries. The insertion of armed British merchants, however, eventually led to marginalizing these networks and a monopolization of the cotton industry to Britain's benefit. Armed merchants stopped non-British merchants from buying cloth and they established themselves as the dominant global buyers of cotton cloth. The British also started cotton plantations in what is now the American south and moved the finishing of cotton into cloth in mills in northwest England. The centre of the cotton industry moved to Manchester, England. British interests misappropriated technology from the Indian weavers to build the industry in Britain. In India, the British got the weavers to work for them rather than independently, effectively as wage labour as did mill workers in the English countryside. The British government also put in place protectionist measures to prevent importation of Indian cloth and the sale of Indian cotton in Britain was eventually criminalized.[52] The British monopolized the market and drove down weaver incomes while driving up the price of cotton cloth.[53] They did so through

[50] ibid 21. [51] What follows is from Beckert (n 2) 31–52.

[52] See HJ Chang, *Kicking Away the Ladder: Development Strategy in Historical Perspective* (Anthem 2002) (rich countries getting rich as a result of policies they now effectively forbid poor countries from implementing).

[53] Beckert summarizes:

> Imperial expansion, slavery, and land expropriations—war capitalism—laid the foundations for the still small and technologically backward domestic cotton industry in Europe. It provided dynamic markets and access to technology and to essential raw materials. It also became a significant engine of capital formation. Mercantile cities such as Liverpool, which

a combination of economic and political power and military might. The French undertook similar measures.[54]

These activities had an obvious economic multiplier effect, producing wealth in commercial interests in insurance, finance, and shipping, areas in which English law retains global importance, and fed into the national tax coffers.[55]

Even after the British banned the slave trade, international trade associated with cotton continued, hence why the British were divided in their support for the Confederacy in the American Civil War.[56] With the prohibitions on slavery in Britain came compensation to British slave owners at £37 billion in today's pounds.[57] The slaves and their families got nothing. Bailouts of the rich are nothing new.[58]

Labour conditions today are not the brutal New World slavery of the past but they reflect a high level of dubious practices nonetheless. Consider as an example the production and supply of lithium ion batteries, necessary for many electronic devices, including mobile phones, tablets, and electronic components in cars.[59] Children and adults, known as artisanal miners, mine cobalt in the Democratic Republic of the Congo (DRC) in extremely hazardous conditions. About one-half of the world's cobalt comes from the DRC and about 20% of that is mined by artisanal miners. These artisanal miners sell to traders who sell the cobalt to a wholly owned Congolese subsidiary of the large Chinese minerals firm, Huayou Cobalt Ltd. Huayou Cobalt processes the cobalt and sells it to battery makers, who then sell batteries to auto and tech companies, including Apple, Microsoft, Samsung, Sony, Daimler, and Volkswagen. Apple, for example, manages a huge supply chain[60] and batteries it needs for making its products will end up at Foxconn, the world's largest

> derived their wealth largely from slavery, became important sources of capital for the emerging cotton industry, and cotton merchants in Liverpool provided ever more credit to manufacturers to enable them to work up the cotton. London merchants, in turn, who sold the yarn and cloth coming from British producers advanced credit to Lancashire manufacturers.

Beckert (n 2) 52.

54 Similar market structures persist today. International trade in coffee is an example, though fair trade organizations have made inroads to produce fairer terms of trade for coffee growers. See CG Gonzalez, 'Institutionalizing Inequality: The WTO, Agriculture and Developing Countries' (2002) 27 Columbia Journal of Environmental Law 433.

55 ibid. As Richard Drayton explains:

> Profits from slave trading and from sugar, coffee, cotton and tobacco are only a small part of the story. What mattered was how the pull and push from these industries transformed western Europe's economies. English banking, insurance, shipbuilding, wool and cotton manufacture, copper and iron smelting, and the cities of Bristol, Liverpool and Glasgow, multiplied in response to the direct and indirect stimulus of the slave plantations.

R Drayton, 'The Wealth of the West Was Built on Africa's Exploitation' *The Guardian* (London, 20 Aug 2005).

56 A Foreman, *A World on Fire: An Epic History of Two Nations Divided* (Penguin 2011).

57 N Draper, *The Price of Emancipation: Slave-Ownership, Compensation and British Society at the End of Slavery* (CUP 2013).

58 See Chapter 6 ('Global Finance') at 177, 204–210 on bank bailouts.

59 The following is primarily from Amnesty International, *'This Is What We Die For': Human Rights Abuses in the Democratic Republic of the Congo Power the Global Trade in Cobalt* (2016).

60 C Minisians, 'Where Are the iPhone, iPad and Mac Designed, Made and Assembled? A Comprehensive Breakdown of Apple's Product Supply Chain' *Macworld* (18 Apr 2016).

maker of electronic and computer products.[61] If you buy an Apple product, the box says 'designed in California' but Apple produces nothing in California, and indeed does not manufacture anything. Apple's profits are largely attributable to its intellectual property, including its trade marks and designs. Apple outsources production to Foxconn, as do other leading brands, such as HP, Intel, and Nokia. Foxconn has over one million workers. It has 'grown into a mega world workshop' with single factories employing about 20,000 and larger compounds at about 400,000. The stresses of the job at Foxconn led a startling eighteen Chinese migrant workers between the ages of 17 and 25 to attempt suicide at Foxconn production facilities. Fourteen died as a result. Evidence shows that rush orders have pushed Foxconn workers 'to their physical and psychological limits, leading to workers' suicides as well as individual and collective resistance in the workplace'.[62] Underage student workers between 16 and 18 years of age and organized by their schools comprise a large segment of the Foxconn workforce.[63] Harsh working conditions are well documented. Foxconn may be one of the better firms for outsourcing in terms of labour protections.[64]

Conceptually like the inside–outside distinction is the distinction western states made between themselves and others outside the West. By today's standards, we might call the very strange doctrine unilateralism in the extreme. There were few trade agreements with discovered peoples because they were considered unnecessary. There was no point in attempting consensual relations with uncivilized peoples who can be forced through superior firepower to bend to your will. The right to force trade and appropriate property provided all the justification needed.[65] It was a form of domination clothed in purported legal and moral authority. While European powers engaged in war capitalism in conquering territories that were not part of 'civilized' states in the Westphalian order, they engaged in treaty making

[61] The evidence to follow is primarily from P Ngai and J Chan, 'Global Capital, the State, and Chinese Workers: The Foxconn Experience' (2012) 38 Modern China 383.

[62] ibid 387–88. [63] ibid 391.

[64] A Lang, 'Trade Agreements, Business and Human Rights: The Case of Export Processing Zones' (Apr 2010) Working Paper No 57, http://www.hks.harvard.edu/mrcbg/CSRI/publications/workingpaper_57_lang%20FINAL%20APRIL%202010.pdf

[65] This norm could be said to continue to have normative force today. As Salomon explains:

> This notion of consent implies a voluntarism, but there is no real freedom of action when choices are between lesser evils ... That participation in the international trading system as currently conceived represents the preferred option to remaining outside of it, where growth opportunity would be curtailed more severely, does not suggest that what they get, for example within the World Trade Organization (WTO), is optimal or even fair. Rational consent should not be mistaken for approval. Moreover, a focus on the problems of membership should not obscure the sacrifices made in seeking eligibility for membership by developing and least developed countries. Policy prescriptions requiring an openness to global economic integration and removal of barriers to market access are imposed as conditions for entry into the WTO and for receipt of funds from international financial institutions even though they may not serve poor countries well.

ME Salomon, 'Poverty, Privilege and International Law: The Millennium Development Goals and the Guise of Humanitarianism' (2008) 51 German Yearbook of International Law 39, 42; see also A Orford, 'Beyond Harmonization: Trade, Human Rights and the Economy of Sacrifice' (2005) 18 LJIL 179.

between themselves. Western states imposed two distinct normative orders, one accepting force as the natural order of things when Europeans encountered non-European peoples, and the other based in an essentially contractual notion of *pacta sunt servanda* between states that the West considered in a position to engage in treaty making. Today, one expression of this application of distinct normative orders might be found in the availability of hard judicial protections when it comes to protecting what is capital (binding dispute settlement and sanctions for non-compliance in international economic law), but weak protections when it comes to diminishing poverty (non-binding, quasi-judicial complaint mechanisms for remedying violations of socio-economic rights).[66] We also see distinct normative expectations play out in in global finance, whereby loan agreements are defended by creditor states and international lenders as binding at all costs, with the principle of *pacta sunt servanda* disregarded when it comes to the tempering effects that human rights obligations of the borrowing state would have on the determination and terms of 'debt sustainability'.[67] While treaty making with non-European peoples was indeed a theoretical possibility for states and their agents in the form of chartered companies of the time, use of force was a default position, ready to be used if those on the other side refused to trade or to trade on terms favourable to Europeans. So, historically, two core normative principles were at work, one justifying force and the other justifying contract. Today, disparate normative forces are still at work, one for the rich and one for others.

War capitalism eventually lost its appeal to lawyers and philosophers. Kant and Rousseau rejected Grotian principles, with Kant labelling Grotius and others who rationalized war capitalism as 'miserable comforters'.[68] With Kant came a move from the right of nations to cosmopolitan right, in which a principle of non-intervention eventually began to develop.[69] But this was a time in which we see the rise of positive law as the hierarchically most important form of law, including positive international law, and lawyer-philosophers were no longer in a position to dispense legal opinions.[70] With the rise of positivism came the rise of the economic treaty. The use of power moved from explicit use of force to another form

[66] ME Salomon, 'The Future of Human Rights' Special Issue on International Law, Human Rights and the Global Economy: Innovations and Expectations for the 21st Century, Guest Editor ME Salomon', 4 Global Policy (Nov 2012) 455, 455–56. 'Put differently, mechanisms have to date been established to provide rigorous safeguards for threats to the maximisation of wealth (largely by the wealthy), but relatively feeble systems are available when it comes to ensuring minimum essential levels of wellbeing for those in need' (ibid 456).

[67] See Chapter 6 ('Global Finance'); see also *Report of the Truth Committee on Public Debt* (Special Committee of the Hellenic Parliament on the Audit of the Greek Debt, 2015).

[68] I Kant, 'Toward Perpetual Peace: A Philosophical Project' in *Kant Practical Philosophy* (tr M Gregor, CUP 1999) 326 (AKA 8: 355). Translations from the German variously use 'sorry', 'miserable', and 'terrible' comforters for *leidige Tröster*.

[69] A Pagden, 'From the "Right of Nations" to the "Cosmopolitan Right": Immanuel Kant's Law of Continuity and the Limits of Empire' in A Pagden, *The Burdens of Empire: 1539 to the Present* (CUP 2015) 201.

[70] See SC Neff, *Justice Among Nations: A History of International Law* (Harvard UP 2014) ch 3; A Orakhelashvili, 'The 19th-Century Life of International Law' in A Orakhelashvili (ed), *Research Handbook on the Theory and History of International Law* (Edward Elgar 2011) 441.

of coercion in the form of state power in treaty negotiations. We now come to the stage from might is right to contract and market over right, with the rise of practical associations between states accomplished in an age of positivism through treaties. Still, treaties maintain coercive power, particularly between rich and poor states and in allocating gains and losses from trade, a subject to which we turn in sections 2 and 3.

2. From War to Contract

Explored here are the norms underlying trade treaties beginning in the mid-eighteenth century, at the beginning of the Industrial Revolution, and before GATT came into existence. While war capitalism provided us with the principle of the right to trade, to be implemented by force if necessary, these periods show a transition to a body of rules of positive law between states as found in a conventional source of law known as treaties. The focus here is on a model of international trade law based on 'trade treaty as contract'. That conception has led us to think of international trade law today in the way we do and why it seems so alien to us to think that justice has anything to do with trade law.[71] To get to a morally acceptable approach to evaluating international trade law, we must reject or at least reconceive the contract model.

The essence of trade treaty as contract is as an international law of practical association, which we elaborate upon in Chapter 2. The contract model of relations between states can be understood along the lines of the famous Coase theorem in law and economics.[72] In a contract account, parties to the contract bargain to the best result they can obtain. In this model, contracting parties are free to be self-interested; it is entirely permissible and expected that they be so. They are not required to be impartial or to take the interests of the other parties into account. They do not have to comply with the moral conditions of reasonable acceptance by all parties and do not have to engage in the form of recognition respect of a morally motivated person or justify their position to others. They are not compelled by the second personal obligations outlined in Chapter 2 ('Confronting the Pathologies of International Law'). Contracting parties, moreover, are free to take full advantage of disparities in bargaining power or inequalities between the parties. The aim of such contracting parties is to extract as much rent as possible from the bargain for themselves. By now it should be clear that the contract model fails to comply with the demands of justice. As explained below, the contract model is no longer feasible or desirable if trade

[71] Trade treaties as incomplete contracts can be understood from the perspective of the contemporary economics literature on incomplete contracts. JP Trachtman, *The Future of International Law* (CUP 2013) 200–01; G Maggi and RW Staiger, 'The Role of Dispute Settlement Procedures in International Trade Agreements' (2011) 126 Quarterly Journal of Economics 475; H Horn, G Maggi, and RW Staiger, 'The GATT/WTO as an Incomplete Contract' (2010) 100 American Economic Review 394; JP Trachtman, *The Economic Structure of International Law* (Harvard UP 2008) 168–69.

[72] R Coase, 'The Problem of Social Cost' (1960) 3 Journal of Law and Economics 1.

treaties are to have a future in which they are reasonably acceptable to states and their citizens.

Another way to understand the contract model is through the general international law principle of *pacta sunt servanda.*[73] If we were simply to replace the natural right to trade with *pacta sunt servanda*, we place in clear exposition competing conceptions of international trade law from the seventeenth century to the present. These principles provide a basic legal frame upon which to model trade relations. *Pacta sunt servanda* can remain an important general principle in international law whilst still having a different, moralized normative foundation for international trade law formed around the demands of justice. Justice does not become a legal rule but a standard by which to evaluate the legitimacy of legal rules. *Pacta sunt servanda* simply has to be put to use in developing fairer treaty frameworks. This is no different from arguing in domestic law contexts that as a matter of policy some matters are just too important to be left only to contract. This recognition led to the regulatory state inside states. It needs to lead to a recognition that an international law of cooperation demands no less.

In the eighteenth century, we begin to see some movement by European powers towards trade architecture more closely resembling those found in the mid-twentieth century, though the relationships are overwhelmingly bilateral at the time and the treaties were overwhelmingly about tariffs, duties, and lifting prohibitions on importing.[74] These treaties should be characterized as reflecting an essentially contractual nature, prioritizing market structuring based on bargaining between states in the interests of their multinational enterprises. If a principle of right could be said to have entered into these treaties, it would be a very limited one based on the notion of respect for formal treaty rights and obligations—*pacta sunt servanda* at its very basic essence.

Economic historians classify trade agreements of the eighteenth and primarily nineteenth centuries along a limited free trade versus protectionist distinction. The free trade–protectionist distinction, as we explore more fully below, provides at best an incomplete understanding of trade agreements. The free trade–protectionist distinction works if we understand treaties from an economic point of view essentially as contracts, but with the rise of social welfare democracies, a positive law of human rights, and the regulatory state, the distinction distorts our understanding of trade treaties. The regulatory state being governed by contemporary trade agreements was unknown until much later and arose gradually in the twentieth century.

The economic narrative around these sorts of treaties work only if we are unwilling to look beyond tariff measures and to peel back the layers of the supply chain to understand how goods are made behind tariff walls. It is thinking about trade treaties as contracts between independent nation states about at-the-border measures only. In the limited case of tariffs or duties, each country has its own goods

[73] Vienna Convention on the Law of Treaties Art 26 codifies the *pacta sunt servanda* principle.

[74] See P Bairoch, *Economics and World History: Myths and Paradoxes* (University of Chicago Press 1993).

that it produces within its own sphere of influence, either in-country or within a global supply chain structure it created in its war capitalism legacy. For example, Britain might have textiles to export to France, but these textiles may have been weaved in Lancashire from cotton produced in a plantation in the American south, a plantation originally created by investments from Britain in its former American colonies and continued by the United States after Independence. In these prior contract-like arrangements, the Westphalian normative order provides states with what Philip Bobbitt calls opaque sovereignty, 'a traditional concept that holds that events within a state's borders are entirely internal matters, beyond the judgment of other states'.[75] To put this in our contract analogy, contract parties do not care how they comply with their contract obligations, so long as they comply.[76]

Contract approaches are put in serious tension when trade treaties regulate behind the border and intrude into regulatory spaces that were developed within the constitutional and administrative traditions of a country's social contract.[77] In these new contexts, the concepts and language of contract fail to provide a way to fix accountability relations and by which to deal with the moral standing of persons to each other through institutions. In the regulatory context, decision-making other than in markets is normatively relevant to the participants. Trade treaties no longer only have direct effects on prices and quantities of goods traded in markets. They now invade decision-making based on democratic deliberation or other forms of public accountability.[78] These are competing and not necessarily complementary forms of decision-making and it is by now well known that not all decision-making should be made according to market principles.[79] Trade treaties regulating behind

[75] P Bobbitt, *Terror and Consent: The Wars for the Twenty-First Century* (Penguin 2008) 469.

[76] Of course, contract parties would want their counterparts to comply within the bounds of the law. A buyer of goods, for example, would not want the seller to sell her fenced goods for the obvious reasons. Treaties like any other legal practice have to comply with the law itself whatever it may be. We do not deal with formal legality in this chapter but with moral evaluation of trade agreements.

[77] These points are often understood in the context of a 'right to regulate'. The WTO Appellate Body said in *China–Audiovisuals* and *US–Clove Cigarettes* that GATT Art XX, which we discuss below, should be understood as a way to preserve WTO members' 'right to regulate'. Appellate Body Report, *China–Measures Affecting Trading Rights and Distribution Services for Certain Publications and Audiovisual Entertainment Products*, paras 136–38, 206–07, 218–33, WT/DS363/AB/R (21 Dec 2009); Appellate Body Report, *United States–Measures Affecting the Production and Sale of Clove Cigarettes*, paras 95–96, WT/DS406/AB/R (4 Apr 2012). Section 5 of China's WTO Accession Protocol, entitled 'Right to Trade' states in part: 'Without prejudice to China's right to regulate trade in a manner consistent with the WTO Agreement, China shall progressively liberalize the availability and scope of the right to trade, so that, within three years after accession, all enterprises in China shall have the right to trade in all goods throughout the customs territory of China, except for those goods listed in Annex 2A which continue to be subject to state trading in accordance with this Protocol.' Accession of the People's Republic of China, Decision of 10 Nov 2001, WT/L/432 (23 Nov 2001). It is unclear whether rights language in these contexts conveys the appropriate meaning. 'Right to trade' sounds reminiscent of the bad old days of war capitalism. Do we really want to use such terminology when referring to China? For a defence of the 'right to trade' as the central human right to address poverty, see JP Chauffeur, *The Power of Freedom: Uniting Human Rights and Development* (Cato Institute 2009).

[78] See J Cohen, 'Deliberation and Democratic Legitimacy' in A Hamlin and P Pettit (eds), *The Good Polity: Normative Analysis of the State* (Blackwell 1989), reprinted in RE Goodin and P Pettit (eds), *Contemporary Political Philosophy: An Anthology* (Blackwell 2006).

[79] See E Anderson, *Values in Ethics and Economics* (Harvard UP 1993) 141–67; M Sandel, *What Money Can't Buy: The Moral Limits of Markets* (Penguin 2013).

the border interact quite directly with social welfare concerns relating to labour,[80] environmental protection,[81] and access to healthcare.[82] It is to these forms of trade treaty making that we now turn.

3. A Future for International Trade Law: Markets with Justice

Trade treaties in the twenty-first century tend to come in three forms: the multilateral, the bilateral, and regional, and what can be called the 'twenty-first-century trade deal', which are something of a hybrid between a regional and multilateral agreement and which include both trade and investment regulation.[83] There can rationally be only one multilateral trading system open for accession to all states if conditions for membership are met and that is embodied in the World Trade Organization and its set of agreements. The bilateral and regional trade agreements tend to be the standard bilateral Free Trade Agreements such as the Korea–European Union Free Trade Agreement or regionally, the North American Free Trade Agreement (NAFTA).[84] In this classification and for trade purposes only the European Union can be classified as a customs union, which makes it different from NAFTA, a free trade agreement.[85]

For the twenty-first century trade deal, 'hybrid' may not fully capture what is happening in terms of membership. These deals are less than multilateral because their aim, at least initially, is not to include all states as members, but they conceivably could expand through accession if they do not maintain eligibility criteria (legal or political) based on the region in which a state happens to be located for accession purposes. An example of a twenty-first-century trade deal is the Trans-Pacific Partnership (TPP). Twelve states have signed the TPP but it is not yet in force: Australia, Brunei, Canada, Chile, Japan, Malaysia, Mexico, New Zealand, Peru, Singapore, the United States, and Vietnam. The total gross domestic product of these states as of

[80] See C Barry and SG Reddy, *International Trade and Labor Standards* (Columbia UP 2008).

[81] E Reid, *Balancing Human Rights, Environmental Protection and International Trade: Lessons from the EU Experience* (Hart 2014); BR Copeland and MS Taylor, *Trade and the Environment: Theory and Evidence* (Princeton UP 2015) (increased international trade *reduces* pollution).

[82] J Gibson, *Intellectual Property, Medicine and Health: Current Debates* (Routledge 2017).

[83] MK Lewis, 'The Trans-Pacific Partnership: New Paradigm or Wolf in Sheep's Clothing?' (2011) 34 Boston College International and Comparative Law Review 27, 28 ('The TPP is a new type of trade agreement. It does not fit into the more common molds of bilateral free trade agreements or plurilateral customs union ... The TPP has the potential to create a new paradigm for trade agreements').

[84] Free Trade Agreement between the European Union and its Member States and the Republic of Korea OJ L127, vol 54, 14 May 2011; NAFTA comprises the following: North American Free Trade Agreement, 32 ILM 289 and 605 (1993); North American Agreement on Environmental Cooperation, 32 ILM 1480 (1993); North American Agreement on Labor Cooperation, 32 ILM 1499 (1993); Understanding between the Parties to the North American Free Trade Agreement Concerning Chapter Eight—Emergency Action, 32 ILM 1519 (1993); Border Environment Cooperation Agreement, 32 ILM 1547 (1993).

[85] Of course, the European Union is much more than a customs union. Any basic text on EU law makes the point. See, eg, P Craig and G de Búrca, *EU Law: Text, Cases, and Materials* (6th edn, OUP 2015), in which the phrase 'customs union' does not appear.

the time of writing is about 40% of global GDP and one-third of world trade.[86] Another twenty-first-century trade deal is the Transatlantic Trade and Investment Partnership proposed between the European Union and the United States, potentially including 50% of global GDP and 30% of world trade.[87] These agreements are fluid and their classifications murky, particularly given recent changes in the Executive Branch in the United States. For example, the TPP may end up transforming into a Free Trade of the Asia Pacific Agreement.[88] These agreements differ from more traditional trade agreements in that they include investment, have more of an explicit focus on regulatory coherence, labour, and the environment, and include chapters on competition policy, small and medium-sized enterprises, state-owned enterprises, and transparency and corruption. They also include both substantial dispute settlement provisions for trade disputes and investor-state dispute settlement institutions for investment disputes.[89]

Beyond their formal structure, twenty-first-century deals are far more ambitious in scope and coverage than the traditional trade agreement.[90] Despite the more ambitious scope of emerging twenty-first-century trade agreements, these new agreements in trade (and investment) leave unchanged the core aspects of standard trade agreements and how they continue to prioritize power over right.[91] If they are to be evaluated by the standards developed in earlier chapters on how international law needs to comply with more robust demands for justice, they are normatively deficient in their core structure. They fail to comply with an insight about markets that is by now very basic: rules implementing non-market values are not exceptions to market rules or exceptional in their application to markets, but are constitutive of markets.[92] These values make markets what they are; they are not exceptions to the basic rules of the market. To conceptualize these values as intrusive in the market is to slip back into the contract model of international trade law critiqued in section 2. Given the move of contemporary trade agreements well inside the regulatory state and the social contract of states, sharp distinctions between global and domestic market institutions have dissolved and trade agreements are not exempt from meeting these moral imperatives. A trade agreement that fails to pay proper respect to non-market values is an intrusion that alienates persons because it violates the basic conditions for justice, whether these conditions are located in the social contract of the societies or in an international law justifiable to each person affected by it.

[86] JP Meltzer, 'From the Trans-Pacific Partnership to a Free Trade Agreement of the Asia-Pacific?' http://www.brookings.edu/blogs/future-development/posts/2015/05/05-tpp-trade-meltzer, 5 May 2015.

[87] Delegation of the European Union to the United States, TTIP fact sheet, http://www.euintheus.org/wp-content/uploads/2013/07/TTIP_Publicatiopn_85x11in_High_res.pdf

[88] See Pacific Economic Cooperation Council, Free Trade Area of the Asia-Pacific, http://www.pecc.org/research/ftaap

[89] For the TPP text, see https://ustr.gov/tpp. See Chapter 5 ('Foreign Investment').

[90] See LC Backer, 'The Trans-Pacific Partnership: Japan, China, the US, and the Emerging Shape of a New World Trade Regulatory Order' (2014) 13 Washington University Global Studies Law Review 49, 63.

[91] See Orford (n 65).

[92] Chapter 2 ('Confronting the Pathologies of International Law') deals with these issues.

One of the core structural defects in international trade agreements is this: international trade agreements allocate—distribute—gains and losses. They structure markets to produce winners and losers.[93] They compensate the winners in the form of market rewards. But they do not compensate the losers. Arguments about comparative advantage and the benefits of trade liberalization proceed on an assumption that states should aggregate gains and losses and justify trade agreements based on net gains to all of society. This sort of aggregation, however, can violate second personal obligations of justice set forth in Chapter 2 ('Confronting the Pathologies of International Law'). They can result in failure to show respect for persons who suffer harm from a trade agreement and have reasonable grounds to complain. When we drill down into the data, we find evidence that mutual gains from trade are not the only phenomenon at work; we also see a distribution of winners and losers that states have failed to evaluate on grounds of justice. States, moreover, have not stepped up in the domestic context to provide adjustment assistance to the losers.[94]

Nothing is stopping us other than our lack of imagination about the structure of cooperation in international trade to prevent us from using these insights to construct new agreements. What humans conceive as plausible for trade agreements is conditioned by the institutional reality of trade agreements that they have created in the past several centuries, as outlined in sections 1 and 2. The current state of affairs for trade agreements is that they fail to meet the demands of justice articulated in previous chapters.

Some twenty-first-century trade deals appear to be moving in the right direction but fall short because they fail to set standards that can be subject to accepted standards of legal accountability. They offer at best hortatory statements about areas the parties to the agreement can collaborate on in the future. They also emphasize that the only real way to structure a prosperous economy is in neoliberal terms and they fail to address the concerns that international economic judicial forums are ill-equipped to evaluate human rights issues (or some attempted equivalent) properly and fairly. The TPP Development chapter 23, with its rhetorical language on broad-based and inclusive growth, on women and growth, and on education, science and technology is an example of such a move. There are, in short, no teeth to any of these provisions. At best, they provide a built-in agenda for possible areas of collaboration between governments in a contingent future, if the TPP were to move forward.

To start with, what will be needed for liberalized trade and investment agreements to meet the demands of justice are institutional structures integrating trade, investment, and social justice into non-fragmented rule regimes. As explained

[93] Recent research on loss of manufacturing jobs as a result of important competition makes this point. JR Pierce and PK Schott, 'The Surprisingly Swift Decline of US Manufacturing Employment' (Apr 2015 draft), http://faculty.som.yale.edu/peterschott/files/research/papers/pierce_schott_pntr_512.pdf; DA Autor, D Dorn, GH Hanson, and J Song, 'Trade Adjustment: Worker Level Evidence' (2014) 129 Quarterly Journal of Economics 1799; I Colantone and P Stanig, 'The Real Reason the UK Voted for Brexit? Jobs Lost to Chinese Competition', *Washington Post* (7 July 2016).

[94] There is plenty of evidence to this effect. For a recent discussion, see 'Collateral Damage: The Impact of Free Trade' *The Economist* (30 July–5 Aug 2016) (discussing OECD findings and findings by economists Colantone and Stanig).

below, fragmentation inexorably leads to competing priorities. Tribunals and other bodies with limited remits are required to privilege their own jurisdiction and rules as supreme to all else. The result can be normative disorder, in which more important moral demands of justice are subordinated to a set of rules about trade or investment. Moral priorities get trumped by contract, with the result that the trade architecture enforces morally perverse principles such as a distributively unjust priority for the better off under which the rich get richer while the poor get poorer, or lead to violations of non-distributive moral principles that relate to the way people in a society understand their freedom, autonomy, and moral responsibilities in the world. Given the current failures to put in place non-fragmented rule regimes that robustly reflect modern conceptions of justice, normative disorder might be approached as a productive symptom of deep malaise that, as James Harrison argues, should not be papered over in an artificial attempt at coherence, but instead confronted to expose a common set of values.[95] This approach avoids legitimating the processes and decisions of tribunals based on purely superficial human rights considerations[96] and begins an honest exploration of frictions between the values and priorities of the different regimes. While it may not resolve the world's problems, it offers a framework of inquiry that opens up the possibility of real reconciliation.[97]

These issues are examined in more detail below in the context of the morals exception found in the GATT Article XX and GATS Article XIV.[98] These exceptions show us not only the way in which so-called 'non-trade values' are dealt with in trade agreements but more generally they offer good illustrations of how trade agreements contribute to a global economic order that subordinates right for a contract conception of the market around neoliberal notions.

These issues are also dealt with in the discussion below on labour standards for trade agreements. We uncover in efforts to regulate labour standards in trade agreements a paradox in the way the regulation of labour has transitioned from war capitalism but has in effect maintained a form of domination over labour. In the war capitalism era, labour migration to support multinational enterprise was often forced, often in the form of the slave trade. With the rise of industrial capitalism, we saw the rise of immigration restrictions. Today, labour is minimally regulated in the global trade order as to standards, but not as to movement, which is strictly the subject of national immigration law. The result is that we have a world of extreme capital mobility and extreme labour rigidity, so that capital, if it is to be used to produce goods and services, can move to where labour is cheapest. Trade agreements thus

[95] J Harrison, 'The Case for Investigative Legal Pluralism in the International Economic Law Linkages Debate: A Strategy for Enhancing International Legal Discourse' (2014) 1 London Review of International Law 115, 139 ('Only when the norms and standards of the two regimes have been applied to the situation in question should the legal inquiry proceed to the second stage, at which point there would be an analysis of whether the differing analytical lenses through which the problem has been viewed allow for a single finding that accommodates both normative visions, or does not').

[96] ibid 125. [97] ibid 135.

[98] General Agreement on Tariffs and Trade (GATT), 30 Oct 1947, 55 UNTS 194, Art XX; General Agreement on Trade in Services (GATS), 15 Apr 1994, 1869 UNTS 183, Art XIV.

create artificial comparative advantages; the structure of markets as determined by legal institutions in turn determines where products get made in the global supply chains that now permeate the globe. Radically liberal immigration policies that open borders to all comers are both politically impractical and insufficient because they do not provide for needed labour standards. Regardless of the immigration policies of states, it is therefore necessary for states to engage in cross-border cooperation on fair labour standards.

This chapter does not deal with provisions in the GATT and the WTO agreements for special and differential treatment for developing countries.[99] Special and differential treatment is principally a failed pre-Uruguay Round approach to promoting the interests of developing countries. In what is probably the most influential study of the old efforts within the GATT of preferential treatment, Robert Hudec characterized these efforts as 'form without substance',[100] devoid of legal language with authoritative force and justiciable standards.[101] At least three problems plague special and differential treatment rules. First, they specify special and differential treatment only for developing countries. Problems of justice found in the current trade architecture apply not only to states as an aggregated whole but to groups and even individuals within states. Second, they specify favoured treatment as something exceptional in the trade architecture. As explained below, one preferable option would be to write rules directly into the code of trade agreements that meet standards of justice. The aim should be to get the basic structure right in the first instance, not to get it wrong and then append dubious fixes. Third, special and differential treatment rules are too narrow because their aim is only to promote trade, when international agreements about trade must get the basic conditions of justice for economic arrangements between states right. Fourth and perhaps most importantly, they fail to produce any meaningful assistance through a predistributive scheme for developing countries. The approach here is to support a normative turn away from non-reciprocity exceptions and towards a basic restructuring of what constitutes an obligation in a trade agreement as a matter of the basic structure of those agreements.

[99] For an extensive treatment, see SE Rolland, *Development at the WTO* (OUP 2012) ch 6. Of course, the classic discussion is RE Hudec, *Developing Countries in the GATT Legal System* (Gower 1987), though Hudec opposed normative fairness standards for evaluating trade agreements. A new edition of Hudec's work was published in 2011, with an introduction by JM Finger. RE Hudec, *Developing Countries in the GATT Legal System* (CUP 2011).

[100] Hudec (n 99) ch 6.

[101] Though we disagree with Hudec's arguments about reliance on open markets alone to promote development, he was writing in the mid 1980s well before neoliberalism came to prominence and was working in the tradition of what John Ruggie calls embedded liberalism. JG Ruggie, 'International Regimes, Transactions, and Change: Embedded Liberalism in the Postwar Economic Order' (1982) 36 International Organization 379. For a masterful account of Hudec's views, and its relevance to contemporary trade order, see CL Lim, 'The Conventional Morality of Trade' in C Carmody, FJ Garcia, and J Linarelli (eds), *Global Justice and International Economic Law: Opportunities and Prospects* (CUP 2012) 129.

3.1 Policy pluralism and trade agreements

The initial chapters elaborated normative principles that should be at work in shaping international economic relations among states. In the international trade area, value pluralism between states has become a matter of some tension. The WTO Appellate Body decision in *European Communities—Measures Prohibiting the Importation and Marketing of Seal Products*[102] is a recent example of how the trade architecture handles conflicts between non-trade moral values and commitments to liberalized trade.[103] In that proceeding, Canada and Norway challenged the EU's ban of the importation of most seal products from these countries. The European Union based the ban at least partly on moral grounds relating to animal welfare. The EU seal regulations banned the importation of seal products into the European Union in all cases except for seal products resulting from hunts by Inuits and other indigenous communities that contribute to the subsistence of these communities. In *Seal Products*, the Appellate Body held that the Technical Barriers to Trade (TBT) Agreement did not apply to the EU seal regulations because they are not a 'technical regulation' under the TBT Agreement. The Appellate Body ruled that the EU regulations violated the most-favoured nation provision found in GATT Article I:1 because the European Union failed to extend the same advantages of the exception 'immediately and unconditionally' to seal products from Greenland. Finally, the Appellate Body ruled that the EU regulations fall within the scope of the public morals exception found in GATT Article XX as necessary to protect public morals, but the regulations lacked a rational relationship to the moral concerns that Europeans had about seal welfare. The defect in the EU regulations, according to the Appellate Body, was that the indigenous communities exception in the regulations failed to comply with the chapeau of GATT Article XX prohibiting arbitrary and unjustifiable discrimination in the application of the exception to WTO members.[104] Though the case could be seen as a partial success by animal welfare activists and those more generally holding the view that the WTO agreements should be more accommodating to non-trade values, the concerns elucidated in this section relate more basically to the structure of trade agreements generally, in which trade values are incorporated as core obligations while non-trade values have to be argued exceptionally and as defences to be justified for abrogating core trade obligations. This basic structure of the trade architecture is problematic from the standpoint of justice.

[102] Panel Report, *European Communities—Measures Prohibiting the Importation and Marketing of Seal Products*, WT/DS400/R (25 Nov 2013); Appellate Body Report, *European Communities—Measures Prohibiting the Importation and Marketing of Seal Products*, WT/DS401/R, 22 May 2014.

[103] As of the time of this writing the WTO Appellate Body issued a decision in *Colombia—Measures Relating to the Importation of Textile, Apparel and Footwear*, the most recent case involving the GATT Art XX(a) morals exception. Panel Report, *Colombia—Measures Relating to the Importation of Textile, Apparel and Footwear*, WT/DS461/R and Add 1 (27 Nov 2015); Appellate Body Report, *Colombia—Measures Relating to the Importation of Textile, Apparel and Footwear*, WT/DS461/AB/R and Add 1 (7 June 2016). The decision confirms the narrow interpretation the Appellate Body places on the public morals exception.

[104] For an explanation of the case, see R Bhala, DA Gantz, SB Keating, and BS Simões, 'WTO Case Review 2014' (2015) 32 Arizona Journal of International and Comparative Law 497.

The world is pluralistic along several lines relating to values and politics. Some societies are pluralistic within their borders, particularly if they embrace some version of a political liberalism in which a government is to strive to remain neutral as to a range of permissible ends of its citizens.[105] A substantial cross-border pluralism also exists, a pluralism among states. So, pluralism exists both within and among states. What precisely does the word pluralism refer to? The prevalent ways to understand pluralism are along political, legal, and moral lines.[106] Without getting bogged down in terminology, references to pluralism here are broadly to a kind of value pluralism as it is expressed in law and public policy. To assist in understanding the tension between trade and non-trade values, this kind of pluralism can be understood as a 'policy pluralism', a term to be used to refer to the differing conceptions of values to be found in what some call 'political' or 'institutional' morality[107] and how that morality either gets incorporated into the institutional structure of a states, including in its sources of law, or actually just *is* that institutional structure.[108] Coherence of the law of a given society with principles of political morality for that society is important. It has to do with the legitimacy of the law in that state to the state's citizens. It is, quite simply, a very basic requirement of any community that the rules applicable to its members be acceptable morally by those members as legitimate.

Policy pluralism plays out in international trade. Consider the basic moral principle of equality of opportunity, an ideal widely accepted in many societies, though widely disrespected in actual practice. The equality of opportunity principle is usually understood as a basic principle of distributive justice. Here is an example. States as diverse as South Africa and the United States implement some aspects of equality of opportunity in their societies through government procurement programmes designed to give preferences in procurement to firms owned by individuals from historically disadvantaged groups.[109] In contrast, the EU procurement Directives

[105] 'Political liberalism' here refers to Rawls' use of the term in his later work. J Rawls, *Political Liberalism* (2nd edn, Columbia UP 2005). A liberal society adheres to a theory of justice that is neutral among competing conceptions of the good. Justice is not based on a comprehensive theory of the good but on principles of right supporting the distribution of basic goods as all-purpose means for citizens to achieve whatever broadly permissible ends they choose to pursue. Political liberalism can support what Rawls called 'reasonable pluralism' in a society. A discussion about what liberalism entails is beyond this chapter's scope. For a recent discussion, see MC Nussbaum, 'Perfectionist Liberalism and Political Liberalism' (2011) 39 Philosophy and Public Affairs 3.

[106] Much has been written about these forms of pluralism. For the distinction between moral and political pluralism, see E Mason, 'Value Pluralism' *Stanford Encyclopedia of Philosophy* (summer 2015 edn), EN Zalta (ed), http://plato.stanford.edu/archives/sum2015/entries/value-pluralism. On legal pluralism, see BZ Tamanaha, 'Understanding Legal Pluralism: Past to Present, Local to Global' (2008) 30 Sydney Law Review 378.

[107] TW Pogge, 'Cosmopolitanism and Sovereignty' (1992) 103 Ethics 48.

[108] Dworkin makes the most well-known argument that law is a branch of morality. For Dworkin's later exposition, see R Dworkin, *Justice for Hedgehogs* (Harvard UP 2011). Another approach is to accept a distinction between law and morality and to argue that an important source of law's authority is in its moral legitimacy, or compliance with moral principles. See J Linarelli, 'Concept and Contract in the Future of International Law' (2015) 67 Rutgers University Law Review 61.

[109] See J Linarelli, 'The Limited Case for Permitting SME Procurement Preferences in the WTO Agreement on Government Procurement' in S Arrowsmith and RD Anderson (eds), *The WTO Regime on Government Procurement: Challenge and Reform* (CUP 2011) ch 15; C McCrudden, *Buying Social Justice: Equality, Government Procurement and Legal Change* (OUP 2007).

generally prohibit EU member states from using such preferences. In the European Union, such preferences are unlawful forms of protectionism. In the current WTO Agreement on Government Procurement context, a WTO member must be a powerful state like the United States to be in a position to resist pressures to dismantle these programmes to comply with GPA commitments. The United States can put sufficient dollar amounts of procurements on the WTO negotiating table yet still carve out these 'set aside' procurements for protected treatment. If the trade architecture relies only on the bargaining power of states to promote these sorts of socio-economic programmes, then only powerful states will be able to maintain these programmes for their people. We have justice only for the rich and powerful. This state of affairs is morally disordered, reducing moral choice to power and interest.

Policy pluralism certainly does include distributive justice, but it also goes beyond it. The *Seal Products* dispute offers an example of law explicitly justified on moral grounds or what Robert Howse, Joanna Langille, and Katie Sykes call 'non-instrumental moral values'.[110] A number of other issues that have come before the WTO Dispute Settlement Body are at bottom about policy pluralism, and often implicate values embedded in the political morality of states as that concept is explicated above.

The European Union has banned hormone-treated beef in various ways since 1981, eventually resulting in rulings from the WTO dispute settlement body in 1997 and 2008, and eventually ending in a memorandum of understanding between the United States and the European Union in May 2009.[111] At issue in the *EU–Beef Hormones* case were not only issues relating to economics and the private interests of powerful interest groups such as EU farmers, but the way that risk is understood in societies and the relationship of culture to food and food security.[112]

Another example of moral values entering into international trade is in the essential medicines debate relating to TRIPs, in which there have been clashes between access to medicines—sometimes framed as the human right to health—and the property rights of owners of intellectual property in pharmaceuticals.[113] The essential medicines–intellectual property clash plays out in a way that mixes power, state interest, lobbying, and interest group capture of public officials, the human right

[110] R Howse, J Langille, and K Sykes, 'Pluralism in Practice: Moral Legislation and the Law of the WTO After *Seal Products*' (2015) 48 George Washington International Law Review 81; R Howse and J Langille, 'Permitting Pluralism: The Seal Products Dispute and Why the WTO Should Accept Trade Restrictions Justified by Noninstrumental Moral Values' (2012) 37 Yale Journal of International Law 367. For a contrasting peremptory norms argument as opposed to a moral values argument, see H Andersen, 'Protection of Non-Trade Values in WTO Appellate Body Jurisprudence: Exceptions, Economic Arguments, and Eluding Questions' (2015) 18 JIEL 383.

[111] For a summary of *European Communities—Measures Concerning Meat and Meat Products (Hormones)* dispute settlement proceedings, see https://www.wto.org/english/tratop_e/dispu_e/cases_e/ds26_e.htm

[112] See MA Echols, *Food Safety and the WTO: The Interplay of Culture, Science and Technology* (Kluwer 2001); J Peel, *Science and Risk Regulation in International Law* (CUP 2010) 220–24.

[113] See DA Desierto, *Public Policy in International Economic Law: The ICESCR in Trade, Finance, and Investment* (OUP 2015) 161–67.

of 'everyone to the highest attainable standard of physical and mental health', and principles of justice on access to healthcare.[114]

These clashes are predictable. Policy pluralism across societies leads to policy clashes internationally because of the way the trade architecture interjects into domestic policy space and the way in which it was developed in parallel to other international legal regimes, such as human rights law. It is intentionally designed to interject into domestic policy space and to operate based on trade values.[115] Political scientist Daniel Kono has shown that democracy in states leads to lower tariff barriers and higher non-tariff barriers.[116] The discussions in the twenty-first century trade deal are dominated by the topics of 'regulatory coherence' or 'regulatory cooperation', which refer to the harmonization of regulatory practices across state borders. Regulatory coherence between the EU and the US regulatory systems is an entire chapter in the proposed TPIP.[117] The proposed TTIP and agreements like it reach far into the regulatory state and affect the principles of political morality that are at play in each state.

The current structure of the trade architecture handles these issues poorly because it still prioritizes the contract approach and its defective understanding of the market above all else, when in fact its reach goes far beyond these concepts. The core misunderstanding of the role of trade agreements is as much in the way they are characterized as about liberalizing and freeing up trade. In substance they go

[114] For early influential treatments of healthcare and justice, see N Daniels, *Just Health: Meeting Health Needs Fairly* (CUP 2008); N Daniels, *Just Health Care* (CUP 1985).

Colombia, for example, advised Novartis it would grant a compulsory licence for generic manufacturers to produce the cancer medicine Gleevec unless Novartis lowered the price of the drug. Colombia argued that the price Novartis charges for Gleevec is extreme and has threatened to bring the Colombian healthcare system into financial crisis. Novartis is a multinational pharmaceutical company headquartered in Switzerland. The pressure on the Colombian government from both the Swiss and US governments was significant. The US government announced it would reconsider granting financial aid for the peace process in Colombia if the Colombian government were to grant the compulsory licence. K Vyas, 'Colombia Threatens to Override Novartis's Patent on Gleevec' *Wall Street Journal* (20 May 2016); E Silverman, 'Colombia Plans to Unilaterally Lower the Cost of a Novartis Cancer Drug' https://www.statnews.com/pharmalot/2016/06/09/colombia-novartis-gleevec, 9 June 2016.

[115] That international trade, as per the Preamble of the Marrakesh Agreement Establishing the WTO, is meant to be a means to the ends of 'raising standards of living, ensuring full employment and a large and steadily growing volume of real income and effective demand, and expanding the production of and trade in goods and services, while allowing for the optimal use of the world's resources in accordance with the objective of sustainable development', is partly a gesture to some minimum form of justice that has not translated into meaningful law. See also the UN Committee on Economic, Social and Cultural Trade imploring that 'Trade liberalization must be understood as a means, not an end. The end which trade liberalization should serve is the objective of human well-being to which the international human rights instruments give legal expression.' CESCR, Statement to the Third Ministerial Conference of the WTO (2000) para 6.

[116] DY Kono, 'Optimal Obfuscation: Democracy and Trade Policy Transparency' (2006) 100 American Political Science Review 369.

[117] See A Alemanno, 'The Regulatory Cooperation Chapter of the Transatlantic Trade and Investment Partnership: Institutional Structures and Democratic Consequences' (2015) 18 JIEL 625; TJ Bollyky, 'Regulatory Coherence in the Trans-Pacific Partnership Talks' in CL Lim, D Elms, and P Low (eds), *The Trans-Pacific Partnership: A Quest for a 21st Century Trade Agreement* (CUP 2012) 171.

far beyond the path dependencies of the contract model. They are also about how governments distribute the burdens and benefits of markets and on what values get prioritized in societies. Trade agreements connect to how governments structure their societies in an important area of human activity that affects not only transactions for goods and services but the core values of societies reaching beyond that which is valued in transactions.

As explained above in connection with the *Seal Products* case, contemporary trade agreements usually contain a 'morals exception' permitting parties to the agreement to deviate from basic trade obligations, but only in limited and exceptional cases. The most prominent of these provisions, addressed in *Seal Products*, is GATT Article XX, entitled 'General Exceptions', provides:

> Subject to the requirement that such measures are not applied in a manner which would constitute a means of arbitrary or unjustifiable discrimination between countries where the same conditions prevail, or a disguised restriction on international trade, nothing in this Agreement shall be construed to prevent the adoption or enforcement by any contracting party of measures ... (*a*) necessary to protect public morals.[118]

General exceptions provisions like GATT Article XX enumerate other exceptions that do not explicitly ground in 'morals' but nevertheless could be said to be so grounded. Clause (b) permits exceptions from trade commitments 'necessary to protect human, animal or plant life or health'. Clause (g) relates to the conservation of natural resources.[119]

In a contract approach to trade treaties, general exceptions articles are meant to deal with the problem of incomplete contracting. Conceptualizing treaties in the economic language of contracts constrains our thinking about trade treaties as involving primarily issues associated with the institutions of transacting and not much else. The general exceptions provisions illustrate problems in the contract approach.

Let us look at the basic structural problems associated with trade agreements to try to bring the problem into clearer focus. Recall the basic features of the contract approach, in which justice is a matter for inside the state only and what happens outside is subject to at most very basic minimum moral demands. We have labelled this the inside–outside distinction in the preceding section. In the prevailing structure of trade agreements, morality comes in as an exception to obligations structuring markets in particular ways under the relevant trade agreement. States are obligated to liberalize as a matter of priority over all else. They agree *ex ante* on what markets they will open to trade. Once markets are structured under a trade agreement, they trump whatever moral concerns might exist or which might later come to exist in domestic regulation or even in constitutions, unless a state can show its non-trade values as expressed in its domestic law are deserving of an exception from the obligations of the trade agreement. The state whose market interests are

118 General Agreement on Tariffs and Trade, 30 Oct 1947, 55 UNTS 194, Art XX.

119 The TBT permits regulation to pursue 'legitimate objectives' to protect human, animal or plant life, or health. Andersen (n 110) 395–96.

adversely affected can initiate a dispute settlement proceeding in which it argues that the other state has breached its obligations under the trade agreement. So, the issues in dispute are drawn between a claimant arguing that core obligations have been violated and that it has been injured and is deserving of a remedy, and between a respondent arguing that some exception applies, relieving it of its obligation to comply with firm obligations found in the trade agreement. In the parlance of litigation, the respondent state argues public morals as a defence against the petitioner state's claim of prima facie violation.[120]

The obligation–exception/defence structure is generalizable beyond the morals exception. The essential medicines provisions in TRIPs share a similar structure, with a broad and vigorous set of property rights taking the centre stage, with exceptions or carveouts for very limited cases demanded by human rights obligations, although not explicitly framed in those terms.[121]

This obligation-exception/defence structure produces a contradiction in the fundamentals of the trade architecture: trade agreements are designed around the notion that justice is a matter for states and their social contracts, but trade agreements regulate justice and can even deny domestic law meant to express the institutional morality of a society its very legality. Trade institutions like the WTO claim not to deal with institutional or political morality but in fact do so very concretely.

One of the argumentative strategies that trade lawyers have used in an attempt to dissolve this contradiction is to develop an argument that states have a 'right to regulate' the domestic policy space.[122] The right to regulate argument is unhelpful because it simply shifts the discussion towards another contradiction between a right to regulate and a 'right to trade'. Though offered benevolently as a way to promote the interests of developing countries,[123] the right to trade argument is problematic because it harkens back to the seventeenth century when states justified using force to open trade routes on grounds of the very strange doctrine discussed above. The right to regulate versus right to trade dichotomy also leads to an infinite regress and imprecision in making these rights equal priorities and in making mysterious the real values at stake that make one or the other, international trade or domestic regulation, subordinate to the other depending on the context. The irony

120 Howse, Langille, and Sykes (n 110) 97.

121 For example, the WTO Doha Declaration on TRIPs and Public Health (WT/MIN(01)/DEC/2, 14 Nov 2001) in which the right of WTO members to use the flexibilities provided in the TRIPs agreement is reaffirmed, and the Amendment to the TRIPs Agreement of 2005 (WT/L/641, 6 Dec 2005) which is meant to make it easier for poorer countries to obtain cheaper generic versions of patented medicines where they lack domestic manufacturing capacity to produce them, include no explicit reference to the human right to health, as found in Article 12 of the International Covenant on Economic, Social and Cultural Rights or Articles 3, 23–25 of the UN Convention on the Rights of the Child.

122 B Rigod, *Optimal Regulation and the Law of International Trade: The Interface between the Right to Regulate and WTO Law* (CUP 2015); JP Trachtman, *The International Economic Law Revolution and the Right to Regulate* (Cameron May 2007). For a related discussion in international investment law, see LW Mouyal, *International Investment Law and the Right to Regulate: A Human Rights Perspective* (Routledge 2016); C Titi, *The Right to Regulate in International Investment Law* (Nomos/Hart 2014).

123 See E Jones, 'The Right to Trade: A Mechanism for Revitalising Pro-Development WTO Negotiations?' (2013) 99 Commonwealth Trade Topics; JE Stiglitz and A Charlton, 'The Right to Trade: A Report for the Commonwealth Secretariat on Aid for Trade' (Aug 2012).

of course is that the right of a government to regulate in the public interest needs to be asserted at all and indicates just how far we have strayed from a justice-based international legal order.

3.2 Labour rights

The relationship between trade agreements and labour exists in a web of rules promoting forms of economic exchange over the rights of persons who depend on employment for basic income and even survival in some cases. Trade agreements and institutions fail on both moral and economic grounds when it comes to labour. The movement to get trade agreements in a position to respect or recognize labour rights offers a classic example of how a limited notion of market trumps right in trade agreements. These are not in any sense 'free' markets as idealized by libertarians and some economists but a highly stylized form of exchange that in crucial respects are involuntary on one side of the exchange. Capital is very mobile and enjoys substantial protections and freedoms, as Chapters 5 ('Foreign Investment') and 6 ('Global Finance') on investment and finance respectively explain, but many individuals working for a wage either as an employee or as an independent contractor enjoys neither such guarantees of protection nor of freedom of movement. We address the trumping of right by contract in two features of the institutional order governing trade: the failure to protect labour and the restrictions on freedom of movement.

The sensible starting point for understanding labour protections would seem to be in human rights law, but human rights approaches seem to have largely failed to deliver, for reasons likely to do with the moral disorder found in institutions of the global economy than with defects in human rights law. The four core labour standards[124] that have traditionally been understood to embody human rights are important and necessary and even while they provide only basic minimums they are still often violated. The core standards express basic human rights obligations because they reflect a widespread consensus, though their breach in practice is all too common. They are widely considered to be part of the panoply of economic and social rights in international human rights law.[125] The International Labour Organization (ILO), the oldest human rights organization, has focused its work on these core standards. The ILO, established in 1919 to eliminate 'injustice, hardship and privation' of workers, was a western response to Communism and the Bolshevik Revolution of 1917.[126] The ILO's work focuses mainly in the progressive

[124] The four core labour rights established in the ILO system are: (1) 'freedom of association and effective recognition of the right to collective bargaining'; (2) 'elimination of all forms of forced or compulsory labour'; (3) 'effective abolishment of child labour'; and (4) 'elimination of discrimination in respect of employment and occupation'. ILO Declaration on Fundamental Principles and Rights at Work and Its Follow-up, 18 June 1998, 37 ILM 1237, annex revised 15 June 2010.

[125] See V Mantouvalou, 'Are Labour Rights Human Rights?' (2012) 3 European Labour Law Journal 151; MA Pagnattaro, 'Labor Rights are Human Rights: Direct Action is Critical in Supply Chains and Trade Policy' (2013) 10 South Carolina Journal of International Law and Business 1.

[126] G Rodgers, E Lee, L Swepston, and J Van Daele, *The International Labour Organization and the Quest for Social Justice, 1919–2009* (Cornell UP/ILO 2009).

development of labour standards and in the monitoring of these standards on the basis of a number of instruments.

This is not the place for a comprehensive review of the progress of labour rights internationally, but suffice it to say that the end result has been a compartmentalization that has served to support a neoliberal international economic order. This claim can be justified on two grounds. First, trade agreements provide no real labour protections. In fact, they do the opposite. Like socio-economic rights more generally, core labour protections are given subordinate status in a trading system that prioritizes particular kinds of economic exchange over right.[127] Second, multinational enterprises have developed and employed strategies effectively to immunize themselves from hard legal obligations related to labour protections through outsourcing and offshoring, at least where relatively unskilled or semi-skilled labour is at issue. Labour rights work against the exploitative demands of international trade has largely been sidelined.

As to the first ground, the WTO website itself says it all, in a clear and candid way, to the effect that the WTO has almost nothing to say or do with respect to labour standards. It explains: 'There is a clear consensus' about 'a narrower set of internationally recognized "core" standards—freedom of association, no forced labour, no child labour, and no discrimination at work (including gender discrimination)' but beyond that no concern exists about the relevance of labour standards to trade agreements.[128] The WTO necessarily concedes that the ILO is the competent body to deal with labour standards and that the two organizations collaborate on matters of 'coherence' in 'global economic policy-making' but 'beyond that it is not easy for them to agree, and the question of international enforcement is a minefield'.[129]

The 1996 Singapore Ministerial Declaration appears to sum up the WTO position:

> We renew our commitment to the observance of internationally recognized core labour standards. The International Labour Organization (ILO) is the competent body to set and deal with these standards, and we affirm our support for its work in promoting them. We believe that economic growth and development fostered by increased trade and further trade liberalization contribute to the promotion of these standards. We reject the use of labour standards for protectionist purposes, and agree that the comparative advantage of countries, particularly low-wage developing countries, must in no way be put into question. In this regard, we note that the WTO and ILO Secretariats will continue their existing collaboration.[130]

[127] This is despite the fact that some free trade agreements outside of the WTO include labour standards, albeit in different forms (http://www.ilo.org/global/standards/information-resources-and-publications/free-trade-agreements-and-labour-rights/lang--en/index.htm) and with little evidence of their effectiveness. On the effectiveness, see F de Ville, J Orbie, and L Van den Putte, *TTIP and Labour Standards*, European Parliament, Directorate-General for Internal Policies, IP/A/EMPL/2015-07, June 2016, http://www.ilo.org/global/standards/information-resources-and-publications/free-trade-agreements-and-labour-rights/lang--en/index.htm

[128] Labour standards: consensus, coherence, and controversy, https://www.wto.org/english/thewto_e/whatis_e/tif_e/bey5_e.htm

[129] ibid.

[130] Singapore Ministerial Declaration, adopted 13 Dec 1996, https://www.wto.org/english/news_e/pres96_e/wtodec.htm

The Declaration sets forth standard neoliberal ideology about the subordination of right to a peculiar notion of market reflecting a view that is now under widespread scrutiny even by economists. It provides for a neoclassical vision of economics that is out of step with contemporary thinking about the role of labour protections in an economy and in a society. Neither economic growth nor increased trade reliably promote labour standards and in fact the causation runs in the opposite direction: labour standards promote economic growth.[131] The Declaration relies on a radically anti-empirical notion,[132] defying what we plainly know about inequality and about how economic measures often aggregate data in ways that mask deep structural injustice.[133] The assertion that labour protections serve as potential protectionist devices reflects a skewed and incomplete view of the role of labour standards, one which takes sides in a manner antithetical to meeting the demands of justice in and across societies. The Declaration relies on an ideological notion that labour protections somehow 'intrude' on markets when in fact they and other rules are actually constitutive of markets.[134] Finally, the comparative advantage argument is a loser, even on the most conservative of economic grounds. Comparative advantage is not at work in trade agreements. Trade agreements are about distribution not economic efficiency. If they were about efficiency, they would liberalize labour movements. They do the opposite. In sum, the Singapore Declaration reflects a way of thinking about trade agreements that is ideological, neither politically nor morally acceptable, inconsistent with international human rights standards and not supported by economic evidence. Perhaps most tragically, the rejection of labour standards in the WTO comes at the behest of developing countries who have ignored findings that compliance with international labour standards often accompanies improvements in productivity and economic performance, and, moreover, have bought into the idea that exploitation can be justified on the basis of aggregate benefit and alleged aggregate benefit at that.[135]

Moving on to business practices, multinational enterprises use trade agreements in combination with domestic law to alter the terms of trade in a way that is severely

[131] For a recent survey of the evidence and literature, see S Deakin, 'The Contribution of Labour Law to Economic Development and Growth' Centre for Business Research, University of Cambridge Working Paper No 478, Mar 2016.

[132] See Somers (n 6) 2.

[133] Though the literature on these issues in political theory has a long vintage (see Chapter 2 ('Confronting the Pathologies of International Law')), the economic literature only began to emerge in the past several years. On the globalization of inequality, see F Bourguignon, *The Globalization of Inequality* (Princeton UP 2015), among other sources. Aggregation has long been a quandary addressed in moral theory. It is only beginning to get attention in economics. Says Angus Deaton: 'Averages are no consolation to those who have been left behind.' A Deaton, *The Great Escape: Health, Wealth, and the Origins of Inequality* (Princeton UP 2013) 219.

[134] See Chapter 1 ('The Legal Rendering of Immiseration') at 20–21 and Chapter 2 ('Confronting the Pathologies of International Law') at 40. A recent very clear explication of these points can be found in R Reich, *Saving Capitalism* (Icon 2016) ch 1.

[135] On the violation of labour rights as well as the rights of women, who make up most workers in Export Processing Zones, see, eg, *Export Processing Zones—Symbols of Exploitation and a Development Dead—End* (International Confederation of Free Trade Unions, Sept 2003), http://www.newunionism.net/library/internationalism/ICFTU%20-%20Export%20Processing%20Zones%20-%202003.pdf.

detrimental to workers. International economic treaties in trade and investment combine in a way that provides many benefits to capital but none to labour: capital is mobile and protected, but labour is immobile and unprotected. Add to this the practice of outsourcing:[136] multinational enterprises use contracting to insulate themselves from legal accountability to workers in an employer–employee relationship.

Companies like Wal-Mart outsource production of their brands to independent contractors in low-wage countries. This is not unique to Wal-Mart. Apple, for example, makes not a single computer, iPad, or other device it sells. Rather, it outsources manufacturing to independent contractors in countries with low labour protections and low wages. There is also the claim that firms like Wal-Mart and Apple 'offshore' jobs away from the United States,[137] but that characterization depends on whether the jobs were ever in the United States in the first place. The typical multinational enterprise knows no patriotic loyalties even though they benefit greatly from protection by their home state. They do not consider themselves as compatriots owing duties of justice to other persons in the political community, however that community is understood. Their multinational status overrides community interests whenever their self-interest so directs. What drives their operations are concepts like cost, profit, and revenue and not allegiance, association, or membership. Apple, for example, made a deal with the Irish government to headquarter its financial holding company for all its international subsidiaries in Ireland and pay only 2% in tax to Ireland.[138] Many companies set up financial holding companies in offshore financial centres like the Cayman Islands, Luxembourg, and Panama.[139]

The US case of *Doe I v Wal-Mart Stores, Inc*[140] offers an example of how multinational enterprises operate in this environment. Employees of Wal-Mart's suppliers in countries such as China, Bangladesh, Indonesia, Swaziland, and Nicaragua sued Wal-Mart in a federal court in California, seeking to hold Wal-Mart liable for injuries the employees suffered as a result of breaches of voluntary codes of conduct by Wal-Mart's suppliers. The essence of the holding by the United States Court of Appeals for the Ninth Circuit was that these employees were not intended to be third party beneficiaries under the contract between Wal-Mart and its suppliers and that any cause of action would be, as a matter of contract, between Wal-Mart and its suppliers. This case illustrates how the contract approach to the trade architecture operates even beyond trade agreements themselves.

The law in this combination results in an institutional structure that fails to comply with the demands of justice. It creates a situation in which economic arrangements of a peculiar kind take priority over principles of right having to do with

136 MJ Zimmer, 'Inequality, Individualized Risk, and Insecurity' (2013) Wisconsin Law Review 1, 9–10.

137 ibid.

138 ND Schwartz, 'Apple's Web of Tax Shelters Saved It Billions, Panel Finds' *New York Times* (20 May 2013).

139 For a recent discussion, see G Zucman, *The Hidden Wealth of Nations: The Scourge of Tax Havens* (University of Chicago Press 2015).

140 572 F.3d 677 (9th Cir 2009).

justice, equality, non-domination, and freedom from exploitation. These economic arrangements are fundamentally distributive at their core, designed to produce disproportionate benefits for multinational enterprises to exploit lax labour protections and low wages.

4. Pathological Politics

Politics within states and the negotiation of trade agreements between states link in various ways. In well-understood models from political economy, organized interest groups use their influence to direct trade policy towards restricting imports, expanding exports, or both.[141] Markets get structured in trade agreements. The distinction between 'free' versus 'protected' markets therefore fails to do much work. Now that trade agreements intrude deeply into domestic policy as a form of regulatory law, as explained above, the role of interest groups in international trade negotiations is becoming less distinct from their role in developing domestic legislation.[142] Power determines how markets are structured. The power in issue is that of powerful states and powerful interest groups within these states.

These arguments are often used to argue in solely economic terms against protectionism. When this literature is examined from the standpoint of a normative model of politics to evaluate what politics ought to be about and to get clear on the moral duties states owe and to whom, the focus shifts to elucidating an important insight about the potential effects of domestic politics on international trade agreements: that of producing trade agreements that harm particular groups and persons. Indeed, some accounts support the argument that trade agreements kill the poor.[143] The result is a situation in which politics is pathological—it brings about real injury and international trade law is a manifestation of this pathology. What might be seen positively as a form of participation in government by corporations is really a form of predation leading to deprivation of those most in need of justice in trade agreements.

The WTO Agriculture Agreement offers a clear example of how a trade agreement can inflict serious harm on the poor in low-income countries. Agriculture is a demonstration of how the world trade architecture is not about free trade but about distribution of advantages and disadvantages through a coercively structured legal order. It cannot be said that comparative advantage or 'free trade' is at work in agriculture. As agricultural economist G Edward Schuch explains: 'much of the world's

[141] For insights from the political economy literature, see GM Grossman and E Helpman, *Interest Groups and Trade Policy* (Princeton UP 2002); ED Mansfield and HV Milner, *Votes, Vetoes, and the Political Economy of International Trade Agreements* (Princeton UP 2012); RE Baldwin, 'The Political Economy of Trade Policy' (1989) 3 Journal of Economic Perspectives 119. See Chapter 6 ('Global Finance') at 208–211 for a similar discussion of regulatory capture by banks.

[142] See S Lester, 'Applying Public Choice Theory to Trade Negotiations and Agreements' draft working paper dated 10 May 2016, http://law.unimelb.edu.au/__data/assets/pdf_file/0005/1954139/Lester,-Public-Choice.pdf

[143] For a survey of the issues, see C Barry and G Øverland, 'Are Trade Subsidies and Tariffs Killing the Global Poor?' (2012) 79 Social Research 865.

agricultural output is produced in the wrong places'.[144] The WTO Agriculture Agreement illustrates how trade agreements are about distribution. The Agreement perpetuates subsidies in rich states, dividing up their markets while failing to deal adequately with the potential for developing countries, in which the agricultural sector accounts for much higher levels of employment, to develop their exports.[145] Powerful states have long maintained a variety of domestic subsidies, price support mechanisms, supply management schemes to deal with overproduction when prices are supported, and direct payments to agricultural producers.[146] The WTO Agriculture Agreement (and agreements like it) imposes a reverse difference principle, a priority for the better off, further enriching the rich at the expense of the poor. The consensus on these points is widespread and accepted by a diversity of sources, from those who argue for market liberalization to those who argue for trade agreements to be subject to the demands of justice.[147]

As discussed, TRIPs is another example of a harm-producing trade agreement.[148] Deaths from HIV/AIDS in developing countries given the unaffordability of antiretroviral drugs under TRIPs is one stark example of the way in which intellectual property rights are protected at the expense of human lives,[149] far beyond what should be tenable in any just community.

Neoliberal domestic politics in high income countries brought this state of affairs into existence. If we look at the state of affairs in politics of high-income countries in the West in the past several decades, we can see powerful interests engaging increasingly in rent-seeking to pressure institutions around neoliberal policies.

[144] GE Schuh, 'Developing Country Interests in WTO Agricultural Economic Policy' in D Kenney and JD Southwick (eds), *The Political Economy of International Trade Law: Essays in Honor of Robert E Hudec* (CUP 2002) 435.

[145] See MJ Trebilcock, R Howse, and A Eliason, *The Regulation of International Trade* (4th edn, Routledge 2013) 467.

[146] MJ Trebilcock and K Pue, 'The Puzzle of Agricultural Exceptionalism in International Trade Policy' (2015) 18 JIEL 233.

[147] For a sampling of research, see CG Gonzalez, 'World Poverty and Food Security' (2015) 3 Penn State University Journal of International Law and International Affairs 56; VH Smith, 'Should Washington End Agriculture Subsidies?' *Wall Street Journal* (12 July 2015); M Risse, *On Global Justice* (Princeton UP 2012) 261–78; Barry and Øverland (n 143); DA Sumner, 'Picking on the Poor: How US Agricultural Policy Hurts the Developing World' in *American Boondoggle: Fixing the 2012 Farm Bill* (American Enterprise Institute 2012); CG Gonzalez, 'Trade Liberalization, Food Security, and the Environment: The Neoliberal Threat to Sustainable Rural Development' (2004) 14 Transnational Law and Contemporary Problems 419; J Norberg, 'American and European Protectionism is Killing Poor Countries and Their People' http://www.cato.org/publications/commentary/american-european-protectionism-is-killing-poor-countries-their-people; Schuh (n 144); CG Gonzalez, 'Institutionalising Inequality: The WTO, Agriculture and Developing Countries' (2002) 27 Columbia Journal of Environmental Law 433.

[148] SK Sell, *Private Power, Public Law: The Globalisation of Intellectual Property Rights* (CUP 2008); TW Pogge, *World Poverty and Human Rights* (2nd edn, Polity 2003) 222–61.

[149] CESCR, General Comment No17, *The right of everyone to benefit from the protection of the moral and material interests resulting from any scientific, literary or artistic production of which he or she is the author (article 15, paragraph 1(c), of the Covenant)* UN Doc E/C.12/GC/17, 12 Jan 2006, para 35. The time it took to facilitate access under TRIPs aside, as described above, strong political pressures remain that limit the use of flexibilities.

International trade was, and remains, at the centre of these moves.[150] The connection back to war capitalism, with the organs of state pushing the commercial interests of their companies even if the outcomes result in injustice, harm, and even death to others, seems evident. International law, albeit in a different and more positive form of law, is used to justify various forms of modern-day war capitalism.

5. Concluding Remarks

Bringing normative ideals beyond those of capitalism into the global trade architecture is an ongoing project. The problem is rooted in history. With its foundations in war capitalism, it has left us with the notion that trade reflects values to be prioritized among all others. It has left us with an outdated structure for trade agreements. It has left us with a limited way of thinking about the kind of global cooperation that is truly needed for international trade. The old models were designed for a world comprising a select club of states concerned primarily with their coexistence so the only real issues are border measures such as tariffs and duties. This is the so-called 'contract' model of trade agreements. But contemporary trade agreements intrude into the regulatory state and the domestic social contract. The old contract-based models cannot be made feasible in a world in need of the kind of cooperation that a contractual bargain cannot provide. Trade agreements have not taken on what might be called a moral consensus that immiserating provisions in trade agreements are impermissible regardless of whose interests they protect and that trade agreements are subject to the demands of justice which would make them far more sensible as instruments for international cooperation.

[150] 'Who Lobbies Most on TTIP?' http://corporateeurope.org/international-trade/2014/07/who-lobbies-most-ttip, 8 July 2014; 'TTIP: A Corporate Lobbying Paradise' http://corporateeurope.org/international-trade/2015/07/ttip-corporate-lobbying-paradise, 14 July 2015; VK Aggarwal and SJ Evenett, 'US Trade Lobbying Strategy for the 21st Century' *Harvard Business Review* (5 July 2011); K Gawande and B Hoekman, 'Lobbying and Agricultural Trade Policy in the United States' (2006) 60 International Organization 527; W Grant, 'The Politics of Agricultural Trade' in M Cardwell, MT Grossman, and CP Rodgers (eds), *Agriculture and International Trade: Law, Policy and the WTO* (CABI 2003) 49–68.

5

Foreign Investment

Property, Contract, and Protecting Private Power

The international law on the protection of foreign investment has been constructed on a series of premises that are reminiscent of the imperial system of international law. The way these premises were developed has been dealt with in Chapters 3 ('The End of Empire and the Search for Justice: NIEO and Beyond') and 4 ('International Trade'). Imperial international law justified colonialism on paternalistic grounds and on grounds of natural rights while controlling vast numbers of people. The labour of the colonial people profited the imperial power in producing new crops like tea, coffee, and rubber, forcing their modes of life and exchange into new modes of economic organization that served the multinational enterprises of the day. European colonial powers forcibly altered existing patterns of land holding to accommodate new crops. Chapter 4 outlines the forcible reorganization of the production and trade of cotton, which required removal of production from India and the creation of the slave economy in the New World to which it was transferred. Sugar required massive numbers of slaves in the Caribbean and elsewhere.[1] Tea was produced in India. The opium grown in India was traded with China. The opium trade was opened through force. It funded the administration of India and other Asian colonies. There was migration of labour within the imperial system so that new crops like sugar could be produced. Such migrations altered the ethnic composition of the colonies. The needs of the colonial people provided markets for traders from the metropolitan states, textiles being the classic example. The natural resources of the colonies provided the raw materials to drive the industries of the imperial states. The structure that was created was wholly beneficial to the imperial state.[2]

International law in its formulation of the time played a substantial role in compelling these modes of economic globalization. The imperial system of international law was constructed on the fictional division of the world based on standards of

[1] See Chapter 4 ('International Trade') at 112–127.

[2] Historian Niall Ferguson seeks to refute these views. His view is that the imperial system benefited the colonies by creating new transport systems such as railways and built up the educational systems of the colonies. N Ferguson, *The Empire: How Britain Made the Modern World* (Allen Lane 2003). There are, however, other more compelling accounts that find the historical evidence to be otherwise. Chapter 4 offers just such an account from S Beckert, *Empire of Cotton: A Global History* (Vintage 2015), identifying an early form of 'war capitalism' associated with empire and colonization. Beckert's work reflects a broader trend towards exploring the connections of contemporary capitalism to slavery.

civilization.[3] European states alone enjoyed personality in international law. They were entitled to subjugate other people on the myth that, enjoying higher standards of civilization, they had a duty to lead the 'lesser breed without the Law'[4] into the same standard of civilization. To accomplish these aims, subjugation was necessary. The justification for conquest of established communities and the occupation of lands of nomadic or aboriginal people on the ground that they constituted *terra nullius* advanced colonialism.[5] And, as explained in Chapter 4, Europeans asserted a natural right of freedom to trade even if that meant forced 'exchange' with non-Europeans. As well, on the ground of establishing trade rules, courts operating on the basis of extraterritoriality were established in lands that were not conquered so that rules favourable to European trade could be administered.[6] These legal strategies denied choice to the peoples of the colonized world on how to order their lives as they pleased. Political philosophers of the age developed a notion of European liberalism that considered such a choice as basic to human freedom and autonomy and necessary for states to respect if citizens were to have a political obligation to support the state and its law. But they were careful to limit their views to the imperial states and not extend them to the colonies. Chapter 4 outlines this 'inside–outside' distinction that is relevant also to this chapter. The recovery of such choice to order political and economic structures was central to the freedom movements in the colonies. It is central to the idea of justice.

No one in modern times seriously argues that the imperial international law accorded with any idea of justice.[7] The later struggle for self-determination by the colonial peoples led to decolonization. The process of decolonization was achieved progressively once the principle of self-determination was established. But whether the imperial system was destroyed or whether it mutated into other forms of control and dominance remains a debatable question. If it does continue, as this chapter argues it does, in the principles and rules on the protection of foreign investment, then the inevitable conclusion is that international law continues to be unjust. The reason for empire and the use of force to acquire and support imperial systems were to promote trade and investment. There can be no justification for the subjection of one people by another people or for the imposition of economic or political inequality through external coercion supported by international law. To the extent that the present system of international law does so, it must be deemed unjust. It

[3] The standard of civilization was the basis on which African and Asian states were denied personality in international law. G Gong, *The Standard of Civilization in International Relations* (OUP 1984). Ironically, the earliest human civilizations were in the areas of Asian and African states.

[4] The words are in a poem written by Rudyard Kipling, 'The White Man's Burden: The United States and the Phillippine Islands' (February 1899) 12 McClure's Magazine 12.

[5] The latter view was reversed by the Australian High Court in *Mabo v Queensland* (1995) 175 CLR 1 in which the High Court held that Australia was conquered from the aboriginal people, not *terra nullius* that was occupied by settlers.

[6] For justifications for empire, see A Fitzmaurice, 'Sovereign Trusteeship and Empire' (2015) 16 Theoretical Inquiries in Law 447.

[7] There are arguments as to whether empire did good. There was infrastructure building and effective administration. But this was to cater for control and trade that advantaged the imperial power. See Ferguson (n 2); Beckert (n 2).

would appear that by using private and public power, acting in tandem, and by using low order sources of international law, a regime has been created to ensure that the modern multinational corporation, the conveyor of foreign investment, is insulated from the control of developing states in their capacity to advance the interests of their public. Multinational enterprises function without any rules in international law as to liability as they are deemed not to have personality in international law.[8] But they can sue host states in which they operate because of a network of regional and bilateral investment treaties giving them standing to sue these states in arbitration for violations of treaty standards.

The claim advanced here is that existing international law has perpetuated many of the features of imperialism thereby enabling the argument that its continued instrumental use undermines justice. Indeed, it may be said that it is a continuation of the objects of the imperial system through more insidious means. The camouflage hiding the intentions of projecting power during modern times are more effective than the feeble recourse of the imperial system to standards of civilization or the 'white man's burden'[9] of civilizing the barbarous peoples of the colonies. The modern system's fiction is couched in sophisticated theories of economic development.[10] The altruistic or paternalistic objective of absolute protection of foreign investment through the law is said to be the economic development of the poorer states. It is claimed that such protection enables flows of foreign investment into developing countries. Consequently, economic development ensues. This questionable hypothesis lies at the root of the international law on foreign investment.[11]

If it can be credibly maintained that the modern system of international law is based on a continuation of the international law of the imperial system under a new guise, the perpetuation of injustice can be easily established. The claim to its reform can be credibly made and the alternative structures for the creation of a new law can be explored. The task of this chapter is to establish such continuation of the imperial system, its essential inequity, and the need for reform.

Section 1 of this chapter offers a way to understand justice that is relevant to the context of the international law on foreign investment. Section 2 deals with the historical circumstances of the international law on foreign investment. It shows us the power imbalances existing at the time of the origin of the law on what is now the international law on foreign investment. The injustice found in the power imbalances that generated the law in the field is exposed. Law resulting from asymmetrical

[8] The curious situation is that it has the right to bring arbitrations unilaterally under bilateral investment treaties and arguments are made that this is a right that inheres in the multinational corporation once the treaty is made.

[9] 'The White Man's Burden' is the title of the poem written in 1899 by Kipling on the occasion of the American colonization of the Philippines. The racist credentials of Kipling are debated in literary circles.

[10] A Escobar, *Encountering Development: The Making and Unmaking of the Third World* (Princeton UP 1995).

[11] There is no uncontested proof that investment treaties enhance investment flows. The many studies in the area are conveniently discussed in LN Skovgaard Poulsen, *Bounded Rationality and Economic Diplomacy: The Politics of Investment Treaties in Developing Countries* (CUP 2015); KP Sauvant and LE Sachs (eds), *The Effect of Treaties on Foreign Direct Investment: Bilateral Investment Treaties, Double Taxation Treaties, and Investment Flows* (OUP 2009).

power balances would be unjust in that it would favour the interests of the strong against the weak. Section 3 deals with the demise of NIEO. The drive towards the universalization of the law was initially espoused by the Latin American states and eventually by African and Asian states and the opposition of these states to the law that was created by the United States and came to be supported by the European capital-exporting states after decolonization. This was the period of the New International Economic Order (NIEO) explored more generally in Chapter 3. The NIEO sought to establish norms that were opposed to the hegemonic norms that arose during the formative period of international law and were challenged by capital-exporting states on the basis of international law. Section 4 deals with the decline of the NIEO with the apparent triumph of neoliberalism in the 1990s and its relationship to the international law on foreign investment.[12] The rapid build-up of the international law on foreign investment during this decade resulting from the increase of bilateral investment treaties and their expansive interpretation by arbitral tribunals is the basis of the reinforcement of injustice in this area. This turn displays how a powerful group of multinational corporations, large law firms, and a select group of arbitrators could exploit the low order sources of international law as they are developed in arbitral awards to create an inflexible system of investment protection to the detriment of developing states. Section 5 critiques the rationales usually offered for the prevailing international investment regime, which include arguments that the regime is good for economic growth because it protects property rights, promotes good governance, and upholds the rule of law. Section 6 concludes with reflections on the resistance to the law that has come about, the changes in treaties due to dissatisfaction with the system even by the developed states, and the nature of the legitimacy crisis the law now faces. The chapter contemplates constructing the international law on foreign investment anew, with the global values of poverty reduction, elimination of morally unjustifiable inequalities, environmental protection, human rights, protection of cultural property, and indigenous rights reflected in the law. These are the primary global values that trump investment protection that serves narrow interests of private power. The final section deals with the possible solutions to the crisis that may bring about a more just legal infrastructure for international investment.

1. Justice in the Context of the International Law on Foreign Investment

As dealt with in Chapter 2 ('Confronting the Pathologies of International Law'), this book seeks to connect theories about justice, particularly those located in normative political theory, more closely to international law. With this book, we are interested

[12] Though neoliberalism started much earlier, Stiglitz regards its highpoint as the last decade of the twentieth century. In terms of the law, this may be accurate as much of the activity inspired by neoliberalism—the trade law and investment laws—were made during this period. JE Stiglitz, *The Roaring Nineties: A New History of the World's Most Prosperous Decade* (Norton 2003).

in offering a lucid account of the drivers of international law's inequities and the justifications for dramatic improvement of the human condition. An aim of this chapter, and the chapters on trade (Chapter 4 ('International Trade')) and finance (Chapter 6 ('Global Finance')), is to develop an account to evaluate the content of international law in each of these areas, to demonstrate how they have failed to meet the demands of justice. Those demands include but are not limited to a requirement that international law serves to alleviate poverty, avoids the support or promotion of inequalities that cannot be justified on moral grounds, and promotes freedom from domination. While international human rights law is the social conscience of international law, Chapter 7 on human rights foregrounds how their deployment needs to be considered against the backdrop of global capitalism, and not merely as a discrete, benevolent response to it. We are preoccupied in that chapter with the ways in which human rights operating under the logic of neoliberalism work against a transformative or radical agenda, to the detriment of their own aims and objectives. The combination of these chapters synthesizes into what might be a pluralistic account of justice about international law in which the context of economic activity in the form of investment, finance, and trade are relevant, and which critiques the negative influences of neoliberalism on international law not only directly in these discrete fields of explicit economic activity but also on international human rights law.

The analysis of the international law on foreign investment that follows concentrates on whether it satisfies core elements of justice that place normative demands on the modern system of international law for compliance. These core elements are moving away from their legacy moorings in eurocentrism.[13] The eventual rise of positivism in Eurocentric international law meant that it did not shoulder the burden of having to justify its content based on moral principles. Power ensured that positivism became a dominant force so that international law could be denuded of its moral elements, though natural law of the prior eras led to grave injustices as well. The instrumental role of international law in developing biased rules and maintaining asymmetrical regimes through its legitimating function is clear. Such regimes lack democratic legitimacy, offend the notion that rules must be of general benefit and not to benefit small groups within it like shareholders of large corporations and be made to the acceptance of all stakeholders. In the existing foreign investment law, a whole industry of legal experts, highly paid to achieve such a task, is at work ensuring that the system survives challenges made based on standards of justice. The industry includes academic lawyers, but in particular practitioners, arbitrators, and judges who willingly subscribe to the norms of the regime as they are not only socialized into its norms but reap personal profits through its operation.

It is necessary to identify some important evaluative criteria for this chapter. One is that truth about the effects of the law must animate the objectives on which the law is founded. Truth has an objective quality. If the policy prescriptions of the law are based on untruths or unprovable hypothesis, then, the law itself will lack

[13] M Sornarajah, 'On Fighting for Global Justice: The Role of the Third World International Lawyer' (2016) 37 Third World Quarterly 197.

legitimacy based on epistemological grounds alone, quite apart from any normative grounds that threaten its legitimacy. Imperial international law was based on the fiction of superiority of civilization as well as on armed power. Such a law or its philosophical bases have lost relevance but today international law relies on the fiction of the equality of states. Imperialism has been dissolved but not power. Power is gradually passing from hegemonic rulers in Europe and North America to other regions. The value of hegemonic law during the period of change to a multipolar world order is an open question.

The fact that law is still based on power brings about a second problem: that the law is not applied equally in that the prescription on which it is based is designed to favour the interests that power supports. This inequality that is created condemns the law as illegitimate, certainly in so far as its interpretation and application does not render it more fair, a central issue for the law on foreign investment. Imperial international law benefited Europe and kept the people of the rest of the world in thraldom. A related factor is that if the law brings disadvantages to the many and profits the few, democratic legitimacy would be lacking in such a law and it loses its validity to be regarded as law. In this context, the view that the international law in this area has often been a purveyor of poverty and other immiserations and the massive distances are emerging within states between the rich and the poor because of its prescriptions is a wholly tenable thesis.[14] If international law is a purveyor of immiserations, the international law on foreign investment demonstrates it very effectively. If it can be so demonstrated, a system that has such a result cannot be based on any sound concept of justice. The law that privileges the rich over the poor or that promotes human greed over human need,[15] that is based on domination or coercion cannot be said to be just on any theory of justice.[16]

The literature on the subject indicates that the principles of the law as well as its founding sources[17] assume that foreign investment flows must be promoted through the protection that international law provides.[18] It is said that the global good of economic development would not occur if not for the inflexible protection of foreign investment through the mechanism of international law. This is the basis of investment treaties. The standard argument is that the aim behind the standards of protection in the treaties leads to the promotion of flows of foreign investment into developing countries. These aims are also stated to be the purpose

[14] There are empirical studies which point to the growing material inequality because of the adoption of neoliberal policies through institutions such as law. These are not 'natural' inequalities but those resulting from the structure of institutions. See, eg, T Piketty, *Capital in the Twenty-First Century* (Harvard UP 2014); B Milanovic, *Global Inequality: A New Approach for the Age of Globalization* (Harvard UP 2016). For more on these points, see Chapter 2 ('Confronting Pathologies of International Law').

[15] M Sornarajah, 'A Law for Need or a Law for Greed? Restoring the Lost Law in the International Law on Foreign Investment' (2006) 6 International Environmental Agreements: Politics, Law and Economics 329.

[16] See Chapter 2 ('Confronting the Pathologies of International Law').

[17] By founding sources are meant the custom, treaties, and writings of publicists supporting the American or western view of international law on the subject. The contrary custom generated by the communist states or developing countries is not taken into account.

[18] The literature is extensive, see, eg, E Neumayer and L Spess, 'Do Bilateral Investment Treaties Increase Foreign Direct Investment to Developing Countries?' (2005) 33 World Development 1567. For a survey of the debate see J Bonnitcha, *The Political Economy of the Investment Regime* (OUP 2017).

of international arbitral mechanisms that have come about in the area, established by treaties. It is in large part the convenience of this position that facilitated the creation of inflexible systems of investment protection through a network of treaties and the expansionary interpretation of the standards of protection in the treaties by arbitral tribunals. The assumption is that investment flows are an economic benefit and will not occur without investment treaties. Foreign investment is accepted as the basis for economic and social development. Its protection, therefore, forms the bedrock of the system that has been built up through international law.

There is increasing evidence that these assumptions are based on false premises, cultivated by institutions and individuals who have promoted a neoliberal vision that global benefits accrue because of the liberalization of flow of assets and investments around the world. There is no doubt that instant creation of capital in the host state is effected when asset flows take place. But it is the later effects of the conduct of foreign investment that must be considered in assessing the benefits of the investment to the host state and its peoples. There is increasing evidence that the net results are not beneficial,[19] and indeed may be detrimental to the economic, social, and environmental aspirations of host states, as well as the human rights of their people. The eventual outflows of profits and resources are shown in studies to be much greater than the initial investment that was brought in. While it is true that employment is created, the possibility that labour is treated otherwise than in accordance with accepted standards creates grave concerns. The environmental depletion that foreign investment may cause must also be factored in. There are malpractices such as corruption, transfer pricing, and tax avoidance that reduce significantly the advantages of foreign investment. The negative effects of foreign investment on local livelihoods, access to food, and the traditional way of life of pastoralist and other communities is also well documented.[20]

Multinational corporations and shareholders reap the benefits of such liberalization. A minority of people in the developed states, who are shareholders of large multinational corporations, benefit from such foreign investments. The other citizens of the developed states might not directly benefit.[21] The clear majority of the citizens of the developing countries into which such investments flow do not benefit from them. Rather, they must shoulder the disadvantages such as displacement (without compensation), lower labour standards, environmental pollution that foreign investors cause, and corruption that they all too often facilitate. The investment flows largely benefit the elite in these states who wield power and can

[19] Economists have heavily contested the assumption in recent times. The monopoly of the subject by economists belonging to neoliberal institutions of the Washington Consensus promoting the regime of laws has been broken as a result. The extensive literature on the subject is dealt with in Poulsen (n 11) in which Poulsen argues that the economic benefits of investment treaties were overestimated by developing countries.

[20] See, eg, O De Schutter, *Report of the Special Rapporteur on the Right to Food: Large-Scale Land Acquisitions and Leases: A Set of Minimum Principles and Measures to Address the Human Rights Challenge* UN Doc A/HRC/13/33/Add 2, 28 Dec 2009, http://www.srfood.org/images/stories/pdf/officialreports/20100305_a-hrc-13-33-add2_land-principles_en.pdf

[21] This is not to say that they are not indirect beneficiaries as increase in national wealth inures to their benefit as well.

make associations with the foreign multinationals. Foreign investment creates an exploitative climate in the host states ensuring that elite and, to a lesser extent, the comprador communities they support receive benefits to the detriment of others within the state, often in particular minority communities. The notion that economic development uniformly results because of the flow of foreign investments is a fiction that is promoted to justify the creation of an international law on foreign investment that is protective of the interests of foreign investors.

The fiction is advanced by credible international financial institutions, like the World Bank and International Monetary Fund, based on theoretical and statistical models linking the flows of foreign investment to economic development. As is well known by now, if the theoretical assumptions are not accepted by states, they are forced to accept them when applying for loans to these institutions, the grant of loans being conditional on the implementation of a package of measures that are prescribed by neoliberal economics. These conditionalities have been challenged for decades, but persist nonetheless.[22] The central tenet of neoliberalism is that an uncontrolled market will ensure that the economy functions efficiently distributing goods according to merit and deciding on modes of production. Left to itself, the market will ensure that there is efficient allocation of resources. This view was to be applied globally and the recognition of market failures has done nothing to address market social failure which remains endemic. Briefly stated, neoliberalism demands at the global level that there be privatization of essential services and liberalization of flows of trade, asset movements, and investments in the state through the acceptance of a package of legal reform measures.

The conditionalities that are imposed on states seeking loans in times of economic stress have been relatively uniform over the years. These conditionalities mandate the usual neoliberal prescriptions including open investment regimes. Economic crises requiring intervention by the World Bank and the IMF usually occur among the poorer nations of the world,[23] but in the case of the IMF European countries are recent borrowers. Similar conditionalities are imposed on all countries, as neoliberal solutions are based on the one-size-fits-all notion that markets can fix all economic problems and ensure fairness. There have been great failures in the developing countries where such programmes (referred to as structural adjustment programmes) have been adopted with inefficient wealth distribution being the result along with grave impacts on the exercise of basic socio-economic rights. In developed countries, where austerity measures have been adopted following neoliberal prescriptions, the measures have had (predictable) deleterious impacts.[24]

[22] See Chapter 6 ('Global Finance').

[23] *World Bank and IMF Conditionality: A Development Injustice* (Eurodad Report 2009).

[24] See ME Salomon, 'Of Austerity, Human Rights and International Institutions' (2015) 4 European Law Journal 521; see Report of the UN Independent Expert on the effects of foreign debt and other related international financial obligations of states on the full enjoyment of all human rights, particularly economic, social and cultural rights: Mission to Greece UN Doc A/HRC/31/60/Add 2, 29 Feb 2016.

In the 1990s, the decade Stiglitz described as the 'roaring nineties',[25] neoliberalism often came to be accepted voluntarily as market capitalism was the only system left standing after the collapse of Communism. The United States, as a hegemonic power committed to neoliberalism, could drive its tenets into the world order through the instrumentality of international law. It benefited itself, its corporations, and possibly, its people. But, such was not the result for the people of the developing world. And of course there is evidence that economic globalization substantially contributed to the significant income inequalities in the United States and precipitated a global economic crisis in 2008 that started in the United States. A result may have been the election of Donald Trump as president. The global economic crisis affected the United States badly but while its economy is said to have recovered relatively quickly, its crisis has left other affected countries, both developed and developing, with what may be a 'lost generation'.[26]

In the area of foreign investment, the neoliberal package requires the adoption of privatization policies insisting on the dismantling of services provided to the public, liberal entry provisions for foreign investment, definite protection for property, the recognition of the sanctity of the foreign investment contract, the equal treatment of local and foreign investment, payment of compensation in the event of expropriation, and, importantly, the existence of a compliance mechanism through unilateral recourse by the foreign investor to external arbitration. The package requires a distinct type of foreign investment law.[27] Such a system of investment law has been brought about in most developing countries because of the pressure to abide by neoliberal prescriptions.[28] Investment treaties bring about a network of rules protecting foreign investment. The focus on the possibility of multinational corporations resorting to arbitration based on these treaties became intense after the decision in *AAPL v Sri Lanka*[29] that admits of such unilateral recourse to arbitration. The expansive interpretation of the treaties ensured inflexible investment protection. It reduces the power of the developing state to act in the interests of its people when occasion demands such a course of action. It ensures private accumulation of wealth in the hands of the foreign investors and the domestic elite with whom they form links, incentives to attract foreign investment often include tax breaks undermining the availability of funds for redistribution. Statistics may show wealth creation but a considerable amount of it flows out of the state and what remains, remains in the hand of a small domestic elite. One criticism then is that neoliberalism creates a disparity in wealth between rich and poor states at the global level. Within states, it creates similar divisions between the rich and the increasing

[25] Stiglitz (n 12).

[26] *Global Employment Trends for Youth 2012* (ILO May 2012), http://www.ilo.org/wcmsp5/groups/public/---dgreports/---dcomm/documents/publication/wcms_180976.pdf

[27] The domestic foreign investment law too will have to reflect the features of the package.

[28] This has led to some writers speaking of a constitutionalism that focuses on property protection as the right to property becomes the central feature of the domestic laws. V Bean and J Beauvais, 'Global Fifth Amendment' (2003) 78 New York University Law Review 30.

[29] (1990) 4 ICSID Rpts 245.

poor. Both globally and domestically, it creates economic structures that perpetuate poverty and inequality.[30]

This chapter considers how the neoliberal package is implemented on the assumption that it facilitates the flow of foreign investment, the effects that such a package produces in developing countries, the injustice it creates by purveying poverty and other immiserations, and the possible ways the laws implementing it could be replaced both at the domestic and international levels. Reinforced by neoliberalism, the justification of this package on the basis that it advances economic development (which, as mentioned, has not been realized) has inappropriately animated the total concentration of the law on investment protection as the sole value to the detriment of other global values including the eradication of poverty and closing the gap in inequality.[31] This sole concentration on investment protection ensures that the host developing state must sit by without interfering and watch while the foreign investor reaps and repatriates profits while desecrating the environment, violating the human rights of workers, disturbing the traditional ways of life of indigenous communities, and more generally producing various forms of immiseration.[32] The system that exists does not comport with any concept of justice. The next section indicates that the origins of the system were flawed and could not but have led to the present situation of injustice.

2. The Flawed Origins

Coercion in the form of imposition through power, a feature of injustice, lies at the very roots of foreign investment protection. The origins of the international law on foreign investment lie in the assertion of an international minimum standard of protection of aliens asserted initially by the United States as a means of protecting its nationals increasingly present trading with and investing in the unstable states of Latin America in the eighteenth century. The system first grew up in the context of Latin America, which had become independent from Spanish rule earlier than in other regions.[33] Africa and Asia were under colonialism during this formative period, where exploitation of their resources and markets continued under imperial law. It was necessary initially to devise a law to provide for the control of investment in Latin America, which was nominally free. The United States, the

[30] The generalized trend is that poverty remains widespread and is now far worse than we have been led to believe. See Chapter 1 ('Legal Rendering of Immiseration').

[31] Economic development in this context meant the initial asset formation taking place at entry without the subsequent factors that may attend the investment later like the outflow of greater capital by way of repatriation of earnings, the environmental and human rights costs, and other harms that the investment may cause.

[32] Chapter 1 deals with the relationship of international law to poverty and related immiserations, and challenges prevailing economic accounts about the positive effects of economic globalization. There is also a far less contested connection between rising wealth inequalities and economic globalization.

[33] M Sornarajah, *Resistance and Change in the International Law on Foreign Investment* (CUP 2015) 32–35.

dominant player in the region, drove the creation of this law. The United States sought to establish an external standard of protection with international arbitration providing the mechanism of achieving such protection. It flew in the face of the obvious principle that an alien is always subject to the jurisdiction of the state that he voluntarily enters. The justification for the external mechanism was that where there was unfair or discriminatory treatment, there was a need to set up an international system of protection to ensure the safety of the alien and his property. The insulation of the alien and his property from the reach of national law was an achievement that was sought through the instrumentality of international law. The Latin American states resisted this innovation through the assertion of the Calvo doctrine, which asserted the continued national control over aliens operating within the territory of a state.[34] Strictly, there was no doctrine necessary to achieve this objective. Foreign investment took place on the territory of the state. It was always subject to the territorial sovereignty of the state. The fact that a doctrine had to be formulated to achieve the obvious indicated the way the basic attributes of the law could be twisted to give protection to foreign investment. Once decolonization was achieved the same tussle resulted between the former imperial states of Europe and the newly independent states of Africa and Asia.

The Calvo doctrine was consistent with every tenet of the then existing international law. It conformed with state sovereignty that was articulated as a basic norm of international law. As foreign investment occurred entirely within the territory of the state, it was subject to the sovereign control of the state. Its laws applied to it. Its courts had jurisdiction over disputes that arise from it. It was consistent with justice as it allocated choice to the people who had sovereignty over the natural resources.[35] It enabled this choice to be exercised in a manner that would promote their interests. The idea that the process of foreign investment should be insulated from the domestic law, subjected to an international minimum standard and disputes relating to the violation of that standard be settled by a foreign and purportedly neutral tribunal was not in accordance with legal notions of territorial sovereignty and with the idea of justice as including non-domination. It was the universally accepted view that a foreigner who voluntarily enters a state is always subject to the law of the state.

The arguments relating the displacement of the application of the host state's laws are themselves based on injustice. That said, they are to be condoned by the situation that existed in Latin America. The regimes in Latin America were largely dictatorships in which seizure of property took place capriciously. Neutral courts

[34] See D Shea, *The Calvo Clause: A Problem of Inter-American and International Law and Diplomacy* (University of Minnesota Press 1955).

[35] Even if, as commentators have pointed out in the context of the NIEO, the claim of developing states to their natural resources understood these raw materials as something to be exploited, as the object of private property, reflecting 'a continuation of, rather than a break with, the colonial interpretation of the earth and what it contains'. S Pahuja, *Decolonising International Law: Development, Economic Growth and the Politics of Universality* (CUP 2011) 125; G Abi-Saab, 'Permanent Sovereignty over Natural Resources' in M Bedjaoui (ed), *International Law: Achievements and Prospects* (UNESCO/Martinus Nijhoff 1991) 600.

did not exist in any meaningful sense. In that context, the rule that the property, and more importantly, the lives of foreign investors should be protected through mechanisms of international law is not unreasonable. The attraction of the rule loses its force when applied to democratic governments. The measures they take to advance social justice or to protect the public interest cannot be treated the same as capricious takings effected in dictatorships. However, progressive governments, which sought to reorganize the economy through a more equitable structure of ownership, also came to be subjected to the same rule.

The Mexican expropriations following the Zapatista revolutions were intended to effect land reforms and reorganize the oil industry.[36] It was in the context of these expropriations that the Hull rule on the payment of prompt, adequate, and effective compensation was created.[37] The rule hindered the possibility of reorganizing the economies of states formed after decolonization because it locked in an unjust state of affairs formed during colonization. African and Asian states consequently rejected this standard, arguing instead for a standard of appropriate compensation. Appropriate compensation reflected the fact that the foreign investor would have reaped sufficient benefits during the colonial times and the payment of full compensation would amount to rewarding him twice over. Besides, the newly independent states had not been left with sufficient money in the coffers by the imperial states to satisfy any requirement of full compensation. Justice related arguments were used to support the norm of appropriate compensation which had been floated in many of the documents associated with the NIEO. These arguments have been detailed in Chapter 3. The issue of compensation was one key element whereby the wider thrust was to articulate the fact that colonialism was based on iniquitous structures that made the colonies vast quarries for raw materials and markets for finished products, ensuring a cycle of dependence. The NIEO sought to break this cycle of dependence.

The NIEO was a package of norms aimed at change. It sought to change the formula of prompt, adequate, and effective compensation, which the developing world could not have met, to a standard of adequate compensation, adequacy being judged by circumstances, such as past exploitation. It asserted permanent sovereignty over natural resources so that past contracts tying up resources could be ended and future contracts could be more equitable.[38] It required that just prices for finished products manufactured within developing countries so that manufacturing could be transferred to the resource-producing states.[39] It required access to markets for these products to the developed world.[40] The NIEO had introduced

[36] N Maurer, *The Empire Trap: The Rise and Fall of US Intervention to Protect American Property Overseas* (Princeton UP 2013) 274–80.

[37] See US Department of State, 3 Digest of International Law—Hackworth (1942) §228 at 655–65.

[38] See Chapter 3 ('The End of Empire and the Search for Justice: NIEO and Beyond') for a discussion of these points.

[39] The NIEO instruments at Art 3(j) linked the prices of raw materials to manufactured goods with the aim of bringing changes in the terms of trade. General Assembly Resolution A/ Res/ 5-6/ 3201, 1 May 1974. Declaration on the Establishment of a New International Economic Order.

[40] NIEO Declaration Art 3(s) required trade on a preferential basis between developed and developing states.

a set of norms in opposition to the norms that had been favoured by the United States and other developed states. As explained in Chapter 3, the NIEO was a singularly important political effort to 'socialize globalization', one that has not been matched since.

3. Dismantling the NIEO

The avowed objective of the developed states, however, was to dismantle the NIEO and its principles. Just principles articulated in the NIEO were to be displaced by principles of power that would be designed to ensure that the multinational corporations of the rich world functioned as before as in the time of colonialism. The resulting situation was in effect what existed under colonialism but now supported through a substantial positive law of treaties, at least for trade and investment. The altruistic or paternalistic justification of colonialism as the white man's burden of gently leading the savage Africans and Asians to a standard of civilization all the while plundering their wealth now became a project of creating a seeming lawful structure of a regime of law based on the promotion of economic development. The regime was constructed under the cover of law with the alleged altruistic object of achieving the economic development of the developing states through foreign investment. It was the cultivated assumption that without such foreign investment economic development would not be possible. While maintaining this façade, there was the same plunder that was taking place. Contracts were made with the pliant ruling elite of resource-producing countries. The resources of the developing states continued to be ravaged. It is interesting to state briefly how this system came to be built.

The dismantling of the NIEO was the first challenge. This was a project that was never completed. While the NIEO was in progress, it had been incorporated into the constitutional systems of most developing countries so that they continue to have authoritative force in these legal systems as a matter of constitutional law, offering aggrieved persons with the potential for justiciable rights but these provisions can only go so far in the legal systems of developing states.[41] The NIEO was largely couched in the form of General Assembly resolutions and this provided an opportunity for attack from the West as to their legal validity. They were challenged on the basis that General Assembly resolutions do not have law-creating effect even where they embody the views of the large majority of the states of the world.[42] It was also decried that the norms of the NIEO are only *lex ferenda*, a contested

[41] The constitutional provision restricting foreign ownership in the Philippines was an issue in the arbitration, *Frapport v Philippines* ICSID Case No ARB/03/25, 16 Aug 2007. Such restrictions on foreign investment entry can also be found in foreign investment laws. See *Rafat Ali v Indonesia* ICSID Case No ARB/11/13,16 July 2013.

[42] B Sloane, *United Nations General Assembly Resolutions in Our Changing World* (Transnational 1991); see, eg, M Oberg, 'The Legal Effects of Resolutions of the UN Security Council and the General Assembly' (2005) 16 EJIL 880.

point.[43] In any case, most principles which constitute the basic norms from which international law derives sustenance are *lex ferenda* yet supply the essential principles of international law. These principles, such as an external minimum standard of protection of aliens based on an early notion of human rights, have been used in the past to justify exploitation and oppression and in some cases in the contemporary period to justify prohibitively stringent levels of investor protection.[44] These arguments, in hindsight, were however mere distractions, although they were made with seriousness. The repetition of the arguments indicated the vigour with which the NIEO was attacked, and the process of dismantling the NIEO accelerated as a new strategy for confronting it came to be made.[45]

The circumstances for the success of the strategy also became more propitious as the immediate age after decolonization passed. The first-generation leaders who led the decolonization movement and held the Third World together either passed away or left the scene. With the petro-dollar loan crisis mounting, the avenues for borrowing from private banks became limited.[46] Aid from developed states dried up as neoliberal leaders of the developed states were averse to such aid.[47] The developing countries had to rely on foreign investment as the sole source of inflow of investment to promote infrastructure growth. The World Bank and the IMF were quick to promote this situation. These changes were vital to the construction of a regime based on neoliberalism that accentuated foreign investment protection, securing profits for multinational corporations but detrimental to the interests of the people of the developing states. It proved to be detrimental to the interests of the developing world.[48] A system supportive predominantly of the interests of multinational corporations is one that cannot be supported in terms of justice as it destroys competing interests, especially the interests of eradicating poverty, eliminating unjustifiable inequalities, protecting human rights, preserving the environment, and preserving the traditional cultures of indigenous peoples. A system that divided the world to privilege a tiny minority of its people, keeping wealth in the hands of the ever-diminishing numbers of the few and impoverishing or making worse off the vast amount of humanity, cannot be just. Yet that is the system on which the international law on foreign investment was constructed.

[43] The NIEO prescriptions were couched in mandatory language, even if not giving rise to binding obligations directly from the text of a resolution. In *Texaco v Libya* (1977) ILR 389, Arbitrator René Dupuy dismissed the General Assembly resolutions on the NIEO and associated resolutions as constituting *lex ferenda*.

[44] Chapter 3 ('The End of Empire and the Search for Justice: NIEO and Beyond') at 83–90 and Chapter 4 ('International Trade') at 112–124.

[45] For a taxonomy of arguments useful in understanding the NIEO, see N Gilman, 'The New International Economic Order: A Reintroduction' (2015) 6 Humanity 1 and a series of articles on the NIEO in a special issue of *Humanity*.

[46] Arab states became enormously rich with cash because of their creation of the oil cartel and the driving up of oil prices. This cash was kept in private banks and given as loans to developing countries, which found it difficult to service the loans. A crisis was generated when the lending banks collapsed. The banks, thereafter, were unable, but in any case unwilling, to lend to developing states.

[47] Thatcher, Reagan, and Helmut Kohl cut aid to their own people, let alone people in developing countries, due to their political inclinations towards neoliberalism which advocated self-help, not state aid.

[48] V Prashad, *The Poorer Nations: A Possible History of the Global South* (Verso 2014) 79–81.

4. Constructing the Neoliberal Order on Investment Protection

The neoliberal order on foreign investment protection was built on notions of global economic governance reminiscent of the old altruistic, paternalistic, or ostensibly other-regarding justification for imperialism. The mission of neoliberalism was to promote the spread of an ideology through the instrumentality of the law. This was done in the areas of international trade[49] and foreign investment.[50] The promise was that economic liberalization and free flow of assets and investment would lead to the development of the poorer world.[51] It was based on trickle-down theory. If wealth accumulates at the top levels of business, it will trickle down to the poor and benefit them. As the American economist, John Kenneth Galbraith famously put it, if you feed fine oats to the stallion, some undigested seeds will pass through in the droppings to feed the sparrows.[52] This cynical view was sold to the world in the construction of the neoliberal thesis that market economics should be the basis on which the global economy is based. The success of the US economy based on market capitalism and the failure of the competing socialist model in Russia was widely accepted as the reason to move towards the only economic system that was left standing after an exhausting contest.[53]

The purpose of the regime was to ensure that the foreign investment process is subject to an external law other than the law of the host state. It is a further manifestation of the inside–outside distinction explicated in Chapter 4 whereby states specify different legal rules for inside and outside the state, with rules for outside the state failing in substantial respects to comply with the requirements of justice. The eventual result that comes about is the insulation of the foreign investment from the sovereign control of the host state. It is reminiscent of the system of extraterritoriality that existed in colonial times in states like China.[54] This system was imposed through a series of wars on China by the United States and the states of Europe. The treaties required that trade with China be open to foreigners and that trade at the important treaty ports be subject not to Chinese law but to the legal system of the foreign traders administered by courts belonging to these legal systems. The contracts and other legal incidents of trade and investment were lifted out of the control of the Chinese law and subjected to foreign law. Any state would have found such a system of trade unpalatable. The Chinese today still express concern

[49] See Chapter 4 ('International Trade'). [50] See Sornarajah (n 33).

[51] The link between foreign investment and economic development were made in many legal instruments, such as, for example, the Preamble of the ICSID Convention (Convention for the Settlement of Disputes between States and Nationals of Other States, 1965). Likewise, the preambles in a large number of bilateral investment treaties make this link.

[52] Though he attributes the saying to others. JK Galbraith, 'Recession Economics' *New York Review of Books* (4 Feb 1982).

[53] The rise of neoliberalism during this period is recounted in many works. M Mandelbaum, *The Ideas that Conquered the World: Peace, Democracy and Free Markets in the Twenty First Century* (Public Affairs 2002); D Harvey, *A Brief History of Neoliberalism* (OUP 2005).

[54] J Lovell, *Opium Wars: Drugs, Dreams and the Making of China* (Picador 2012); J Spence, *The Search for Modern China* (Norton 2013) 161–63.

about the inequity that had been put upon them through this system of extraterritoriality.[55] The system was colonialism in all but name as the fiat of the Chinese state did not run in areas that affected foreign trade and investment. China had passively to watch while its people suffered because of vast quantities of opium brought into China by the foreign traders. The insulation of the trade achieved through extraterritoriality ensured that the Chinese state could not protect its people from the consequences of opium use.[56] The current system of foreign investment protection that has come about is like the older version of extraterritoriality as it insulates the foreign investment from the control of the host state. The present system is not maintained through the force of arms but through the sophistry of the law and legal arguments that the system of power provides.

The insulation of foreign investment is principally achieved in the modern system in two ways. The first method is based on the argument that the foreign investment contract made in a state is subject to an international or supranational system on the ground that the contract contains relevant clauses that seek to remove the contract from host state regulation through a foreign arbitration clause,[57] a choice of law clause indicating the application of general principles of law[58] and a stabilization clause.[59] These clauses are said to ensure that the contract is externalized through the countering of any idea that there is local control over the foreign investment as legislative power to affect the contract, it is said, is removed by the stabilization clause and judicial power is removed through the choice of law and foreign arbitration clauses.

The second system is through the network of regional and bilateral investment treaties. The treaties create standards of treatment for investments. The treaties are not uniform though they share common features. Though there are over 3,500 treaties, there is an important line of argument that they do not create customary international law based on the position that the language in the treaties contain variations.[60] They provide for dispute settlement through arbitration. Consequently, they do have an effective compliance mechanism, at least for foreign investors and multinational corporations, who can enforce arbitral awards through the New York

[55] Lovell (n 54); Spence (n 54).

[56] The poignant results of the massive addiction to opium that resulted are recorded in Lovell (n 54).

[57] There are many works which explain this technique of internationalization of the foreign investment contract. The highpoint of the technique is its acceptance in the award of Professor René Dupuy in *Texaco v Libya* (1977) 104 Journal du Droit International 350, translated in (1979) 17 ILM 1. Since then, there have been several arbitrations which have used the arguments considered in that award. Because of their low visibility, the extent of these awards is difficult to determine.

[58] Since reference is to general principles of law which is a source of international law, the argument is made that the system chosen as the applicable law is international law, a system that cannot be changed by the host state law.

[59] The stabilization clause seeks to freeze the law of the host state as at the time of entry so that future laws cannot affect the contract. Whether such a feat can be achieved is a matter for conjecture as several queries arise. Principal among them is the doubt whether a contractual provision between parties can exclude the constitutional powers of the state.

[60] The issue whether the treaties create customary international law is a contested one. See, eg, P Dumberry, *The Formation and Identification of Rules of Customary International Law in International Investment Law* (CUP 2016).

Convention.[61] The treaty regime now constitutes the principal means of foreign investment protection.

The way investment treaty arbitration has worked has been to create new rules of protection through interpretation of treaties. The expansion of the treaty rules to create stricter principles of investment protection has ensured that the neoliberal project is furthered. The technique has been to bring about rules at the international level that would bind the conduct of states towards foreign investors. The violation of the rules will create state liability. Often, the damages that are imposed are staggering.[62] As a result, states become constrained by the rules. They act in accordance with the neoliberal prescriptions even where such restraint is not in the public interest. A regulatory chill comes about.[63] The system created is one which can readily further investment protection to the detriment of the public. Thus, the state is pressed to avoid taking measures that are needed to prevent poverty and encourage sustainable social development through distributive methods of taxation, environmental measures, and observance of human rights standards where those might impact on the foreign investors profits. As the law on investment protection operates in its own silo fragmented from other areas of international law, arbitrators hold that it is not within their province to consider interests other than investment protection.[64] Such fragmentation becomes a technique whereby neoliberal principles are furthered and the disregard for other interests is deemed reasonable. In no way can this situation be described as just. The new treaties which recognize a right to regulate will not change the situation as arbitrators have begun to apply a proportionality test to determine the extent of the validity of the regulation.[65]

An unjust body of principles has been created that deter states from acting in the public interest. These interpretations have become a course of precedent and have taken the form of hard law. It is necessary to examine how through treaty interpretation the system of protection of foreign investment has been significantly expanded. This expansion provides the best evidence for the building up of neoliberal principles in this area of international investment law.

[61] Arbitral awards in the investment regime are enforced by national courts under various conventions on international arbitration. See the Convention on the Recognition and Enforcement of Foreign Arbitral Awards, 10 June 1958, 21 UST 2517, TIAS No 6997, 330 UNTS 38.

[62] Some recent examples include the *Yukos v Russia* arbitration where damages exceeding US$50.2 billion were awarded. *Yukos v Russia* UNCITRAL PCA Case No AA 225, Award on 18 July 2014. A district court at The Hague set aside the award on 20 April 2016 but there are enforcement proceedings in other jurisdictions.

[63] K Tienhaara, *The Expropriation of Environmental Governance: Protecting Foreign Investors at the Expense of Public Policy* (CUP 2009).

[64] In *Von Pezoid v Zimbabwe* (2015) ICSID ARB 10/15, 29 July 2015, arbitrators stated that the history of exploitation by foreigners in Zimbabwe is not a matter for their consideration. In *Santa Helena v Costa Rica* ICSID Case No ARB/96/1, 17 Feb 2000 the protection of wildlife given as a reason for rescinding the foreign investment was held not to be relevant.

[65] On the use of the test, see C Henckels, *Proportionality and Deference in Investor-State Arbitration* (CUP 2015).

The methods of insulation of foreign investment that have been detailed above have been made to support the building up of a system of rules that are intent on providing as much protection as possible to foreign investment through the machinery of international law. The nature of the extensions that have been made are set out to demonstrate that none of the theories that have been stated in justification of the regime formation can support the acceptability of the extensions that have been made. Constraints of space require that they be stated only briefly.[66] As explained above, the core problem at hand is one of institutional design, on getting the investor-state arbitration provisions of investment treaties to constrain arbitral tribunals from interpreting the provisions to implement a particular version of a neoliberal state and a neoliberal order of relations between states.

4.1 The expansion of investment protection: extensions of jurisdiction

It is axiomatic that jurisdiction in arbitration depends entirely on consent. Since the holding in *AAPL v Sri Lanka*[67] that the investor-dispute settlement provision creates jurisdiction in arbitration tribunals whose jurisdiction is unilaterally invoked by the foreign investor, there has been a spate of arbitrations using this technique. The assumption is faulty as the creation of rights in third parties, often not yet in existence, through contract or treaties was hardly known in many domestic law systems or in international law. Despite the adoption of this contentious technique, arbitrators have been wont to expand jurisdiction even further. They have used the most favoured nation clause to construct new types of jurisdiction not found in the treaty on the basis of which they operate by latching onto other treaties of the respondent state that contain more favourable statements on jurisdiction.[68] They have generally permitted multinational corporations to incorporate in other states on the basis of a surprising theory of corporate migration so that they could take advantage of more favourable treaties of the new state in which they incorporate postbox subsidiaries.[69] The technique of expanding the meaning of foreign investment in the treaties to include types of transactions, which would not traditionally fall within the meaning of investments, is also a contested feature of investment arbitrations.

[66] For detailed statement of these issues, see Sornarajah (n 33).

[67] (1990) 4 ICSID Rpts 245.

[68] Two lines of cases have developed as to whether such a technique is permissible. For an example of the use of the technique, see *Maffezini v Kingdom of Spain* ICSID Case No ARB/97/7, 25 Jan 2000. For an example of a refusal to follow this technique, see *Plama Consortium v Bulgaria* ICSID Case No ARB/03/24 27 Aug 2008. J Maupin, 'MFN-based Jurisdiction in Investor-State Arbitration: Is There Any Hope for a Consistent Approach?' (2011) 14 JIEL 157.

[69] See, eg, *Conoco Phillips v Venezuela* ICSID Case No ARB/07/27, 10 June 2010. The strategy does not always work. The awards conflict.

The most glaring of these extensions relates to the establishment of jurisdiction in the case of bonds issued in foreign markets by a state to raise capital. These instruments have been held to amount to investments protected by treaties.[70] A series of awards have held that jurisdiction could arise under the treaties based on these instruments despite the traditional indicia for investments not having been satisfied. As they freely circulate in international markets with no requirement as to how long they should be held, they do not have the requisite duration to be regarded as investment. They are in the nature of loans rather than of investment, a clearly distinct category of transaction which could not possibly have been thought of as an investment by the states concluding treaties. They are sold under foreign laws. The crucial defect in the argument that these debt instruments could amount to foreign investment in terms of international law is that the holders and the assets may not even have entered the respondent states. Foreign direct investment, whether in the economic or the legal sense, is when the investor and the investment enter a state to make a long-term economic transaction involving construction, extraction of resources, or manufacture within the boundaries of a state. The debt instruments do not contain any of these essential characteristics. The absence of a territorial link itself is a sufficient reason to conclude that such instruments do not fall within the scope of treaty protection. Besides, the state does not even know at any given time to whom it owes responsibility as the bonds are freely circulating instruments. The nexus is between the issuing bank and the holder of the instrument. Yet, it is surprising that a series of cases should have concluded that these transactions fall within the terms of treaty protection in the face of widespread dissent. It is difficult to explain this reasoning except based on arbitral misfeasance, though, of course, systemic and structural biases in international law towards neoliberal tenets provides arbitrators with the institutional environment in which they rule. It is difficult to conclude that the objective is other than to build up a law through precedent among like-minded arbitrators to advance an ill-judged project that favours multinational corporations.[71] It appears to be a self-interested effort at promoting the scope of the business of investment arbitration knowing that several economic crises are looming in the horizon that could generate a plethora of cases in which investors and multinational enterprises will be the only real recipients of protection.

70 The inclusion of free-floating financial instruments as investment is the most stunning innovation. See *Abaclat v Argentina* ICSID Case No ARB/07/05, 4 Aug 2011; *Ambiente Ufficio v Argentina* ICSID Case No ARB O8/9, 8 Feb 2013. *Deutsche Bank v Sri Lanka* ICSID Case No ARB/09/02, 31 Oct 2012. There were strong dissents in the three awards. They indicated the absurdity of such instruments, created under other legal systems and bought by persons who had no relationship with the host state other than the purchase of the instruments in foreign states, being protected under the treaties. In *Postova Bank v Greece* ICSID Case No ARB/13/8, 9 Apr 2015 the tribunal denied jurisdiction because the instruments were not protected. *Ping An Life Insurance v Belgium* (Unreported, 2015), which involved financial instruments jurisdiction was denied on other grounds.

71 This charge has been made in several publications. Studies point out that a limited number of arbitrators command the whole field ensuring that the awards made by the select group are followed within the group. Large law firms make repeat appointments so that there could be a reaffirmation of the favourable rules that have been made. S Puig, 'Social Capital in the Arbitration Market' (2014) 25 EJIL 387.

This tendency again is deeply questionable in terms of justice. States and their people are imperilled at a time of economic crises so that a small coterie of arbitrators and lawyers who work in the field, and multinational corporations, profit at their dismay.[72] An award arising from the Greek economic crisis might contribute to the end of this particular arbitral charade.[73] The holding was that the shareholders do not have protection in respect of the assets of the company and that government bonds do not fall within the definition of investments. This, however, brings no comfort to states and their people that have already been affected by the extension.

It is true that the expansion of the scope of jurisdiction has met with dissent from within the rank of arbitrators.[74] But, the fact that the majority of the arbitrators have been inclined to interpret treaty provisions to expand jurisdiction evidences a bias or error, or a defect in treaty provisions, towards certain dispositions that favour the interests of multinational corporations. They show the shoring up of a system that is geared to the promotion of neoliberal ideologies where they play their role in the building up of an external standard of governance that ensures the protection of property, the promotion of the sanctity of property, and the liberalization of flows of foreign investment. The same rationalizations also support the expansion of substantive law under the treaties. Much of the law that has come about has been made by a handful of arbitrators who have been repeatedly appointed to tribunals, which means that repeat interpretations tend to harden the law towards particular interpretations. It is plausible to maintain the view that there has been a purposeful shaping of the law to enhance investor interests, though the reasons for this shaping are likely the result of an acceptance of particular neoliberal ideologies as the underlying purposes of investment treaties.[75]

4.2 The expansion of investment protection: The substantive law on investment arbitration

There has been more virulent activity in the extension of substantive principles of investment arbitration well beyond the manifested intentions of the signatories to investment treaties and to the detriment of host states. This is apparent as the extensions go well beyond what the language in the treaties can support. Studies on the interpretation of investment treaties indicate that the nature of the interpretations made in the awards of the provisions of the treaties do not accord with

[72] A sociolegal account of the role of international arbitrators can be found in Y Dezalay and BG Garth, *Dealing in Virtue: International Commercial Arbitration and the Construction of a Transnational Legal Order* (University of Chicago Press 1998).

[73] *Postova Bank v Greece* (n 70).

[74] Some arbitrators have limited the extensions made, as evidenced, for example, by the tussle among arbitrators as to the use of the most-favoured-nation clause to extend jurisdiction, or by the use of corporate nationality to establish jurisdiction by nationals of the respondent state and routing the investment from a treaty partner of their own state. For a survey of the dispute as to the use of most-favoured-nation clauses, see Maupin (n 68). On the use of corporate nationality, see S Schill and H Bray, 'Good Faith Limitations on Protected Investments and Corporate Restructuring' in A Mitchell, M Sornarajah, and T Voon, *Good Faith and International Economic Law* (OUP 2015) 88.

[75] M Waibel (ed), *The Backlash against Investment Arbitration* (Kluwer 2010).

the standard formulae prescribed for the interpretation of treaties in the Vienna Convention on the Law of Treaties.[76] These interpretations are guided by the views of the arbitrators as to what the state making the treaties intended or should have intended, usually reliant on the formula that since economic development of developing countries was the desired goal of all their investment treaties, an extension of any substantive rule that can be alleged to accord with this objective, should fall within the intention of the parties.[77] Only a few of these expansionist views are stated as illustrations of the nature of the extensions of the law they contain and the reactions to them.

First, as to the expansions to the law on expropriations and the reactions to these extensions, the linear developments are easy to record. The broad intention of the treaties was clearly to codify the western understanding of what the law on expropriation of foreign property should be.[78] No writer on international law looking at the treaties prior to the expansionary phase had treated the provisions on expropriation as anything other than a codification of the western views on expropriation. The debate between the West and the developing countries had centred around the issue of compensation. The treaties evidence a distinct preference for the western view that prompt, adequate, and effective compensation must be paid upon expropriation. The compensation debate had become a dormant grievance as a result. The developed countries wanted the acceptance of the norm of full compensation. This has been achieved through a network of investment treaties. But, despite this, the norm has not become customary international law.[79] Since there were also no large-scale nationalizations based on which the law had been constructed in the past, attention shifted to the types of expropriation under the treaties and it was here that there was scope for expansion.

The focus was on what amounted to a taking. The idea behind the expansion was to ensure that all measures that a state takes against property could be captured under the term expropriation and compensation be demanded whenever such measures are taken against foreign investment. These interpretations support the foreign investor and the interests of their home states. Treaty language distinguished between direct, indirect, and measures tantamount (or equivalent) to an expropriation. The latter category of what was tantamount to an

[76] TH Yen, *The Interpretation of Investment Treaties* (Brill 2014).

[77] Why arbitrators take particular interpretative positions, it is difficult to conclude with certainty. Apart from personal bias towards ideological positions and self-interest in ensuring repeat appointments, there could be other explanations for arbitral behaviour. They could have been socialized into conforming behaviour as in the case of judges or the fact that they have spent much time as commercial arbitrators may have induced a behaviour conducive to business certainty. Answers to these questions will depend on the disciplinary approach used to investigate them. A political economist, for example, might look very closely at the interests of arbitrators.

[78] Many of them repeat the Hull standard of compensation. Some conclude that the repetition is taken as confirming its status as customary law. This is incorrect. The treaty only applies to the specific types of investment that it protects.

[79] For one thing, treaties qualified the types of investment that was to be protected. For another, the balance in the different treaties were differently struck so that even the practice of one states differed according to the other party and according to the period at which the treaty was negotiated.

expropriation was a surplusage awaiting exploration by the expansionist. The neoliberal dissection of what constitutes taking had been attempted earlier in an article that had received little attention at the time of its writing. In due time however it became a focus for the argument—subsequently endorsed by many an arbitrator—that taking did not involve dispossession from property but that lesser invasions of a bundle of rights that constitute ownership could amount to expropriation. The novelty of the argument extended to cover any acts attributed to the state which resulted in a depreciation in the value of the property. Thus, in *Ethyl v Canada*,[80] the strategy of litigation was that the announcement of the consideration of a ban in the future of a carcinogenic substance amounted to a depreciation of value of the shares in the only foreign company manufacturing the substance and was therefore a compensable expropriation. The expansion held that compensation was required for the value of the foreign investment affected by any measure. The scope of this rule was great. The parties settled so we do not have a definitive arbitral ruling, but states (notably western states) reacted to it by removing the phrase 'tantamount to an expropriation' from their treaties and arguing the dormant domestic law on regulatory takings that provided that regulatory measures, taken in the public interest affecting property rights, are non-compensable.[81] The award in *Methanex v United States*[82] was based on the principle of regulatory expropriation. Here it was decided that a ban of a carcinogenic substance produced by the foreign investor did not carry an obligation of compensation as the measure was a regulatory measure taken to protect the health of the public. These developments narrowed the law on expropriation, confining it to situations of direct dispossession of property. Such dispossession hardly takes place in modern times.[83]

But the story does not end there. The narrowing of the neoliberal interpretation of the law on expropriations would have rendered expropriation nugatory in modern law as direct expropriations seldom took place in modern times. But arbitrators kept the law that they have made alive by staying one step ahead of states which do not want to cut the Gordian knot by withdrawing from the system of investment arbitration altogether.[84] They have now introduced the notion of proportionality into the law on expropriation so that they could determine whether a regulatory expropriation was proportionate to the object that was sought to be achieved through the taking.[85] In this way, neoliberal protections remain relevant even where

[80] (1999) 38 ILM 708.

[81] By this time, developed states also began being targets of expansionary views especially under NAFTA. See ibid. They led the reaction which led to the formulation of the regulatory expropriation exception.

[82] UNCITRAL Award, 3 Aug 2005.

[83] There are instances, but they are clearly due to dictatorial tendencies in some countries. See *Von Pezoid v Zimbabwe* (n 64).

[84] The technique adopted lately has been to use defences to liability in the so-called balanced treaties. This may not prove sufficient. It will also prolong litigation.

[85] On the impact of proportionality see C Henckel, *Proportionality and Deference in Investor-State Arbitration* (CUP 2016).

the state believes that the taking it had affected was a regulatory expropriation and in the public interest.

The other major doctrine created through interpretation was the waking up of the dormant, fair, and equitable treatment standard. It had remained unused for over half a century of its existence in BITs so that it was possible to state in 1999 that the phrase had no definite meaning.[86] It was given several meanings in arbitral awards in quick succession since then so that by 2005 it was possible to state that the phrase had a distinct meaning.[87] The most important meaning that was given to it was that where commitments made to the foreign investor at the time of the investment were later broken so that his legitimate expectations came to be sundered, there was a violation of the standard, giving rise to liability.[88] This newly formed doctrine, plucked out of thin air, became the staple of many arbitral awards. It was quickly followed by academic writing that bolstered the creation of the doctrine. One witnesses a technique at work.[89] Decisions of tribunals and writings of publicists—are used to create new doctrines. That has been the traditional technique of law creation employed by the agents of private power. The same technique is employed to create the doctrine of legitimate expectations which becomes the staple basis for the arbitral awards in the first decade of the twenty-first century. The door of expropriation closes. A new door is opened through the doctrine of legitimate expectations.

It is easy to criticize the perversity that attends such lawmaking. No reasonable drafter or state official agreeing to the fair and equitable language in an investment treaty would have predicted such a meaning would be ascribed to the phrase. No academic writer had ascribed such a meaning to the words prior to these awards except Professor Orrego-Vicuna who sat as arbitrator in a series of awards in which the view was made the main reason for the award.[90] Thus, a rule on legitimate expectations was created in investment arbitration.[91] The legitimacy of the process of the creation of the rule is suspect. The rule ties down the state to the expectations of the foreign investor in situations where circumstances change

86 Its use begins with reference to a standard of fairness in the Havana Charter on the International Trade Organization in 1948. In 1999, in an article in the British Yearbook, Stephen Vascianne concluded that the phrase had no definite meaning in the law. S Vascianne, 'The Fair and Equitable Standard in International Investment Law and Practice' (1999) 70 BYIL 99. In just a few years, it was given meaning so that in 2005, it was possible for commentators to state the new meanings of the phrase. See especially, C Schreuer, 'Fair and Equitable Treatment in Arbitral Practice' (2005) 6 Journal of World Investment and Trade 357.

87 Writers had begun to state that a system of precedent had emerged in investment arbitration. The rapid development of the rule relating to legitimate expectations was used as an example. Y Banifitemi, *Precedent in International Investment Law* (Juris 2008).

88 The many assertions of this rule in arbitral awards are discussed in Sornarajah (n 33) 257–81.

89 The technique is to find stability as the aim of investment treaties and to achieve that objective through interpretation accommodating the rule on legitimate expectations. Then, a doctrine of precedent serves to justify the earlier awards containing the interpretation being followed. As Arbitrator Nikken pointed out in his dissent in *Suez v Argentina* ICSID Case No ARB/03/19, 30 July 2010 the use of such a technique was never intended by the states making the treaties.

90 See Sornarajah (n 33) 266–67.

91 For a more elaborate treatment of this point, see ibid.

from the time of its entry and necessitate the state to act in the public interest. The expectations of the foreign investor, which were allegedly raised, were all based on general statements of policy. It is unthinkable that states can be tied down to statements of policy made at a time for the future as a state must change policies for a variety of legitimate reasons, quite apart from crises that take place. This was precisely the situation of the Argentine economic crisis. Earlier general promises to investors made in statements promoting Argentina as an investment destination could not be kept because of changes effected by the crisis. The doctrine of legitimate expectation was designed almost precisely to fit the circumstances of that crisis. Later, schisms developed between arbitrators some of whom saw that the use of the doctrine worked injustice. Limitations came to be stated.[92] Some arbitrators refused to conclude that the expectations of the foreign investor were legitimate when the investor went into a risky country like the former East European states which were transforming to capitalist systems.[93] Was Argentina, which had undergone successive undemocratic governments, coups and economic crises in its history, a country which an investor enters with secure and legitimate expectations? No arbitrator who made the awards in the Argentinian cases paused to consider such a question simply because there was a need to make a law that would fit the fifty-two cases that had been brought after the Argentinian crisis. More importantly, there appears to have been a definite project on the part of these arbitrators to build up a structure for the protection of the interests of foreign investment and thereby support an aspect of the neoliberal project—the unhindered flow of foreign investment seeking profits around the world under a regime of protection provided by international law. Such cynicism is justified in the way the law has been made in this area. For the more recent instances and future directions of the law, the Trans-Pacific Partnership (TPP) and the Transatlantic Trade and Investment Partnership (TTIP) are instances in which the rules designed to entrench the neoliberal regime that has been built up become more entrenched.

It is difficult to justify the system that has been created in terms of justice. The initial justification in terms of economic development is hollow. It would be incredible to suggest that the economic development of Argentina was promoted by the system. At the time of its crisis, Argentina faced the prospect of fifty-two arbitrations with multimillion dollars in awards made against it. The Argentinian episode illustrated how arbitrators scurried to develop expansive doctrines to ensure that a state that had suffered a setback is taken advantage of at the time of its crisis through claims that were based on extensive theories of liability that came to be approved.

The only economic development that seems to have taken place because of the system is that arbitrators, lawyers, and multinational corporations had become richer because of its existence. Poverty remains endemic in the main capital-importing countries of the South despite the existence of investment treaties for over sixty

[92] See C McLachlan, L Shore, and M Weineger, *International Investment Arbitration: Substantive Principles* (OUP 2008) 225.

[93] *Saluka Investments v Czech Republic* UNCITRAL PCA, 17 Mar 2006, para 304; *Electrabel v Hungary* ICSID Case No ARB/07/19, 30 Nov 2012.

years. Yet the system that has been created continues to be justified in theoretical terms and sanctioned under international law. It is necessary to turn to these theoretical justifications to determine whether they are maintainable in terms of justice.

5. The Rationalization of the Regime

The series of rationales provided in the recent literature for this system need to be examined. It has been observed that neoliberalism uses the technique of processing its favoured rules through judicial processes to give them legitimacy.[94] The technique in domestic law is to use administrative tribunals which administer the law as washing machines through which unpalatable rules are laundered to give them a sense of cleanliness.[95] The claim is that domestic judges belong to a distinct class socialized into distinct rules of propriety, particularly when it comes to commercial dealings and cannot act except in ways that support business interests with whom a class interest is shared.[96] A similar technique is worked out in international law where arguments, seemingly jurisprudential, are used to rationalize a neoliberal system of investment protection that advantages multinational corporations. There are two principal arguments that seek to rationalize the system. They relate to arguments based on property rights as essential to global economic governance and rule of law considerations. They are arguments made on the need to provide justice and legitimacy to the system that has been built up. In that sense, they seek to anticipate any arguments relating to the view that the system is not based on considerations of justice. These arguments are considered in turn.

5.1 The property rights and good governance argument

This argument presupposes that a regime of protection of property is essential for good governance and that it should be promoted through the recognition of the protection of property at the global level. Protection of property is seen as the basis of the organization of society in this vision. It is also seen as essential to economic development as there will be no striving for wealth unless the property acquired through effort is protected both from covetous acquisition by others and expropriation by the state.[97] The state must provide for order ensuring such acquisition by others. If it is necessary for the state to acquire property for any public purpose such as the building of infrastructure, such acquisition must be accompanied by the payment of full compensation. To a large degree, the American Constitution embodies

[94] R Hirshl, *Towards Juristocracy: The Origins and Consequences of New Constitutionalism* (Harvard UP 2004); D Schneiderman, *Resisting Economic Globalization* (Palgrave 2013).

[95] Hirshl (n 94). [96] See, eg, J Griffiths, *Politics of the Judiciary* (Fontana 1997).

[97] The idea is traced to John Locke's *Fragment on Property*. Absolute property has not been accepted in any constitutional system. Yet, such an absolute right to property dominates the neoliberal vision as the fundamental basis of the capitalist society. The protection of this right is central to the neoliberal vision.

these values of property. The Lockean prescription that property is central to the devising of any rules relating to the place of the individual in society animates this vision. It was to be later taken over as one of the fundamental tenets of neoliberalism which stressed individual effort at acquiring property as the basis of the progress of society.[98] Society's progress was understood as the outcome of the collectivity of individual efforts. The centrality of property to this vision requires that the law should protect property as an absolute value in itself. The United States tends to adhere to this vision in its constitutional law. Some constitutional lawyers would doubt such a statement.[99] It is not essential to any society that a system based on individual ownership of absolute property should be imposed upon it devoid of an element of public interest. Indeed, property and contract exist only because a state permits such concepts to exist to the extent they do not conflict with the public interest. The balance is worked out in each system.[100] It is not a constant balance imposed from above but one that is worked out by each society according to its ideological, historical, and societal predispositions.[101]

Absolute sanctity of property is a heavily contested vision. Community of property rather than individual property still holds sway in traditional and tribal societies.[102] The fallen ideology of Communism is still in existence in an attenuated version in socialist states.[103] Most legal systems recognize that the notion of individual property can exist in a society only to the extent it is permitted by the state. The idea of a natural right to property has long since been discredited.[104] The idea of the welfare state at least partly rests on the notion that economic liberties, which would include strong property rights protections, must give way to values of fairness and equality.[105] In this context, it would be invidious to say that there is a single vision of governance that privileges the right to property. There is no constitutional system in the world that is premised on such an absolutist vision of property.[106]

Those who support investment treaties argue that they contain standards that seek to universalize accepted premises on the treatment of the foreign

[98] For the view that the international investment law is modelled on American constitutionalism, see D Schneiderman, *Constitutionalizing Economic Globalization: Investment Rules and Democracy's Promise* (CUP 2008).

[99] See, eg, T Allen, 'Liberalism, Social Democracy and the Value of Property' (2010) 59 ICLQ 1053.

[100] See Chapter 2 ('Confronting the Pathologies of International Law') for further elaboration of these points.

[101] For comparative studies on the right to property, see A Vander Walt, *Constitutional Property Clauses: A Comparative Analysis* (Kluwer 1999); T Allen, *The Right to Property in Commonwealth Constitutions* (CUP 2000).

[102] L Benton, *Law and Colonial Cultures* (CUP 2001).

[103] Though China introduced a right to property into its constitution, it is not strictly enforced in the law.

[104] The conflict between this idea and inflexible right to property and the qualifications of these rights as subject to a social function is inherent in American law. *Kelo v City of New London* (2005) 545 US 469; see N Davidson, 'Sketches for a Hamiltonian Vernacular as a Social Function of Property' (2011) 80 Fordham Law Review 1053.

[105] G Alexander and E Penalver (eds), *Property and Community* (OUP 2009).

[106] G Alexander, *Global Debate over Constitutional Property: Lessons from American Takings Jurisprudence* (University of Chicago Press 2001) 21: 'In its failure to openly recognize that the individual owners owe duties to maintain the common welfare of their communities, the American constitutional property clause lags behind the rest of the world. It is time to catch up.'

investor's assets by imposing uniform standards on expropriation of property and its treatment within the host state.[107] The treaty's prescription of various standards of treatment are intended to secure foreign investment through the neutralization of the power of the state to take measures that would be harmful to such investment. The argument is that the existence of such standards at the international level ensures its political acceptability at the domestic level. In such a view, the external standards are used to justify the inevitability that the state must conform to them in order to avail itself of advantages of belonging to the international community, like access to financial institutions for loans or access to markets. Acceptance therefore becomes necessary and from it are raised arguments that this wide acceptance has consequences. The supporters of the system would argue that the network of these treaties creates customary international law[108] or multilateralize the norms of investment protection through the most-favoured-nation clause.[109] But the project of formulating a multilateral agreement has met with serial failures indicating that states of both the North and the South do not agree upon a global order on investment protection. These are back-door efforts at bringing about such multilateral norms on investment protection hearkening back to the same notion of unreasonable levels of property protection. They align with arguments that the norms of public law on property protection are globally uniform and that these norms mandate property protection or at the least, judicial review when property is subjected to harm. Such a principle may be present in some western legal systems but it is difficult to demonstrate that other systems have evolved similar principles. So, as the system of investment protection under treaties becomes subject to attack on the ground of legitimacy, there is a resort to weak and implausible arguments to shore it up. The governance argument and its various manifestations are too weak to sustain the legitimacy of a system which is geared to the protection of the interests of a minority within the international community. If rules are to be internationalized in the form of governance it is a system of law grounded in appropriate principles of justice that account directly for humanity that needs to be given that status so that the law may truly serve the function of bringing adequate living standards to all. This cannot be said of ideologically driven rules favoured by private or public

[107] This tendency is strong among writers who believe that modern international investment law is based on public law systems. See S Schill (ed), *International Investment Law and Comparative Public Law* (OUP 2010).

[108] This is a fallacious argument. The existence of some 3,500 bilateral treaties, containing a variety of formulations resulting in subtle differences, is insufficient to create customary international law. Despite this fact, writers take the view that there is a 'BITs revolution' creating customary international law. This unfortunate view is taken in the 2012 edition of *Brownlie's Principles of Public International Law*, reversing Brownlie's own long-held view that the investment treaties do not create customary international law. J Crawford, *Brownlie's Principles of Public International Law* (8th edn, OUP 2012) 31, 626.

[109] The argument is that the best protection offered in treaties linked through signatories could become the common norm as it would constitute the best norm of protection that becomes transferred to all the signatories through the operation of the clause. This is an equally fallacious argument for treaties must have remarkable similarity for this exercise to be performed. It is not an idea taken seriously. It was given up no sooner than it was formulated. S Schill, *The Multilateralization of International Investment Law* (CUP 2009).

power. A distinction must be made. Those rules cannot contribute to the formation of constitution-like norms that lead to principles accepted by nations. The argument that globalization will create pressures towards common constitutional norms like the right to property and its protection, must be resisted. The focus on this contested right to the exclusion of other political rights as well as socio-economic rights in the making of this argument is unfortunate. The argument is that states seeking foreign investment will want to ensure that the right to property is kept strong in the hope of attracting foreign investment.[110] As indicated, this neoliberal argument offers an unconvincing hypothesis which is increasingly coming to be suspected.

5.2 The rule of law argument

The rule of law argument is like the standard of governance argument. The weighty principle accepted by all lawyers as a protection of the citizen from the power of the state is called into aid and morphed as a principle which favours the protection of the foreign investment of multinational corporation. The picture of the powerful multinational corporation in need of protection against a developing state devoid of funds and legal expertise is not apposite. The origin of the argument lies in an early effort by the World Bank to argue that the rule of law ensures the protection of foreign investment.[111] The difficulty with the argument is that it may be the citizen of the developing country which stands in need of the protection of the human rights and environmental abuses of the foreign investor. There is an evident subversion of the notion of the rule of law as recognized by its founding treatises like those of Dicey.[112] The concept has been subverted to serve the interests of the powerful by its diversion to serve the interests of multinational corporations.[113]

The view is stated that unless the host state maintains the rule of law there will be no flows of foreign investment into the state.[114] It also argued that investment will not flow into states which do not abide by the rule of law. The ensuring of political and economic stability through the maintenance of the rule of law is the sure way of attracting and maintaining foreign investment, according to this argument. The maintenance of the rule of law of the variety that promotes stability for foreign investment is a recipe for fascism.[115] It ensures that trade unions are suppressed, political freedoms are curtailed, and the legal system is geared to furthering the

[110] M Tushnet, 'The Inevitable Globalization of Constitutional Law' (2009) 49 Virginia Journal of International Law 985; DS Law, Globalization and the Future of Constitutional Rights (2008) 102 Northwestern University Law Review 1277.

[111] S Schill, 'The Fair and Equitable Treatment: The Rule of Law and Comparative Public Law' in Schill (n 107) 151.

[112] S Humphries, *The Theatre of the Rule of Law: Transnational Legal Intervention in Theory and Practice* (CUP 2010).

[113] The novel concept of the rule of law geared to business promotes the interests of elite groups within the host state and their partnership with foreign multinational companies.

[114] This argument is a restatement of the view that legal and political stability are necessary to attract foreign investment.

[115] It is necessary to reconcile the fact that China has attracted foreign investment without maintaining the rule of law understood as involving democratic values. See R Peerenbom, *China's Long March Towards the Rule of Law* (CUP 2007).

interests of the dominant groups so that foreign investment can be furthered. The system is best promoted in situations of dictatorships. The rule of law of this variety may advance foreign investment goals but is disastrous for the vast majority of the people of the developing world whose lives become geared to the protection of foreign investment. It is premised on the idea that foreign investment is a panacea to the ills of poverty, but the theory has never been established in the long years it has been in existence. The restoration of the rule of law to its original position as a principle that protects against power and the rejection of its subversion as a notion that promotes the interests of private power are essential to the achievement of justice.

6. Concluding Remarks

While some governments have pushed back on an international law on foreign investment that gives primacy of norms to the protecting the rights of investors at the expense of the public interest, recent developments show that existing treaty regimes and thinking about investment treaties remain resistant to change. The vitality of the perpetuation of neoliberal ideas is present in the efforts at creating mega-regional treaties like the TPP and the TTIP.[116] They contain the same substantive principles as the model treaties of the large capital-exporting states. But the real change is that they seek an approach of bolstering up the neoliberal order through the development of norms on dispute settlement. Knowing that investor-state arbitration has been a heavy target of attack the attention is now shifted to the setting up of investment courts. Such a proposal has been made by the negotiators for the European Union and Canada.[117]

The proposal for a multilateral investment court is a red herring. The central issue is whether investment treaties should exist in the form and substance they do at all. As explained in this chapter, investment treaty investor protections have been developed in a manner to be so broad as to curtail substantially the ability of states to regulate inside their borders. The secondary issue is whether, if investment courts do come to be, they are better than the present system for the settlement of disputes through investor-state arbitration. An investment court would provide a forum for cloaking the neoliberal prescriptions that are made with greater legitimacy as a permanent court will have the opportunity to make hard law more expeditiously and with more certainty.

International investment law is in the throes of a tussle between forces that seek to change the order based on its prescriptions and the forces that seek to entrench its gains and further stabilize the regime. The outcome of the tussle is yet unclear but

[116] With the election of Trump, the possibility of these treaties is now remote, but not for the right reasons. See Presidential Memorandum Regarding withdrawal of the United States from the Trans-Pacific Partnership Negotiations and Agreement, 23 Jan 2017.

[117] European Commission—Fact Sheet, 'A Future Multilateral Investment Court: The European Commission and the Canadian Government are Working Together to Establish a Multilateral Investment Court' 13 Dec 2016, europa.eu/rapid/press-release_MEMO-16-4350_en.htm

the withdrawals from the system, the return to national legislation, the termination of treaties, and the narrower grounds for claims as stated in the newer treaties point to efforts to resist neoliberalism. Unless this is done, justice will be a distant vision as states will be unable to calibrate their economic policies to the differing circumstances of their economies. This shift would not mark the end of neoliberalism but perhaps the beginning of acknowledging anew the sacred place of democratic governance and of the market as subservient to society.

6

Global Finance

Riches for the Few; Harm for the Many

The global financial architecture that was put in place when neoliberalism overtook efforts to achieve the New International Economic Order (NIEO) was a radical departure from what existed previously. A neoliberal form of financial globalization now dominates the global economic scene.[1] The financial globalization existing today reflects an extreme version of global capitalism. It is accomplished through a legal and institutional order referred to in this chapter as the global financial architecture, encompassing a range of hard and soft law initiatives applicable to banks, financial institutions that are not traditional banks, capital markets, financial services, sovereign debt, and many other activities relevant to global finance.

The numbers are staggering. Cross-border financial flows increased dramatically after liberalization of the rules permitting such flows in the late 1980s and early 1990s. Cross-border financial flows rose from about 5% of world GDP in the mid 1990s to about 20% in 2007. In that period, they rose three times faster than cross-border trade flows.[2] A significant decline in cross-border financial flows occurred during the most recent global economic crisis, but the growth has resumed although at lower than pre-crisis levels, but this may change as the salience of the crisis wanes through time.[3] Debt is also an indicator of financial globalization. It is the major source of profits for rich investors at the expense of poor consumers, with the substantial cost of systemic risk imposed on the overwhelming majority of people in the world who gain few if any benefits from financial globalization. The modest deleveraging (reduction of the use of debt to make profit) that occurred right after the most recent crisis appears to have been a temporary reaction. Since 2007, global debt has grown to $57 trillion, resulting in an increase in the debt to GDP ratio by

[1] Financial globalization is an umbrella concept that is typically used to refer to the rise of cross-border financial flows and how those financial flows create linkages between states and peoples. See ES Prasad, K Rogoff, SJ Wei, and MA Kose, *Effects of Financial Globalization on Developing Countries Some Empirical Evidence* (IMF 2003) 1–2.

[2] Many sources for this data exist. See *OECD Economic Outlook* No 89 (OECD 2011); OECD, *International Capital Flows: Structural Reforms and Experiences with the OECD Code of Liberalisation of Capital Movements* (June 2011) (Report from the OECD to the G-20 Subgroup on Capital Flow Management).

[3] One place for this data is McKinsey Global Institute, *Financial Globalization: Retreat or Reset?* (Mar 2013).

17%. Global debt as of 2014 was $199 trillion, which was 286% of world GDP in that year. Debt has increased since 2007, when it was $142 trillion and 269% of GDP. China's debt has quadrupled since 2007 in a period in which it has emerged as the largest trading nation.[4] Taking a brief look at the large banks tells us a much about financialization. The largest banks are global operators, outstripping the capacities of many governments to regulate or subsidize them. Though not the case historically, banks are now significantly larger than non-financial firms. The top three largest firms in the world are Chinese banks and seven of eleven of the largest firms in the world are banks.[5] The fourth, Berkshire Hathaway, is a holding company with some ownership interests in insurance and financial firms. The largest bank in the world, Industrial and Commercial Bank of China, has about $3.4 trillion in total assets.[6] Compare it to the largest carmaker in the world, Toyota, which has about $407 billion in total assets.[7] HSBC, the largest bank headquartered in the United Kingdom, holds about $2.6 trillion in assets, roughly the same size of the UK's GDP.[8] The balance sheets of UK banks have been measured at about twenty times that of total wages paid in the United Kingdom.[9] UK bank capitalization has been measured to be about 450% of UK GDP.[10]

With financial globalization, the global financial architecture has become dangerous to inhabit. With it came more severe and frequent asset bubbles threatening the stability of economies. A direct link exists between the law, institutional design, and economic crises. The data shows flat lines for crises during the period of liberal Keynesianism implemented by the Bretton Woods institutions. Though the gold standard and the Bretton Woods order had their problems, no economic crises of any kind occurred in this period, post-war until the mid 1980s.[11]

[4] See McKinsey Global Institute, *Debt and (Not Much) Deleveraging* (Feb 2015); *Debt and Deleveraging: Uneven Progress on the Path to Growth* (Jan 2012); *Debt and Deleveraging: The Global Credit Bubble and Its Economic Consequences* (July 2011).

[5] See S Schaefer, 'The World's Largest Companies 2016' *Forbes* (25 May 2016). Eleven rather than ten firms are evaluated because two firms—Toyota and ExxonMobil—are tied for ninth place.

[6] ibid. [7] ibid.

[8] O Bush, 'Why Is the UK Banking System So Big and Is That a Problem?' (2014) Q4, 54(4) Bank of England Quarterly Bulletin 385.

[9] O Burrows and K Low, 'Mapping the UK Financial System' (2015) Q2, 55(2) Bank of England Bulletin 114.

[10] Bush (n 8).

[11] CP Kindleberger and RZ Aliber, *Manias, Panics, and Crashes: A History of Financial Crises* (6th edn, Palgrave 2011); M Obstfeld and AM Taylor, 'Globalization and Capital Markets' in MD Bordo, AM Taylor, and JG Williamson (eds), *Globalization in Historical Perspective* (University of Chicago Press 2003) 121. Reinhart and Rogoff explain:

> [C]onsonant with the modern theory of crises is the striking correlation between freer capital mobility and the incidence of banking crises ... *Periods of high international capital mobility have repeatedly produced international banking crises, not only famously, as they* did in *the1990s, but historically.*

They continue: 'One common feature of the run-up to banking crises is a sustained surge in capital inflows', which has been termed a 'capital flow bonanza'. CM Reinhart and KS Rogoff, *This Time Is Different: Eight Centuries of Financial Follies* (Princeton UP 2009) 155, 157. The criticisms of Reinhart and Rogoff's link between high government debt and slow growth are not relevant here. See, eg,

The kind of risk at issue in global finance is not only simple market risk, which is a risk only between the parties to a transaction. It is not simply risk between the buyers and sellers of financial products. It includes systemic risk.[12] Systemic financial risk imposes what economists call negative externalities on persons who have nothing to do with the financial practices causing the risk and who often have no stake in any potential gains accumulating from these practices. The victims of financial globalization mainly receive burdens and not benefits—too many downsides and too few, if any, upsides. Systemic financial risk has the potential to inflict substantial harm, particularly on the poor and the vulnerable, and disproportionately on debtors relative to savers and investors. The mitigation of systemic risk is a significant collective action problem for regulators.

Contemporary debates about regulating global finance focus almost exclusively on financial stability.[13] Financial stability is the *grundnorm* for all post-crisis financial regulation.[14] Financial stability is necessary and important, but it is an incomplete focus. A focus on financial stability leads regulators to ignore concerns about justice and fairness. We focus on a significant set of problems with the global financial architecture: the injustices the architecture imposes on states and their peoples. Governments and international rule-makers need to explore how to achieve financial stability in ways that are sensitive to concerns of justice. Each of the fundamental pillars in the architecture make it susceptible to reasonable rejection by those who bear its burdens. The current architecture imposes insecurity in a manner that makes the rich richer and the poor poorer. It permits the free flow of capital in a

T Herndon, M Ash, and R Pollin, 'Does High Public Debt Consistently Stifle Economic Growth? A Critique of Reinhart and Rogoff' (2014) 38(2) Cambridge Journal of Economics 257.

[12] J Linarelli, 'Luck, Justice, and Systemic Financial Risk' (2017) 34 Journal of Applied Philosophy 331.

[13] See, eg, M Adenas and I H-Y Chiu, *The Foundations and Future of Financial Regulation: Governance for Responsibility* (Routledge 2014) 8–9 (on the 'public good' of stability). Other goals may be important as well. See, eg, L Garciano and RM Lastra, 'Towards a New Architecture for Financial Stability: Seven Principles' in T Cottier, JH Jackson, and RM Lastra (eds), *International Law in Financial Regulation and Monetary Affairs* (OUP 2012) 72. Other goals are not well understood and tend to get subsumed into the stability goal.

[14] See International Monetary Fund, Global Financial Stability Report (Oct 2016), https://www.imf.org/external/pubs/ft/gfsr/2016/02; European Central Bank, Financial Stability Review (Nov 2016), https://www.ecb.europa.eu/pub/fsr/html/index.en.html; Bank of England, Financial Stability Report (Nov 2016), http://www.bankofengland.co.uk/publications/Pages/fsr/default.aspx. These reports are issued on a periodic basis. The Bank of England's definition of financial stability is available at http://www.bankofengland.co.uk/financialstability/Pages/default.aspx. The Dodd–Frank Wall Street Reform and Consumer Protection Act, Public Law No 111–203 (21 July 2010), 124 Stat 1376 (2010), the comprehensive post-crisis legislation in the United States, uses the phrase 'financial stability' ninety-seven times. The first sentence of Dodd–Frank states: 'To promote the financial stability of the United States by improving accountability and transparency in the financial system, to end "too big to fail", to protect the American taxpayer by ending bailouts, to protect consumers from abusive financial services practices, and for other purposes.' As explained below, the Financial Stability Board, established in April 2009, forms a pillar of the current global financial order, succeeding the Financial Stability Forum. Financial stability has been the subject of attention of the Bank for International Settlements and the Basel Committee on Banking Supervision for some time. There is a journal dedicated to financial stability: *Journal of Financial Stability*, published by Elsevier.

way that allows sophisticated market actors to extract rents from the system using unsustainable levels of leverage, risking asset valuation bubbles that disproportionately benefit the affluent and disproportionately harm those on the financial margins. It permits banks to be so highly leveraged as to be a danger to societies, with the rewards of subsidies and government guarantees, all paid for by taxpayers. It is unjust in the way that it structures sovereign debt to impose misery on citizens to enrich creditors. The global financial architecture, in sum, is designed to increase the financialization of the global economy leading to an accumulation by dispossession, a movement of wealth from poor to rich, from marginalized and middle-class households to market sophisticates, from the public to the private. It is an institutional order to govern the wealth of a community that can be reasonably rejected by persons motivated by concerns of justice.

Any financial architecture worthy of support needs to do more than avoid crises. It could achieve crisis-free conditions in a totally unjust manner. Or financial stability could come at the expense of access to credit in the banking system and with serious adverse consequences for economic welfare. It is not that financial stability should be abandoned as a goal, but how financial stability is achieved along with other important policy goals needs to be investigated. If, for example, financial stability could be achieved by means that impose fewer harms on less well-off groups, or which contribute less to income inequality, then these means need to be identified and prioritized, just as minimum standards under international human rights law require, a topic that is explored further in section 3. The focus has been almost entirely on keeping the banking system sound and capital markets confident but without regard to the consequences of policies to those who need credit most in societies.

Banking and capital markets need to be better understood from the standpoint of social value. They are not only accumulations of private rights and liabilities in a market. They are also the financial wealth of a community, which the community can rightly use to promote social and not merely private ends and going beyond mere accumulation by the owners of the assets. In a capital market, assets are individually owned in a system that protects property rights and pooled into markets as tradable securities. But the pool is not simply an aggregation of private wealth. These markets are made possible only through law. Finance is entirely legally constructed.[15] It exists only in the form and substance that we make of it through our institutions, in the allocation of risk, rights, and liabilities in contract and regulation. In a fair scheme of social cooperation, the creators of these norms, the people of the community, should benefit from the existence of these markets. The rules need to meet the standard of reasonable acceptance set forth in Chapter 2 ('Confronting the Pathologies of International Law'). No community member should have a reason to reject the organization of market institutions, regardless of whether they own any assets in the market. And

[15] See K Pistor, 'A Legal Theory of Finance' (2013) 41 Journal of Comparative Economics 315.

because banking and capital markets now exist on a global scale, the community must be understood globally.[16]

Apart from concerns about the justice of the global financial architecture, it fails on its own terms. It imposes financial *instability.* Even stability is at risk in the current global financial architecture. Rule-making ostensibly designed to achieve financial stability often gets captured by powerful financial interests and the result is rules and policies that fail to achieve their intended purpose. It is widely accepted, perhaps not by lawyers but certainly by a large consensus of economists and other social scientists, that the current global financial architecture is poorly designed but politics prevents its fixing. The consensus seems to be that the current arrangements will fail to stabilize the global economy in downturns.[17]

The rules affecting financial globalization at the international level are a hodgepodge of norms that cannot always be classified as falling within recognized sources of international law.[18] Traditional treaty instruments are remnants of a prior age when cross-border financial flows were restricted. These rules have a characteristic of international law known as fragmentation, a subject that has received considerable attention in the past decade.[19] At the risk of oversimplification, fragmentation in international law can be understood as a description of international law as not comprising a single normative order within an overarching normative framework with systemic properties. In the norms governing global finance, fragmentation goes even further, to include at its core extralegal norms that are not formal law or legally binding in a traditional sense. Most of the discussion about fragmentation tends to locate in legal theory and not in normative theory. Legal theory deals with ontological questions and ignores questions going to the values that we need to explore here.[20] Going beyond legal theory, approaches influenced by game theory and economics have been offered as a way to understand fragmentation.[21] None

[16] Paul Tucker, former Deputy General Governor of the Bank of England, has referred to a 'banking social contract'. P Tucker, *Regimes for Handling Bank Failures: Redrawing the Banking Social Contract* (British Bankers' Association Annual International Conference, 30 June 2009). Tucker employs the concept in a different way from a philosopher would.

[17] A good sampling of the literature is covered in the sections to follow.

[18] C Brummer, *Soft Law and the Global Financial System: Rule Making in the 21st Century* (2nd edn, CUP 2015).

[19] Not least, M Koskenniemi et al, Report of the Study Group of the International Law Commission, *Fragmentation of International Law: Difficulties Arising from the Diversification and Expansion of International Law* International Law Commission, 58th session, General Assembly, A/CN.4/L.682, 13 Apr 2006.

[20] On the ontological nature of the question, see R Michaels and J Pauwelyn, 'Conflict of Norms or Conflicts of Law? Different Techniques in the Fragmentation of Public International Law' in T Broude and Y Shany (eds), *Multi-Source Equivalent Norms in International Law* (Hart 2010) 19–44.

[21] Law and economics, at least its rational choice version, gives primacy to private bargaining. Persons, firms, and states can privately bargain to an efficient result when transaction costs of bargaining are low enough and no social costs in the form of externalities on third parties will result from the bargain. This is a standard Coase theorem argument and it forms the foundation for much of rational choice theory about the law. Municipal law may be necessary when persons do not bear the full social costs for their actions or when transaction costs prevent private bargaining. Similarly, international law may be necessary when states do not bear the full social costs for their actions, such as when they impose risks on other states and their peoples from their activities. States can cooperate, however, without international law, such as through soft law, and in fact there is an argument that informal

of these approaches offers the range of insights needed to fully understand what is going on in global finance. The concern exposed in this chapter in the global financial architecture is not conceptual but practical: a focus on the moral disorder of global finance in the form of disjointed norms that makes bankers and financial interests the real makers and beneficiaries of these norms while making everyone else passive recipients of norms that can in many cases reasonably be rejected by these passive recipients because of the very real and serious risks that these norms pose to their lives, their families, and their communities.

If a classic example exists of where the national and international dissolve and puts the practical association point, discussed in Chapter 2, into serious doubt, global finance is it. It is an area in which the distinction between international and domestic law does not deserve the respect it might in other areas. David Graeber's description of what happens when the International Monetary Fund (IMF) imposes conditions in sovereign debt restructuring makes the point:

> there [is] a difference between refinancing loans, and demanding that in order to obtain refinancing, countries have to follow some orthodox free-market economic policy designed in Washington or Zurich that their citizens never agreed to and never would, and that it was a bit dishonest to insist that countries adopt democratic constitutions and then also insist that, whoever gets elected, they have no control over their country's policies anyway.[22]

Trying to neatly separate the national and the international in finance risks fetishizing the conceptual over the pragmatic and the masking of real harm in an analysis of formal categorization of rules over moral problematizing of the rules. To understand the consequences of financial regulation we cannot isolate law along the old categories. Global finance challenges these old categories.

This chapter proceeds as follows. Section 1 explains the history of the global financial architecture from the latter nineteenth century to the present. Primarily soft law standard-setters are now at the centre of the global financial architecture, designed substantially around the regulation of banks, with liberalized cross-border financial flows as a dominant feature of the architecture. It is important to discovering how we got to an institutional state of affairs, entirely of our own doing, that promotes financial instability, benefits the few who participate in the financial system, and harms the rest who in the main do not participate. Section 2 critiques this institutional state of affairs, mainly on grounds of justice. Section 3 deals with problems associated with the regulation and supervision of banks, which now is the foundation of the soft law found in the global financial architecture. Banking regulation is inadequate—banks are dangerous. They use too much debt to finance their operations. The result is recurring failures and risks of failures of banks. Banks,

institutions lower the costs of cooperation. C Brummer, *Minilateralism: How Trade Alliances, Soft Law and Financial Engineering Are Redefining Statecraft* (CUP 2014). The concern in the economics of international law is whether the rules in question are efficient. The focus is on the conditions for cooperation, not so much on the terms of that cooperation. See JP Trachtman, *The Future of International Law: Global Government* (CUP 2013) 168.

[22] D Graeber, *Debt: The First 5,000 Years* (Melville House 2011) 3.

moreover, have played a substantial role in creating a shadow banking system to avoid regulation, increasing risk to societies and globally. Section 3 also explores how the power of global finance makes real reform at either the domestic or international level very difficult. Section 4 exposes injustices associated with the resolution of sovereign debt crises, with a focus on the recent crisis for Greece. Section 4 sets out how an international law approach designed around the notion of contract offers creditors, states, and the IMF the means to resolve crises in a manner in which the less advantaged are made much worse off through the discredited economic policy of austerity. The Greek crisis was an example of how an inadequate global financial architecture internalizes domination: rich EU member states and the IMF dictated the terms of the resolution to the Greek state, causing harm to the Greek people. It is a classic example, as is sovereign debt restructuring more generally, of how differentiated notions of justice as between states and the global must necessarily fail. The normative bottom line for the global financial architecture is that it offers great benefits to the few, very little to the rest, while putting everyone at risk of serious economic harm. It constitutes a classic case of a set of morally disordered institutions. The global financial architecture, is, in sum, not only a practical failure, but a moral failure too.

1. Designed to Harm: The Global Financial Architecture

The global financial architecture was until recently not the subject of much attention except for insiders and technocrats. Its lack of transparency is partly a result of its fragmentation across a variety of institutional contexts but also because of its variegated form, a good deal of which is so-called soft law,[23] its technical nature, but perhaps more significantly, its considerable change since 1944, with the relegation in the 1990s of the IMF and the World Bank, two well-known intergovernmental organizations, to secondary status in global finance,[24] albeit with important gatekeeping roles and considerable influence over poor (including indebted) countries.[25] No multilateral treaty governs global finance. There is no World Financial Organization nor do strong prospects exist for one in the future.[26] According to Chris Brummer, for global finance, 'institutions of various sizes, shapes, and objectives participate in the regulatory process—and no one institution has a monopoly (or even explicit authority) over the day-to-day activities of all others. As such,

[23] Some parts of the soft law aspects of the international financial architecture, notably those dealing with banking, usually get implemented in the traditional forms of domestic law. For example, in the United States, banking regulation is mainly administrative law.

[24] See E Helleiner, *States and the Reemergence of Global Finance: From Bretton Woods to the 1990s* (Cornell UP 1994).

[25] See, eg, C Tan, 'Mandating Rights and Limiting Mission Creep: Holding the World Bank and the International Monetary Fund Accountable for Human Rights Violations' (2008) 2 Human Rights and International Legal Discourse 1, 79.

[26] See RM Lastra, 'Do We Need a World Financial Organisation?' (2014) 17 JIEL 787.

new forms can be created, launched, and reformed, just as responsibilities can be shared or moved from one institution to another in the face of novel regulatory challenges.'[27] The global financial architecture is so unlike that for trade and investment. States have not sought to govern the field through plurilateral, regional, and bilateral agreements. No country is proposing anything like 'mega-regionals' despite the global financial crisis, which led to the Great Recession of 2009. But whatever the institutional architecture for global finance is or will become it must comply with basic moral demands for justice.

Modern global finance has two periods in which exchange rates were not managed and cross-border financial flows were liberalized. The first was the period between about 1870 to 1914, when a significant number of states pegged their exchange rates to the market value of gold, and when cross-border financial flows were substantial. The second period is from about 1974 to the present. Exchange rates now freely float and cross-border financial flows are substantial once more.[28] There are two periods of financial globalization in the modern history of states, one in the age of unfettered capitalism, before the First World War, and the second in an era of neoliberal capitalism, after the cold war.

A key qualitative difference between these two periods of financial globalization is in the kinds of cross-border financial flows that occurred in the late-nineteenth-century period of financial globalization and in the current period.[29] Cross-border financial flows today are designed primarily for investors to achieve diversification of assets, in the form of asset swapping by investors in high-income countries. Their purpose is to hedge and share risks among the rich and not for long-term finance or to match the supply of savings with the demand for investment among countries. In contrast to financial flows in the current period, late-nineteenth-century cross-border financial flows were about accumulation and investment, though of course, that investment was in large part to further colonization and empire. A considerable body of evidence informs us that low-income countries are marginalized in the current global financial architecture, with very low inbound financial flows. In the late-nineteenth-century era of financial globalization, they were major recipients of foreign capital, accounting for almost half of inward financial flows before the First World War.[30] Obstfeld and Taylor explain: 'Globalised capital markets are back,

[27] Brummer (n 18) 65.

[28] There are many economic sources that explore this history in much greater detail. See, eg, Helleiner (n 24); A Elson, *Governing Global Finance: The Evolution and Reform of the International Financial Architecture* (Palgrave 2011); M Obstfeld and AM Taylor, *Global Capital Markets: Integration, Crisis, and Growth* (CUP 2005); B Eichengreen, *Globalising Capital: A History of the International Monetary System* (2nd edn, Princeton UP 2002). There are no accounts of the *legal* history of international financial law. This is likely due to the lack of formal law on the subject. Much of the history of the subject must be dealt with as a matter of political economy or institutional economics. To conceptualize international finance only from the perspective of law would produce serious gaps in the discussion.

[29] Obstfeld and Taylor (n 11); M Schularick and TM Steger, 'Financial Integration, Investment, and Economic Growth: Evidence from Two Eras of Financial Globalisation' (2010) 92 Review of Economics and Statistics 756; M Schularick, 'A Tale of Two Globalisations: Capital Flows from Rich to Poor in Two Eras of Global Finance' (2006) 11 International Journal of Finance and Economics 339; see also A Samuels, 'The Epicenter of American Equality' *The Atlantic* (23 Sept 2016).

[30] Schularick (n 29) 340.

but with a difference: Capital transactions seem to be mostly a rich-rich affair, a process of "diversification finance" rather than "development finance". The high-impact creditor–debtor country pairs involved are more rich-rich than rich-poor, and today's foreign investment in the poorest developing countries lags far behind the levels attained at the start of the last century.'[31]

Cross-border financial flows in the contemporary global financial architecture are designed to making the rich richer and result in serious capital deprivation where it is most needed and could be put to more productive uses.[32] No claims are made that the late-nineteenth-century period of financial globalization was free of exploitation or injustice. It was a period in which empire and colonization were ascendant. We isolate a single empirical insight here to make the point that the global financial architecture in its current form is not improving the lives of people in low- and some middle-income countries, and indeed may be making their lives worse. Diversification finance solves the problem of market risk for rich investors but has aggravated exposure of everyone to the substantial social costs associated with systemic risk. The costs associated with systemic risk tend to be borne disproportionately by marginalized peoples and groups. Those excluded from or not participating in the global financial order bear substantial risks of harm.[33]

Some economists have sought to show that the reason for lack of investment in low-income countries is due to 'poor institutional quality'.[34] This argument fails to account for the features of diversification finance. Investing for diversification pushes capital to profit-making away from investment and towards trading and speculating—in essence gambling—in the major capital markets in London, New York, Hong Kong, and elsewhere, where it takes the form of tradable securities for the rich. These activities make capital markets more like casinos than sources of community wealth. For example, securities can be created by pooling residential mortgages or any other asset that produces a cash flow, and these securities, if backed by mortgages, are known as mortgage-backed securities, which can be sold to investors. This is known as securitization, the most prominent form of shadow banking.[35] There are benefits associated with this financial practice. Banks benefit from securitization to diversify risk. But with financial globalization, mortgage-backed securities have been used to produce new securities called collateralized debt obligations on top of collateralized debt obligations. For example, the mezzanine or middle tranche of a mortgage-backed security, which might be rated BBB,[36]

31 Obstfeld and Taylor (n 11) 175–76.

32 They also exhibit very strongly the Lucas paradox which is that capital does not flow from developed to developing countries, despite the fact that developing countries have low levels of capital per worker and therefore infusions of capital should result in higher returns, given diminishing marginal returns on capital. R Lucas, 'Why Doesn't Capital Flow from Rich to Poor Countries?' (1990) 80(2) American Economic Review 92.

33 See section 1.2.

34 L Alfaro, S Kalemli-Ozcan, and V Volosovych, 'Why Doesn't Capital Flow from Rich to Poor Countries? An Empirical Investigation' (2005) 90(2) Review of Economics and Statistics 347.

35 See (n 141) for authorities on shadow banking.

36 Credit ratings are evaluations of credit risk, which is the risk of default of a debtor. The role of credit ratings agencies has been under considerable investigation after the most recent global financial

could then be divided into senior, mezzanine, and junior tranches, and the mezzanine tranche of this collateralized debt obligation could then be divided again into senior, mezzanine, and junior tranches, all with new credit ratings.[37] These derivative instruments are designed mainly to produce returns for investors. They produce no new social value. Any socially useful functions of this financial engineering, such as in producing liquidity in markets or opening financing for housing, were accomplished by the initial securitization. Firms that produce these sorts of derivatives look to produce them in capital markets that have high institutional quality, such as in New York or London. Institutional quality beyond these established capital markets may not bear much relevance when investors predominantly trade for diversification. Moreover, given financial globalization, investors who want to raise capital for investment in low- and middle-income countries can do so in any capital market. The problem is that development finance is simply far less important today.

How did the international financial architecture get to where it is today? After the era of financial globalization lasting until 1914, from about 1914 to 1945, finance was in a relatively autarkic state because of two world wars. The discussion to follow skips the war periods and starts with the Bretton Woods system.[38]

On 1–22 July 1944, the United Nations Monetary and Financial Conference was held at the Mount Washington Hotel in Bretton Woods, New Hampshire. Delegates from forty-four states created a new international monetary system which came to be known as the Bretton Woods system. Of course, politics and power played significant roles, with the United States and the United Kingdom the most influential actors. But the effort was ideationally centred in a form of enlightened Keynesianism. The key architects were John Maynard Keynes, the lead British representative and Harry Dexter White, the lead US representative.

The Bretton Woods agreements established two intergovernmental organizations: the IMF and the International Bank for Reconstruction and Development (IBRD).[39] The Bretton Woods institutions were initially viewed as a comprehensive and integrated governance architecture designed to avoid the problems that arose

crisis. The US Financial Crisis Inquiry Commission concluded that 'the failures of credit ratings agencies were essential cogs in the wheels of financial destruction'. Financial Crisis Inquiry Commission, 'The Financial Crisis Inquiry Report: Final Report of the National Commission on the Causes and Consequences of the Financial and Economic Crisis in the United States' Jan 2011, at xxv, https://www.gpo.gov/fdsys/pkg/GPO-FCIC/pdf/GPO-FCIC.pdf

37 See F Partnoy and D Skeel Jr, 'The Promise and Perils of Credit Derivatives' (2007) 75 University of Cincinnati Law Review 1019.

38 For an overview of the Bretton Woods institutions, see AF Lowenfeld, *International Economic Law* (2nd edn, OUP 2008) 593.

39 The IBRD has since evolved into the World Bank Group. The World Bank is currently comprised of two units: the International Bank for Reconstruction and Development (IBRD), which lends to low- and middle-income countries and the International Development Association (IDA), which provides interest free loans (credits) and grants to the poorest countries. The World Bank Group is comprised of five units, the two forming the World Bank, plus the Multilateral Investment Guarantee Agency (MIGA) and the International Centre for the Settlement of Investment Disputes (ICSID). MIGA provides political risk insurance to investors and lenders. Beyond the 'hard' lending and financing programmes the World Bank and IMF undertake, they have also undertaken to provide monitoring, policy advice, and research.

in international monetary affairs between the two world wars.[40] IMF policies were central to an approach to monetary cooperation that restricted cross-border financial flows for almost thirty years after the Second World War.

Bretton Woods put in place a system of exchange rate controls. IMF members were required to peg the par value of their currency in terms of the value of gold or the US dollar.[41] In addition to currency exchange controls, no IMF member could impose restrictions on payments and transfers for current international transactions without IMF approval.[42] In the Bretton Woods system, the free movement and convertibility of funds for current transactions is to be contrasted with the substantial controls on the movement and convertibility of capital. According to Keynes: 'Nothing is more certain than that movement of capital funds must be regulated ... which in itself will involve far-reaching departures from laissez-faire arrangements'.[43] The United Kingdom was concerned about further depletion of capital in the country and so the prohibition on exchange controls was not made to apply to capital transfers. For capital transfers, IMF members could freely devise 'such controls as are necessary to regulate international capital movements'.[44]

[40] See P Coggan, *Paper Promises: Money, Debt and the New World Order* (Allen Lane 2011).

[41] Pegging at par value simply meant that the currency value was set at a value equal to whatever other currency (or gold), serves as the benchmark. The US dollar's value was in turn pegged to the value of gold as of the first day of the Bretton Woods conference, 1 July 1944. Each state was required to maintain the value of its currency within 1% below or above its par value. To maintain this pegging of the value of a currency to the US dollar, states were required to purchase or sell their currency with reserves of fully convertible currency. If a state lacked the reserves, it could draw on IMF resources so long as the IMF determined that the need was temporary and the state would pursue policies, usually within three to five years, to overcome the shortfall. This marked the beginning of the concept of IMF conditionality. The IMF would conduct *ex ante* reviews before a drawing was needed and enter stand-by arrangements with countries. A stand-by arrangement is a commitment to a drawing if and when needed, usually within six to twelve months. Performance targets were specified on such matters as budget deficits, tax collection, pension policy, inflation rates, and trade balances. The drawing was in form a purchase of currency but in substance a loan. The IMF had the resources to do this because IMF members were required to pay the IMF a subscription based on a quota, reflecting voting strength in IMF governance, comprising 25% in gold or US dollars, with the rest in its own currency. Revaluation of par value was permitted only to correct a 'fundamental disequilibrium' and after consultation with the IMF. 'Fundamental disequilibrium' was not defined in the IMF Articles of Agreement but it was generally understood to mean a situation not correctible within three to five years, ie, the time that resources of the IMF would normally be available to members. Revaluation did not resort to floating exchange rate but to a new par value.

[42] IMF Articles of Agreement, Art VIII(2). A number of states maintained a transition status permitting exchange controls on current transactions for some years after 1944. Some justified these restrictions on grounds that unemployment would become substantial if they lifted the controls. In actual practice, exchange controls were more substantial than a reading of the rules in IMF's Articles of Agreement would suggest.

[43] DE Moggridge, *Keynes* (3rd edn, University of Toronto Press 1993) 673, quoted in CL Lim and B Mercurio, 'The Fragmented Disciplines of International Economic Law after the Global Financial and Economic Crisis: An Introduction' in CL Lim and B Mercurio (eds), *International Economic Law after the Global Crisis: A Tale of Fragmented Disciplines* (CUP 2015) 12.

[44] IMF Articles of Agreement, Article VI(3). Of course, regulatory arbitrage might result in circumvention of capital controls. Capital transfers were made during this period through the timing of import and export payments. Kindleberger and Aliber (n 11) 229–30. But this was not really movement of capital but returns on short-term investment of funds. Capital mobility was still quite low in the Bretton Woods period. Obstfeld and Taylor (n 11).

The system was designed to facilitate international trade in goods but not international flows of capital. Financial flows had to be restricted if the fixed exchange rate system was to work.[45] A 'natural corollary' of exchange rate controls were restrictions on the availability of credit within a national economy.[46] In the period of fixed exchange rates, credit availability was restricted and managed in many of the major economies. The Bretton Woods era was a time when banks were domestic enterprises that engaged only in commercial banking.[47] There was no shadow banking. Liberal domestic credit was a threat to fixed exchange rates; it would be difficult to maintain an exchange rate at a particular par value if credit increased imports to the extent that a current account deficit became unsustainable.[48]

How did countries emerging from colonialism get financing in a world of capital controls?[49] International commercial lending practically did not exist from 1914 until it resumed in the Eurodollar market in the 1960s. Private financial flows in whatever form were much smaller than official flows from multilateral institutions and from governments as creditors. Private financial flows in the Bretton Woods period were low in comparison to these public financial flows.[50] Recall that the World Bank was one of two key institutions in the Bretton Woods system. A system of regional development banks also came into existence, which provided smaller-scale lending.[51]

By the early 1970s, it became unsustainable for the US dollar to be fixed at its value as at 1 July 1944. The system of fixed exchange rates collapsed in the early 1970s. The United States terminated its treaty obligations to maintain the dollar as a reserve currency in August 1971. IMF members tried various amendments to the IMF Articles of Agreement but the result was a move from managed to floating exchange rates. The managed exchange rate features of the Bretton Woods system are now history, no longer forming the current set of rules and policies in the global financial system.

Though gold standard was far from desirable[52] no financial crises occurred in the period of Bretton Woods exchange controls.[53] By 'financial' crisis we here mean the varieties of crises that can occur in a global economy, including but not limited to sovereign and other debt crises, banking crises, bursting of asset price bubbles,

[45] A Turner, *Between Debt and the Devil: Money, Credit, and Fixing Global Finance* (Princeton UP 2016) 90–91.

[46] ibid.

[47] Brummer (n 18) 10 ('For much of the postwar period up through the 1980s, the objects of financial regulation—banks, the buyers and sellers of securities, and insurance companies—were primarily domestic actors').

[48] Coggan (n 40); Turner (n 45) 90–91.

[49] Chapter 5 ('Foreign Investment') deals with the separate questions associated with foreign direct investment law.

[50] The above is based on JD Sachs, 'Developing Country Debt' in M Feldstein (ed), *International Economic Cooperation* (University of Chicago Press 1988) 233.

[51] See SD Krasner, 'Power Structures and Regional Development Banks' (1981) 35 International Organization 303.

[52] For a recent critique see Y Varoufakis, *And the Weak Suffer What They Must? Europe, Austerity, and the Great Threat to Global Stability* (Vintage 2017).

[53] Kindleberger and Aliber (n 11); Reinhart and Rogoff (n 11).

and currency devaluation crises.[54] There are a variety of reasons for this stability. Private debt was relatively low in the period, and sovereign debt was in the process of accumulating. There could be no real possibility of asset price bubbles because of capital controls. Currency could not rapidly devalue because exchange rates were managed. Banks were basically domestic actors and did not engage in speculative financing, did not carry tradable assets on their books, and did not seek to avoid regulatory limitations through regulatory arbitrage in the form of shadow banking.

At the same time the Bretton Woods architecture of exchange rate control and restrictions on cross-border financial flows was disintegrating, the NIEO debates began in the United Nations. The NIEO received its official start with the adoption in 1974 by the United Nations General Assembly of the Declaration for the Establishment of a New International Economic Order.[55] The fixed exchange rate system came to an end in the period 1968–73, when the United States delinked the value of the dollar to the value of gold. At the time when the Bretton Woods system was adapting to change and its institutions becoming essentially secondary actors in global finance, developing countries sought to influence the agenda in global finance towards a fairer set of norms for the global economy.

The NIEO agenda was relevant to the reformulation of the global financial architecture in several ways. Developing countries were not well represented at Bretton Woods.[56] The NIEO provided developing countries with a focal point at a time when the global financial architecture was up for reform. The NIEO identified economic development, equity, and distribution as relevant concerns in the reform of the global financial architecture, at a time when powerful banking and financial interests sought to influence governments towards a liberalized laissez-faire structure of largely unregulated cross-border financial flows.

IMF members formed a Committee of Twenty (C20) to hold discussions in 1972–74. Though the C20 comprised a broader representation of interests than Bretton Woods, its agenda was largely controlled by the United States, Western Europe, and Japan. The C20's 'Outline for Reform' addressed the interests of developing countries, though this was mainly token as the liberalization agenda of high-income capital-controlling countries managed the outcome of the C20 report issued in June 1974.[57] Developing countries were also interested in the management of commodity markets to foster economic development, given that many of them were commodity exporters. Finally, developing countries were interested in more legal than informal mechanisms to deal with sovereign debt restructuring.

But change in the aftermath of the Bretton Woods regime moved in the opposite direction from the NIEO proposals. It did not move from a liberal Keynesianism of cooperation in international monetary affairs to a more robust fair and equitable framework in which a law on global finance could be of benefit to those most in need of capital and less harmful to those who are less able to bear the systemic

[54] See Reinhart and Rogoff (n 11) ch 1 for a taxonomy.

[55] Resolution Adopted by the General Assembly, 3201 (S-VI) Declaration on the Establishment of a New International Economic Order, A/Res/S-6/3201, 1 May 1974.

[56] What follows is guided by Elson (n 28).

[57] See Helleiner (n 24) ch 5.

risk associated with capital liberalization. Rather, it moved to what Benjamin Cohen has described as a 'neoclassical or neoliberal policy framework' which 'gained strength from the pre-existence of a sophisticated epistemic community of central bankers based around the Bank for International Settlements (BIS).'[58] The second amendment of the IMF Articles of Agreement, which entered into force on 1 April 1978, reflects this approach in its opening sentence, 'that the essential purpose of the international monetary system is to provide a framework that facilitates the exchange of goods, services, *and capital* among countries'.[59] The opportunity for a robust legal form of cooperation in global finance was lost.

Predictably, capital account liberalization led to a credit bonanza which in turn led to the first post-war crisis, the Mexican debt crisis of 1982, caused by a steep rise in debt-servicing costs as a result of interest rate increases by creditor countries to combat inflation, along with a collapse in commodity prices. Other countries suffered similar crises. The Asian Debt Crisis in the 1990s was the result of attempts to peg currency values to the US dollar, leading to a crisis in confidence and a failure to prop up currency values.[60]

After Bretton Woods, the IMF undertook a new role as a structural adjustment lender, with a substantial increase in conditions it imposed on its lending. The conditions required a much-reduced role for the state in borrower societies, limits on domestic credit, and reductions of budget deficits.[61] The IMF and the World Bank are responsive to 'interest group' pressure.[62] These interest groups include its powerful shareholder countries and the global banks headquartered in those countries that lend to low- and middle-income countries. Structural adjustment lending led to the flow of capital from poor to rich countries because it is designed to enable debtor countries to generate sufficient foreign exchange to pay debts owed in and to creditor countries.[63] It was lending leading to great hardship and very little to help people in low- and middle-income countries. In the 1990s the IMF ostensibly moved away from structural adjustment and towards a strategy of poverty reduction, but criticisms have remained extensive.

In an institutional order in which exchange rates float and cross-border financial flows are unrestricted, the focus of global regulation fell on large, systemically important financial institutions, in particular banks and bank holding companies.[64]

[58] BJ Cohen, 'Phoenix Risen: The Resurrection of Global Finance' (1996) 48 World Politics 268, 271.

[59] IMF Articles of Agreement, approved 30 Apr 1976, entered into force 1 Apr 1978, 15 ILM 546 (1976).

[60] Kindleberger and Aliber (n 11) 3–4, 184, 233, 278; Reinhart and Rogoff (n 11) 16–17.

[61] A Dreher, 'A Public Choice Perspective of IMF and World Bank Lending and Conditionality' (2004) 119 Public Choice 445; RP Buckley, 'The Direct Contribution of the International Financial System to Global Poverty' in KN Schefer (ed), *Poverty in the International Economic Legal System* (CUP 2013) 278. The World Bank and the regional development banks also departed from their traditional project lending role and began to make policy-based loans as well.

[62] See, eg, Dreher (n 61).

[63] Buckley (n 61) 279–86.

[64] Brummer (n 18) 213. Other areas of focus include credit rating agencies and accounting practices.
Systemically significant banks tend to be organized in a bank holding company structure. The typical structure is one of parent–subsidiary relationships, where a holding company owns domestic banks

BIS serves as the clearing bank for central banks, with its membership of over sixty member central banks representing 95% of the global economy.[65] It played a supporting role during the Bretton Woods period but eventually became one of the central governing forum so much that its website now says that 'the BIS is the new financial architecture', in the wake of the Asian Financial Crisis in 1997.[66] Atop the global financial architecture sits the Financial Stability Board (FSB), created in 2009 as a successor to the Financial Stability Forum.[67] The FSB coordinates national regulation and international standards, as well as assesses vulnerabilities in the global financial system. In 1974, the G-10 states and the IMF created the Basel Committee on Banking Supervision. The Basel Committee 'was one of the first concerted forms of international administrative rulemaking'.[68] The Basel Committee serves as a 'think tank' on banking regulation.[69] It has now expanded to G-20 membership.[70] While its charter declares it to be the 'primary global standard setter for the prudential regulation of banks', it has no formal legal status and its decisions lack formal legal authority.[71] It is the drafter of Basel Accords I, II, and III, recommendations for domestic banking regulation with a principal focus on bank capital adequacy. The Committee also has produced the 2008 Principles for Sound Liquidity Risk Management and Supervision.[72] These instruments are not treaties. They do not comprise formal rules of international law.

The Basel Accords form a key set of these soft law instruments. They are designed primarily around a method for evaluating the riskiness of bank assets to determine minimum capital requirements for banks. Capital adequacy rules are supposed to be part of a system of reducing risks in the global economy. The Accords deal with how banks fund themselves—with the mix of debt and equity in their capital structure. They also are intended to create a level playing field between banks internationally, to equalize capital adequacy across borders. If a single country unilaterally makes its capital adequacy rules stricter for its own banks, other countries, under pressure from their own banks, have an incentive to free-ride and to maintain laxer capital adequacy rules for its own banks. Either some banks will still pose too much risk, or a select few countries end up bearing the costs of mitigating risk to the global economy. This is precisely what happened when Japan in the 1980s opted to maintain lax capital adequacy standards for its banks. The United Kingdom and the United States

as subsidiaries, as well as foreign banks as subsidiaries and possibly a range of other subsidiaries engaged in financial services or investment banking but not traditional commercial banking. This reflects the now pervasive model of universal banking, a model rising to significance at about the same time as the rise of the neoliberal global financial order.

[65] About BIS, https://www.bis.org/about/index.htm?l=2andm=1%7C1

[66] https://www.bis.org/about/history_5new_fin_architecture.htm

[67] http://www.fsb.org/about/history [68] Brummer (n 21) 100.

[69] JH Dalhuisen, *Dalhuisen on Transnational Comparative, Commercial, Financial and Trade Law*, vol 3 (5th edn, Hart 2013) 627; see E Avgouleas, *Governance of Global Financial Markets: The Law, the Economics, the Politics* (CUP 2012) ch 5.

[70] Plus Hong Kong and Singapore.

[71] Basel Committee Charter, arts 1, 3 (updated Dec 2016), https://www.bis.org/bcbs/charter.htm

[72] www.bis.org/publ/bcbs144.pdf

pressured Japan, Japan relented, and the Basel I Accord was finalized in 1988.[73] Basel I was 'viewed as one of the marquis achievements in financial statecraft'.[74]

In 2008, the Basel II Accord replaced the Basel I Accord. Basel II was not fully implemented, but it proved inadequate as the most recent financial crisis began in 2007. Basel II has been characterized as an 'immediate flop',[75] coming out in 2008, during crisis. Nouriel Roubini has argued that '[a]ll of the pillars of Basel II have already failed even before being implemented'.[76] The G-20 agreed on the Basel III Accord in 2010–11. Basel III was to be introduced into domestic law from 2013 until 2015. The implementation phase was ultimately extended to March 2019 because of amendments to the Accord.[77]

There are a host of other associations, including the International Organization of Securities Commissions (IOSCO), the International Association of Insurance Supervisors, the International Accounting Standards Board, the International Federation of Accountants, the Committee on Payment and Settlement Systems, the International Association of Deposit Insurers, and the International Swaps and Derivatives Association.[78] These associations promulgate guidance for members.[79]

Perhaps the most telling illustration of the fundamental change of the architecture since Bretton Woods is the total inversion of the structure. Organizations once forming the foundations of the architecture have been moved to the side and no longer form the core of the global financial architecture. At the foundations are the producers of informal norms, basically clubs. Somewhere off to the side are the old Bretton Woods institutions, the IMF, and the World Bank, initially conceived as the most important of international organizations for a legal system of formal law for global finance, now serving the clubs as monitors of compliance, though the IMF maintains a strategic role in managing sovereign debt crises and both continue to have considerable influence over development policy in many low-income countries. More generally, however, the IMF and the World Bank are characterized by other influential actors in global finance as 'no longer the primary originators of financial market policy' but mainly 'observers of policy compliance'.[80] Unlike in the Bretton Woods era, exchange rates are now a matter for domestic policy, not international law or policy.[81] The IMF has made some significant mistakes harmful to people affected by structural adjustment, particularly so in the area of structural adjustment, and the IMF appears to have effectively continued these policies as the recent eurozone crisis, dealt with in section 3, illustrates.

From the standpoint of institutional design, financial regulation has moved in the opposite direction from trade. Trade has moved from what Richard Shell

[73] Brummer (n 21) 101. [74] ibid. [75] Dalhuisen (n 69) 628.

[76] *Financial Times* (London, 9 Feb 2009).

[77] See K MacKenzie, 'European Bank Deleveraging: Basel III Edition' *Financial Times* (London, 24 Oct 2012).

[78] See Brummer (n 18) 67–95, 233–44 (discussion of the roles of these entities).

[79] The ISDA produces a standard form contract, a 'Master Agreement' for over-the-counter derivatives transactions, http://www.isda.org/publications/isdamasteragrmnt.aspx

[80] ibid 69. [81] ibid 90.

described as 'trade realism' to 'trade legalism'. [82] John Jackson called this the move from power to rule orientation in trade,[83] though, of course, power still plays a dominant role in setting the rules. Finance, in contrast, has moved from 'finance legalism' to 'finance realism'. No intergovernmental organization with supervisory and enforcement capabilities exists at the international level. The G-20 is not a formal intergovernmental organization with legal personality.[84] In 2013, the G-20 described itself as 'the premier forum for international cooperation on the most important issues of the global economic and financial agenda'.[85] In 2015, the description narrowed to 'the premier forum *for its members'* international economic cooperation and decision-making'.[86] It is, however, difficult to use language like 'describes itself' and 'regulator' to describe the G-20 because it is not an entity in a formal legal sense but only an aggregation of interests. Neither the FSB nor any other institution fills the gap.

The soft law or 'extralegal' norms dominating in the global financial architecture result in a situation in which no single organization exists to conduct both surveillance and enforcement and to issue authoritative rulings on law and policy, though as is argued in this chapter, conceptual questions about institutional structure do little work in helping us to evaluate the justice of these institutions. No normative claims are made here about the relative superiority or inferiority of hard or soft law based on some autonomous understanding of legal theory and there is no suggestion that a body charged with issuing authoritative rulings would remedy the problems identified in this chapter. Rather, the focus on what is 'better' or 'worse' should be a question about the substance of the law and policy under consideration and not about legal conceptualism. It is entirely possible for soft law to be more just or fair if suitably designed though it is very improbable for global financial norms to meet such standards because vast swaths of the global financial architecture are outsourced to financial interests or to entities captured by those financial interests.

The current state of affairs reflects an assemblage of norms and organizations that create instability and serve the powerful. The current set of rules and policies are usually referred to with the metaphor 'architecture' and this terminology is used in this chapter, but it is really quite inaccurate. As architecture, it is unstable. To refer to it as architecture is to admit its fragility. It effectively falls upon G-20 states, and in particular, a few powerful G-20 members, to maintain the legal and institutional state of affairs at the international level existing today. This is financial statecraft or financial diplomacy in its benign characterization or financial power imposition in its critical characterization, but not financial law if we understand law in its conventional forms. While no

[82] GR Shell, 'Trade Legalism and International Relations Theory: An Analysis of the World Trade Organization' (1995) 44 Duke Law Journal 829.

[83] JH Jackson, *The Jurisprudence of the GATT and the WTO: Insights on Treaty Law and Economic Relations* (CUP 2000) 7–9.

[84] CD Zimmerman, *A Contemporary Concept of Monetary Sovereignty* (OUP 2013) 194.

[85] ibid citing 'What Is the G-20' http://www.g2o.org/docs/about/about_G20.html.

[86] http://g20.org.tr/about-g20, accessed 16 Jan 2016 (emphasis added).

critique is offered on conceptual grounds here, there has been little attention paid to concerns around the impact of decisions promoting powerful financial interests on basic expectations of justice or on accountability for the harms generated.[87]

2. Assessing Harm

2.1 The futility of legal conceptualism

Legal conceptualists come in a variety of stripes, either as analytical legal philosophers, legal theorists who tend to treat law as an autonomous discipline, and functionalists who investigate compliance. A legal conceptualist might find the soft law of global finance problematic on grounds of a lack of universality and comprehensiveness, lack of pedigree as duly enacted law, and problems with its resistance to traditional means of legal enforcement.[88] These conceptual concerns will be less important if one takes an approach based in the social sciences, examining the function of extralegal norms like formal legal rules, which might have even more significance than formal legal rules. Research influenced by game theory and the analytical social sciences investigates compliance with norms lacking the status of formal law, which are usually described in this literature as 'extralegal' or informal norms.[89]

Conceptualist approaches do not get us to where we need to be. Functionalist approaches, the more recent and perhaps most influential of conceptualist approaches, can make normative questions obscure and fetishize compliance as the principal issue at stake. These approaches tell us about the compliance of club members with rules of the club but little else. But what does it mean 'to comply'? To illuminate the limits of conceptualism, think of it in the context of this question: are there not important distinctions between withdrawing from a treaty or breaching is provisions on the one hand,[90] and on the other hand declining to adhere to an extralegal norm or modifying that norm in some way in the process of implementing it? There may be reputational sanctions for breaches of extralegal norms that are serious in their consequences, but reputational sanctions also apply

[87] For a recent and scathing critique of the IMF, see *The IMF and the Crisis in Greece, Ireland, and Portugal: An Evaluation by the Independent Evaluation Office* (8 July 2016). Civil society organizations working in the area of human rights protection and promotion are increasingly focusing on global finance.

[88] Rolf Weber may not accept these arguments but he has articulated them well in RH Weber, 'Does Financial Law Suffer from a Systemic Failure? A Study of the Fragmentation of Legal Sources' in Lim and Mercurio (n 43) 35.

[89] There have been many discussions of these methodological points. For a survey by social scientists, see EM Hafner-Brown, DG Victor, and Y Lupu, 'Political Science Research on International Law: The State of the Field' (2012) 106 AJIL 47. A vast literature exists on the economics of norms, mainly from the 1990s. See N Mercuro and SG Medema, *Economics and the Law: From Posner to Postmodernism and Beyond* (2nd edn, Princeton UP 2006) ch 7 (social norms and law and economics).

[90] See LR Helfer, 'Exiting Treaties' (2005) 91 Virginia Law Review 1579.

to treaty exit and breach contexts too. If we dig deeper, we might find that compliance is difficult to assess, and that causation might be working in the opposite direction: norms in the global financial architecture might be complying with domestic law. What matters more is *what* is being complied with—the substance of the rules themselves and how they do things like make more efficient, distribute resources or welfare, impose vulnerability, facilitate domination, or misallocate resources from the poor to the rich.

Conceptualism helps us to understand the global financial architecture in only a limited sense. It may tell us something analytical or conceptual about fragmentation in international law. It will likely inform us that the rules of clubs are authoritative only to the clubs they serve. Extending out of the analytical framework, this means that the rules may not serve broader interests or reflect values beyond the interests and values of the club's members. These kinds of norms are often accepted into a legal system to govern so-called private activity, as in the case of norms governing contracts and exchange, but they neither have nor claim to be superior or higher in rank to the law itself, which can be used to place restrictions on the rules, unless they are incorporated into the law through an authoritative pronouncement to that effect in the legal system in question.[91] For example, professional associations often promulgate standard terms and conditions that legal systems will enforce, not as law applicable to everyone but as the private law of the contract between the parties.[92] In the global financial context, the club rules take on a public law significance, but they are still rules of the club. The club comprises mainly states with financial markets and banking systems of systemic significance. The club rules they generate in the global financial architecture will likely serve the interests of these states and their financial institutions. The club rules have to comply with domestic regulatory bargains struck by governments and their financial institutions and not the other way around. This is indeed what is occurring. The capital adequacy requirements in the Basel Accords, for example, are not primarily based on any sound empirical or 'scientific' analysis informing governments and the Basel Committee how to set the ratios to mitigate risks to the financial system or the global economy. Rather, they are based primarily only on what the big banks are able, or perhaps more accurately, willing, to do to their capital structures, and what a select group of powerful countries are willing to hold them to.[93]

[91] See J Raz, *The Authority of Law* (2nd edn, OUP 2009) 118–19.

[92] J Linarelli, 'Analytical Jurisprudence and the Concept of Commercial Law' (2009) 114 Penn State University Law Review 119.

[93] See section 2 for more on capital adequacy. One take on this point is A Admati and M Hellwig, 'The Parade of the Bankers' New Clothes: 31 Flawed Claims Debunked' (Dec 2015), http://bankersnewclothes.com/wp-content/uploads/2016/01/Parade-Continues-2015.pdf. This paper provides:

> Flawed Claim 19: Basel III and capital regulation as implemented in different jurisdictions, are based on careful scientific analysis of the cost and benefits of different levels of equity requirements, whereas the rough numbers of those who advocate much higher requirements cannot guide policy because they are not supported by scientific calibration. What's wrong with this claim? Basel III, and regulations as implemented, appear to be the result of a political process much more than of valid scientific analysis . . . [T]he studies that support the Basel III rules are based on flawed models and their quantitative results are meaningless.

Paradox is at work in global financial regulation. Historically, banking and finance are core necessities for the very existence of modern states.[94] They are part and parcel of state power. But banks and financial markets cannot exist without states. Moreover, in the way that the global economy now operates, banking and finance are areas in which domestic and international law must ground in a closely related set of policies, interests, and values. The efficacy of state regulation depends on how other state regulate. Whether exchange rates are managed or float freely, decisions on monetary policy, and the freedom or restriction of cross-border financial flows all have substantial domestic and international effects, and all may be regulated by domestic or international law. Economists contend that three policies operate in a monetary trilemma: a state cannot simultaneously pursue freedom of cross-border financial flows, fixed exchange rates, and an independent monetary policy. Governments can only pursue two of these policies at once.[95] There is

> For example, they assume that the required return on equity is independent of risk; one paper purports to derive the 'optimality' of Basel III without even considering the costs that bank failures can impose on the rest of the financial system and the economy. The 'scientific' papers that discuss costs and benefits of different capital requirements also ignore the distinction between private and social costs, the distortions in investments associated with high leverage, and the problems with risk weights, discussed below.
>
> The fact that studies end up with precise numbers for 'optimal' capital regulation is irrelevant if the foundations of the studies are shaky. We are not aware of any theory or model that would provide appropriate estimates of the costs and benefits to society associated with different funding mixes for banks. Despite this, we are confident in asserting that equity levels of three percent of total assets, as admitted by Basel III, are unsafe, and that a significant increase will substantially improve the health and safety of the financial system. Low levels of equity expose the banks and the economy to unnecessary risk. Allowing banks to rely as much on subsidized borrowing distorts and harms the economy. Countering the banks' incentives to choose unsafe levels by effective regulation is essential, because ... markets fail to produce an efficient outcome both privately for all of banks' investors and socially. A significant challenge in specifying any specific capital ratio has to do with setting the appropriate numerator and denominator, which have to do with valuations of the relevant assets and liabilities. Accounting conventions matter greatly, including how to deal with off-balance sheet exposures and derivatives ... [T]he key to capital regulation is high requirements for genuine, loss absorbing equity, and prompt intervention by regulators if equity is depleted through losses. (emphasis and footnotes omitted)

For a 'law and economics' take on these questions, see EA Posner, 'How Do Bank Regulators Determine Capital Adequacy Requirements?' (2015) 82 University of Chicago Law Review 1853. JC Coates IV, 'Cost–Benefit Analysis of Financial Regulation: Case Studies and Implications' (2015) 124 Yale Law Journal 882 (questioning effectiveness of cost–benefit analysis for financial regulation: 'Finance is at the heart of the economy; is social and political; and is characterized by non-stationary relationships that exhibit secular change'). A recent issue of the *Journal of Legal Studies* deals with cost–benefit analysis of financial regulation. 'Benefit–Cost Analysis of Financial Regulation: A Conference Funded by the Alfred P. Sloan Foundation and Supported by the Coase-Sandor Institute for Law and Economics' (2014) 43(S2) Journal of Legal Studies. Another set of conference papers is in 'The Administrative Law of Financial Regulation' (2015) 78(3) Law and Contemporary Problems.

[94] See CW Calomiris and SH Haber, *Fragile by Design: The Political Origins of Banking Crises and Scarce Credit* (Princeton UP 2014).

[95] Obstfeld and Taylor (n 11) 127–33. The origins of trilemma theory are understood to be in the work of economists Marcus Fleming and Robert Mundell. R Mundell, 'Capital Mobility and Stabilization Policy under Fixed and Flexible Exchange Rates' (1963) 29 Canadian Journal of Economic and Political Science 475; MJ Fleming, 'Domestic Financial Policies under Fixed and Floating Exchange Rates' (1962) 9 IMF Staff Papers 369.

also a second, financial policy trilemma, that states cannot simultaneously pursue a national financial policy, international financial integration, and financial stability.[96] Finance often overrides sovereignty. The most compelling fact of interdependence is systemic risk associated with government policy and financial activity, as was made very clear in the most recent global crisis. The interconnectedness of domestic and international financial law means that attempting to evaluate the law or to formulate legal solutions based on conceptual distinctions between national and the international law becomes a costly distraction, an unrealistically utopian exercise that we undertake at our peril.

2.2 Injustice in the global financial architecture

Turning to a moral assessment of the global financial architecture,[97] let us first explore briefly a few procedural wrongs. We will then move on to substantive wrongs. 'Procedural wrong' refers to the legitimacy of the processes used to produce, apply, and enforce the rules and the standards of public accountability these rules comply or do not comply with.[98] 'Substantive wrong' refers to the legitimacy of the rules themselves from the standpoint of the principles of justice laid out in Chapter 2 ('Confronting the Pathologies of International Law').

Many low- and some middle-income countries are excluded from the process of creating and developing the global financial architecture. Qualification requirements prevent these countries from participating in making the norms that apply to them and their citizens: the club nature of the G-20 and subsidiary institutions in the global financial architecture, some of which do not even have state membership yet perform important functions with effects going well beyond effects on their membership. As David Held and Kevin Young explain: 'most institutions of financial governance have promulgated an exclusionary model for participation when it comes to dealing with problems which are, at the end of the day, quintessentially global'.[99] While these exclusions reduce the transaction costs of agreement and facilitate cooperation, they have a moral cost: they do so at the expense of fairness and inclusivity. To focus only on the transaction costs of compliance is to omit several other important variables relating to fairness of process and on having all of the stakeholders at the table who will bear the social costs of the rules being produced.

BIS claims that the countries whose central banks comprise its membership constitute 95% of the world's GDP. BCBS membership is comprised of the G-20 states. The G-20 comprise the nineteen largest national economies and the European Union,

[96] M Obstfeld, 'Trilemmas and Trade-offs: Living with Financial Globalisation' BIS Working Papers No 480, Jan 2015.

[97] This section does not deal with issues of justice relating to sovereign debt. These are dealt with in section 3.

[98] MS Barr, 'Who's in Charge of Global Finance?' (2014) 45 Georgetown Journal of International Law 971, 973–74.

[99] D Held and K Young, 'The World Crisis: Global Financial Governance: Principles of Reform' LSE Ideas (2009).

accounting for 65% of the world's population and 84% of world GDP.[100] The IMF is a multilateral organization but most of the voting power, determined by quotas of contributions to the IMF's SDR facility, are heavily weighted in favour of the United States and other large economy states.[101] This is inadequate participation for at least two reasons. First, why focus on GDP and central bank representation? It is remarkable that 35% of the world's population has no say through their governments in financial policy making on the world stage. Add to this that some of the institutions that are commonly included in descriptions of the global financial architecture are private bodies whose members come from industry. In addition, in many cases, given the nature of contagion in financial crises, even small states can have systemic significance, as the recent sovereign debt crisis in Greece has demonstrated and as the Mexican and Asian crises demonstrated in prior decades, well before the G-20 was a concept that included these states in the membership.

The IMF, one of the few institutions in the global financial architecture that is an intergovernmental organization formed by treaty, is dominated primarily by the interests of the United States and other select high-income countries. Basel Committee membership was very narrow until June 2009, when its membership expanded beyond the longstanding domination of the Committee, since its founding in 1974, by the G-10 states. The Committee had no choice but to expand membership. At the time of expansion, many non-European states without any formal Committee representation had more capital in their banking systems than those represented on the Committee.[102] Many of those excluded were countries with fast growing economies exceeding or projected to exceed the GDP of several European countries.

It is one thing to promulgate rules imposing burdens, vulnerabilities, or in economic language, negative externalities, on countries and their populations and quite another to do so without meaningful participation by their governments. Few low- and middle-income countries were able to take advantage of credit policies that caused the most recent global economic crisis, but the crisis and the response was global: these countries were affected by the crisis, though some less than others,[103] and also by policies implemented in the global financial architecture after the crisis that reduced credit availability.[104] History repeats itself. The financial crises of the 1990s brought about a number of changes to the global financial architecture that had substantial deleterious effects on low- and middle-income countries but these countries had really no input into the making of these policies. For example, the Basel II Accords largely served the interest of powerful market actors and only served to increase cost and

[100] The G20 economies explained in twelve charts, https://theconversation.com/the-g20-economies-explained-in-12-charts-33887

[101] https://www.imf.org/external/np/sec/memdir/members.aspx

[102] ibid.

[103] See Chapter 5 ('Foreign Investment'). See, eg, SG Checchetti, MR King, & J Yetman, 'Weathering the Financial Crisis: Good Policy or Good Luck?, BIS Working Paper No 351 (12 Oct 2011); & AK Rose & MM Spiegel, 'Cross-Country Causes and Consequences of the 2008 Crisis: International Linkages and American Exposure' (2010) 15 *Pacific Economic Review* 340; P Berkman, G Gelos, R Rennhack, & JP Walsh, 'The Global Financial Crisis: Explaining Cross-Country Differences in Output Impacts', IMF Working Paper, WP/09/280 (Dec 2009).

[104] See Held and Young (n 99).

reduce availability of domestic and external financing for these countries.[105] It is too early to assess the effects of the Basel III Accords on these countries, since countries do not have to implement the norms in the Accords fully for several years.

Arguments to the effect that these countries are not interested in participating or lack the knowledge or regulatory capacity to participate miss the point that knowledge and capacity are questions of means that do not override questions about the aims and ends of global norm making and norm applying processes. Knowledge and capacity, moreover, can only develop through participation.[106] The argument of a lack of interest in participation is, moreover, questionable, because governments often have incentives to comply with these norms to signal 'institutional quality', even if participation may not be in the national interest.[107] The major norm producers in the global financial architecture are all located in either Europe or the United States, making it difficult for countries with limited institutional capacities and resources to be able meaningfully to participate in these organizations.[108]

The extralegal nature of the norms of the global financial architecture raise transparency concerns. Rules that clubs create tend to be transparent only to club members. They are, after all, rules for the club. But in the case of the global financial architecture, these rules are meant for the global economy. In the context of one of the centrepieces of the global financial architecture, the FSB, the G-20 has taken a more prominent role, but that clearly is insufficient.[109] Part of the FSB's mission is to pressure for compliance even by non-member states who may not seek to cooperate.[110] Regional consultative groups going beyond FSB membership and even expanding FSB membership may be insufficient.[111]

From the standpoint of substantive moral wrong, we briefly explore here three related features of the global financial architecture that make it susceptible to reasonable rejection by those who bear its burdens. First, it produces insecurity particularly for those least able to be bear financial risk. Second, the current architecture is morally perverse in its structuring actual redistributions in the wrong direction, from poor to the rich, from the less well-off to the least well-off, in ways that produce disproportionate benefits to the more affluent and disproportionate harm to those on the financial margins. It is a classic case of injustice. These redistributions are accomplished, moreover, not as a result of choice by those affected, but as a result of the choice of those who benefit within a legal and policy structure that produces perverse redistributions. Third, the current architecture produces real concerns about domination.[112]

Jonathan Wolff and Avner de-Shalit argue that a 'pervasive aspect of disadvantage' is that 'very often people are disadvantaged because they are exposed to risks which they would not have taken had they had the option or are forced to take risks that in one way or another are bigger than others they are being exposed to or

[105] S Claessens, GRD Underhill, and X Zhang, 'The Political Economy of Global Financial Governance: The Costs of Basel II for Poor Countries' (2008) 31 World Economy 313.

[106] See A Walter, 'Emerging Countries and Basel III: Why Is Engagement Still Low?' Centre for International Governance Innovation, New Thinking and the New G20 Series, Paper No 4, 13 Mar 2015.

[107] See at 172–73 on institutional quality.

[108] Barr (n 98) 1003.

[109] ibid 1002–03.

[110] ibid 1002.

[111] ibid 1003.

[112] The groundwork for this discussion is laid out in Chapter 2 ('Confronting the Pathologies of International Law').

take'.[113] They argue that 'exceptional risk and volatility' is a disadvantage, even if the feared event does not actually happen.[114] For exposure to risk to be a disadvantage of the kind to trigger egalitarian concerns, it has to be involuntary.[115] To force someone to take a risk means the risk cannot be reasonably avoided because there is no reasonable alternative.[116] Kantian inspired approaches to risk offer similar insights. Carl Cranor's work on non-consequentialist approaches to risk offers clarity on precisely what sorts of risk it is morally acceptable to impose on persons, though his work might not reflect an explicit egalitarian focus.[117] The focus here aligns with that of Chapter 2 in evaluating a global institutional order in ways that require these institutions to be accountable to each person affected by them. The move here is to reject financial stability, as discussed in the Introduction to this chapter as the *grundnorm* for financial regulation, as inadequate on its own because it impermissibly aggregates and permits substantial harm to vulnerable persons, even if that means that the rich benefit, so long as the financial order is 'stable'.

What is the main moral concern about insecurity in the global financial architecture? To the extent that the architecture maintains unacceptable levels of systemic risk, it produces insecurity. Policy makers fail to address the core problems associated with unregulated cross-border financial flows. We can drill down into these financial flows. Section 2, for example, partly deals with problems associated with shadow banking and ineffective regulation of bank capital. When a focus on these flows exists, it tends to be on controlling mainly consumer debt, only one piece of the crisis puzzle, the control of which can produce hardship on the middle- and lower-income brackets of a society, particularly when a society is set up essentially to mandate debt taking as the route to social mobility and improvement of living standards.[118] Financial crises, moreover, have adverse effects on social protections governments provide to the vulnerable.[119] The risks associated with the current global financial architecture are accepted as a fait accompli, a danger we have to live with, as if capital markets are inevitable, like planets, when they are really just legal constructions. So, the fait accompli argument goes, we must live with the fact that rich investors are entitled to get richer and the rest of us must suffer what we must. It is the classic argument of the Athenians to the Melians that starts Chapter 2. The main worry of governments seems to be to shoring up banks, so that they will continue to function through the inevitable crises brought upon by unregulated financial flows, and even shoring up banks, as we explore in the next section, is risky and inadequate.

[113] J Wolff and A de-Shalit, *Disadvantage* (OUP 2013) 66–67. Wolff and de-Shalit base their arguments on a capabilities account, an approach not adopted in this book, but which bears complementarities to the core arguments in this book.

[114] ibid. [115] ibid. [116] ibid.

[117] CF Cranor, 'Toward a Non-Consequentialist Approach to Acceptable Risks' in T Lewens (ed), *Risk: Philosophical Perspectives* (Routledge 2007).

[118] See A Mian and A Sufi, *House of Debt* (University of Chicago Press 2014) (on the harshness of debt in crises to persons of limited means who depend on debt).

[119] Overseas Development Institute Briefing Paper, 'The Global Financial Crisis: Poverty and Social Protection' (Aug 2009) (on the effects on government resources available to the vulnerable in economic crises); A Elson, *The Global Financial Crisis in Retrospect* (Palgrave 2017) (on the effects of the global financial crisis on income inequality).

Second, the current global financial architecture imposes what is effectively an unjust difference principle. It promotes a priority for the *better* off. It seems to implement what is known in political circles as a reverse Robin Hood principle.[120] Another way to understand these is as accumulation by dispossession, a concept made popular by David Harvey and whose origins can be traced to violent upheavals in history to create markets.[121]

How do these morally perverse redistributions occur in finance? First, in guarantees, both explicit and implicit, to large financial institutions, that governments are providing insurance against insolvency risk for these institutions. The costs associated with this insurance are real. Given the structure of the global financial architecture, a significant body of expertise supports the proposition that crises are inevitable. In the current financial architecture, governments seek to reduce the probabilities, but they still exist and many powerful arguments are being made that capital adequacy rules for banks are inadequate.[122] The guarantees are basically guaranteed transfer payments to financial institutions. In the event of crisis, which has been made inevitable, there will be transfer payments—from the public purse—to 'save the system'. Before a crisis, these future transfer payments have expected values and they lower the costs of borrowing for banks, who then look to lower cost of credit to capitalize themselves with borrowing. No one else is getting these sorts of guarantees of transfers to transform their balance sheets, and certainly not individual debtors.

Another example of a morally perverse difference principle is in the now enormous cross-border financial flows in diversification finance. With the changes to the global financial architecture explained above, cross-border financial flows have become a substantial part of the global economy.[123] We identified the trilemmas for policy makers above, and how crises will be inevitable with substantial cross-border financial flows. Substantial cross-border capital inflows can fuel extreme volatility in asset pricing, asset bubbles, severe exchange rate fluctuations, and depletion of foreign reserves.

The quantity of cross-border financial flows is not the only issue at stake. The quality and characteristics of these cross-border financial flows has been mainly in

[120] American politicians, including Barack Obama and Bernie Sanders, have used the 'reverse Robin Hood' argument. Its origins are unknown. Its original use has been attributed to George Meany, former president of the AFL-CIO, in reaction in 1971 to an economic policy of Richard Nixon. R Frank, 'Robin Hood in Reverse: The History of the Phrase' CNBC, 7 Aug 2012.

[121] K Polanyi, *The Great Transformation: The Political and Economic Origins of Our Time* (Beacon 1944) (markets do not arise spontaneously and require the use of official force and social dislocation).

[122] For discussion of these issues see A Admati and M Hellwig, *The Banker's New Clothes: What's Wrong with Banking and What to Do about It* (Princeton UP 2013), ch 9. Section 2 deals with capital adequacy in more detail.

[123] See, eg, A Feibelman, 'The IMF and Regulation of Cross-Border Capital Flows' (2015) 15 Chicago Journal of International Law 409; K Gallagher, 'Regulating Capital Flows for Development' G-24 Policy Brief No 76, 4 July 2012; JA Ocampo, 'The Case for Regulating Cross-Border Capital Flows' International Monetary Fund Macro Conference, https://www.imf.org/external/np/seminars/eng/2011/res/pdf/AOpresentation.pdf.; A Viterbo, *International Economic Law and Monetary Measures: Limitations to States' Sovereignty and Dispute Settlement* (Edward Elgar 2012) 39; International Monetary Fund, 'The Fund's Role Regarding Cross-Border Capital Flows', 15 Nov 2010.

financing for diversification and not for development.[124] Diversification financing has serious implications for distributive justice as well as for insecurity.[125] Diversification finance is dangerous but also primarily benefits only those who participate in it. As economist Moritz Schularick explains, 'financial integration today is essentially uncorrelated with investment rates, presumably the main channel through which foreign capital would spur economic growth'.[126] So, financial globalization serves no robust economic welfare aims. Global finance principally benefits the rich. It is used for asset swapping. When understood in a moral context, discussions of 'innovation' in financial markets and the need to protect incentives of managers of financial firms to innovate are mainly but not exclusively about how to protect one set of rich investors against another. In a very complex architecture, transaction structures are established so that securities and their derivatives are traded back and forth numerous times between multiple institutions. It is not 'real economy' finance, or at least not primarily so. Credit default swaps, for example, can allow banks to hedge credit risk, but they also enable banks and other investors and securities dealers to profit from taking positions in the market. The value of credit default swaps grew from zero in 1990 to almost $60 trillion by 2007, on the eve of the most recent crisis.[127]

Beyond the lack of overall welfare gains through economic growth in an economy, diversification finance contributes to inequality. The inequality it produces is a creature of law. These inequalities are classic socially created and not natural inequalities.[128] The most recent economic crisis offers examples. In search of returns, global credit markets were created to diversify risk associated with home mortgages in the United States, the United Kingdom, and elsewhere. While the mortgages were located in countries with high levels of private home ownership, the investors in the securities created through securitization of these mortgages were global. Deutsche Bank, for example, was one of the largest investors in this market,[129] even though Germany has historically had relatively far less private home ownership by owner-occupiers than other countries such as the United States, the United

[124] See at 172–173. Adair Turner has argued that the investments should be in productive assets and not real estate for example, Turner (n 45) ch 9 entitled, 'Too Much of the Wrong Sort of Capital Flow'. Some real estate investments may be economically beneficial and socially desirable, such as when they meet demand for housing or promote home ownership in countries in which private home ownership is a significant aspect of household wealth.

[125] There is also an argument, from a macroeconomic perspective, that capital flows prompting the most recent financial crisis were from the relatively poor (perhaps at the time) to rich, from China to America, in which China financed easy credit to finance consumption by US consumers to buy Chinese goods. N Ferguson and M Schularick, 'Chimerica and the Global Asset Market Boom' (2007) 10 International Finance 215.

[126] M Schularick, 'The End of Financial Globalisation 3.0' *Economists' Voice* (Jan 2010) 3.

[127] Turner (n 45) 26.

[128] We do not take a position on whether governments should neutralize natural inequalities because we are dealing with inequalities of a social kind here, inequalities that we create and perpetuate in the structure of societies. Omitted is discussion of issues that do not have to do with institutions. There are many competing theoriesin economics about the good or bad of financial globalization. See D Rodrik and A Subramanian,'Why Did Financial Globalization Disappoint?' (2009) 56 IMF Staff Papers 112.

[129] ibid.

Kingdom, and other countries.[130] The end result of the collapse in house prices supporting mortgage-backed securities was severe aggravation of already substantial inequalities in the United States and in other countries affected.[131] The credit bonanza created by a mix of government policies and financial engineering led to an asset bubble in the form of inflated house prices. The collapse in home prices in the crisis hit low-income households the hardest. There is a serious downside risk to debt, a leverage multiplier. Mian and Sufi explain that 'a fundamental feature of debt' is that it 'imposes enormous losses on exactly the households that have the least. Those with the most are left in a much better relative position because of their senior claims on the assets in the economy.'[132] The rich have senior claims because they are the investors who lend to the less affluent through the financial architecture. As succinctly put by Atif Mian and Amir Sufi, 'a poor man's debt is a rich man's asset'.[133] The result is disproportionate benefits for the rich and disproportionate burdens for the poor and other persons of limited means.

Completing the moral evaluation, the global financial architecture has the potential to lead to domination if the vast inequalities associated with it leads to significant disparities in political influence in a society. As explained in prior chapters, domination is a situation in which one agent has power over the life of another person on an arbitrary basis. To dominate arbitrarily means to do so with impunity or at the will of the dominating agent. One might be tempted to think that the arbitrary wielding of such power is rare in democracies, which require powerful interests to seek what they want in a political process they do not totally control. The relationship of domination to regulatory capture seems apparent. But a financial architecture in which diversification finance is the norm, which imposes high concentrations of debt on the less affluent, and high concentrations of assets in the few, shares similarities to debt servitude, or forms of peonage found in former Spanish colonies in Latin America.[134] Maurizio Lazzarato makes a forceful case for the creditor–debtor relation as the defining feature of global capitalism today, a

[130] M Outlanders, 'Why Is the German Homeownership Rate So Low?' (2009) 24 Housing Studies 355; M Phillips, 'Most Germans Don't Buy Their Homes, They Rent. Here's Why' *Quartz*, 23 Jan 2014, http://qz.com/167887/germany-has-one-of-the-worlds-lowest-homeownership-rates. This may be changing. C Jones and J Shotter, 'German Push for Home Ownership Drives Price Bubble Fears' *Financial Times* (London, 5 Jan 2017).

[131] See, eg, Elson (n 28); Mian and Sufi (n 118).

[132] Mian and Sufi (n 118) 24–25.

[133] ibid 20.

[134] Harvey on financialization:

> Deregulation allowed the financial system to become one of the main centres of redistributive activity through speculation, predation, fraud, and thievery. Stock promotions, ponzi schemes, structured asset destruction through inflation, asset-stripping through mergers and acquisitions, the promotion of levels of debt incumbency that reduced whole populations, even in the advanced capitalist countries, to debt peonage, to say nothing of corporate fraud, dispossession of assets (the raiding of pension funds and their decimation by stock and corporate collapses) by credit and stock manipulations—all of these became central features of the capitalist financial system.

D Harvey, *A Brief History of Neoliberalism* (OUP 2007) 161. Deregulation may not be the only way or even the best way to describe what is happening with financialization, but rather *the wrong kind of regulation*. See at 209–210.

relationship wiping out future alternatives.[135] If we want an international financial architecture that is just, in the first instance, we shall have to develop institutions in a manner that is sensitive to minimizing domination.

3. Dangerous Banks

As explained in the preceding section, the FSB and the BCBS now form the cornerstone of the global financial architecture. They are engaged, along with governments, in lawmaking to deal with the very substantial risks to persons and societies associated with activities of large, systemically important financial institutions. But as we have seen, the international standard-setters do not regulate states and banks through a formal legal source such as a treaty. Rather, they produce guiding principles, and formulate standards for cooperation and oversight, which can be understood as soft law. There has been, moreover, widespread criticism of the Basel Accords and the domestic law that is meant to track them.[136] Banks remain what Charles Calomiris and Stephen Haber call 'fragile by design'[137] even though we need them to be durable by design. Indeed, banks are dangerous in a financial sense. Despite post-crisis regulation ostensibly regulating bank balance sheets through capital adequacy ratios, stress tests, macro-prudential regulation, and other regulatory schemes, the big banks continue to impose unacceptable risks of falling like dominoes, a systemic risk that can crash the global economy. When they are regulated, they engage in regulatory arbitrage to promote shadow banking activities that avoid regulation but pose dangers to persons and societies. The dominoes effect is a real possibility, despite the new post-crisis regulatory regimes.

These real and very significant dangers implicate the moral concerns that were raised in the prior section. They are indeed part and parcel of it, as they contribute substantially to insecurity particularly for those unable to protect against the risks, and because they contribute to the kind of reverse difference principle or accumulation by dispossession effects that now are core aspects of the global financial architecture.

Why are banks dangerous? They are dangerous for two reasons. First, they are dangerous by design. Any financial institution that engages in maturity mismatch or maturity transformation, in which short-term debt is used to make money from long-term investments, be it a traditional bank or a shadow bank, if the institution is large enough, poses risk beyond their own failure, to the global economy. Second, banks rely too much on debt to fund their operations. Their capital structures are pathologically harmful as well, heaping balance sheet risk on top of credit intermediation risk. These two dangers are explored in more depth below.

[135] M Lazzarato, *Governing by Debt* (JD Jordan tr, semiotext(e) 2013).

[136] A significant line of attack is that the current regime permits banks to be leveraged to dangerous levels. Admati and Hellwig (n 122).

[137] Calomiris and Haber (n 94).

The problem of maturity mismatch can be understood as one of liquidity risk or cash flow insolvency, the inability to pay debts as they come due. Liquidity risk is inherent in banking. Cash flow insolvency is the 'normal state of affairs' for banks.[138] Liquidity risk and cash flow insolvency are partly why banks are inherently fragile. Deposits are a major funding source for traditional banks. Let us look at traditional banking very briefly, though we must admit that bank holding companies make money in a variety of ways and not only from traditional banking. Traditional depository banking, however, provides us with the clear insights on maturity mismatch. Banks engage in credit intermediation: they repackage deposits to make loans, which produces liquidity in the economy in the form of spending power for borrowers. A maturity mismatch occurs in this intermediation. Deposits are mostly short term while loans tend to have longer maturity periods. Maturity mismatch causes liquidity risk. Banks take several steps to mitigate liquidity risk. They maintain reserves in the form of cash or as deposits with the central bank, which the bank can draw as cash. They borrow short term from each other in the interbank market. They may invest in relatively liquid and 'safe' tradable assets, such as government bonds. As a last resort, they borrow short term from the central bank. Governments can bail out banks to resolve liquidity crises when the central bank can do no more.

Banks are vulnerable to panics, which can be understood as rational and coordinated in situations of bank runs, when large numbers of depositors withdraw their short-term loans (deposits) at once, disrupting the longer-term lending functions of banks and the payment systems that banks provide to societies and globally. This can result in systemic shocks rippling through the banking system, making banks insolvent on a balance sheet basis, causing them to collapse. The contagion effect in the banking system, because banks and payments are interdependent, is a systemic risk to the financial system, which governments now try to mitigate through macro-prudential regulation.[139]

Governments have sought to regulate liquidity risk. For example, in 2008, the BCBS issued guidance on the use of two ratios to regulate liquidity risk for banks with international operations. The liquidity coverage ratio would require that banks have sufficient 'high quality' liquid assets in place to survive an acute stress scenario lasting a month. The net stable funding ratio would require that banks have stable funding for the longer term to cover liquidity needs.[140] The main source of

[138] Dalhuisen (n 69) 439; Calomiris and Haber (n 94) ch 2.

[139] RM Lastra, 'Systemic Risk and Macro-Prudential Supervision' in N Moloney, E Ferran, and J Payne (eds), *The Oxford Handbook of Financial Regulation* (OUP 2015) 309; S Schwarcz, 'Systemic Risk' (2008) 97 Georgetown Law Journal 193; Group of Thirty, Enhancing Financial Stability and Resilience: Macroprudential Policy, Tools, and Systems for the Future, October 2010, http://group30.org/images/uploads/publications/G30_EnhancingFinancialStabilityResilience.pdf; P Tucker, 'Macroprudential Policy at the Bank of England' Quarterly Bulletin 2013 Q3, http://www.bankofengland.co.uk/publications/Documents/quarterlybulletin/2013/qb130301.pdf; European Systemic Risk Board, Flagship Report on Macroprudential Policy in the Banking Sector, Mar 2014, ttps://www.esrb.europa.eu/pub/pdf/other/140303_flagship_report.pdf

[140] See H Scott, 'Regulating Systemic Risk Through the Reform of Capital Regulation' in Cottier, Jackson, and Lastra (n 13) 222.

regulation of liquidity risk, however, are not these international initiatives, which are driven by central banks in any event, but in explicit and implicit guarantees provided by government of deposit protection and bailouts. In other words, subsidies are of overriding importance when it comes to liquidity risk. These subsidies illuminate that liquidity ultimately depends on solvency. Illiquidity often masks a bigger problem of potential balance sheet insolvency looming on the horizon, when a bailout may be necessary.

So far, the discussion has been on traditional banking, but the discussion of risk associated with maturity mismatch should extend to shadow banking, which played a significant role in the financial crisis of 2007–09. While a plurality of views exists in what a shadow bank is, the prevailing definition seems to be that a shadow bank is any financial institution that performs credit intermediation through maturity transformation, but which is not a traditional bank.[141] Perhaps the classic or most common example of shadow banking is securitization of home mortgages, funded by short-term commercial paper. There was an explosive pre-crisis growth of shadow banks, likely the result of regulatory arbitrage by banks to move financial activity off their balance sheets to avoid regulation of their on-balance sheet activity. The search for yields by hedge funds, pension funds, and other institutional investors likely also produced incentives for banks to engage in shadow banking.[142] Widespread consensus exists that these shadow banks contributed substantially to bring about the most recent global financial crisis.[143]

The regulation of the capital adequacy of banks is a central focus of banking regulation. Regulatory failure seems to be significant when it comes to bank capital adequacy. Banks should hold considerably more equity in their capital structure, to ensure their funding can pay for losses in the bad economic times that are plainly foreseeable in a neoliberal world of financial globalization. The main provisions of the Basel Accords regulate capital adequacy through specification of capital adequacy ratios, which are ratios of equity in a bank's capital structure to the bank's risk weighted assets. Anat Admati and Martin Hellwig explain that the Basel III Accord 'eliminates some abuses' but 'fails to address the basic problem that banks can easily game

[141] See M Ricks, *The Money Problem* (University of Chicago Press 2016); LE Kodres, 'What Is Shadow Banking?' (2013) 50 Finance and Development 42–43, https://www.imf.org/external/pubs/ft/fandd/2013/06/basics.htm; 'The Economist Explains: How Shadow Banking Works' *The Economist* (1 Feb 2013), http://www.economist.com/blogs/economist-explains/2016/02/economist-explains-0; Shadow Banking, http://ec.europa.eu/finance/general-policy/shadow-banking/index_en.htm; Z Pozsar, T Adrian, A Ashcraft, and H Boesky, 'Shadow Banking' (2013) 19 Economic Policy Review, http://ssrn.com/abstract=2378449; A Bouveret, 'An Assessment of the Shadow Banking Sector in Europe' 6 July 2011, http://ssrn.com/abstract=2027007; T Burns, 'The Shadow Banking System as a New Source of Financial Turmoil' in K Alexander and R Dhumale (eds), *Research Handbook on International Financial Regulation* (Edward Elgar 2012) 30–41.

[142] See P Lysandrou and A Nesvetailova, 'The Role of Shadow Banking Entities in the Financial Crisis: A Disaggregated View' (2015) 22 Review of International Political Economy 257 for synthesis of 'endogenous' (to banking) and 'exogenous' explanations for shadow banking.

[143] There are many sources on the connection of shadow banking to the most recent global financial crisis. See, eg, authorities cited in (n 141); Financial Crisis Inquiry Commission (n 36); Avgouleas (n 69) 89–154; GB Gorton, 'Slapped in the Face by the Invisible Hand: Banking and the Panic of 2007' (9 May 2009), https://ssrn.com/abstract=1401882 or http://dx.doi.org/10.2139/ssrn.1401882.

the regulation. Banks' equity can still be as low as 3 percent of their total assets. It is not clear that anything would have been substantially different in the 2007–2009 crisis had Basel III already been in place.'[144]

As explained above, despite the need for more equity in their capital structure, banks are highly leveraged institutions. Compare the financial data of publicly traded non-financial firms and banks. For example, compare the capital structure of Walmart, the largest publicly traded company in the United States and in the world in terms of revenues, and JPMorgan Chase, the largest US bank. As of the writing of this chapter, Walmart's debt to equity ratio was 0.58 and equity comprised approximately 29.3% of its capital structure. These are conservative figures, as we are using liability data from Walmart's balance sheet, which includes items that do not bear interest, such as accounts payable. Turning away from balance sheet accounting and to market valuation, Walmart's market capitalization at the time of this writing in late December 2015 was approximately $189 billion. As of the date of this writing, JPMorgan Chase's debt to equity ratio was 1:38 and its equity comprised approximately 9% of its capital structure. These are not risk-weighted Basel Accord compliant ratios but simple financial ratios. JP Morgan's debt to equity ratio is almost twice that of Walmart's and its capital structure comprises more than three times more debt than Walmart's. JPMorgan Chase's market capitalization at the time of this writing is $237.2 billion, fairly high for the company historically.[145] The current JPMorgan Chase CEO says that his bank has a 'fortress balance sheet'.[146] Relying on Admati's and Hellwig's characterisation, it seems a fragile fortress.[147] For those concerned with how the global financial architecture works against the vulnerable, these dangerously leveraged positions represent an accumulation by dispossession, a threat of domination in the event the banks need bailouts at the expense of everyone else.

Widespread unease persists about the state of banking regulation. Commentators have recommended various reforms of the banking system, some representing quite dramatic change. A few are summarized here. Some have argued for 100% reserve banking.[148] Others have recommended a move towards narrow banking, in which banks can invest deposits only in 'safe' government bonds.[149] In these proposals, banks lose their lending function. They would not create credit or money through

[144] Admati and Hellwig (n 122) 96.

[145] The sources for this data are Market Watch and Yahoo Finance, as of late December 2015. While debt to equity ratios rely on book values, market capitalization is the market value of equity. The numbers here are only a snapshot on at a particular time and historical data may be more helpful, but they are indicative of a basic point: banks are much more leveraged than non-financial firms.

[146] See Admati and Hellwig (n 122) 82–87 for these references.

[147] ibid 83–82.

[148] The idea of 100% reserve banking originates in the Chicago Plan, recommended in 1933 to US President Franklin D Roosevelt by University of Chicago economists. F Knight, 'Memorandum on Banking Reform' Franklin D Roosevelt Presidential Library, Personal File 431, Mar 1933, as discussed in Turner (n 45) 187–88. See also AJ Levitin, 'Safe Banking: Finance and Democracy' (2016) 83(1) University of Chicago Law Review 62.

[149] J Kay, 'Narrow Banking: The Reform of Banking Regulation' http://www.johnkay.com/wp-content/uploads/2009/12/JK-Narrow-Banking.pdf; KR James, 'The Case for Narrow Banking' http://www.bcb.gov.br/Pec/seminarios/SemMetInf2007/Port/KevinJames.pdf

debt. The proposals would require a substantial move of financial intermediation activities to the financial markets, so that borrowers could tap into these markets for debt finance. Financial markets would fundamentally change in character and the focus of regulation would shift to these markets. These proposals do not address the very real dangers of shadow banking—if banks are regulated too much then credit intermediation can simply move elsewhere. Another proposal is that governments should only assist banks in protecting against liquidity risk.[150] In these proposals, guarantees, bailouts, and other subsidies provided by taxpayers should only protect bank depositors and the payment system but not the bank's shareholders and long-term creditors. So, the bailouts in the last crisis to the tune of about $11 trillion, which went well beyond protecting the payment system, would be much lower in the future.

Most of that $11 trillion bailout was paid to banks by the United States and the United Kingdom. The United Kingdom bailout amounted to over 94% of the country's GDP, which on a per capita basis is $50,000 per person.[151] Soon after the bailout, US bank executives took huge bonuses.[152] Government bailout guarantees for banks are subsidies for bank shareholders and some bank creditors and if the efficient capital market hypothesis has any measure of correctness then the value of these subsidies is reflected in the prices of bank shares.[153] These bailout funds could have been used to jump-start consumption if paid to consumers and homeowners in distress.[154]

While alternatives are often posited, in real-world politics, the banks will get most of what they want. It is also doubtful shadow banking activities will be curtailed if they are important to banks or institutional investors. In many states, banks serve quasi-sovereign functions for states and therefore link closely to the role of the state in providing the goods that finance can buy (resources and material welfare) for people and firms. Historically, a strong linkage between the state and its financiers has always been evident because of the importance of banks to the social contract. In the contemporary version of the state, markets are vehicles for success, wealth, and power. Government needs its financiers to fund not only their operations but also to underwrite the welfare of the government's constituencies. Along with a system of tax and transfer, banks are an important institution in the financing of the social contract.

Beyond maintaining the payment system, banks engage in two socially significant functions. First, they engage in credit creation. Credit is necessary given the way that economies are organized today. No high-income country exists today without banks providing a significant amount of credit to firms and households.[155] In the

[150] Mian and Sufi (n 118) 121–23.

[151] 'Follow the Money' http://news.bbc.co.uk/1/hi/business/8249411.stm, 10 Sept 2009.

[152] Bank executives expressed surprised at the outcry. RG Rajan, *Fault Lines: How Hidden Fractures Still Threaten the Global Economy* (Princeton UP 2010) 154–55.

[153] See Admati and Hellwig (n 122) ch 9, entitled 'Sweet Subsidies'.

[154] Mian and Sufi (n 118) 126: 'So while any policy that would have helped home owners was shelved, governments bailed out bank creditors and shareholders using taxpayer money.'

[155] See JR Barth, G Caprio Jr, and R Levine, *Rethinking Bank Regulation: Till Angels Govern* (CUP 2008) 1–3.

current global economy, poor countries suffer from under-banking—insufficient credit.[156] Says Calomiris and Haber, 'There is no avoiding the government–banker partnership.'[157]

With credit creation comes money creation, historically a function exclusively reserved to the state. When banks lend to borrowers, they create deposits in the borrowers' bank accounts, effectively expanding the money supply. Most money is created this way. In the United Kingdom, 98% of money is in the form of bank-created money, while only 2% comprises notes and coins issued by the Bank of England.[158] So, governments cede control of a core sovereign function to banks. Says Beth Simmons, 'Sovereign control over money is one of the most closely guarded national prerogatives. Creating, valuating, and controlling the distribution of national legal tender is viewed as an inherent right of the nation-state in the modern period.'[159] Simmons may sound unfashionably out of date with the rise of the eurozone but the same reasoning applies, *mutatis mutandis*, to the eurozone. Some of the tensions about private and public debt and banking in the eurozone is likely attributable to destabilizing stresses on the government–banker partnership.

A commercial bank creates money as debt of the borrower and it becomes debt of the bank when deposited into the borrower's account. It is money creation through private debt, to be distinguished from fiat money printed by the central bank,[160] which would be necessary with 100% reserve banks. Note the multiplier effect: the loan creates more deposits for more loans. If this strikes you as a Ponzi scheme, you are right.[161] A major downside of this process of money (and credit) creation is that it is pro-cyclical: banks lend liberally during good economic times and restrictively during bad economic times. Add to this that the significant downsides of debt to the borrower in bad times when asset prices fall.[162]

Continuing to explore the banks' role in financing the social contract, banks perform several socially significant distributive functions. Banks must decide who gets the money they allocate. In a state that is classically liberal or libertarian in approach, governments will only support traditional notions of property rights in the credit markets.[163] In such states, banks allocate loans to 'deserving' borrowers based principally on the criterion of creditworthiness or the ability to repay a

156 Calomiris and Haber (n 94) 7–9, 46–47, 412, 449. 157 ibid 27.

158 See Z Jakab and M Kumhof, 'Banks Are Not Intermediaries of Loanable Funds—And Why This Matters' Bank of England Working Paper No 529, May 2015; Turner (n 45) 58.

159 BA Simmons, 'The Legalization of International Monetary Affairs' (2000) 54 International Organization 573.

160 See Turner (n 45) 111–13, 187–88, 239–40 on fiat money. See also Admati and Hellwig (n 93) (flawed claim 5: 'banks are special because they create money').

161 'Did Hyman Minsky Find the Secret Behind Financial Crashes?' http://www.bbc.co.uk/news/magazine-26680993, 24 Mar 2014; 'Ponzificating: Is the Financial System a Confidence Trick?' *The Economist* (15 Mar 2007).

162 See, eg, Anat and Hellwig (n 122) ch 2 for an accessible discussion of the downsides of rigid debt contracts.

163 There may be limit cases in which banks perform few domestic functions or do no not engage in much retail banking for individuals. We have in mind here banking centres like Hong Kong. Still a government–banker partnership exists.

loan when payment is due. The ability to repay in turn depends on the system of property rights the state provides to banks to obtain security, such as in the form of collateral, and to enforce delinquent loans by use of the legal system. The liquidity risk banks face in maturity mismatching requires creditworthiness to be the principal criterion. In a state that governs by notions of justice or egalitarianism in some form, the creditworthiness criterion may be altered by government policy, such as when governments choose to implement policies that promote just or egalitarian aims through guarantees or subsidies to support lending to the poor, the disadvantaged, or the less affluent, or to support citizens in their life projects, such as with subsidized loans to students, or to assist in the revitalization of socially or economically distressed communities. To classify these functions only as bargains struck by government officials with voters misses an important normative point: at least some of these policies are associated with fairness and distributive justice in society.[164] Governments can engage in these policies as a matter of predistribution rather than or in addition to redistribution via tax and transfer.[165] So, banks play an important distributing function, distributing the money they create either on the basis of market considerations, through implementation of government policy, or through a combination of these factors. In sum, banks perform a quasi-governmental role in a market-oriented society. In the EU context, to the extent that supranational EU law interferes in any such distributive functions, the risk of destabilizing the government–banker partnership increases.[166]

If banks are so important, why are they so fragile? The prudential supervision of banks has never successfully prevented the collapse of large banks.[167] Would it not be in the public interest for governments (and their agents, such as the European Union) to regulate banks in a way that makes them safer? Serious pathologies appear to be at work in rulemaking on banking. A relevant concept from political economics is rent-seeking. Very basically, rent-seeking is the notion that powerful interests can use the lawmaking process to transfer wealth from others, usually the public at large, to themselves, through lobbying and influence over regulatory design.[168] A related concept is regulatory capture, a situation in which banks use their political influence to get regulators to write rules that take into account the banks' interests and not those of society, and which often result in wealth transfers from citizens to banks.[169] Regulatory capture can be accomplished in a pecuniary context, such as

[164] Here one can disagree with Calomiris and Haber (n 94), or at the very least this work explores different problems.

[165] See Chapters 1 ('Legal Rendering of Immiseration') and 2 ('Confronting the Pathologies of International Law') on predistribution.

[166] See Varoufakis (n 52).

[167] Dalhuisen (n 69) 540.

[168] The modern origins of the concept of rent-seeking is traceable to G Tullock, 'The Welfare Costs of Tariffs, Monopolies, and Theft' (1967) 5 Western Economic Journal 224. Anne Krueger coined the phrase. AO Krueger 'The Political Economy of the Rent-Seeking Society' (1974) 64(3) American Economic Review 291. On the political economy of financial regulation, see R Litan, 'The Political Economy of Financial Regulation After the Crisis' in AS Blinder, AW Lo, and RM Solow (eds), *Rethinking the Financial Crisis* (Russell Sage 2012).

[169] See L Lessig, *Republic Lost: 2.0* (rev edn, Twelve 2015); D Carpenter and DA Moss (eds), *Preventing Regulatory Capture: Special Interest Influence and How to Limit It* (CUP 2014); LG Baxter, 'Capture of Financial Regulation: Can We Redirect It Toward the Common Good?' (2011) 21 Cornell Journal of Law and Public Policy 175.

in the case of the revolving door. Raghuram Rajan describes Goldman Sachs as 'a bank with alumni in every corner of the government'.[170] After all, '[r]egulating and supervising an industry requires some expertise' and that expertise is often shared between industry and government.[171] In the United States, bank CEOs sit on the boards of the federal reserve banks.[172] There can also be what Stiglitz calls 'cognitive capture', where the thinking of the regulator and the regulated are shared.[173] Financial institutions maintain a substantial lobbying apparatus in national capitals and in some countries financial contributions to the campaigns of politicians are permitted.[174]

A substantial consensus exists across a range of disciplines that political influence is very much at work in the making of law on banking and finance.[175] As Stiglitz explains:

> Government never corrects market failures perfectly, but it does a better job in some countries than in others ... Deregulation in the 1980s led to scores of financial crises in the succeeding three decades ... But those government failures were no accident: the financial sector used its political muscle to make sure that the market failures were *not* corrected, and that the sector's private rewards remained well in excess of their social contributions—one of the factors contributing to the bloated financial sector and to the high levels of inequality at the top.[176]

It is unclear whether deregulation is the culprit, or bad regulation, or a combination of the two amounting to bad deregulation: lower levels of regulation but regulation put in place that fails to protect households, consumers, vulnerable people, and communities.

Research by IMF economists reveals a 'striking picture' of the financial institutions that lobbied the US Congress on mortgage lending and securitization legislation also maintaining risky mortgage lending strategies right before the crisis.[177] Between 2000 and 2006, lenders that lobbied the most extensively to prevent a

[170] Rajan (n 152), 154.

[171] Admati and Hellwig (n 122) 204.

[172] ibid 204–06.

[173] JE Stiglitz, *The Price of Inequality* (Princeton UP 2013) 59–60.

[174] ibid 60. 'The bankers have unleashed enormous numbers of lobbyists to persuade any and all who play a role in regulation that they should not be regulated—an estimated 2.5 for every U.S. representative'. On campaign contributions, see Lessig (n 169).

[175] In addition to authorities cited throughout this section, see also Calomiris and Haber (n 94); L Kostovetsky, 'Political Capital and Moral Hazard' (2015) 116(1) Journal of Financial Economics 144; M Behn, R Haselmann, T Kick, and V Vig, 'The Political Economy of Bank Bailouts' (2015) Institute for Monetary and Financial Stability, University of Frankfurt, Working Paper Series 86; D Igan and P Mishra, 'Three's Company: Wall Street, Capitol Hill, and K Street' (2014) 57 Journal of Law and Economics 1063; N McCarty, KT Poole, and H Rosenthal, *Political Bubbles: Financial Crises and the Failure of American Democracy* (Princeton UP 2012); A Khwaja and A Mian, 'Rent Seeking and Corruption in Financial Markets' (2011) 3 Annual Review of Economics 579; N McCarty, KT Poole, T Romer, and H Rosenthal, 'Political Fortunes: On Finance and its Regulation' (2010) 139 Daedulus 61; A Mian, A Sufi, and F Trebbi, 'The Political Economy of the US Mortgage Default Crisis' (2010) 100 American Economic Review 1967.

[176] Stiglitz (n 173) 43.

[177] D Igan, P Mishra, and T Tressel, 'A Fistful of Dollars: Lobbying and the Financial Crisis' NBER Working Paper No 17076 (May 2011), IMF Working Paper 09/287.

tightening of mortgage lending law also originated mortgages with higher loan to income ratios than other lenders, engaged in securitization practices more frequently than other lenders, and had faster growing mortgage portfolios than other lenders. The evidence seems clear that lobbying by financial institutions contributed to the increasing of systemic risk before the most recent crisis. Beginning in 2002, the mortgage industry increasingly targeted contributions to the political campaigns for members of the US Congress who represented districts with large numbers of subprime borrowers. Voting on legislation relevant to housing and foreclosure could be predicted by these campaign contributions.[178]

Banks have engaged in 'intense lobbying' on the Basel Accords too.[179] Recent research tells us that large internationally active banks have manipulated the Basel Accord norm making process to get norms advantageous to them but disadvantageous to other stakeholders.[180] Some research indicates banks may have had less lobbying influence in recent years at the international level.[181] Influence at the Basel Committee level has to be understood within the context of regulatory arbitrage and the government–bank partnership we have outlined above. Lobbyists will focus efforts where they are most effective and least transaction costly. Lobbying for international norms often gets accomplished domestically, through government representatives who serve at the international negotiating table, representing the interests of financial institutions headquartered within the borders of the states they represent. Lobbying for international norms therefore may be hidden and less transparent. Moreover, if the financial industry does not get what it wants internationally, it may thwart efforts to implement the international norms domestically.

Anecdotal evidence suggests that no or very little compliance pull can be associated with the Basel Accords or other Basel guidance. Rather, compliance works in the opposite direction. As explained above, compliance with Basel guidance does not require a significant departure from what states and the European Union would do or are already doing anyway.[182] Moreover, the Accords and other Basel policies are drafted by a Committee (the BCBS) comprised of national regulators in substantially broad language of guidance. They allow for 'substantial national discretion' in application, which national regulators may use to support the government–bank partnership.[183] The Basel III Accord contains six references to national discretion.[184] Regulators have

[178] A Mian, A Sufi, and F Trebbi, 'The Political Economy of the Subprime Mortgage Credit Expansion' (2013) 8 Quarterly Journal of Political Science 373; see also M Dorsch, 'Bailout for Sale? The Vote to Save Wall Street' (2013) 155 Public Choice 211 (campaign contributions influenced US congressional voting on bailout).

[179] Admati and Hellwig (n 122) 96. See generally W Mattli and N Woods (eds), *The Politics of Global Regulation* (Princeton UP 2009).

[180] R Lall, 'From Failure to Failure: The Politics of International Banking Regulation' (2012) 19 Review of International Political Economy 609.

[181] See K Young, 'Empirical Examination of Transnational Lobbying Over the Basel Committee on Banking Supervision' (2012) 19 Review of International Political Economy 1.

[182] See JV Stein, 'Do Treaties Constrain or Screen? Selection Bias and Treaty Compliance' (2005) 99 American Political Science Review 611.

[183] DE Ho, 'Compliance and International Soft Law: Why Do Countries Implement the Basle Accord?' (2002) 5 JIEL 647.

[184] It is well understood that the Basel Accords include what the BCBS characterize as 'national discretions.' See Basel Capital Framework National Discretions (Nov 2014), https://www.bis.org/bcbs/publ/d297.htm.

used this discretion to produce weaker standards for banks.[185] While more empirical research is required on these issues, a reasonable inference is that the BCBS policies on bank capital and liquidity are coordinating mechanisms, designed to promote level playing fields between banks than as hard-core substantive obligations for governments to impose on banks. They follow but do not lead. To talk about the global financial architecture on banking is really to talk about domestic banking law.

The above linkage between banks and governments makes banks relatively resistant to regulation at the international level. Why would a powerful government cede the control of the banks serving these functions to an international regulator? So the result is there is no forum, domestic or international, that is effectively regulating banks to make them less dangerous. The potential for inadequate domestic regulation of large systematically important banks whose activities risk the propagation of negative spillovers with potential to cause grave economic harm on a global scale is very significant. Moreover, if the analysis is correct, the global financial architecture relevant to banking implements an agenda created by the central bankers of economically powerful states. International norms in such contexts are more likely to be epiphenomenal, implementing the deal that banks have cut with their host governments. They contribute to a situation of fragmentation of norms producing moral disorder—a moral failure contributing to insecurity and misallocation of resources from poor to rich.

In conclusion, what appears to be at work in banking regulation is a dangerous cocktail of policies that are bound to fail and cause grave harm. Capital adequacy rules clearly do not go far enough. Banks are inherently dangerous by their very nature, and attempts to regulate them produce responses in the form of regulatory arbitrage to divert maturity transformation functions to off balance sheet vehicles, which simply move the risk around but do not mitigate it and indeed make it worse to the extent that this outsourcing means less effective regulation of global finance. Banks are important to the social contract and this creates a situation in which it is difficult to regulate them effectively either domestically or internationally. All of this becomes part and parcel of a larger problem of lots of risk in transborder financial flows that benefit the affluent but which put everyone else at risk. Insecurity, vulnerability, and perverse maldistributions of wealth result.

4. Injustices of Sovereign Debt: The Case of Greece

Here this chapter homes in on the recent sovereign debt crisis that afflicted Greece and the institutional responses to it. The aims are to foreground in the context of a case study some of the central problems raised when it comes to injustice in the institutions of global finance. The failure to respect the life prospects of persons and to recognize and account for burdens imposed through legal constructs dedicated to governing what are inappropriately characterized as private activities of contract

[185] Ho (n 183) 665–66.

and exchange is one of these problems. Others are the commodification of politics and its democratic deficits, the accepted practice of domination, as well as the lack of accountability.

Issues of justice associated with sovereign debt are well overdue for evaluation. There has been considerable discussion on the need for a sovereign debt restructuring mechanism, along the lines of a sovereign insolvency statute, but it has gone nowhere.[186] Neoliberal ordering of the global economy has resulted in a 'contractual' approach to sovereign debt restructuring, which means that all creditors must voluntarily agree to a restructuring. The contractual approach has been inadequate. It suffers from collective action failures and produces creditor holdouts. The rise of vulture funds is an example of why the contractual approach fails. With the issuance of Brady bonds in the 1980s came the rise of bond financing for sovereign debt, a source of funding in addition to traditional bank loans. Vulture funds are hedge funds that buy sovereign debt on the secondary market at highly discounted prices only in order to sue to compel sovereign debtors to use some of the savings associated with the restructuring to pay them off rather than to use the funds in the service of the state. The result is a transfer of resources from populations, often of low- and middle-income countries, to hedge fund investors in Manhattan. Another problem is with the length of proceeding through a contract-oriented resolution, meaning that states lack funding and the debt situation is only exacerbated, hence, the phrase 'too little too late'.[187] The UN General Assembly has called for reform, which explicitly criticize hedge funds as professional litigants, but has not gotten matters going yet towards a fair and effective resolution mechanism.[188]

Developments in Europe over the past few years offer a substantial yet unfortunate opportunity to evaluate aspects of sovereign debt restructuring from the standpoint of human rights and justice. The concern addressed here is the pernicious roles played by public international institutions in the Greek affair, institutions that have acted as if representing solely private interests. The human impacts that the global financial crisis and the international and institutional responses to it brought to bear on Greece (and not only Greece) have exposed, in the starkest terms, injustices associated with the law applied to sovereign debt. Of course, foreign debt and the familiar responses to it by international institutions of restructuring economies through economic policy conditionalities according to neoliberal prescriptions, including austerity, have plagued the people of developing countries

[186] See M Guzman and JE Stiglitz, 'Creating a Framework for Sovereign Debt Restructuring that Works' in M Guzman, JA Ocampo, and JE Stiglitz (eds), *Too Little, Too Late: The Quest to Resolve Sovereign Debt Crises* (Columbia UP 2016) 3; S Brooks and D Lombardi, 'Sovereign Debt Restructuring Issues Paper' CIGI Paper No 64, April 2015, https://www.cigionline.org/sites/default/files/cigi_paper_no.64web.pdf; CW Mooney Jr, 'A Framework for a Formal Sovereign Debt Restructuring Mechanism: The KISS Principle (Keep It Simple, Stupid) and Other Guiding Principles' (2015) 37 Michigan Journal of International Law 57.

[187] See Guzman, Ocampo, and Stiglitz (n 186).

[188] United Nations General Assembly Resolution, Basic Principles on Sovereign Debt Restructuring Processes, A/Res/69/319, 29 Sept 2015.

since the 1970s.[189] The European debt and justice crisis has made it a first world issue; perhaps now it will receive the kind of attention that can compel change.

Why does the issue of sovereign debt and responses to it need to be evaluated using principles of justice and what does justice require? Let us begin with the first question. The recent case of Greece provides insight. Prior to the first Greek bailout in 2010, the IMF Executive Board agreed to circumvent its 'exceptional access policy' to lend to a country with 'unsustainable debt'[190] (as conventionally defined, here 'sustainable' debt is understood as 'the ability of a country to meet its debt obligations without requiring debt relief or accumulating arrears',[191] a narrow definition to which we will return). The first loan came from the pooled bilateral loans of eurozone states and the IMF and went to shield German, French, and Greek banks holding Greek bonds from losses. In this way, private (commercial) debt held by these banks was replaced by taxpayer's money from the eurozone lenders and from the IMF.[192] The loan converted private debt into public debt—now owed (with interest) to the disgruntled taxpayers of eurozone countries and to the IMF.[193] Among the conditions that came with the loan was austerity. Austerity focuses on the reduction of wages, prices, and public spending to restore competitiveness, which is supposedly best achieved by cutting the state's budget, debts, and deficits.[194] Austerity in times of recession has received extensive criticism as a policy response evaluated on its own terms—for taking the wrong approach to promoting growth and investment. One of many critical interventions on this issue came by way of an open letter by one hundred US economists in 2012 using examples

[189] There is an abundance of literature, including empirical. See, eg, Harvey (n 134).

[190] 'These terms refer to restrictions the Fund imposed on itself in the aftermath of one of its worst debacles, an effort in 2001 to rescue Argentina that ended a few months later in an economy-crushing default and currency collapse. Under the No More Argentinas rule [ie the exceptional access policy], the IMF could make large loans only to countries whose debt was deemed sustainable with "high probability"'. P Blustein, 'Behind the Scenes at the IMF on a Fateful Day in the Greek Crisis' Centre for International Governance Innovation, 7 July 2015, https://www.cigionline.org/blogs/global-economy/behind-scenes-imf-fateful-day-greek-crisis

It is not insignificant that the IMF staff 'silently' inserted the change into the paper going to the executive board for decision, a concern raised by the Swiss executive director and supported by the Australian, Brazilian, and Iranian executive directors. Office Memorandum on the IMF Board meeting of 9 May 2010 on Greece's request for a Stand-by Arrangement ('Strictly Confidential'). On file with authors.

[191] Development Finance International, http://www.development-finance.org/en/topics-of-work/debt-strategy-information/debt-sustainability.html

[192] The euro area member states other than Greece concluded to this effect an intercreditor agreement, allowing them to pool their bilateral loans to Greece and agreed to provide a total of €80 billion in loans through this channel with the understanding that the IMF, to which Greece had also turned for assistance, would provide another €30 billion. So far there have been three loans to Greece each managed through a different formal mechanism but with all loans funded by the eurozone states along with the IMF.

[193] 'It was declared that initiating these loans with a high interest rate would act as an "incentive to return to market-based financing as soon as feasible". Because of this policy choice €2,614 billion of interest payments were made to the member states by March 2012.' From May 2010 to 2015 over €3 billion was paid in interest and charges to the IMF (footnotes omitted). *Report of the Truth Committee on Public Debt* (Special Committee of the Hellenic Parliament on the Audit of the Greek Debt, 2015) 23–24, http://cadtm.org/IMG/pdf/Report.pdf.

[194] See, eg, M Blyth, *Austerity: The History of a Dangerous Idea* (OUP 2013) 2.

from Britain, Ireland, Spain, and Greece to argue that 'inflicting austerity on a weak economy leads to deeper recession, rising unemployment and increasing misery'.[195] A study undertaken in 2014 by the IMF's Independent Evaluation Office (IEO) concluded that the IMF's call for fiscal consolidation in the euro economies was premature.[196] The conclusion of Greece Prime Minster Alexis Tsipras by April 2016 was that the IMF–eurozone strategy brought 'six years of deep and prolonged recession, during which the economy lost a quarter of its GDP'.[197]

The IMF executive directors knew that the money was not to rescue Greece but to rescue banks and several non-European IMF executive directors, as well as the Swiss, spoke out against it at the time.[198] During that fateful meeting of the executive board on 9 May 2010, Brazil's executive director Paulo Nogueira Batista expressed the following categorical concern: 'The risks of the program are immense ... As it stands, the programs risk substituting private for official financing. In other and starker words, it may be seen not as a rescue of Greece, which will have to undergo a wrenching adjustment, but as a bailout of Greece's private debt holders, mainly European financial institutions.'[199] The Australian executive

[195] 'Jobs and Growth, Not Austerity' open letter signed by US economists, Institute for America's Future (Dec 2012), http://jobsnotausterity.org. See also JF Weeks, *Economics of the 1%* (Anthem Press 2014) 180–81: 'The fakeconomics narrative tells us that inefficiencies generated by the welfare state caused the euro crisis, and the solution required public sector spending cuts. In reality German trade policies caused the euro crisis. German mercantilism provided the "backstory" of the euro crisis, a beggar-thy-neighbour trade policy. Through tight monetary and fiscal policy combined with wage restraint, the German government successfully achieved export-led growth. No need to be an expert in economics to know that success in export-led growth by one country will result in import-led recessions for the trading partners when global demand declines, as it did in 2007'. RH Wade, 'Income Inequality: Should We Worry About Global Trends?' 23 European Journal of Development Research 4 (2011) 513, at 519: '[B]etter in German eyes to blame profligate Greeks, Portuguese and Irish, and demand Versailles-type austerity, in order to shield from view the role of German banks in lending to these countries and helping the market for German exports, as well as the role of German wage compression in making it difficult for them to increase their exports.'

[196] S Dhar, 'IMF Macroeconomic Policy Advice in the Financial Crisis Aftermath' (8 Oct 2014) IMF Independent Evaluation Office Background Paper, BP/14/07, vii. Moreover, the author points out that: 'In contrast to the conclusions of most academic researchers with similar findings, the IMF did not conclude that the shift to fiscal consolidation had been premature ... [instead, for example, the IMF] framed the debate in terms of *pace* of fiscal consolidation, rather than *whether* such consolidation should have been undertaken in the first place ... This manner of framing the debate essentially ignores the work of those who view the advent of post-stimulus fiscal consolidation to have been premature' (ibid para 60).

[197] A Tsipras, 'Greece Has Defied Doom-Mongers—Now the IMF Must Do Its Bit' *Financial Times* (London, 14 Apr 2016). In short, 'The required fiscal austerity was simply too great, causing the economy to collapse.' A Mody, 'The IMF's Big Greek Mistake' *Bloomberg* (21 Apr 2015), https://www.bloomberg.com/view/articles/2015-04-21/imf-needs-to-correct-its-big-greek-bailout-mistake

[198] 'IMF Documents Excerpts: Disagreement Revealed' *Wall Street Journal* (7 Oct 2013), http://blogs.wsj.com/economics/2013/10/07/imf-document-excerpts-disagreements-revealed; also at IMF Office Memorandum (n 190).

[199] *Wall Street Journal* (n 198); IMF Office Memorandum (n 190).

Here is the summary by the former IMF mission chief for Germany and Ireland, worth reproducing at some length:

> Greece's onerous obligations to the IMF, the European Central Bank (ECB) and European governments can be traced back to April 2010, when they made a fateful mistake. Instead of allowing Greece to default on its insurmountable debts to private creditors, they chose to lend it the money to pay in full. At the time, many called for immediately restructuring

director criticized the European Commission for 'conditionality that seems like a shopping list',[200] with the IMF staff acknowledging that 'the program will certainly test Greek society'. According to the then IMF Deputy Director for Europe (now Director of the European Department), Poul Thomsen, the programme for Greece would be 'tough, difficult and painful'.[201] With forceful backing by the Europeans, in particular Germany,[202] the loan was nonetheless approved. The IMF Board unanimously approved Greece's request for a three-year Stand-By Arrangement (SBA) amounting to EUR 30 billion, the largest loan ever approved by the IMF.[203] The pooled bilateral loan from the eurozone states was for EUR 80 billion. In 2015 Panagiotis Roumeliotis, Greece's former alternate executive director at the IMF from 2010–11, was called to testify before the Special Committee of the Hellenic Parliament on the Audit of the Greek Debt. He offered the following summary regarding the decisions of 9 May 2010: 'We asked Greek society to pay for the losses of the banks ... along with the hidden interests of enforcing strict austerity as a warning to other Eurozone countries'.[204]

To advance the bank bailout plan debt restructuring was rejected by Germany and France, as well as Greece, and at least 86% of that so-called bailout package went to German, French, and Greek banks not to the Greek state and its people.[205] In reference to that decision, IMF staff provided the following frank account in May 2013 of the 2010 period:

> [M]any commentators considered debt restructuring to be inevitable. With debt restructuring off the table, Greece faced two alternatives: default immediately, or move ahead as if debt restructuring could be avoided. The latter strategy was adopted, but in the event this only served to delay debt restructuring and allowed many private creditors to escape ... An upfront debt restructuring would have been better for Greece although this was not acceptable to the euro partners. A delayed debt restructuring also provided a window for private creditors to reduce exposures and shift debt into official hands.[206]

Ashoka Mody, the former IMF mission chief for Germany and Ireland offers a summary of the past six years, and in introducing what change to the current

> privately held debt, thus imposing losses on the banks and investors who had lent money to Greece. Among them were several members of the IMF's board and Karl Otto Pohl, a former president of the Bundesbank and a key architect of the euro. The IMF and European authorities responded that restructuring would cause global financial mayhem. As Pohl candidly noted, that was merely a cover for bailing out German and French banks, which had been among the largest enablers of Greek profligacy.

Mody (n 197).

[200] IMF Office Memorandum (n 190). [201] ibid.

[202] Hearing of the Special Committee of the Hellenic Parliament on the Audit of the Greek Debt: Panagiotis Roumeliotis, 15 June 2015. Notes on file with authors.

[203] *The IMF's Annual Report 2010: Supporting Balanced Global Recovery*, 24, http://www.imf.org/external/pubs/ft/ar/2010/eng/pdf/ar10_eng.pdf; see also IMF Office Memorandum (n 190).

[204] Hearing of the Special Committee of the Hellenic Parliament (Roumeliotis) (n 202).

[205] See *Report of the Truth Committee on Public Debt* (n 193) 23; European Commission, Economic Adjustment Programme for Greece, Fifth Review, Oct 2011. Yanis Varoufakis, the former Greek finance minister would later use the figure of 90%.

[206] IMF, 2013. Greece: Ex Post Evaluation of Exceptional Access under the 2010 Stand-By Arrangement, IMF Country Report No 13/156, paras 56–57.

dysfunctional system would require, states quite simply: 'the Fund's major shareholders must leave the building'.[207]

This fairly technical account hardly masks the nature, scale, and ambition of the domination over Greece at the hands of its *public* international creditors.[208] And while the IMF and its member states are directly implicated, the commentator Paul Blustein endorses a widely accepted view that the eurozone states 'can be fairly accused of having been the primary drivers of an approach that caused more suffering for the Greek people than was necessary'.[209] While the past few years have seen produced a range of publications estimating the human harms inflicted on the people of Greece, here we want to introduce some recent findings in order then to offer observations on what justice requires in the circumstances.

Since the contested bailout arrangements economic output shrank by roughly one-quarter with, as Blustein writes, a 'correspondingly wrenching impact on living standards'.[210] To this was added austerity as official policy with the following figures providing just the tip of the iceberg: There has been an 'unprecedented rise in unemployment' in Greece since 2008,[211] with recent accounts providing a figure of 27.5%, 6.5% higher for women, and at close to 50% for youth.[212] The number

207

> The IMF's subordination to its major shareholders became painfully clear when it parachuted into the euro crisis in 2010 ... The greatest failure was in Greece, where, rather than forcing a restructuring of debt, the Fund and its European partners relied on ever deeper fiscal austerity. The Fund continued to back the European orthodoxy that austerity in Greece would help to restore growth by reviving investor confidence, even as its own research—including a seminal paper by Blanchard and his colleague Daniel Leigh—showed that austerity was counterproductive. The Fund never wavered from its basic approach—more official loans for more Greek austerity. True, in 2012, Greece's private creditors finally took losses. But, it was too little too late. Driblets of relief on official debt payments followed, but continuing austerity made a return to growth impossible. Thus, even as the Greeks cut spending deeply and raised taxes, the debt-to-GDP ratio kept climbing. Finally, after a prolonged standoff with the Greek government through the first half of 2015, the IMF publicly stated that Greece's official debt was unsustainable and a large chunk needed to be written off. But the Fund *still* refused to back off on austerity ... [A] month after Greece's embattled finance minister, Yanis Varoufakis, resigned, Mohammed A. El-Erian came to his defense. '[P]olicymakers must recast the country's austerity program, couple pro-growth reforms with greater social justice, and secure additional debt relief'

A Mody, 'Saving the IMF' *Project Syndicate* (9 Apr 2016), https://www.project-syndicate.org/onpoint/saving-the-imf-by-ashoka-mody-2016-04.

208 Domination comes in two main forms, coercion and manipulation. For international law to be morally legitimate, it must comply with moral principles that prevent or minimize domination. See Chapter 2 ('Confronting the Pathologies of International Law').

209 P Blustein, 'The Greek Crisis: Human Errors—And Divine Forgiveness' Centre for International Governance Innovation (20 Feb 2015), https://www.cigionline.org/articles/greek-crisis-human-errors-and-divine-forgiveness. Most of Greece's massive debt is owed directly or indirectly to its eurozone partners.

210 ibid.

211 End of Mission Statement, UN Independent Expert on the effects of foreign debt and other related international financial obligations of States on the full enjoyment of all human rights, particularly economic, social and cultural rights: Mission to Greece, 22–26 April 2013, http://www.ohchr.org/EN/NewsEvents/Pages/DisplayNews.aspx?NewsID=13272andLangID=E

212 Report of the UN Independent Expert on the effects of foreign debt and other related international financial obligations of states on the full enjoyment of all human rights, particularly economic, social and cultural rights: Mission to Greece UN Doc A/HRC/31/60/Add2, 29 Feb 2016, para 57: 'Overall about one million jobs have been lost since the beginning of the crisis, resulting in an unprecedented unemployment rate of 27.5% in 2013 which has only dropped slightly to 24.0%

of people who live in households that cannot keep their home adequately warm doubled since 2010 from 15.4% to 32.9% in 2014.[213] Public health expenditures were cut by 42% within a five-year period.[214] Cutbacks in health expenditure have resulted in figures that point to a 200% rise in the incidence of HIV/AIDS,[215] the return of mother-to-child transmission of HIV,[216] and the return of malaria.[217] Education expenditure decreased heavily between 2009 and 2013, for example with spending on secondary schools reduced by 24.4%.[218] In its 2015 Concluding Observations on Greece, the UN Committee on Economic, Social and Cultural Rights (CESCR) noted that the population at risk of poverty or social exclusion increased severely since 2010, reaching 36% in 2013.[219] In the area of labour rights, the Committee recommends appropriate measures are taken 'to prevent the practice of replacing fixed-term contracts by part-time contracts and other flexible forms of employment with lower pay, including by creating decent work opportunities that offer job security and adequate protection of workers, with a view to respecting their labour rights'.[220] The Committee also highlights its concern at the reductions on the minimum wage as a consequence of the austerity measures taken, noting that the current level of the minimum wage is insufficient to provide workers and their families with a decent living,[221] just as it takes issue with the new legal framework introduced on the right to collective bargaining that could disadvantage employees in their negotiations on wages and conditions.[222] In drawing attention to the restructuring of the state party's social security system as a consequence of the austerity measures, the CESCR concludes—like many judicial, political, and civil society bodies before it—that it has led to drastic cuts in social security benefits and restrictive entitlements and conditions. Moreover, the Committee highlighted its concern that current social security coverage and benefits are inadequate to ensure even a decent living for the recipients and members of their families in contravention with rights protected under the Covenant.[223]

during the 3rd quarter of 2015. Unemployment of women has remained 6.5% higher than men, and youth unemployment (age 15–24) remains with 48.8% at inacceptable proportions undermining the prospects of an entire generation. Job seekers have to accept increasingly part-time or unstable work. The number of persons who have never worked reached 23.6% of all unemployed and 73.7% of all unemployed are in the meantime long-term unemployed. No significant reduction of unemployment is forecast for 2016–2017.'

213 ibid para 69.

214 'At the same time demand for public health care services increased, as more people could no longer afford private health care. Nobody disputes that a reform of the Greek public health care system was overdue and that cost reduction measures needed to be taken to improve its efficiency or reduce the cost of medicines. However, the excessive austerity in the public health care sector literally killed first nurses and doctors before treating the patient ... it is impossible to undertake such drastic cuts in a short period without jeopardizing the right to health in all its dimensions, which include accessibility, affordability, acceptability and quality' (ibid para 35).

215 D Stuckler and S Basu, *The Body Economic: Eight Experiments in Economic Recovery from Iceland to Greece* (Penguin 2013) xiv.

216 ibid 91. 217 ibid xiv.

218 Report of the UN Independent Expert on the effects of foreign debt (n 212) para 36.

219 CESCR, Concluding Observations: Greece UN Doc E/C.12/GRC/CO/2, 9 Oct 2015, para 29.

220 ibid para 18. 221 ibid para 19. 222 ibid para 21. 223 ibid para 23.

There is little doubt that prior to the debt–austerity catastrophe Greece was in need of cleaning up its affairs by addressing extensive corruption, including overspending on defence,[224] illicit financial outflows, and its bloated public sector.[225] But there can be no justification for the assault on the people of Greece, including via the imposition of austerity, which was built on a categorical misrepresentation of the economic policies of the European South[226] and unsupported by sound logic or data,[227] exposing motives ulterior to saving Greece. It may have been a desire by the international creditors to punish the Greeks for their 'profligacy',[228] and/or to crush the rising left of Europe, or due to some other nefarious motive. Or it may be that we need only look to recent history for the most telling deduction: simply that the practice of the IMF of prioritizing the needs of the banks and financial institutions while diminishing the standard of living of the debtor country is well established.[229] Whatever the explanations, there can be no justification that comply with standards of justice for the widespread human rights harms summoned and the absence of effective legal, as well as administrative, accountability.[230] What the IMF and eurozone states did to the people of Greece was tantamount to collective punishment, an act categorically outlawed in international law and reflective of a general principle applicable at *all* times.[231]

[224] Notably the Debt Truth Committee highlights that, 'Most of this spending is due to large-scale contracts for the purchase of military equipment supplied by companies based in current creditor countries.' *Report of the Truth Committee on Public Debt* (n 193) 13.

[225] The Debt Truth Committee offers the following summary: 'The increase in debt was not due to excessive public spending, which in fact remained lower than the public spending of other Eurozone countries, but rather due to the payment of extremely high rates of interest to creditors, excessive and unjustified military spending, loss of tax revenues due to illicit capital outflows, state recapitalization of private banks, and the international imbalances created via the flaws in the design of the Monetary Union itself.' ibid (Executive Summary).

[226] On the comparative finances of the Southern European countries and Germany: 'According to the mainstream narrative, in the European South people were paid too much, worked too little, received excessive public benefits and retired too young ... To begin with the most obvious fallacy: the crisis-hit countries did not have excessive social protection or high social expenditure ... At 25% of national product, German social spending exceeds that of all the putatively spendthrift PIIGS.' Weeks (n 195) 174–84.

[227] For a clear account, see Stuckler and Basu (n 215) 140.

[228] Blustein (n 209).

[229] For an account covering the past several decades, see Harvey (n 134) 73–74.

[230] On the latter, the IMF's Independent Evaluation Office offers recommendations based on its very critical assessment of the procedural and substantive deficiencies by the IMF in its handling of the crisis in Greece, including that 'The Executive Board and management should reaffirm their commitment to accountability and transparency and the role of independent evaluation in fostering good governance'. *IMF and the Crisis in Greece, Ireland, and Portugal* (n 87) paras 130 and 141.

[231] In the context of the laws of war, Convention (IV) respecting the Laws and Customs of War on Land and its annex: Regulations concerning the Laws and Customs of War on Land. The Hague, 18 Oct 1907 (Hague Regulations) Art 50; Convention (III) relative to the Treatment of Prisoners of War. Geneva, 12 August 1949 (Third Geneva Convention) Art 87, third paragraph; Convention (IV) relative to the Protection of Civilian Persons in Time of War. Geneva, 12 Aug 1949 (Fourth Geneva Convention) Art 33: 'No protected person may be punished for an offence he or she has not personally committed. Collective penalties and likewise all measures of intimidation or of terrorism are prohibited. Pillage is prohibited. Reprisals against protected persons and their property are prohibited.' See also, UN Human Rights Committee, General Comment No 29, States of Emergency (Art 4) UN Doc CCPR/C/21/Rev.1/Add 11, 31 Aug 2001, para 11: 'States parties may in no circumstances invoke article 4 of the Covenant as justification for acting in violation of humanitarian law or peremptory norms of international law, for instance by taking hostages, by imposing collective punishments ... '; and

The handling of the Greek sovereign debt crisis is notable for its subversion of democracy and the authoritarian tactics deployed by public international institutions functioning as creditors. This authoritarianism was made manifest by the secret meetings in Washington hotel rooms to lock in the bank bailout plan of 2010, to the effective rebuff by the international creditors of the Greek referendum in July 2015 after the Greek people rejected the terms of the third bailout. The responses included the ECB immediately cutting off liquidity to Greek banks in a shameless act of collective retribution and political manipulation. While the IMF is a strong advocate of democracy in borrowing countries (as is the European Union in its development cooperation), the values it seeks to export are not reflected within the institution, a point long recognized by law and development scholars and most recently by the IMF's own Independent Evaluation Office.[232] As is addressed in Chapters 2 ('Confronting the Pathologies of International Law') and 4 ('International Trade'), this 'inside–outside' distinction is part of international law as we know it: the values exported need not be the values deployed at home in lending countries or by the institutions over which they exercise great influence.

In important ways, our so-called public international institutions are 'public' only in name. They have not shown themselves to represent the public interest in the countries in which they operate so intrusively. That international law ought to be understood as a law of cooperation does not mean that it functions well as a law of cooperation; it is at best a differentiated law of cooperation applicable to rich states and some emerging states with another approach reflective of domination by the strong against the weak.[233] In the regulation of sovereign debt, the IMF has demonstrated clearly that it faces a conflict of interest in that it is too closely affiliated with its creditors while it is a creditor itself. These democratic deficits are not remedied by changes to the IMF's weighted voting system which is essentially dedicated to determining which countries will wield influence that reaches deep into borrowing states.[234] What we have is what Lazzarato refers to as the coupling of economic expropriation with democratic expropriation.[235] Put differently, the most significant problem faced by justice is first and foremost the commodification of politics: the capture of economics and politics by private interests. What justice requires is democratic institutions for a post-democratic age.

Mody argues that addressing the conflict of interest would require replacing the Fund's executive board, which represents shareholders, with a board of independent, professional directors.[236] There are other suggestions. For current purposes, the core issue is what this story represents for international law given that the situation can hardly be considered just. Two reflections are offered in this regard.

analogously Protocol No 4 to the European Convention on Human Rights (1963), Art 4: 'Collective expulsion of aliens is prohibited'.

[232] *IMF and the Crisis in Greece, Ireland, and Portugal* (n 87).

[233] See further Chapter 2 ('Confronting the Pathologies of International Law').

[234] Mody (n 207). [235] Lazzarato (n 135) 28. [236] Mody (n 207).

The familiar claim that international law has ushered in a rules-based system that replaces an international anarchic order where 'might makes right' is grossly overstated. While this is overstated as a description of international law in general, in the realm of global finance the system more readily reflects an order based on supremacy: 'rule by a bloc of forces that clearly serves partial or particular interests, and this is experienced by subordinates as involving coercive, corrupt forms of rule that lack legitimate appeal and credibility'.[237] These features are at work in the global financial architecture, as explained in the sections above. What becomes apparent from a consideration of the Greek sovereign debt and austerity crisis is the adherence to a contract approach whereby the legal system governs seemingly private activities as if those activities are purely a matter of contract and exchange. A result is that while the decisions and arrangements have enormous public significance—not least for the people of borrowing states but also for the people of the lending states—the public dimensions are ignored. The use of what is effectively a contract approach may offer one explanation as to why international human rights obligations were not at all factored in to methods of addressing the sovereign debt crisis in Greece, including why the loans were not used for the benefit of the Greek population. Of course states cannot contract out of their human rights obligations, and the human rights obligations of states continue even after their transfer of competences to international organizations, such as the IMF.

The idea of international law and practice as consent-based exists only in so far as the fiction of functional or formal equality among (so-called) sovereign states is maintained. This contract approach takes this fiction one step further by endorsing the creation of rules overtly based on domination, including coercion and manipulation. What the Greek debt debacle highlights is how coercion is an international custom tacitly or explicitly allowed by law. There is little doubt that what this case study indicates, perhaps more than any other development, is that as a matter of current international law, economic coercion is an approved practice. Needless to say, this fails the test of justice.

The second reflection on what this Greek tragedy represents for international law is that impunity would seem to be part of global finance. The former IMF official and mission chief for Germany and Ireland calls for accountability when he accuses the IMF of 'serial mistakes in the conduct of the Greek program'.[238] But with little optimism Mody concluded in the latter part of 2015 that: 'Of course, the most likely outcome is that Greece will continue to borrow new money from the creditors to pay its old debts to those creditors. As it undertakes more austerity, Greek output and prices will fall, making its debt burden greater. That will be blamed on Greek intransigence.'[239] Mody is clever, but this

[237] S Gill and AC Cutler, 'New Constitutionalism and World Order: General Introduction' in S Gill and AC Cutler (eds), *New Constitutionalism and World Order* (CUP 2014) 1, 15.

[238] A Mody, 'Wolfgang Schauble, Debt Relief and the Future of the Eurozone' *Bruegel Blog* (6 Aug 2015), http://bruegel.org/2015/08/wolfgang-schauble-debt-relief-and-the-future-of-the-eurozone

[239] ibid.

was not prescience. As an IMF insider he was easily prepared to argue as to what the economic outcome would be; as for international law, even a cursory mapping in this area suggests that there will be no legal accountability when it comes to the IMF for the harms brought to bear on the people of Greece.[240]

For decades, international human rights lawyers have quite tirelessly written on the need for accountability of international financial institutions for the human rights harms with which they are implicated. And it was back in 2001 when Philippe Sands and Pierre Klein concluded in *Bowett's Law of International Institutions* that: 'It has been suggested that, for example, the World Bank is not subject to general international norms for the protection of fundamental human rights. In our view that conclusion is without merit, on legal or policy grounds.'[241] Recently the same argument regarding the IMF has been elaborated in the context of the Greek crisis.[242] The European Court of Human Rights (ECtHR) for its part has repeatedly held that the obligations of contracting states continue even after the transfer of competences to international organizations.[243] Compliance by member states with their human rights obligations requires that the relevant organization is considered to protect the fundamental rights that bind the states in question (in this case under the European Convention on Human Rights), as regards both the substantive guarantees offered and the mechanisms controlling their observance, in a manner which can be considered 'at least equivalent' to that for which the Convention provides.[244] The IMF offers no such guarantee or remedy.[245] Similarly,

[240] Let's see what happens in the European Union where recently a Grand Chamber of the Court of Justice of the European Union (CJEU) recognized that EU institutions are bound by EU law (thus including the Charter of Fundamental Rights and Freedoms) also when acting outside of the European Union (the Commission and ECB were 'borrowed' by the European Stability Mechanism (ESM). The ESM is an international organization of eurozone states established for financing the bailouts). The CJEU decision further shows that individuals can challenge the EU institutions' bailout actions by means of an action for damages. Joined Cases C-8/15 P to C-10/15 P, *Ledra Advertising v the European Commission and European Central Bank*, 20 Sept 2016.

[241] P Sands and P Klein, *Bowett's Law of International Institutions* (5th edn, Sweet & Maxwell 2001) 459. Making a point that applies equally to the IMF given its structure as an international organization.

[242] ME Salomon, 'Of Austerity, Human Rights and International Institutions' (2015) 21 European Law Journal 521; O De Schutter and ME Salomon, 'Economic Policy Conditionality, Socio-Economic Rights and International Legal Responsibility: The Case of Greece 2010–2015' Legal Brief prepared for the Special Committee of the Hellenic Parliament on the Audit of the Greek Debt, 15 June 2015, http://www.lse.ac.uk/humanRights/documents/2015/SalomonDeSchutterGreekDebtTruth.pdf

[243] ECtHR, *Mathews v United Kingdom*, Appl No 24833/94, Grand Chamber Judgment of 18 Feb 1999, paras 29, 32, and 34; ECtHR, *Waite and Kennedy v Germany*, Appl No 26083/94, Grand Chamber Judgment of 18 Feb 1999, para 67; ECtHR, *Bosphorus Hava Yollary Turizm ve Ticaret Anonim Sirketi v Ireland*, Appl No 45036/98, Grand Chamber Judgment of 30 June 2005, paras 152–56. See also Maastricht Principles on Extraterritorial Obligations of States in the Area of Economic, Social and Cultural Rights (2011) Principle 15.

[244] *Bosphorus Airways v Ireland* (n 243) para 155; ECtHR, *Gasparini v l'Italie et la Belgique*, Requête No 10750/03, Deuxième Section, Décision de 12 mai 2009.

[245] This is unlike the World Bank Group's International Finance Corporation that has a complaint mechanism (the Compliance Advisor Ombudsman) providing a forum in which stakeholders can seek to have their claims addressed. But like the Bank's other mechanism, the Inspection Panel, this is not a legal enforcement mechanism and the IFC board is entitled to ignore its findings and recommendations. See DD Bradlow, Brief as Amicus Curiae in support of Plaintiffs–Appellants in *BI Jam, KA*

There have been repeated calls by the UN Committee on Economic, Social and Cultural Rights over a period of decades that state parties should ensure rights in the Covenant are respected in the lending policies, credit agreements, and in structural and/or fiscal adjustment policies pursued under the auspices of international financial institutions of which they are member, recommendations that are yet to be heeded.[246]

It is also the case that, as regards the IMF *qua* the IMF, the Articles on the Responsibility of International Organizations[247] do not address the real obstacles preventing individuals from holding international organizations to account, such as the lack of available judicial forums or procedural obstacles such as their immunity before domestic courts.[248] International organizations have effectively converted the immunity that was put in place primarily to shield them from interference by member states 'into a sword' with which they can ward off attempts by individuals to hold them accountable for their actions.[249] And while a member *state* of an international organization would seem not to incur international responsibility when aiding and abetting an international organization of which it is a member when it acts *in accordance with the rules of the organization*, even if those acts violate its other international obligations, the state is not free to ignore its other international obligations, for example in the area of human rights, for which it would incur responsibility for a breach of those obligations as part of the law on state responsibility.[250] Still, there are few judicial avenues to make this legal fact stick. In short, the right to a remedy for victims of human rights violations incurred through the decisions of the IMF or its member states—including as regards the conditionality imposed on Greece—are simply not available. The consequence is a lack of legal accountability and no reparation for injury caused, including guarantees of non-repetition. This is despite the fact that the obligation to provide a right of access to an effective remedy is so widely recognized by states that it has become part of customary international

Manjalia, SK Jam, R Jadeja, N Panchayat, and MAS Sanghathan (Plaintiffs–Appellants) v International Finance Corporation (Defendant–Appellee), On Appeal from the United States District Court for the District of Columbia, No 15-cv-00612. Document No 1630690, Filed 16 Aug 2016.

246 A recent articulation is as follows: 'States parties acting as members of relevant international organizations should also respect the right [to just and favourable conditions of work]. States parties that are members of international financial institutions, notably the IMF, the World Bank, and regional development banks, should take steps to ensure the right is taken into account in their lending policies, credit agreements and other international measures. They should also ensure that the policies and practices of international and regional financial institutions, in particular those concerning structural and/or fiscal adjustment, promote and do not interfere with the right'. CESCR, General Comment No 23, Right to Just and Favourable Conditions of Work (Art 7) UN Doc E/C.12/GC/23 (2016) para 71.

247 International Law Commission, Draft Articles on the Responsibility of International Organizations with Commentaries 2011 (A/66/10). Hereafter, DARIO.

248 J Wouters and J Odermatt, 'Are All International Organizations Created Equal?' (2012) 9 International Organizations Law Review 8, 10; A Reinisch and J Wurm, 'International Financial Institutions before National Courts' in DD Bradlow and D Hunter (eds), *International Financial Institutions and International Law* (Kluwer 2010) 103; S Herz, 'Rethinking International Financial Institution Immunity' ibid 137.

249 Bradlow (n 245).

250 See DARIO (n 247) Art 58(2) at 91, para 5. See also DARIO, Art 59(2).

law.[251] We cannot be surprised that, as a former vice president of the World Bank remarked recently: 'Lessons have not been learned and structural adjustment policies being imposed on Europe now by the IMF are very similar to those that were being pushed on developing countries in the 70s and 80s by the World Bank and IMF.'[252]

The adoption in September 2015 by the UN General Assembly of Principles on Sovereign Debt Restructuring Processes might represent a notable move away from an exclusive focus on the priorities of creditors to a wider set of procedural and substantive values that protect a greater set of interests.[253] As argued earlier in this chapter, justice would require precisely a move away from the contract approach to those that might more readily accommodate principles of justice. And it is reasonable to assert that 'the human rights revolution' challenges—or should challenge—business as usual in sovereign debt repayment, restructuring, and in the very definition of sustainability[254] to include what the UN Independent Expert on Foreign Debt and Human Rights refers to as the 'social sustainability of debt'.[255] But we should be reminded that the resolution saw the major developed countries vote against it,[256] with the European Union emphasizing that any discussion around a debt restructuring framework is best pursued in the IMF, explaining its position as such: 'The IMF is ... the main forum for discussing technical capital market issues related to restructuring sovereign debt. It is also a forum where the influence of the

[251] See Bradlow (n 245).

[252] I Goldin, 'Divided Nations: Why Global Governance Is Failing and What We Can Do About It' LSE public lecture, 20 Mar 2013, http://www.lse.ac.uk/publicEvents/events/2013/03/20130320t1830vHKT.aspx. Harvey remarks: 'in 1984 the World Bank, for the first time in its history, granted a loan to a country in return for structural neoliberal reforms. De la Madrid then opened Mexico to the global economy by joining GATT and implementing an austerity programme. The effects were wrenching.' Harvey (n 134) 100.

[253] See, eg, JP Bohoslavsky and M Goldmann, 'An Incremental Approach to Sovereign Debt Restructuring: Sovereign Debt Sustainability as a Principle of International Law' (2016) 41 Yale Journal of International Law 13.

[254] R Howse, 'Concluding Remarks in Light of International Law' in C Esposito, Y Li, and JP Bohoslavsky (eds), *Sovereign Financing and International Law: The UNCTAD Principles on Responsible Sovereign Lending and Borrowing* (OUP 2013) 385, 386. GA Res 69/319 (n 188) para 8: 'Sustainability implies that sovereign debt restructuring workouts are completed in a timely and efficient manner and lead to a stable debt situation in the debtor State, preserving at the outset creditors' rights while promoting sustained and inclusive economic growth and sustainable development, minimizing economic and social costs, warranting the stability of the international financial system and respecting human rights.'

[255] UN Independent Expert on the effects of foreign debt and other related international financial obligations of states on the full enjoyment of all human rights, particularly economic, social and cultural rights, Mission to Greece cover note, 14 March 2016: 'During the discussion of the report at the Human Rights Council the Government of Greece made a statement in support of the report acknowledged that the economic crisis has had a very severe impact upon the situation of human rights in the country, in particular as regards to the enjoyment of social and cultural rights. Greece said further that no programme of reforms and fiscal adjustment can be effective without society's support. The Government also concurred with my finding that, to date, no comprehensive ex-ante human rights impact assessments of the three economic reform programmes have been carried out. Greece argued that there is an urgent necessity to assess debt issues in relation to social needs, thus introducing into the public debate the notion of social sustainability of debt.'

[256] Canada, Germany, Israel, Japan, United Kingdom, United States.

EU and of its Member States is significant, in contrast with the EU's structural difficulty to orient the work in the UNGA.'[257]

That the IMF has long resisted calls to consider human rights in the execution of its mandate and its member states have failed to honour the human rights obligations they have when making decisions within the IMF seemed not to influence the EUs position paper, nor did the IMF's categorical disregard for socio-economic rights in Greece. Instead, the European Union followed the line it has taken for years when the possibility of reforming international economic affairs in the interest of justice has been broached at the UN: one that seeks precisely to continue to keep economic and 'non-economic' matters apart and to ensure that decisions on the former take place in venues where they hold the balance of power.

In 2016 the IMF's Independent Evaluation Office began an in-depth assessment of the IMF on Social Protection. This represents an opportunity to call the bluff of the European Union and for the IEO to recommend precisely that the IMF is long overdue in bringing the matter of social sustainability and human rights in-house. This would include a robust assessment of how the real public interest is *directly* accounted for and how human rights harms might in future be directly remedied. It would also represent an important step in redressing the post-war institutional order that endorsed the bifurcation of the economic and 'non-economic' realms, one that decades later any reasonable account of justice is still struggling to see transcended.[258] The proposals to emerge from our consideration of the Greek crises are relatively modest, but the dysfunction of the current global financial system in this area by any standard of justice is so fantastic that even moderate improvement would, on one definition, represent radical improvement.

5. Concluding Remarks

The global financial architecture offers regrettable instances of injustice and immiseration. With the fall of the Bretton Woods institutions, and the eventual faltering of the NIEO, global finance moved to an extreme version of capitalism, in which financialization became ascendant, which brought on liberalized financial flows, a push to securitize many forms of finance, and moves of finance away from investment in development and towards diversification and profit-making on trading. Banks and shadow banks continue to pose substantial risks of harm with risky capital structures. The result is a dangerous mix of policies and practices that threaten systemic forms of instability with the potential to do serious damage to the living standards of those who do not participate or at best only marginally benefit from global finance. Add to the mix a contract

[257] EU common position on the UN draft resolution A/69/L.84 on 'Basic Principles on Sovereign Debt Restructuring Processes' Council of the European Union, Cover Note 11705/15, 7 Sept 2016, 4.

[258] The IEO evaluation was released as this book went to press. It falls short of recommending meaningful change.

approach to sovereign debt restructuring that prioritizes power and creditors over welfare and citizens, with an international organization, the IMF, coordinating sovereign debt restructuring in ways that suggest it places too much power in the hands of creditors. The potential for the global financial architecture to impose misery on many people remains very significant. In sum, the global financial architecture in its current state is a moral failure.

7

Human Rights

Between the Radical and the Subverted

International law is too market-oriented. In the areas of trade, investment, and finance international law focuses on how the rules serve the economy, how they stimulate wealth creation, and how they encourage economic growth presenting these ends as if they are of singular importance and of common benefit. But as the other chapters in this book explore in detail, the global economy functions in a manner that imposes needless risk on the wider international society and on those least likely to benefit, wealth creation happens by making the rich richer, and the dedication to profit generation is through the expansion of markets that fail to take inclusive, fair, or sustainable growth into account. The particular means through which these ends are advanced include trade liberalization aimed at the distribution of the world's resources,[1] an investment regime that solely protects transnational corporate interests under a system of reverse (and perverse) international redistribution,[2] and substantial cross-border capital flows directed not at development but at diversifying the assets of investors in high-income countries.[3] This toolbox also includes spending cuts and the dismantling of the welfare state, 'flexible' work practices aimed at deregulation in favour of profit generation through labour insecurity,[4] and a dedication to privatization.[5] It is no

[1] M Somers in Conversation with J Curtis, 'Socially Embedding the Market and the Role of Law' Series on Economics and Law in Conversation, Laboratory for Advanced Research on the Global Economy, Centre for the Study of Human Rights, LSE (Mar 2016) 12, http://www.lse.ac.uk/humanRights/research/projects/theLab/Economics-and-Law-in-Conversation---Interview-with-Margaret-Somers-FINAL.pdf. Trade agreements carve up markets to the benefit of the constituents of rich states, which are often multinational enterprises. See Chapter 2 ('Confronting the Pathologies of International Law'), Chapter 3 ('The End of Empire and the Search for Justice: NIEO and Beyond'), and especially Chapter 4 ('International Trade').

[2] See Chapter 5 ('Foreign Investment').

[3] See Chapter 6 ('Global Finance').

[4] Or 'flexicurity'. 'In many instances, the focus is on how best to provide an environment which can increase (local and multinational) corporate profits through flexible work practices while workers' rights (or security of employment) are often viewed as obstacles in these processes ... [O]n the whole flexicurity has meant de-regulation in favour of increased flexibility and devaluing security.' R Kurian, 'Lab Views, Laboratory for Advanced Research on the Global Economy Interview 2' Centre for the Study of Human Rights, LSE (Mar 2014), http://www.lse.ac.uk/humanRights/documents/projects/LABViewsKurian.pdf

[5] On the links between spending cuts and a pro-corporate agenda: '[T]hose who are smart enough to know that [austerity] doesn't work [especially in the middle of an economic downturn] still would use it because it is a very good way of shrinking the state (and thus giving more power to the corporate sector, including the foreign one) and changing the nature of state

exaggeration to suggest that global capitalism as practised has exceeded the morally odious condition of having society subordinated to the market.[6] As Chapter 1 ('Legal Rendering of Immiseration') explains, in important ways this model is failing to achieve even its purported objectives from the claim of shared gains to the promise of economic redemption through iterations of neoliberal shock therapy.[7] Meanwhile, widespread poverty persists and the general trend is against signs of its overall reduction (even based on the inadequate international poverty line of US$1.25 per day), just as material inequality has exploded within countries with any figures pointing to the closing of the global gap necessarily qualified.[8] As if poverty and unjustifiable inequality aren't enough, they are accompanied by a host of alienations, dispossessions, and immiserations: from the process of 'depeasantization' that sees land effectively stolen from the poor as its value increases,[9] to the destruction of indigenous cultures through the forced shift from non-market to market-based economies, to the conditions that encourage greater market concentration and the entry of large foreign chain stores at the expense of local family-owned businesses,[10] to the rural flight of small-scale producers and the corresponding feminization of capital-intensive farming.[11] People are being crushed under the dominance of this economic project of globalized capital accumulation and the centrality and tenacity of *homo economicus*.[12] As the other chapters in this book have demonstrated, from

activities into a pro-corporate one (eg it is almost always welfare spending that goes first). In other words, austerity is a very good way of pushing through a regressive political agenda without appearing to do so.' CJ Polychroniou, 'Exposing the Myths of Neoliberal Capitalism: An Interview with Ha-Joon Chang' *Truthout* (8 Feb 2017), http://www.truth-out.org/opinion/item/39393-exposing-the-myths-of-neoliberal-capitalism-an-interview-with-ha-joon-chang

[6] See F Block, 'Introduction' in K Polanyi (ed), *The Great Transformation: The Political and Economic Origins of Our Time* (Beacon Press 2001 edn) xxiv.

[7] A recent case is that of Greece at the hands of its international creditors but there is a long and tragic history of neoliberal shock therapy.

[8] Milanovic concludes that global inequality (income inequality among the citizens of the world) has fallen dramatically among nations, but due to rising incomes in China and India, while inequality has soared within nations. B Milanovic, *Global Inequality: A New Approach for the Age of Globalization* (Harvard U Press 2016) 19–22.

[9] F Magdoff, 'Multiple Crises as Symptoms of an Unsustainable System' (2010) 33 Review: Fernand Braudel Center, Special Issue on Food, Energy, Environment: Crisis of the Modern World System 103, 107. Magdoff's use of the term 'depeasantization' is taken from Araghi.

[10] Y Varoufakis, 'Commentary to the 3rd Memorandum of Understanding between the European Commission Acting on Behalf of the European Stability Mechanism and the Hellenic Republic and the Bank of Greece' (11 Aug 2015).

[11] 'Critical parts of food systems are becoming more capital-intensive, vertically integrated and concentrated in fewer hands. This is happening from input provisioning to food distribution. Small-scale producers and landless households are the first to lose out and increasingly seek employment opportunities outside of agriculture. This is driving increased migratory flows, especially of male members of rural households, which is leading, in turn, to the "feminization" of farming in many parts of the world.' UN Food and Agriculture Organization, *The Future of Food Agriculture: Trends and Challenges* (FAO 2017) xi.

[12] We agree that, '[D]espite abandonment of some unrealistic assumptions, *homo economicus* was retained ... post Washington Consensus.' B Akbulut, F Adaman, and YM Madra, 'The Decimation and Displacement of Development Economics' (2015) 46 Development and Change 733, 746. And despite *homo economicus* being widely challenged in terms of behavioural assumptions.

the past to the present, international law has formalized the terms under which this project of immiseration is facilitated and sanctioned.[13]

Against this backdrop, international human rights law is generally posited as a counter-hegemonic force, limiting harm and confronting deprivations. Indeed, human rights—normatively and practically—provide significant protections to people and it would be an error to disregard their contribution to human well-being since the modern human rights project was elaborated in the post-Second World War era. Yet, human rights exist within this extreme capitalist global economy and their deployment needs to be considered against that backdrop, and not merely as a discrete, benevolent response to it. To that end, this chapter interrogates whether human rights have settled for preventing and mitigating deprivations but not changing the terms under which that suffering is not only made possible but is reproduced, including by reinforcing the structural features that engender it. Taking that inquiry one step further, we are interested here in the ways in which human rights work against a transformative or radical agenda,[14] to the detriment of their own aims and objectives. A subsequent question is whether human rights when seen to be effective are more than merely redistributive: whether they incorporate what we call here the predistributive demands of justice as expressed through law: priorities, the rules and their application, and systems and structures.[15] Taken together the various chapters in this book offer a critique of the negative influences of neoliberalism on international law not only directly in the discrete fields of explicit economic activity in the form of trade, investment, and finance, but also on international human rights law. Human rights are being circumscribed by the justifications, logic, and dynamics of contemporary global neoliberalism supported, as the previous chapters in this book have shown, by the instrumental use of international economic law to those ends. It is under this dominant narrative of global capitalism that the transformative potential of human rights is considered.

1. The Dominance of Global Neoliberalism

The majority of people globally, including those of the industrialized world, oppose capitalism as it is currently practised. The fierce appropriations and commercialization of neoliberal capitalism, its manufactured desperation, and its gross material inequality are despised by the multitudes. There is disgust at the categorical embrace of a 'commercial morality'[16] for a social one and the capitulation of democratic

[13] On the history and making of international commerce as law, see especially Chapter 3 ('The End of Empire and the Search for Justice: NIEO and Beyond'), Chapter 4 ('International Trade'), and Chapter 5 ('Foreign Investment').

[14] These terms are used interchangeably.

[15] See Chapter 1 ('Legal Rending of Immiseration') and Chapter 2 ('Confronting the Pathologies of International Law'): the aim of predistribution is to make international law just in a structural sense, *ex ante*, so that the elements of international law relevant to the global economy are designed to make it structurally impossible for injustice to exist in the global economy in any material sense. The aim would be for international law to be structured to eliminate or, given the limitations of the law as an instrument to effectuate change, to make it exceedingly difficult for powerful actors to dominate in the global economy.

[16] CB Macpherson, *The Rise and Fall of Economic Justice and Other Papers* (OUP 1985) 7.

governance to corporate interests and motives; there are wide-ranging denunciations of economic rationalizations and justifications operating as the universal lodestar. Yet this widespread condemnation has not been nearly enough to challenge the onslaught against principles of social justice based on a tireless commitment to profit and the unbounded expansion of markets. Neoliberalism as a system of normative reasoning,[17] as policy and as practice delineates existence like no other contemporary value; with economic globalization as its conduit, and international economic law as its ally, it orders economic and social life on the planet and, in important ways, political life too.

Even the global financial crisis of 2008, a product of the neoliberal commitment to the deregulation of financial activity (or as Radhika Balakrishnan, Diane Elson, and Raj Patel prefer—'profit-led regulation'),[18] perhaps remarkably resulted in the strengthening of neoliberalism by elites in western countries. A recent example of neoliberalism's staying power is demonstrated by the insistence on fiscal contraction and austerity by Europe's international creditors, measures that have deeply damaged European debtor economies and decimated socio-economic rights in the process.[19] The answer to the question as to *why* we have seen this commitment to

[17] '[A]s a normative order of reason developed over three decades into a widely and deeply disseminated governing rationality, neoliberalism transmogrifies every human domain and endeavour, along with the humans themselves, according to a specific image of the economic. All conduct is economic conduct: all spheres of existence are framed and measured by economic terms and metrics, even when those spheres are not directly monetized. In neoliberal reason and in domains governed by it, we are only ever *homo oeconomicus*.' W Brown, *Undoing the Demos: Neoliberalism's Stealth Revolution* (Zone Books 2015) 9–10.

[18] 'Neo-liberal economists tend to argue that markets and property should be regulated in ways that promote flexibility and make it easier for businesses to invest and make profits (this is often called "deregulation", but might more appropriately be called "profit-led regulation"'. R Balakrishnan, D Elson, and R Patel, 'Rethinking Macroeconomic Strategies from A Human Rights Perspective' (2010) 53 Development 27, 35. Kadri rejects the language of deregulation altogether and points instead to a regulatory shift in society towards benefiting the ruling class: 'What these supposed de-regulatory measures do is not to de-regulate, but to shift the power to regulate the flow of resources in society from the working class to the ruling class. As such, these are re-calibrations of the accounting parameters that allow value, signified in the money form, to wash back and forth within certain degrees between labour and capital; in the neoliberal case, it is capital that makes the bigger share.' A Kadri, 'Lab Views, Laboratory for Advanced Research on the Global Economy Interview 3' Centre for the Study of Human Rights, LSE (July 2014) 1, 3, http://www.lse.ac.uk/humanRights/documents/projects/LABViewsKadri.pdf

[19] See RH Wade, 'Capitalism and Democracy at Cross-Purposes' (2013) 28 New Zealand Sociology 208, 211: 'Contrary to the pattern in earlier bouts of hard times, elites in western countries have even strengthened their commitment to neoliberalism since the global financial crisis of 2008 and subsequent long slump. Neoliberalism supports the macroeconomic agenda known as "expansionary austerity" or "fiscal consolidation" applied through much of the western world and now increasingly in developing countries too (amplifying recessionary and unequalising tendencies on a world scale).' On the deployment of austerity as a response to the crisis in Europe, see ME Salomon, 'Of Austerity, Human Rights and International Institutions' (2015) 21 European Law Journal 521; C Crouch, *The Strange Non-death of Neoliberalism* (Polity 2011) viii: 'Whereas the financial crisis concerned banks and their behaviour, resolution of the crisis has been redefined in many countries as a need to cut back, once and for all, on the welfare state and public spending'; J Fischer, 'The Return of the Ugly German' *Project Syndicate* (23 July 2015), http://www.project-syndicate.org/commentary/return-of-the-ugly-german-by-joschka-fischer-2015-07#f57p7PUqpSWtxs1y.99: 'Greece could either exit (in full knowledge of the disastrous consequences for the country and Europe) or accept a program that effectively makes it a European protectorate, without any hope of economic improvement. Greece is now subject

neoliberalism imposed on flailing European countries when it failed so egregiously on its own terms in the past[20] has thrown up any number of viable explanations—political expedience in certain lending countries,[21] populists politics, disciplining other borrowers, quashing the rising left in Europe, vested interests and personal gain,[22] or flagrant coercion.[23] But the key lies in the question posed: what to the many is a crisis of (global) neoliberalism—its accumulation by dispossession,[24] by displacement,[25] through encroachment,[26] its support for corporate capital accumulation and profit-led regulation—has not failed all of *us*. As Colin Crouch frames it, the global financial capital class is the dominant class[27] and, as such, 'neo-liberalism

to a cure—further austerity—that has not worked in the past and that was prescribed solely to address Germany's domestic political needs.'

[20] For case studies on its failures, see D Stuckler and S Basu, *The Body Economic: Eight Experiments in Economic Recovery from Iceland to Greece* (Penguin 2013).

[21] 'If Schäuble is acting tough with Greece right now, it is because his electorate wants him to act that way; it's not just that he doesn't care about the Greek people, he wants people to believe he doesn't care, because he sees the political advantage in it.' D Laabs, 'Why Is Germany So Tough on Greece? Look Back 25 Years' *The Guardian* (London, 17 July 2015).

[22] Stuckler and Basu (n 20) 140: 'Ultimately austerity has failed because it is unsupported by sound logic or data. It is an economic ideology. It stems from the belief that small government and free markets are always better than state intervention. It is a socially constructed myth—a convenient belief among politicians taken advantage of by those who have a vested interest in shrinking the role of the state, in privatizing social welfare systems for personal gain.'

[23] Paul De Grauwe offers an outline as to what the European Central Bank (ECB) could have done, and should have done to address the Greek banking crisis in mid July 2015, instead of announcing that it would cap the amount of liquidity available to the Greek banks, causing panic in Greece and a run on the banks: 'The correct announcement of the ECB should be that it will provide all the necessary liquidity to the Greek banks.' De Grauwe goes on to conclude the following: 'I would be very surprised if the very intelligent men (and one woman) in Frankfurt did not know these first principles. This leads me to conclude that the ECB has other objectives than stabilizing the Greek banking system. These objectives are political. The ECB continues to put pressure on the Greek government to behave well. The price of this behaviour by the ECB is paid by millions of Greeks.' P De Grauwe, 'The ECB Doesn't Learn from Past Mistakes' *Ivory Tower* (16 July 2015), http://escoriallaan.blogspot.be/2015/07/in-2011-at-height-of-sovereign-debt.html

[24] D Harvey, *A Brief History of Neoliberalism* (OUP 2005).

[25] F Araghi, 'The End of "Cheap Ecology" and the Crisis of "Long Keynesianism"' (2010) 45 Economic & Political Weekly 39, 40.

[26] 'Any particular bloc of capital can grow, conceptually, in two ways. One is by reinvesting its surplus value and thereby growing bigger; the other is by annexing other blocs of capital, or by taking over common property, or the property of non-capitalist petty producers, or that of the state. The first of these constitutes "accumulation through expansion"; the second constitutes "accumulation through encroachment" ... Taking the entire bloc of capital in the world economy, its accumulation through expansion necessarily has to be complemented by a process of accumulation through encroachment ... An example can make the point clear. The capitalist sector can meet, say, its raw cotton requirements in any one of two ways: if the peasant agricultural sector increases its supply to match the requirement of the capitalist sector; or if some traditional cotton manufacturers are thrown out of their occupation and the raw cotton they were using becomes available to the capitalist sector. Since it is in the nature of capitalism to capture markets from pre-capitalist producers, its "normal" functioning will entail its meeting its raw cotton needs through the second route. And this very fact will foreclose the first route, which, in any case, it is not in the nature of capitalism to follow. Accumulation through encroachment therefore is an intrinsic property of capitalism, which is based not on balanced but on uneven development of the different segments of the world economy.' P Patnaik, 'The Accumulation Process in the Period of Globalisation' (2008) 43 Economic & Political Weekly 108.

[27] R Hyman, 'Markets, Crouch and Neo-Liberalism: Praising with Faint Damns?' (2012) 10 Socio-Economic Review 610, 619 (review symposium, citing Crouch 1997).

persists because it is in the *interests* of the economically powerful, and their economic power shapes political outcomes'.[28] These conclusions are captured in Slavoj Žižek's cogent summary of the three tendencies that unite to describe contemporary capitalism: the unaccountable expansion of the reign of the market, the circumscription of the public—from enclosures of public space to cuts in public services—and a rising authoritarianism in the functioning of political power.[29] As this book is being written, Greece continues to implode under the weight of the bias of twenty-first-century 'cruel capitalism' but it is clear that many states are not able, no less civil society, to rein in its relentless assault on social values.[30] In its struggle for social justice there was a moment when Greece carried the hopes of the global majority in inaugurating the defeat of global capitalism. But even a state in industrialized, 'Social Europe' fights the behemoth 'armed only with sticks and rocks'.[31]

With the end of the cold war socialism lost its power of persuasion but as Michael Freeman points out the ethical questions about capitalism remained. That void was filled in important ways by human rights, the concept of which has replaced socialism as the main language through which capitalism is critiqued.[32] There are many reasons to question whether human rights today can meet the expectations of providing an ethical 'barrier to a worldwide, voracious, and highly divisive brand' of transnational capitalism.[33] Capitalism is a powerful adversary given its ability to create wealth.[34] It is a powerful force also because of the incommensurability of

[28] ibid 611. Further, 'The Marxian observation here is that those sectors of society having real weight in political decision-making tend to win the conditions of freedom relevant to those sectors. The primary condition of freedom for those with command over resources is the protection of the individual from state encroachment, whereas the primary condition of freedom for the have-nots is an end to economic deprivation and insecurity and to social disempowerment and exclusion.' BR Roth, 'Marxian Insights for the Human Rights Project' in S Marks (ed), *International Law on the Left: Re-examining Marxist Legacies* (CUP 2008) 220, 243.

[29] See N Tolokonnikova and S Žižek, *Comradely Greetings: The Prison Letters of Nadya and Slavoj* (Verso 2014) Slavoj to Nadja 74.

[30] Parts of Latin America may represent certain uneven exceptions but as José Mujica the President of Uruguay put it recently: 'I am just sick of the way things are. We're in an age in which we can't live without accepting the logic of the market. Contemporary politics is all about short-term pragmatism. We have abandoned religion and philosophy ... What we have left is the automatisation of doing what the market tells us.' J Watts, 'No Palace, No Motorcade, No Frills: Meet Uruguay's Unique President' *The Guardian* (London, 14 Dec 2013). Today, the initiative by Ecuador and South Africa to secure a treaty on business and human rights through the UN is reflective of a response to transnational neoliberalism as advanced through international investment law (and meeting with hostility by capital-exporting states). In Latin American countries perhaps the most sustained resistance to global neoliberalism has come from below.

[31] 'It is revealing of the political landscape in Europe—indeed, the world—that everyone's dreams of socialism seemed to rest on the shoulders of the young Prime Minister of a small country. There seemed to be a fervent, irrational, almost evangelical belief that a tiny country, drowning in debt, gasping for liquidity, would somehow (and that somehow is never specified) defeat global capitalism, armed only with sticks and rocks.' A Andreou, 'Alex Tsipras: Hero, Traitor, Hero, Traitor, Hero' *Byline* (13 July 2015), https://www.byline.com/column/11/article/164

[32] M Freeman, 'Beyond Capitalism and Socialism' in J Dine and A Fagan (eds), *Human Rights and Capitalism: A Multidisciplinary Perspective on Globalisation* (Edward Elgar 2006) 3, 25.

[33] CA Gearty, 'Human Rights' in A Kuper and J Kuper (eds), *The Social Science Encyclopedia*, vol I (3rd edn, Routledge 2004) 468, 470–71.

[34] Freeman (n 32) 26.

democracy and wealth concentration: the political costs of income concentration at the top is that the rich get their preferences translated into government policy, a danger long-recognized.[35] Inequality figures today are as shocking as they are familiar: 80 people have the same wealth as 3.5 billion people[36] with the top 10% of the world population owning 86% of global wealth.[37] Capitalism as practised has introduced this indefensible inequality.[38] Moreover, it is not just the *outcomes* that are egregious for their excess, but the *processes* of alienation, dispossession, and immiseration that make the elite accumulation of money and capital possible.

Under capitalism today the terms by which success is measured pose a direct challenge to a model that values inclusive decision-making, respect for people, and socio-economic well-being as means and end. Central to these terms is economic growth; so essential to capitalism is this capital accumulation that it has become an unqualified objective 'which is then taken to justify otherwise unjustifiable means'.[39] Growth (and profits, which are for all intents and purposes the same thing) is a condition for the survival of capital. Far-reaching cross-border trade, investment, and finance is thus judged successful to the extent that it leads to more capital accumulation for the owners and managers of capital.[40] Since securing socio-economic rights could challenge the flow of capital and the march of liberalization as currently practised and might reduce the rate of return,[41] there remains a disincentive to secure those rights. There are inherent forces working against socio-economic rights because of the insubordination their philosophy represents to capitalism's alleged spontaneous and beneficent tendencies, and due to the threat that they are seen to pose to capital accumulation.[42] As addressed throughout the book, this separation of the economic and 'non-economic' realms is the basis upon

[35] Captured in the famous remark by US Supreme Court Justice Louis Brandeis, 'We must make our choice. We may have democracy, or we may have wealth concentrated in the hands of a few, but we can't have both.' See also Wade (n 19).

[36] 'Wealth: Having It All and Wanting More' Oxfam Issue Briefing (Jan 2015), https://www.oxfam.org/sites/www.oxfam.org/files/file_attachments/ib-wealth-having-all-wanting-more-190115-en.pdf

[37] Compared to barely 1% for the bottom half of all adults. Credit Suisse, *Global Wealth Report 2013*.

[38] Indefensible inequality in that it 'give[s] the few far more reward than is necessary to encourage productivity, while denying the vast majority of the [global] population the essentials (health care and educational opportunity, for example) necessary for them to develop their full capacity for productivity'. TM Franck, *Fairness in International Law and Institutions* (Clarendon Press 1995) 20.

[39] Macpherson (n 16) 29; see further the example by Eva Pils on the drive for rapid urbanization in China and state-orchestrated landgrabs whereby the 'public interest' is thought to be justified by reference to a general desire for GDP growth. E Pils, 'Voice, Reflexivity and Say: Governing Access to and Control of Land in China' in O de Schutter and K Pistor (eds), *Governing Access to Essential Resources* (Columbia UP 2015) 127.

[40] '"The market" is the polite way of referring to "the owners and managers of capital, especially financial capital".' Wade (n 19) 209.

[41] While reducing the rate of return would not be an unjustifiable trade-off, findings show that securing socio-economic rights is very good for the economy and the sharing of its gains. See SA Ramirez, 'Taking Economic Human Rights Seriously after the Debt Crisis' (2011) 42 Loyola University Chicago Law Journal 713; OHCHR Background Paper, 'Promoting a Rights-based Approach to Economic, Stabilization, Recovery and Growth' (OHCHR 2013); on investment in health and education acting as the greatest fiscal multipliers, see Stuckler and Basu (n 20) 65.

[42] See P Patnaik, 'A Left Approach to Development' (2010) 45 Economic & Political Weekly 33, 35.

which the modern international legal and institutional architecture was built. One outcome of this separation is that human rights are not recognized as constitutive of markets.[43]

As a result of this separation between the economic and so-called non-economic realms and the dominance of the former, we have also seen the risk of the overt appropriation of human rights by the ethos of capitalism. It is in this vein that Upendra Baxi elaborated a concern around what he signalled as the emergence of 'market-friendly human rights' under globalization, whereby rights crafted for the attainment of human dignity, well-being, and security were being reoriented under conditions of economic globalization to protect and promote the 'collective human rights of global capital'.[44] In his description of market-friendly human rights, Baxi offers a range of examples that have the promotion and protection of human rights possible only when 'the order of rights for global capital stands fully recognized'.[45]

This chapter is likewise concerned with the appropriation of human rights but foregrounds a different, more covert, model through which this arrogation is achieved. Here consideration is given in section 2 not only to how human rights are being circumscribed by the logic and force of contemporary capitalism, nor how their terms are challenged and misappropriated to those ends, but also how they are co-opted in sustaining capitalism through their perceived *successes*. Building on what has come before, section 3 revisits the extraterritorial requirements under international human rights, including obligations of international cooperation towards rights for all, for insights into the way in which socio-economic rights are being sidelined. In assessing the subversion of human rights to the predilections of global capitalism, this chapter explores: capitalism's dedication to economic growth and its implications for human rights; the reproduction of the causes of poverty and inequality through the Sustainable Development Goals (SDGs) and its social protection floors; and what the cosmopolitanism of human rights obligations is up against in its efforts to unsettle global capitalism.

[43] Another outcome, as addressed earlier in this book, is that human rights have been situated in relation to international economic law either as exceptions to the rules of the market or, worse, breaches of those rules.

[44] U Baxi, *The Future of Human Rights* (3rd edn, OUP 2008) 273.

[45] ibid 299–300. For example, the right to health as contingent on 'the research and development rights of pharmaceutical and diagnostic industries'; sustainable development requiring 'rights and processes [that] depend on technological fixes and corporate technosciences'; the right to food (or food security) best served 'by the protection of the rights of agribusiness corporations' (ibid 299). In an insightful early piece on the topic, Alston recognizes an omission in law and globalization thinking that sees globalization as devoid of values. Instead the shift noted is that it is not enough to identify that relevant practices under globalization run counter to socio-economic rights, instead the weight accorded rights increasingly depends on a demonstration that they are also not 'offensive to the imperatives of economic efficiency and the functioning of the free market'. In this regard, Alston notes: 'In at least some respects the burden of proof has been shifted—in order to be validated, a purported human right must justify its contribution to a broader, market-based "vision" of the good society.' P Alston, 'The Myopia of Handmaidens: International Lawyers and Globalization' (1997) 3 EJIL 435, 442.

2. Chronicles of Globalization and the Fragilities of Human Rights

2.1 Economic growth and its discontents

The drive for economic growth is rife and so far no philosophical or empirical challenge has meaningfully tempered it as the golden chalice to which all countries and the global community relentlessly strive. Growth, usually measured in the form of gross domestic product (GDP), is the total monetary value of what has been produced (goods and services) in a country over a particular period of time. Growth takes place in the form of the expansion of markets with sacrifices required to ensure it.[46] It is constantly measured (quarterly or monthly) in anticipation of gains, and it remains largely unquestioned in the corridors of power.

There are many concerns about the commitment to economic growth, one familiar critique being that which it includes in the count. In a famous speech at the University of Kansas in 1968, US Senator Robert Kennedy lamented the huge US gross national product—over US$800 billion per year—which included in the count air pollution and cigarette advertising, special locks for doors and jails for the people who break them, the destruction of the redwood, and the loss of natural wonder, napalm, and nuclear warheads.[47] In highlighting societal values that are ignored in this slavish dedication to growth, Senator Kennedy drew attention to what is not factored in to the gross national product when recalling that: it 'does not include the beauty of our poetry or the strength of our marriages, the intelligence of our public debate or the integrity of our public officials. It measures neither our wit nor our courage; neither our wisdom nor our learning ... [I]t measures everything, in short, except that which makes life worthwhile.'[48] A related and current criticism is that the focus on measuring growth ignores much of what people value but cannot be measured, or not easily measured, like happiness.[49] Another concern around the indiscriminate commitment to economic growth is that, as currently practised, it is environmentally unsustainable. Some countries have already passed the point at which the extra environmental costs of growth exceed the extra production benefits that it produces.[50] Finally, and importantly, growth as pursued today seeks endlessly to accumulate for some on the basis of the dispossession of others.

[46] 'Another mechanism in capitalism that drives expansion is credit ... Promises of repayment can, however, only be kept if there is growth; credit is nothing else than anticipated growth'. W Streeck, *How Will Capitalism End?: Essays on a Failing System* (Verso 2016) 201, 206.

[47] Robert F Kennedy, Remarks at the University of Kansas (18 Mar 1968), JFK Presidential Library and Museum, http://www.jfklibrary.org/Research/Research-Aids/Ready-Reference/RFK-Speeches/Remarks-of-Robert-F-Kennedy-at-the-University-of-Kansas-March-18-1968.aspx

[48] ibid.

[49] R Layard, *Happiness: Lessons from a New Science* (Allen Lane 2005); and see JE Stiglitz, A Sen, and J-P Fitoussi, *Mismeasuring Our Lives: Why GDP Doesn't Add Up* (New Press 2010) on, inter alia, the importance of also measuring multidimensional well-being.

[50] HE Daly, 'A Foreword' in T Jackson, *Prosperity without Growth: Economics for a Finite Planet* (Earthscan 2009) xii. HE Daly, 'Uneconomic Growth and the Illth of Nations: Defining the Optimal

For our immediate purposes, there are several inter-related concerns to highlight. That growth is not questioned as a foundational assumption of contemporary economics renders it seemingly apolitical, beyond contestation and, as Bengi Akbulut et al point out, 'insulated from any critical engagement with the myriad contradictory effects that economic growth necessarily entails'.[51] A result is that where the object of intervention is poverty alleviation—an objective of the World Bank's development work since 1973—*poverty reduction itself* became a product of growth fetishism thereby legitimizing processes of capital accumulation through the usual practices of dispossession and extractionism.[52] Poverty alleviation that does not account for these structural elements becomes a reliable tool for its reinforcement. Put differently: on these terms what is sold as development in fact creates underdevelopment.[53]

A similar problem arises with the various ways in which the downsides of growth have been addressed. The now largely discredited claim that rapid expansion of GDP would automatically 'trickle down' to those in need easily justified a high growth rate of GDP. Now the idea is that while trickle down can't be expected to happen automatically, a larger GDP (implying a high rate of growth GDP) will enable the state to garner larger resources through taxation, and hence to spend more for the benefit of the poor. So if a high rate of GDP was once considered a sufficient condition for development and addressing the needs of the poor, under this latter account growth is a necessary but not a sufficient condition to address poverty.[54] But a larger GDP does not guarantee higher resources through taxation. Over the past three decades trade in goods and services have been profoundly liberalized on the logic that markets and prices must be left to do their job with as few distortions as possible, with redistribution at best something that comes in

Scale of the Macro Economy' Beatty Memorial Lecture (McGill University, 27 Mar 2003), 35 *McGill Reporter* (3 Apr 2003): '[T]he economy does not grow in a vacuum. It is a subset of the larger ecosystem which is finite, materially closed and governed by the laws of thermodynamics. When the economy expands, it further encroaches on the ecosystem.'

[51] Akbulut, Adaman, and Madra (n 12) 734. The authors develop their detailed and thoughtful thesis in the context of development economics specifically. In the context of postcolonial developmentalism, Sundhya Pahuja similarly provides that 'the commitment to growth required nothing less than faith in it as the rightful path to salvation. This faith, rapidly shared by people of all political persuasions, removed the axiom of economic growth per se from the field of political contestation and left only the question of how to achieve it.' S Pahuja, *Decolonising International Law: Development, Economic Growth and the Politics of Universality* (CUP 2011) 93.

[52] Akbulut, Adaman, and Madra (n 12) 734.

[53] A conventional understanding of development is 'first and foremost as economic progress, which in turn translated into industrialization and rising real income' and as a 'process of technological progress, industrialization and economic growth' (ibid). When reviewed more broadly, there are diverse definitions of development: 'For many, development is the ineluctable strategy by which poor countries need to modernize; for others, it is an imperial imposition by the rich capitalist countries on the poor ones, and as such it should be opposed; ... for many common people the world over, finally, development has become either a reflection of their aspirations to a dignified life, or an utterly destructive process with which they have to coexist, and not infrequently at the same time.' A Escobar, 'Development, Critiques of' in G D'Alisa, F Demaria, and G Kallis (eds), *Degrowth: A Vocabulary for a New Era* (Routledge 2015) 29. On development as underdevelopment, see Akbulut, Adaman, and Madra (n 12) 735.

[54] P Patnaik (n 42) 33.

'the second instance'. But as Thomas Piketty indicates, '[T]he "second instance"—greater redistribution—never came. Just the opposite: international tax competition has hammered progressive levies ... The richest benefited from sharp cuts in tax, even though they were already the main beneficiaries of trade liberalization and globalization ... Instead of a more equitable sharing of the gains from liberalization, tax redistribution has, on the contrary, tended to worsen its inegalitarian effects.'[55] As Prabhat Patnaik similarly remarks, the idea that this surplus value will be taxed by the government to be spent on the poor may never get realized, moreover, the condition for this growth might well be the offer of corporate enticements and investment 'incentives' in terms of disciplining workers and limiting their rights.[56]

The move to 'pro-poor growth'[57] and 'growth with equity' is another example of how the downsides of growth have been approached and is reflective of a recent shiftless shift where the commitment to growth under the current model of capital accumulation remains firmly in place. While under this approach we get so far as to see that capitalist growth is not sufficient to alleviate poverty, there remains a failure to account for the fact that the growth inevitably *creates* poverty.[58] Furthermore,

[55] T Piketty, *Chronicles on Our Troubled Times (Protectionism: A Useful Weapon ... For Lack of Anything Better, 20 Dec 2011)* (S Ackerman tr, Viking 2016) 92.

[56] Speaking of India but with application generally, Patnaik (n 42) 34. See also an overview of Myanmar's 'celebrated' Foreign Investment Law of November 2012: 'The most eye-catching incentive is the increase from a three year to a five year tax holiday that begins when the enterprise starts production or services activities. Another interesting improvement is the granting of customs duty and internal tax exemption for the expansion of an existing investment, which was painfully absent from the 1988 law.' P Grewal and MM Kyi, 'New Foreign Investment Law with Extensive Tax Incentives Enters into Force' *Myanmar Legal Wire* (20 Dec 2012), http://www.vdb-loi.com/mlw/new-foreign-investment-law-with-extensive-tax-incentives-enters-into-force

[57] For example, the UK Department for International Development's policy links liberalized trade, investment, and finance with the (dubious) post-Washington Consensus idea of 'pro-poor' policies—see ME Salomon, 'You Say You Want a Revolution: Challenges of Market Primacy for the Human Rights Project' in W Vandenhole (ed), *Challenging Territoriality in International Human Rights Law: Building Blocks for a Plural and Diverse Duty-Bearer Regime* (Routledge 2015) 188. Land titling and other reforms as a pro-poor policy meant to convert otherwise 'dead capital' into new sources of wealth, as advocated by the economist Hernando de Soto and championed by the World Bank, have been accused of being 'uncongenial to traditional land ownership patterns, entitlements and uses ... [with] land titling reforms ... often explicitly designed to interrupt such uses and entitlements, and for this reason they systematically disfavour subsistence activities and non-tradable production as compared to commercial ventures that are measurably growth-enhancing'. R Buchanan, H Kijo-Bisimba, and K Rittich, 'The Evictions at Nyamuma, Tanzania: Structural Constraints and Alternative Pathways in the Struggles Over Land' in LE White and J Perelman (eds), *Stones of Hope: How African Activists Reclaim Human Rights to Challenge Global Poverty* (Stanford UP 2010) 91, 100–01. On the World Bank casting trade and financial liberalization and privatization as pro-poor policies under the post-Washington Consensus, see A Ruckert, 'Towards an Inclusive-Neoliberal Regime of Development: From the Washington Consensus to the Post-Washington Consensus' (2006) 39 Labour, Capital and Society 36.

[58] Akbulut, Adaman, and Madra (n 12) 748. The authors take Amartya Sen's capabilities and entitlements approach to task which adopts the premise that (capitalist) growth is not sufficient to alleviate poverty, but is criticized for not going further and addressing its role in inevitably creating poverty. More generally, as Pogge would have it: '[Pro-poor growth and growth-with-equity] ... is crucial to [those economists who support it and] their theological role of appeasing the conscience of their wealthy constituents and of reconciling rich and poor alike to the great globalization push of the last twenty-five years'. TW Pogge, 'Growth and Inequality: Understanding Recent Trends and Political Choices' (2008) 55 Dissent 66.

it may well be the case that poverty and immiseration is seen 'helpfully' to precede growth, demonstrated through the familiar commitment of reducing the costs to capital.[59]

Part and parcel of this shiftless shift is the perpetuation of a bias in favour of commercial activities at the expense of non-commodified economies and more generally a commitment to the fierce imposition of so-called modernization that capitalist growth and the global economy will (allegedly) achieve.[60] Even findings that demonstrate how particular policy choices—notably investment in public health programmes and education—can boost growth (and reduce debt) without human costs have been ignored, as countries that embraced austerity policies in the recession following the 2008 crisis demonstrated.[61] As many commentators have highlighted, there is always a risk that the means will overwhelm the ends,[62] when it comes to growth this is a consequence that follows from the fact that capitalists must compete for higher profits.

A current danger in perpetuating the status quo is by co-opting the poor through a neo-Gramscian strategy of economic concessions that offer them real material benefits and incentives while at the same time serving to mollify and defer challenges to business as usual[63] (we return to this below when considering the SDGs and the dangers of the social protection floors). Through this method, the various 'dislocations and antagonisms' produced by capital accumulation are managed and the strategy invariably becomes an indispensable aspect of sustaining the processes of capitalist exploitation, dispossession, and accumulation.[64] This is what Gramsci referred to when he wrote of a passive revolution—socialization and cooperation by the ruling class in the sphere of production that nonetheless does not touch upon their appropriation of profit nor their control over the 'decisive nucleus of economic activity', thereby ensuring that the elite interests prevail.[65] In the same

59 Growth requires that the political and social conditions for growth are put in place. States and international organizations at the behest of capital are known to do what is possible to reduce the costs to capital, for example lowering environmental standards, busting unions to lower wages, etc.

60 The 'ostensibly scientific account of the causes of underdevelopment in the non-European world ... were widely adopted by scholars in the West from the 1950s onwards. In broad terms, this view held that the lack of development was attributable to the backward cultural, political and economic systems in the Third World. Of course, it was recognized that colonial excesses might have hindered progress; but once these were negated—and this was achieved, it was asserted, by granting independence to colonial states—then indigenous conditions and incapacity were to blame. This set of views was embodied by "modernization theory", as it was termed by political scientists and economists, who then formulated the corresponding policies necessary to modernize backward societies ... [I]ntegration into the global economy [was posited as being] the best means of achieving this goal of becoming "internationalised."' A Anghie, *Imperialism, Sovereignty and the Making of International Law* (CUP 2004) 207.

61 Stuckler and Basu (n 20); Salomon (n 19).

62 Rajagopal drawing on Hannah Arendt in B Rajagopal, *International Law from Below: Development, Social Movements and Third World Resistance* (CUP 2003) 197; Stuckler and Basu (n 20) 145.

63 JJ Wills, 'The World Turned Upside Down? A Critical Enquiry into the Counter-Hegemonic Potential of Socioeconomic Rights Praxis in Global Civil Society' PhD thesis, School of Law, University of Leicester (Jan 2014). (*Contesting World Order: Socioeconomic Rights and Global Justice Movements* (CUP 2017)).

64 Akbulut, Adaman, and Madra (n 12) 748–49.

65 A Gramsci, *Selections from the Prison Notebooks*, ed and trans Q Hoare and G Nowell Smith (Lawrence & Wishart 1971) 119–20; 161. Istvan Mészáros and others go further on this: capital

vein, Arne Ruckert speaks of a 'minor victory' in the fight against poverty reduction in his critique of the post-Washington Consensus. Drawing on the World Bank's *Sourcebook for Poverty Reduction Strategies*, he highlights how the inclusive strategies of compensation and subsidization do not fundamentally challenge 'the neoliberal logic of commodification and market colonization of all aspects of social life' offering instead an 'inclusive-neoliberal' development model promoted as part of a reformed Washington Consensus.[66] Kerry Rittich is right to question whether a commitment to alleviating poverty might better invite a goal not of poverty reduction per se, given the dubious policies it can spur, but of identifying and tackling the problem of growing inequality, and in particular access to power and resources within and across states.[67]

The second International Monetary Fund (IMF) Memorandum of Understanding (MoU) with Greece of 2012, underlining the terms of its loan package, captures well the commitment to growth just described and an unbridled dedication to violent neoliberal restructuring in order to achieve it. Moreover, it does this without even a nod to whom it is this imagined future robust economy was meant to serve.[68] In the hands of the international creditors 'saving' Greece from its debt has become the vehicle through which alienation, dispossession, poverty, and inequality was bestowed upon the majority.[69] The MoU states: 'To restore competitiveness and growth, we will accelerate implementation of far reaching structural reforms in the labor, product, and service markets . . . To bring the fiscal deficit to a sustainable position, we will implement bold structural spending and revenue reforms. The adjustment will be achieved through permanent expenditure reductions . . . We remain

forsakes profits for long periods in order to uphold its sociological basis, which is the form of social control exercised through the state that readies society for exploitation by subjugating labour.

66 Ruckert (n 57) 59.

67 K Rittich, 'Governing by Measuring: The Millennium Development Goals in Global Governance' in R Buchanan and P Zumbansen (eds), *Law in Transition: Human Rights, Development and Transitional Justice* (Hart 2014) 165, 178–79.

68 It is the third MoU of August 2015 between the international creditors and Greece that provides a reference to social justice and fairness, albeit an unconvincing one. Former Greek finance minister Yanis Varoufakis added his commentary (in square brackets) highlighting the real—and largely irreversible—objective of this plan for so-called social justice: The MoU states: 'The recovery strategy takes into account the need for social justice and fairness, both across and within generations . . . Product market reforms seek to eliminate the rents accruing to vested interest groups "[as long as they are not the large scale rent seekers, who are to be fully protected and, indeed, assisted through the creation of conditions encouraging greater market concentration and large chain stores; e.g. the legislation that targets family owned pharmacies, granting licences to nonpharmacists to bring multinationals like CVS and Boots into the market]" '. Further, the reference in the MoU to the need for 'social justice and fairness both across and within generations' can be understood as an endorsement of austerity on the argument that '[d]eficits are considered to represent sinful profligate spending at the expense of future generations who will be left with a smaller endowment of invested capital'. Varoufakis (n 10). See further, O Komlik (on William Vickery, 1998), 'Get Free from the Dogmas of the Apostles of Austerity: Fifteen Fatal Fallacies of Financial Fundamentalism' (15 Aug 2015) Economic Sociology and Political Economy, https://economicsociology.org/2015/08/15/get-free-from-the-dogmas-of-the-apostles-of-austerity-fifteen-fatal-fallacies-of-financial-fundamentalism

69 On the evolution of the Greek public debt, see *Report of the Truth Committee on Public Debt* (Special Committee of the Hellenic Parliament on the Audit of the Greek Debt, 2015) chs 1 and 2, http://cadtm.org/IMG/pdf/Report.pdf

committed to our ambitious privatization plans.'[70] The number of people facing material deprivation in Greece doubled between 2009 and 2014 (the years covering the Troika's first two MoUs) rising from 11% to 21.5% of the population.[71]

Doctrinaire economists remain committed to growth as a panacea and politicians cling to it as a secular religion despite the various ways in which today's model of economic growth is not serving most of the world's people and destroying the environment that sustains us all in the process.[72] The natural dynamic of the capitalist model is expansion on the terms described or collapse[73] but alternatives are hardly garnered by the elite.[74] The continuing dominance of a neoliberal capitalist economy and its institutions offer an aggressive form of capitalist expansion with fierce means of achieving it. Growth as practised is largely silent on the harms that capital accumulation invites and indicates little about distribution and the relative share of the poorest. All the while increases in inequality are not captured in the conventional measure of growth. Where some of those considerations are factored in, the idea of 'inclusive capitalism' forecloses structural change and avenues that support alternative meanings of development all the while reproducing the dispossession and exploitation that makes the growth

[70] IMF, Greece: Letter of Intent, Memorandum of Economic and Financial Policies (15 Mar 2012). As this book goes to press little has changed.

[71] UN Independent Expert on the effects of foreign debt and other related international financial obligations of states on the full enjoyment of all human rights, particularly economic, social and cultural rights, End of Mission Statement: Greece, 'Human Rights Pose Limits to Adjustment—Debt Relief for Inclusive Growth in Greece' 8 Dec 2015.

[72] 'Technological innovation permitting nonmaterial, nonpolluting growth could very well continue indefinitely. But only if we come up with clean energy sources, which can't be taken for granted.' Piketty (n 55) 122.

[73] Jackson (n 50) 64.

[74] On alternatives: 'Since freedom is incompatible with the "spontaneity" of capitalism, it requires going beyond capitalism to a system where people, organised politically, control their own destinies, by setting up an economic arrangement that is amenable to political control instead of being driven by its own inner logic.' Patnaik (n 42) 37. 'In a world without Wall Street, the economy is still largely controlled by the "market". But these markets are for the first time truly transparent, regulated by democratic negotiation among genuine social partners ... it is the financial "market"—opaque by nature and subjected to the requirements of management for the benefit of the monopolies—that is abolished. We could even explore whether it would be useful or not to shut down the stock exchanges, given that the right to property, both in its private as well as social form, would be conducted differently. We could even consider whether the stock exchange could be re-established to this new end.' S Amin, *The Implosion of Capitalism* (Pluto 2014) 142–43. On reorienting development economics: 'not only laying bare the distributional and ecological conflicts caused by all that is done in the name of development, but also by incorporating these very conflicts as its privileged subject matter, ... the recognition and incorporation of forms of sociality beyond the aggregation of individual agendas [and, in tandem, for] development economics to acknowledge the sphere of economy as one of diversity in order to move beyond individualism and to begin to render visible and make sense of a diverse array of community and solidarity economies that can be found in all types of social formations ... Thirdly, and relatedly, development economics should confront its explicit or implicit prioritization of economic growth as essential precondition of human betterment. In addition, such a confrontation should move beyond a critical stance that (merely) unveils the unwanted socio-ecological costs of economic growth, and take steps towards rendering visible and reclaiming already-existing forms of social existence and development that do not fetishize growth. Development economics should thus be democratized to allow voices from social movements that demand and articulate different ways of dignified living to permeate its disciplinary field.' Akbulut, Adaman, and Madra (n 12) 754–56.

possible. It is within this climate and labouring under these assumptions, influences, and interests—borne of the ideology bequeathed to us by a history won and written by them[75]—that international human rights and the law that provides for them are meant to be advanced.

2.2 Neoliberal capitalism and the subversion of human rights

The values that bolster a capitalist, commercial, competitive ethic feature more strongly than any other set of values and international human rights law and the human rights project is subjected to this overriding narrative in a variety of ways. There would be no reason to assume that human rights are immune from the assumptions and pressures of neoliberal globalization and its allegiance to transnational commercial organization. Indeed, while human rights remain in important ways a language and tool of justice, we can see how the assumptions and priorities of global capitalism shape them in dangerous ways.[76]

There are a number of lessons to emerge from this consideration of the ways in which human rights are subverted when up against global capitalism. To begin with, the most radical challenges posed by human rights have been those most contested by the same forces that advance extreme capitalism precisely for their potential to unsettle it. We see this just below in the considerations of the right to development (RTD) when it comes to redistribution and, more profoundly, in relation to RTD's extraterritorial duties of international cooperation. Next, in important ways human rights—like all other narratives that might challenge globalization—are at risk of being a handmaiden to the priorities of global capitalism. Here we see how growth and the ubiquitous role of the market is a precondition for the realization of human rights and other ways in which this growth narrative has been used to misappropriate the socio-economic rights narrative and the rights themselves. This line of argument is developed by focusing on the neoliberal co-optation of human rights and the defeat of transformative solutions under the redistributive scheme of the SDG's social protection floors initiative. Here the internalization of capitalism's assumptions by the UN Committee on Economic, Social and Cultural Rights (CESCR) is revealed and the 'neutrality' of socio-economic rights as avowed by CESCR is challenged. Together these examples covered in sections 2.2.1–2.2.4 reflect ways in which the enfranchising capacity of human rights is subverted by the interests of global capitalism.

[75] As eloquently put by Ali Kadri during a conversation.

[76] For an excellent overview and analysis of the various ways in which the relationship between (human) rights and capitalism has been conceived, see Freeman (n 32). Notably, Freeman convincingly exposes how the theoretical argument that insists the commitment to rights entails a commitment to private property and is thus complicit in the violation of human rights is inaccurate. He argues that the real story 'provides a coherent theoretical basis for the critique of capitalism from a human rights perspective ... [even if] there is currently no plausible economic alternative to capitalism, and because liberalism and its concept of rights have grown up historically with capitalism, albeit in a complex and tense relationship, the human rights perspective on contemporary capitalism is reformist' (ibid 6–7 and 25).

2.2.1 Challenges to redistribution and international cooperation

The radical elements of the 1986 right to development lie in its demands for effective international cooperation toward development objectives, its recognition that development is geared towards the improvement of human well-being, including by the exercise of human rights, and that this is achieved through the fair distribution of benefits. According to the Declaration on the Right to Development (DRD),[77] national equal opportunity measures are a requirement, and these include access for all not only to 'basic resources' but to the 'fair distribution of income'.[78] Moreover, and quite radically, 'economic and social reforms' are envisaged 'with a view to eradicating all social injustices'.[79] *Fair* distribution can be a challenge to inequality,[80] the hallmark of global neoliberalism whereby the latest figures continue to display its grotesque rise and concentration among a very small minority of people.[81] The Declaration's centre of attention on national and international norms of distributive justice for development situates human rights beyond its more narrow concerns of fulfilling basic needs to the greater project of reducing material inequality.[82]

When it comes to giving effect to socio-economic rights, international human rights law requires that we look at the entire distribution of activity and resources in society, both domestically and internationally. That being the case, in its interpretation of the International Covenant on Economic, Social and Cultural Rights

[77] DRD, GA Res A/RES/41/128, 4 Dec 1986, Annex 41 UN GAOR Supplement (No 53) 186 UN Doc A/RES/41/53 (1986).

[78] DRD, Art 8(1). [79] ibid.

[80] But see the need for predistribution outlined below.

[81] The figures include the following: 3.5 billion people (50% of the global population) share between them the same amount of wealth as that of the wealthiest 80 people, with 5.5% of global wealth owned by 80% of people in the world. Oxfam notes, moreover, that if this trend of an increasing wealth share to the richest continues, the top 1% will have more wealth than the remaining 99% of people by 2016. Even if we are prepared to take some meagre comfort in the argument that the total wealth of the poorest half of the world had been increasing at the same rate as that of the billionaires between 2002 and 2010, from 2010 it has been decreasing. Oxfam (n 36) 3. On the effect of inequality on poverty reduction: 'the higher the inequality, the smaller the effect of each increment of growth in reducing the poverty rate' and further on how global trends and their mechanisms set limits to what national governments can do, RH Wade, 'Income Inequality: Should We Worry About Global Trends?' (2011) 23 European Journal of Development Research 513. On income inequality between countries: 'Of course, fast growth in China and India is a major contributor to human well-being, given that they contain 37 per cent of the world's population, as against the West's 11 per cent. But the globalization argument is wrong to say or imply that convergence is a widely dispersed phenomenon. Most developing countries in Latin America, sub-Saharan Africa, the Middle East and North Africa, as well as South Asia outside of India, have not been converging.' On income inequality within countries: '[D]eveloped and developing countries alike have moved together in their internal inequality' (ibid 515).

[82] ME Salomon, 'Why Should It Matter That Others Have More: Poverty, Inequality and the Potential of International Human Rights Law' (2011) 5 Review of International Studies 2137, 2153. As Craven has rightly highlighted, this emphasis on the *international* environment shifts the focus of the problem from one of scarcity, and places greater importance instead on the question of distribution. M Craven, 'The Violence of Dispossession: Extraterritoriality and Economic, Social and Cultural Rights' in MA Baderin and R McCorquodale (eds), *Economic, Social and Cultural Rights in Action* (OUP 2007) 71, 86.

(ICESCR),[83] a far greater focus has nonetheless been placed by the CESCR on the minimum exercise of rights 'rather than a fuller bodied egalitarianism',[84] with a key risk being that the approach to basic needs reproduces the violent appropriations that engender the poverty in the first place, an issue we explore below in our coverage of the SDGs Social Protection Floors. Invariably, the Committee has been up against some entrenched positions that have sought to limit redistribution towards even that 'minimum' approach including decades of international programmes aimed precisely at undermining redistributive programmes, from structural adjustment in developing countries from the early 1980s[85] to the recent conditionality imposed on Greece along with other European debtor countries by international creditors.[86] The Northern countries in the recent period that have been pushed into adopting policies that fall foul of even the minimum requirements are the borrowers Cyprus, Greece, Ireland, Portugal and Spain[87] whereas other countries have jumped.[88] International tax competition and the race to the bottom in incentivizing investment have also served redistribution poorly and worsened national inegalitarian effects,[89] and there are many other such examples.[90] While redistributive requirements towards meeting basic rights should hardly be considered radical[91]

[83] International Covenant on Economic, Social and Cultural Rights (1966), entered into force 3 Jan 1976, GA Res A/RES/2200A (XXI), 993 UNTS 3.

[84] S Moyn, 'A Powerless Companion: Human Rights in the Age of Neoliberalism' (2014) 77 Law and Contemporary Problems 147, 161–62; Salomon (n 82) 2137.

[85] See the findings of Abouharb and Cingranelli: 'Based on an analysis of outcomes in 131 developing countries between 1981–2003, we show that, on average, structural adjustment has led to less respect for economic and social rights, and worker rights.' MR Abouharb and D Cingranelli, *Human Rights and Structural Adjustment* (CUP 2007) 4ff.

[86] Salomon (n 19).

[87] See the European Parliament Report 2009–14 on the inquiry on the role and operations of the Troika (ECB, Commission, and IMF) with regard to the euro area programme countries (2013/2277 (INI)), A7-0149/2014, 28 Feb 2014; and *The Impact of the Crisis on Fundamental Rights across the Member States of the EU*, Study for the LIBE Committee Directorate-General for Internal Policies (2015). See also the Statement by CESCR, 'Public Debt, Austerity Measures and the International Covenant on Economic, Social and Cultural Rights' UN Doc E/C.12/2016/1, 24 June 2016; and, inter alia, CESCR, Concluding Observations: Ireland UN Doc E/C.12/IRL/CO/3, 8 July 2015: 'The State party's response to the crisis has been disproportionately focused on instituting cuts to public expenditure in the areas of housing, social security, health care and education, without altering its tax regime' para 11(a); 'The Committee encourages the State party to ensure that, before entering into any agreement with or implementing any fiscal consolidation policy prescribed by international organizations, including international financial institutions such as the International Monetary Fund, such agreement or policy is in compliance with its obligations under the Covenant' (para 35).

[88] CESCR, Concluding Observations: the United Kingdom of Great Britain and Northern Ireland' UN Doc E/C.12/GBR/CO/6, 14 July 2016.

[89] Piketty (n 55) 92.

[90] On other global policies that are serving within-country inequality well: 'The common pattern indicates that the major causes of [unequalizing] changes in within-country inequality are linked less to characteristics or policies of the country concerned, and more to factors with wide geographic distribution—including global financial regimes, global commodity regimes (price rises boost the income of producers and curb the income of consumers), and the trend towards more "open" national economies (which drives increases in national inequality).' Wade (n 81) 516.

[91] On how positive international human rights law can be applied beyond efforts at poverty alleviation to accommodate a doctrine of fair global distribution, see Salomon (n 82) 2137.

and, moreover, can be criticized for falling short of more robust egalitarian expectations of social justice, they are perhaps radical when weighed against the despairing reality.

As for the radical demands of international cooperation, Ian Brownlie concluded in the years following the DRD's adoption that 'the right constitutes a general affirmation of a need for a programme of international economic justice.'[92] The DRD drew inspiration from the UN's purpose to achieve international cooperation in solving economic and social problems and promoting and encouraging respect for human rights[93] and its commitment to promoting social progress through international cooperation.[94] Article 28 of the Universal Declaration of Human Rights (UDHR) offered the next basis for the juridical claims eventually found in the DRD.[95] It recognizes that for human rights to be fulfilled a suitable national, as well as international, order is necessary. In short, human rights anticipate claims on our political, economic, and social arrangements at both levels, and articulate those requirements as constituting nothing less than an actual entitlement. The DRD demands not merely cooperation for the achievement of human rights central to the alleviation of poverty and human-centred development, but also changes to the system of structural disadvantage that characterizes the international order,[96] an obligation provided for in article 2(1) of the Covenant and elaborated as part of the fulfilment of economic, social and cultural rights.[97] The idea of structural change at the international level harnessed and promulgated by the Declaration has made radical normative demands on the human rights project: the idea of the right of everyone to change in global power relations.[98]

While the right to development exists as a result of, and in relation to, the international community, and can only be achieved through the shared effort of that community,[99] what if anything does that tell us about whether this idea of development as a right embraces or departs from conventional practices? The right to development is people-centred and demands that socio-economic disadvantage is addressed also in terms of the international structures of political economy—this is

[92] I Brownlie, 'The Human Right to Development' (Commonwealth Secretariat 1989) 8.

[93] Charter of the United Nations (1945), entered into force 24 Oct 1945, 59 Stat 1031, TS 993, 3 Bevans 1193, Art 1(3).

[94] UN Charter Arts 55 and 56.

[95] Universal Declaration of Human Rights, GA Res 217A (III), 10 Dec 1948, UN GAOR, 3rd session resolutions, Pt 1, 71 UN Doc A/810 (1948).

[96] ME Salomon, *Global Responsibility for Human Rights: World Poverty and the Development of International Law* (OUP 2007).

[97] For a detailed overview, see Maastricht Principles on Extraterritorial Obligations of States in the Area of Economic, Social and Cultural Rights (2011); and O De Schutter, A Eide, A Khalfan, M Orellana, ME Salomon, and I Seiderman, 'Commentary to the Maastricht Principles on Extraterritorial Obligations of States in the area of Economic, Social and Cultural Rights' (2012) 34 HRQ 1084.

[98] See SP Marks, 'Foreword' in Salomon (n 96).

[99] H Gros Espiell, 'Community-Oriented Rights: Introduction' in M Bedjaoui (ed), *International Law: Achievements and Prospects* (Martinus Nijhoff 1991) 1167, 1170. See also SP Marks, 'Emerging Human Rights: A New Generation for the 1980s?' (1981) 33 Rutgers Law Review 435.

a notable dimension of its normative promise. Like other significant interventions into the development debate, the right to development also shifted the focus of development from economic growth to enhancing human well-being, with a central focus on participation.[100] Linking the realization of the right to development to social, political, and economic contexts nationally and, especially, internationally would seem to leave open an interpretation of the right to development that recognizes that human development and capitalist development might be incommensurable;[101] its particular 'growth with equity' thesis explored below advances this position. But for all its potential the RTD global justice agenda falls short of offering up a radical programme in two ways: first in its partial focus on securing a bigger share of the pie, an approach inherited from the New International Economic Order (NIEO), and second, due to the political antagonisms of industrialized countries to its most progressive demands: international cooperation to the ends of structural change.

On the first point, like the NIEO from which it gains inspiration, access to markets and the right or opportunity to share in the benefits of economic growth (that is capital accumulation), are woven into its central aims.[102] As explored in Chapters 1 ('Legal Rendering of Immiseration') and 3 ('The End of Empire and the Search for Justice: NIEO and Beyond'), the NIEO reflected the acceptance by the Third World of the economic ideology promulgated by the advanced capitalist world, bolstering the commitment to universally recognized value of foreign capital including exploitation of local labour in the periphery.[103] While fundamentally the NIEO embraced the logic of the capitalist world economy, its demands in the 1970s by developing countries for a new international economic order in the wake of decolonization continues to represent the high water mark of challenging international law even if it didn't achieve its aims of a different form of global economic integration with equality between states and whereby the South could catch up with the North. If the ideas and practice of NIEO didn't take the world and its disenfranchised where many hoped it would, it did take us somewhere notable. The NIEO was a rejection of colonialism (even if not of an imperialist international law); it represented

[100] Akbulut on Sen, Akbulut, Adaman, and Madra (n 12) 748 '[Sen's] capabilities approach, [was] widely celebrated primarily for shifting the focus of development from economic growth to enhancing individuals' opportunities and choices'.

[101] cf Sen's capabilities approach as critiqued by Akbulut: 'Formulating the question of development primarily as one about individuals whose capabilities can be enhanced while leaving the broader social, political and economic contexts intact, Sen's conceptualization implies that human development and capitalist development are commensurable' (ibid 748). Similarly, Pahuja remarks: 'Sen's notion of "capabilities" and the way they relate integrally to the realization of freedoms ultimately boils down to access to markets and the right or opportunity to share in the benefits of economic growth'. Pahuja (n 51) 247.

[102] On calls for a new international economic order see the DRD Preamble and Art 3(3). See also DRD Preamble and Art 1(2) on demands for sovereignty over natural resources. DRD Art 4(2) provides that: 'Sustained action is required to promote more rapid development of developing countries' capturing what Rajagopal refers to as the Declaration's 'catching up rationale'. Rajagopal (n 62) 222.

[103] See BS Chimni, 'The Principle of Permanent Sovereignty over Natural Resources: Toward a Radical Interpretation' (1998) 38 IJIL 208; AG Frank, 'Rhetoric and Reality of the New International Economic Order' in H Addo (ed), *Transforming the World Economy: Nine Critical Essays on the New International Economic Order* (United Nations University 1984) 165.

an effort to assert the sovereign autonomy of the non-western world; and it was an attempt to redirect international economic governance towards distributional equity and fairness. The Declaration on the Right to Development while caught up in the concessions of the NIEO nonetheless goes further by directing the ends of NIEO to the realization of human rights[104] including through a critique of conventional growth strategies.

A prominent approach to RTD as advanced by the former UN Independent Expert on the Right to Development has been that of 'growth with equity'. The growth with equity approach acknowledges that development should not solely centre on growth; on this account growth is necessary but not sufficient for the realization of human rights. Here RTD risks falling into the same trap that Akbulut et al raise in the context of the trajectory of development economics, including its most progressive intellectual intervention—the 'critical liberalism' of Sen and Nussbaum's capabilities approach:[105] while its premise is that growth is not sufficient to alleviate poverty, it remains something of an open question as to whether RTD addresses how it inevitably *creates* poverty. That said, 'equity and justice' in the Independent Expert's account of the right to development (which remains the only official attempt to elaborate a conceptual approach), provides, not insignificantly, that the 'whole structure of growth will have to be determined and reoriented by them'.[106] The focus on equity or 'the reduction of disparities' would imply 'a change in the structure of production and distribution in the economy to ensure growth was equitable'. It would 'entail a programme of development and investment that may require substantial international cooperation and not rely on the market'.[107] While here the important conclusion by Arjun Sengupta, the former UN Independent Expert on the Right to Development, moves RTD as a radical project forward, not surprisingly the potential of the right to development as a transformative political initiative was left in limbo.[108]

The commitment to equity as directing growth would have poverty reduction understood not as something that happens independently of growth, but is instead sensitive to the ways in which growth can lead to poverty. In line with this logic, Sengupta's approach explicitly makes growth part of the formal record

[104] DRD, Preamble: 'Aware that efforts at the international level to promote and protect human rights should be accompanied by efforts to establish a new international economic order.'

[105] See S Hickey, 'Relocating Social Protection within a Radical Project of Social Justice' (2014) 26 European Journal of Development Research 322, 324.

[106] Independent Expert on the Right to Development, 4th Report UN Doc E/CN.4/2002/WG.18/2, 20 Dec 2001, para 12.

[107] ibid para 11.

[108] In its concluding report, the UN High-level Task Force on the Implementation of the Right to Development offered the following reflection: 'The greatest challenge for the implementation of the right to development, in theory and practice, is to reconcile a holistic vision of human rights, implying indivisible and interdependent norms aimed at maximizing the well-being of all individuals and peoples, with development, which requires sound economic policies that foster growth with equity. It is easier to affirm their mutually reinforcing nature in principle than to apply this principle to decisions of policy and resource allocation.' Consolidation of findings of the UN High-Level Task Force on the Implementation of the Right to Development UN Doc A/HRC/15/WG.2/TF/2/Add 1, 6th session, 25 Mar 2010, para 6.

and something to be accounted for against the demands of justice, rather than an indisputable good.[109] Moreover, he anticipates structural reform of production and distribution to ensure equitable growth. This account would accommodate what Nancy Fraser sees as 'transformative' and not merely 'affirmative remedies': going beyond merely increasing the consumption share of economically disadvantaged groups by 'transforming the underlying political-economic structure'.[110] There are a range of alternative approaches to the status quo that could inform this right to development effort as against, as Fred Magdoff would frame it, a status quo based on 'greed, individualism, competitiveness, exploitation of others, and consumerism'.[111] To name but a few: the global eco-socialism of Farshad Araghi to replace the 'social system that is parasitically consuming life, labour, and nature as it is dying'[112] and the social and solidarity economy of the United Nations Research Institute for Social Development (UNRISD) that advances explicit social and often environmental objectives and follows principles of cooperation, democratic self-management and new thinking on time use.[113]

The Declaration on the Right to Development points human rights in the direction of transformative change in its national commitment to 'equality of opportunity for all in their access to basic resources, education, health services, food, housing, employment and the fair distribution of income'.[114] It also has equality of opportunity as a prerogative of states in their international relations.[115] It compels international cooperation to these ends recognizing the symbiotic relationship between the national and international levels under conditions of globalization and the power and influence of states other than the right-holders own on the exercise of human rights. This extraterritorial dimension of the right to development that implicates (mainly) Northern states in poverty and underdevelopment beyond their borders has always been zealously contested by those states.[116]

[109] Akbulut drawing on Sanyal offers a critique of the capabilities approach on that basis: 'grounding the poverty driven approach in the concepts of entitlement and capability served to situate "the space of poverty" independently from that of growth (that is capital accumulation), masking the ways in which growth and accumulation can lead to poverty'. Akbulut, Adaman, and Madra (n 12) 748.

[110] 'By restructuring the relations of production, these remedies would not only alter the end-state distribution of consumption shares; they would also change the social division of labour and thus the conditions of existence for everyone.' N Fraser, 'From Redistribution to Recognition: Dilemmas of Justice in a "Post-socialist" Age' (July–Aug 1995) New Left Review 68, 84. As provided by Fraser, 'transformative remedies typically combine universalist social-welfare programmes, steeply progressive taxation, macroeconomic policies aimed at creating full employment, a large non-market public sector, significant public and/or collective ownership, and democratic decision-making about basic socioeconomic priorities' (ibid 85).

[111] Magdoff (n 9) 123. [112] Araghi (n 25) 41.

[113] K Hujo and G Koehler, 'Beyond 2015: The Sustainable Development Agenda from Inspiration to Action' Brief 06 (UNRISD Sept 2015). On the key elements of Gustav Cassel's market socialism under his 'socialistic' community model which advocated a 'self-contained exchange economy in which the entire production is conducted by and for the community itself through officials appointed for the purpose, and all the material means of production are the property of the community: but in which there is still freedom of work and consumption to the extent to which it is essential to an exchange economy', see J Bockman, 'Socialist Globalization against Capitalist Neocolonialism: The Economic Ideas behind the New International Economic Order' (2015) 6 Humanity 109, 120.

[114] DRD, Art 8(1). [115] DRD, Preamble.

[116] For a fuller exploration, see Salomon (n 96).

So, while its shortcomings inherited by the NIEO don't go far enough in challenging the central tenets upon which the capitalist global economy functions, its radical inclinations to international cooperation and structural change have left the right to development as the most contentious and least operationalized of all human rights. It is small comfort but Balakrishnan Rajagopal was right when he noted almost fifteen years ago that the right to development represents the only attempt by international lawyers 'to compel human rights law to take the violence of development seriously'.[117]

2.2.2 *The ubiquitous market and the misappropriation of human rights*

Any attempt at advancing principles that might drive a human-centred agenda will have to confront directly the logic and means of neoliberalism in its global and national manifestations. The challenges are great: all too often the realization of human rights (including the money needed to fund them) are argued to be tied so tightly to the role of the market—economic rationalization and the outcomes of transnational market exchanges—that we could almost be forgiven for internalizing the dubious counsel that there can be no socio-economic rights without extreme capitalism.[118] Here human rights risk being resituated so as to be understood as dependent upon the capacity of the capitalist order thus inverting the logic that underpins human rights as first order principles the realization of which should shape our economic arrangements. What becomes increasingly hard to secure is what Wolfgang Streeck refers to as 'non-market notions of social justice' aimed at resisting forceful efforts at economic rationalization in the age of neoliberalism.[119] Non-market notions of social justice would foreground, as Streeck describes it: 'the social over the economic; [. . .] social commitments and obligations being protected from market pressures for "flexibility"; and society honouring human expectations of a life outside the dictatorship of ever-fluctuating "market signals" '.[120]

The relentless dedication to economic growth is of course part of this narrative but in so far as it is desirable or even necessary[121] its fetishization cannot be

[117] Rajagopal (n 62) 173. [118] Salomon (n 57).

[119] W Streeck, 'The Crisis of Democratic Capitalism' (Sept–Oct 2011) 71 New Left Review 5, 8.

[120] ibid.

[121] 'Instead of GDP growth rate becoming the main focus, under the chimerical assumption that it will bring about development, this [left approach to development] strategy directly addresses the problem of development; the growth that occurs is a fallout of it. And in the worst-case scenario, even if no growth occurs, addressing the question of development directly is still preferable on grounds that John Stuart Mill had made famous, when he had declared his unconcern over the "stationarity" of a "stationary state" as long as the workers were better off in it.' Patnaik (n 42) 35. Escobar captures the ideas well in his summary of 'postdevelopment': 'Postdevelopment was generally meant as an era in which development would no longer be the central organizing principle of social life. In this way, it is related to two other emerging imaginaries, that of postcapitalism (questioning capitalism's ability to fully and naturally occupy the economy, with the concomitant visualization of an array of diverse economic practices) and post- or degrowth (decentring growth from the definition of both the economy and social life) . . . At least for many social movements and for transition advocates, whatever form "development" or alternatives to development take will have to involve more radical questionings of growth,

justified—that is, to disregard that it has emerged from the ideology and priorities of capitalist society with all that implies and that its espousal is offered up as an end in itself, to which everything else may appropriately be subordinated.[122] The CESCR pushed back against precisely this tendency when it highlighted in its Statement to a World Trade Organization (WTO) Ministerial Conference that 'Trade liberalization must be understood as a means, not an end. The end which trade liberalization should serve is the objective of human well-being to which the international human rights instruments give legal expression.'[123] But that would represent a very different kind of trade liberalization. As Oscar Schachter argued some forty years ago, if we are to treat 'need' as a basic principle of international law it is quite clear that states will have to diverge from other principles. And if the aim is to reduce the gap between rich and poor ('real equality in the satisfaction of basic needs'), international action will require *dirigiste* policies over reliance on market forces and international trade.[124] Instead, the reality to which human rights are exposed is that capitalist growth is seen as a precondition of development, well-being, poverty reduction, social justice and all else; negative impacts of growth as such become justifiable, and growth becomes self-perpetuating and in the first (and often only) instance judged successful largely to the extent that it leads to more capital accumulation.

As the law and development literature has pointed out a more nuanced neo-liberalism emerged by the new millennium, one that includes poverty-reduction objectives and the move from a raw form of capitalism under the Washington Consensus to focus on the legal and regulatory framework within which economic transactions are conducted and whereby institutions matter.[125] As that literature has highlighted, here however, economic development requires respect for the rule of law understood as protection of property and other investors' rights along with anti-corruption measures. This 'frank instrumentalism' is driven by the idea—as promulgated by the World Bank—that law reform is to be undertaken in order to achieve growth through a climate of stability and predictability conducive to domestic and foreign private investment.[126] There has also been a general shift in the past decades to questioning market fundamentalism and admitting to market failures; but while this adjustment recognizes the requirement to mitigate market 'externalities', including actively to protect the vulnerable, addressing market

extractivisim, and even modernity than ever before.' Escobar (n 53) 31–32. Here the main attempt is to shine a light on growth fetishization.

[122] Macpherson (n 16) 29.

[123] CESCR, Statement to the Third Ministerial Conference of the World Trade Organization UN Doc E/C12/1999/9, 26 Nov 1999, para 6.

[124] O Schachter, 'The Evolving International Law of Development' (1976) 15 Columbia Journal of Transnational Law 9–11.

[125] See K Rittich, 'The Future of Law and Development: Second-Generation Reforms and the Incorporation of the Social' in DM Trubek and A Santos (eds), *The New Law and Economic Development: A Critical Appraisal* (CUP 2006) 203, 210.

[126] S Humphreys, *Theatre of the Rule of Law: Transnational Legal Intervention in Theory and Practice* (CUP 2010) 139. See also Chapter 5 ('Foreign Investment') at 169–173.

economic failures doesn't require that we confront the system of global economic relations in which those harms are produced nor the fact that production is internationalized and hence at the lower echelons of the production process there is tremendous social failure.[127] In short, market *social* failure remains endemic. At root, the arguments for market regulation is an argument for enhancing competitiveness and the efficiency of markets;[128] and the protection of the vulnerable is drawn from the orthodoxy that advocates that they connect themselves to markets and to global growth to pull themselves out of poverty.[129] The structural impediments are further occluded through the turn to focus on the national level roles as an alleged response to the control of external actors, for example the 'country ownership' of the World Bank and IMF. That shift functions to blame maldevelopment on the failures of governance by the state itself, ignoring how the globalized economy and its international rules shape domestic policy options.[130]

This dominance of the market and growth narrative also facilitates the wholesale misappropriation of justice narratives, such as that of human rights, to its own ends. In this regard, attention has been drawn to the prioritization of rights by international financial institutions that facilitate economic growth and achieve poverty reduction, diluting the basic tenets of human rights and watering down the scope of legal obligations.[131] In other instances, 'rights' are singled out, and advanced, that are in fact no more than economic freedoms, ie those that are needed to satisfy the conditions of efficiency in production and exchange and maximize profits and growth. On this account, 'rights' are understood as personal choice, voluntary exchange, freedom to compete, and the protection of persons and property.[132] The concerns raised herein over these misappropriations are not motivated by a puritanical commitment to human rights conventionally understood (although it may be that too), in that the evolutionary and teleological approach of human rights interpretation is one of its most noteworthy strengths. The risk is that human rights become detached from their foundations in human dignity, and instead are reduced merely to instrumental means in the achievement of (neoliberal) economic policy

[127] 'The transaction costs are the real world, while the algebraic model coming into some steady state is the fiction. The perniciousness of such an approach is that if the market model failed to reach equilibrium, it did so because there were conditions in actuality—namely, all of reality—which were unaccounted for and had caused the system to fail. This is a failure of theory at its inception and before it becomes subjected to interpersonal comparisons (as in theoretical nihilism). Selecting some of the real but distorting conditions that stand in the way of equilibrium and including them as additional variables in a model is theory by convenience.' A Kadri, 'The Islamic World and Capitalism: Military Routs, Not Formal Institutions' in ES Reinert, J Ghosh, and R Kattel (eds), *Handbook of Alternative Theories of Economic Development* (Edward Elgar 2016) 161, 181.

[128] Rittich (n 125) 212.

[129] See Moore developing the point in relation to rural economies. HL Moore, 'Global Prosperity and Sustainable Development Goals' (2015) 27 Journal of International Development 801.

[130] See Rittich (n 125) 211; Salomon (n 19).

[131] GA Sarfaty, 'Why Culture Matters in International Institutions: The Marginality of Human Rights at the World Bank' (2009) 103 AJIL 647, 677.

[132] JP Chauffeur, *The Power of Freedom: Uniting Development and Human Rights* (Cato Institute 2009); See ME Salomon and C Arnott, 'Better Development Decision-Making: Applying International Human Rights Law to Neoclassical Economics' (2014) 32 Nordic Journal of Human Rights 44.

objectives; as Philip Alston has pointed out, individuals would become the object of rights rather than the holder of them.[133] A second concern emerges, that in the absence of proof that there will be suitable economic gains, it might seem justified and legitimate to reject human rights on the basis of that particular cost–benefit analysis, thereby disregarding other 'pay-offs' or values.[134]

A dominant theory in development economics sees costs incurred as tradable with the benefits that accrue to other groups[135] or accepts that costs are made to disappear via the notion of (hypothetical) compensation.[136] Human rights theory challenges the postponement of rights for pronounced greater objectives, for example increased national wealth or for benefits anticipated at some indeterminate time in the future; trade-offs are carefully considered and never at the expense of ensuring the minimum essential level of socio-economic rights in the first instance. Human rights are anti-utilitarian requiring that where a utilitarian calculation is to be made it is tested carefully against the sacrifices transacted. The work of Akbulut et al is instructive here in pointing out how the utilitarianism of the collective welfare serves analytically to postpone the contradictions and antagonisms—for example, impoverishment, dispossession, social rights violations, disruption of the social fabric—generated by the processes of accumulation that accompany the modernizing character of so-called development[137] (or in the case of European countries, under the guise of fixing the economy). Dedication to the maximal market and the misappropriation of human rights offers one story. Postponing but also reproducing antagonisms through the co-optation of human rights and justice efforts is another and is the focus of the next two sections.

2.2.3. Co-optation: the right to social security, the social protection floors, and the Sustainable Development Goals

The International Labour Organization (ILO) has done much to mobilize international attention and support around social security and most recently that of social protection floors. According to the International Labour Conference Recommendation 202 (2012), 'social protection floors are nationally defined sets of basic social security guarantees which secure protection aimed at preventing or alleviating poverty, vulnerability and social exclusion'.[138] The basic social security guarantees that comprise the social protection floors entail 'access to essential health care and to basic income security which together secure effective access to goods

[133] P Alston, 'Resisting the Merger and Acquisition of Human Rights by Trade Law: A Reply to Petersmann' 2002 13 EJIL 815, 843.

[134] See P Alston, *Report of the Special Rapporteur on Extreme Poverty and Human Rights* UN Doc A/69/297, 11 Aug 2014, http://www.ohchr.org/EN/NewsEvents/Pages/DisplayNews.aspx?NewsID=13341&LangID=E

[135] Akbulut, Adaman, and Madra (n 12) 742.

[136] Salomon and Arnott (n 132) 65–66.

[137] Akbulut, Adaman, and Madra (n 12) 742.

[138] R202—Social Protection Floors Recommendation, 2012 (No 202) Recommendation concerning National Floors of Social Protection Adoption, 101st ILC session (14 June 2012) para 2.

and services defined as necessary at the national level'.[139] Just as the ILO now takes a rights-based approach to social security,[140] the official human rights community has endorsed fully the idea of the ILO's social protection floors. In a 2013 contribution to the post-2015 development agenda, seventeen UN Special Rapporteurs recommended that the SDGs should include 'a goal on the provision of social protection floors, explicitly referencing the right to social security and a human rights-based approach to social protection.'[141] In April 2015 CESCR offered its endorsement when it issued a statement on 'Social protection floors: an essential element of the right to social security and of the sustainable development goals'.[142] In September 2015 the SDGs were adopted with the first Goal to 'End poverty in all its forms everywhere'. Among the key SDG tools to achieve that noble ambition is the target to 'Implement nationally appropriate social protection systems and measures for all, including floors, and by 2030 achieve substantial coverage of the poor and the vulnerable'.[143] However, with social protection and the social protection floors as recently endorsed we see social justice interventions that are conservative (including neoliberal) and liberal but hardly radical,[144] in particular they fail to confront the structural features of poverty and may serve to support them. Furthermore, the indifference of the SDGs to confronting the status quo and indeed to *sustaining* it elsewhere in the Goals, fails to offer an account of the *causes* of poverty and inequality and as such risks advancing them.

First, we see advanced in the endorsement of social protection what has elsewhere been referred to as 'methodological individualism'[145]—targeting the needy

[139] ibid para 4. Paragraph 5 elaborates on paragraph 4, providing the most basic social security guarantees, namely: '(a) access to a nationally defined set of goods and services, constituting essential health care, including maternity care, that meets the criteria of availability, accessibility, acceptability and quality; (b) basic income security for children, at least at a nationally defined minimum level, providing access to nutrition, education, care and any other necessary goods and services; (c) basic income security, at least at a nationally defined minimum level, for persons in active age who are unable to earn sufficient income, in particular in cases of sickness, unemployment, maternity and disability; and (d) basic income security, at least at a nationally defined minimum level, for older persons'.

[140] ILO Recommendation 202 reaffirms that the right to social security is a human right in its Preamble and in 2001 the International Labour Conference affirmed that social security 'is a basic human right and a fundamental means for creating social cohesion'. See further B Saul, D Kinley, and J Mowbray, *The International Covenant on Economic, Social and Cultural Rights: Commentary, Cases and Materials* (OUP 2014) 621.

[141] Statement by 17 Special Procedures Mandate-holders of the Human Rights Council on the Post-2015 Development Agenda, 21 May 2013.

[142] CESCR, Statement on Social Protection Floors: An Essential Element of the Right to Social Security and of the Sustainable Development Goals UN Doc E/C.12/2015/1, 15 Apr 2015.

[143] Transforming Our World: The 2030 Agenda for Sustainable Development, A/Res/70/1, 25 Sept 2015, SDG Target 1.3.

[144] For a very helpful typology of the ideological terrain of social justice in the area of social protection, see Hickey (n 105). In Hickey's typology, 'conservative/neoliberal' social justice theory and their social protection implications would include market failures and individual frailty, followed by various liberal approaches ('responsible, social, and critical'). Radical approaches associated with the views of Forst, Fraser and Young, would be more fully transformative (ibid 324). See also S Devereux and JA McGregor, 'Transforming Social Protection: Human Wellbeing and Social Justice' (2014) 26 European Journal of Development Research 296, 298.

[145] 'This ontological position can be identified in the World Bank's endorsement of social protection as a set of tools for managing individualised risk (World Bank, 2001) and more recently as a vehicle

individual and diagnosing injustice as a result of market failure and individual frailty[146] while ignoring the more complex explanations of root causes, of how poverty is produced and reproduced, and the significance of power to the equation. The turn to the technocratic interventions offered by 'social protection' takes the individual or the household as the unit of intervention and has been criticized for inviting a conception of poverty that situates poverty in the personal characteristics and circumstances of individuals and households.[147] This concentration on direct and technocratic intervention might allow people 'at least essential health care, basic shelter and housing, water and sanitation, food and the most basic forms of education'[148] but it obfuscates how poverty is created and sustained and it obscures the role of power and institutions at all levels.[149] Second, the focus on social protection and a universal social protection floor while attempting to cushion the worst effects of policies that engender poverty and inequality—through the very protections they offer—*bolster* political support to them;[150] with transfer by the state of the profits of the capitalist growth economy to the subsistence economy legitimating the capitalist growth economy.[151] In the same vein, the widespread turn to social protection does not challenge the commitment of international financial institutions (and of many states) to liberalization and privatization—controversial prescriptions that continue unabated—instead support to basic social services is reflective merely of an awareness that extremely poor people are unable to pay for those services at market-determined rates and as such cannot become customers.[152]

for reducing household income poverty (World Bank, 2012).' Devereux and McGregor (n 144) 298. On the IMF, see R Rowden, *The Deadly Ideas of Neoliberalism: How the IMF Has Undermined Public Health and the Fight against AIDS* (Zed 2009) 149.

[146] Hickey (n 105) 324.

[147] Devereux and McGregor (n 144) 297. And for a critique of the ways in ILO Recommendation 202 is 'ungendered' due its liberal economic bend, rendering women invisible and 'simply lumped within the broad category of "vulnerable persons" in need of social protection', see L Lamarche, 'Unpacking the ILO Social Protection Floor Recommendation from a Women's Rights Perspective' in B Goldblatt and L Lamarche (eds), *Women's Rights to Social Security and Social Protection* (Hart 2014) 65, 68.

[148] CESCR, Statement on Social Protection Floors (n 142) para 8.

[149] See B Fine, 'Entitlement Failure' 28 Development and Change (1997) 617. Similarly, on how technical problems and solutions serve as a distraction from the larger framework within which those vulnerabilities are systematically reproduced, see S Marks, 'Human Rights and Root Causes' (2011) 74 MLR 57, 71, and on locating poverty as an outcome of 'local dysfunction' instead of 'determinate forces and relations, including forces and relations that stretch across the world' (ibid 67).

[150] This was an explicit critique of the earlier 'social safety net approach' that sought merely to cushion temporarily the effects of structural adjustment. See Report of the Social Protection Floor Advisory Group, *Social Protection Floor for a Fair and Inclusive Globalization* (ILO 2011) 12–13, http://www.ilo.org/global/publications/ilo-bookstore/order-online/books/WCMS_165750/lang--en/index.htm

[151] P Chatterjee, 'Foreword' (2013) in K Sanyal, *Rethinking Capitalist Development: Primitive Accumulation, Governmentality and Post-Colonial Capitalism* (Routledge 2007) xii. Chatterjee writes of the establishment of the 'legitimacy of postcolonial capital'.

[152] Ruckert (n 57) 42; see also the study by Rittich, who concludes: 'Since at least 1997, the Bank has rejected a purely minimalist or night watchman conception of the state and recognized that a variety of distortions, market failures, and externalities may warrant intervention and regulatory action in at least some instances ... The arguments for regulation, however, remain securely tethered to the goals of enhancing competitiveness and efficiency of markets.' Rittich (n 125) 212.

The celebrated Bolsa Família conditional cash transfer programme made famous in Brazil has been critiqued for turning 'the miserable into consumers'[153] offering what a conservative Mexican commentator notes is an 'innovative welfare programme that is as neoliberal as one can get'.[154] What Ruckert refers to as a 'shallow compromise' does not aim to decommodify social rights but only to subsidize impoverished consumers under conditions of privatization.[155] This is not a scheme to decommodify the core provisions of health, education, housing, and social insurance by removing them from the effects of the market, it is based on an 'enabling state' there to facilitate the role of market forces;[156] as social provisions become strong, the idea of universal rights to decommodified public services wanes.[157] The neo-Gramscian twist comes with the risk of winning over the subaltern classes to neoliberalism through consent instead of coercion by means of material concessions[158] and of pleasing both the left and right, but not without its costs. Here,

[153] L Lavinas, Professor of Welfare Economics, Federal University Rio de Janeiro as cited in J Tepperman, 'Brazil's Anti-Poverty Breakthrough: The Surprising Success of Bolsa Família' (Jan–Feb 2016) 95 Foreign Affairs 34, 41. According to the ILO, '[T]he *Bolsa Família* programme of cash transfers in Brazil is estimated to have accounted for 15 per cent of the improvement in the Gini coefficient for that country between 1999 and 2009 and for a reduction of the poverty gap by 12 per cent between 2001 and 2005'. Report of the Social Protection Floor Advisory Group (n 150) 38.

Lavinas offers these insights: '[I]t is primarily rising labour earnings that have accounted for the decline in poverty in Brazil, as was the case elsewhere in Latin America. Brazil is also no exception to the wider continental tendency to concentrate social spending on cash transfers rather than expanding provision of decommodified services, such as public health, education, sanitation and other basic social goods'. L Lavinas, '21st Century Welfare' (Nov–Dec 2013) 84 New Left Review 5, 32. 'The runt of the litter here is health spending: not only did it grow at a rate below average, but it also saw its share in federal social spending reduced from 13 per cent in 2001 to 11 per cent in 2010. By that time federal expenditures on education and welfare benefits amounted to 1 per cent of GDP, whereas sanitation and housing received only 0.1 and 0.8 per cent of GDP. Little wonder, then, that Brazil ranks so low with respect to living conditions ... Access to consumer goods such as cell phones, washing machines and computers, on the other hand, has soared: an amazing 86 per cent of households have at least one cell phone, up from 31 per cent in 2001, and one in two have a washing machine—though only 2 in 3 households have adequate sanitation. There was no change in the availability of clean water over the entire decade' (ibid 33). 'In short, in Brazil as elsewhere in Latin America, social infrastructure and access to state-provided, decommodified goods and services are growing at uneven tempos, exacerbating inequalities ... In 2009, private spending on health reached 5.3 per cent of Brazilian GDP while public expenditures amounted to only 3.5 per cent. The commodification of health in Brazil seems inexorable, reflecting the grip of the financial markets' (ibid 34). For another insightful study, see A Saad-Filho, 'Social Policy for Neoliberalism: The Bolsa Familia Programme in Brazil' (2015) 46 Development and Change 1227: '[S]ocial policy under neoliberalism remains a tool of poverty management: a palliative addressing only the most urgent symptoms of poverty and inequality while subsidizing their reproduction' (ibid 1247–48).

[154] Tepperman (n 153) 41. 'Lula had also realized that the wave of privatizations that had swept Latin America in the 1980s and 1990s—as governments sold off everything from airlines and energy producers to utility providers—had left hundreds of millions of citizens stranded, too poor to participate in the expanding market economies. Lula and his advisers reckoned that, rather than go through the nightmare of renationalizing big businesses, the best and simplest way to reverse the poor's exclusion was to put a little cash in their pockets' (ibid 38).

[155] Ruckert (n 57) 63. [156] Lavinas (n 153) 6. [157] ibid 34.

[158] See RW Cox, 'Gramsci, Hegemony and International Relations: An Essay in Method' (1983) 12 Millennium: Journal of International Studies 162, 163.

predistribution is attenuated for a form of redistribution that entrenches the predistributive neoliberal status quo.

The methodological individualism of the social protection floor is criticized for disregarding macroeconomic processes that are implicated in the poverty and inequality that the social protection floors seek to address.[159] The SDG Goal to 'reduce inequality between and among nations' important as it is, then offers for its part the target to 'Adopt policies, especially fiscal, wage and social protection policies, and progressively achieve greater equality'.[160] While the SDG goal on reducing inequality within and among countries fills a gap left by the MDGs, it is not clear how the micro fix offered by the social protection focus in the SDGs will be reconciled with the reform of international and institutional economic governance needed to address poverty, inequality, and their root causes. Indeed no attention seems to have been given to how the two might work against each other.

In so far as social protection aims and succeeds in confronting economic injustice,[161] it leaves intact the 'deep structures' allowing for the perpetual regeneration of the root causes of poverty and inequality and thus the need for 'surface reallocations time and again'.[162] That social protection can function as an 'automatic stabilizer' of economies,[163] contribute to reducing global imbalances, and has 'the *added* virtue of opening the way to improved human development'[164] highlight benefits just as they affirm the limits of its transformative agenda. Despite its claims, the SDG commitment to social protection is, as Jayati Ghosh cogently captures,

[159] J Ghosh, 'From "Development" to "Poverty Alleviation": What Have We Lost?' *Frontline* (4 Sept 2015), http://www.networkideas.org/news/aug2015/Development.pdf. 'Macroeconomic processes are entirely ignored: patterns of trade and economic activity that determine levels of employment and its distribution and the viability of particular activities, or fiscal policies that determine the extent to which essential public services like sanitation, health and education will be provided, or investment policies that determine the kind of physical infrastructure available ... or financial policies that create boom and bust volatility in various markets.'

[160] SDG Target 10.4.

[161] In Brazil, it has reached more than one-quarter of the population and 85% of the poor. By 2014, 36 million Brazilians had been lifted out of poverty and Brazilians living in indigence had effectively been eradicated. As for inequality, the overall income gap was reduced by one-third. Tepperman (n 153) 41.

[162] Fraser (n 110) 85. Fraser also highlights the group tensions that these social assistance interventions create: 'Far from abolishing class differentiation per se, these affirmative remedies support it and shape it. Their general effect is to shift attention from the class division between workers and capitalists to the division between employed and nonemployed fractions of the working class. Public-assistance programmes "target" the poor, not only for aid but for hostility. Such remedies, to be sure, provide needed material aid. But they also create strongly cathected, antagonistic group differentiations' (ibid).

[163] JE Stiglitz, 'The Global Crisis, Social Protection and Jobs' (2009) 148 International Labour Review 1. Emphasis added.

[164] Report of the Social Protection Floor Advisory Group (n 150) 57–58. 'The main impact of social protection measures has been to maintain the consumption capacity of lower-income households, and the domestic goods they consume typically have high employment multipliers' (ibid 53); 'Affirmative remedies for such injustices have been associated historically with the liberal welfare state. They seek to redress end–state maldistribution, while leaving intact much of the underlying political–economic structure. Thus they would increase the consumption share of economically disadvantaged groups, without otherwise restructuring the system of production. Fraser (n 110) 84.

ameliorative of the conditions of those defined as poor, rather than transformative of the economies in which they live.[165]

2.2.4 Internalizing capitalism: social protection and the subversion of human rights

Article 22 of the Universal Declaration of Human Rights recognizes that 'Everyone, as a member of society, has the right to social security and is entitled to realization, through national effort and international co-operation.' The UDHR also provided for a right to social security in Article 25 in the contexts of, inter alia, unemployment, sickness, disability, widowhood, old age, as well as for mothers and childhood.[166] Article 9 of the International Covenant on Economic, Social and Cultural Rights provides that, 'The States Parties to the present Covenant recognize the right of everyone to social security, including social insurance'[167] and notably, the rights in the Covenant may give rise to obligations of international assistance and cooperation.[168] In its interpretation of the provision, the Committee takes the view that 'social security should be treated as a social good, and not primarily as a mere instrument of economic or financial policy'.[169]

Despite the best efforts of NGOs and others, the references to social protection and the social protection floors in the SDGs are not framed in terms of a 'human right' to social security as many lawyers would argue is essential to shift the terms of the debate.[170] While much of the debate has thus turned around the failure to

[165] Ghosh (n 159). 'These silences enable a rather two-dimensional view of the poor, who are given the dignity of being treated as subjects with independent decision-making power, but apparently inhabiting a world in which their poverty is unrelated to a wider social, political and economic context, but is more a result of their own particular circumstance and their own often flawed judgements' (ibid).

[166] UDHR, Art 25(1) 'Everyone has the right to a standard of living adequate for the health and well-being of himself and of his family, including food, clothing, housing and medical care and necessary social services, and the right to security in the event of unemployment, sickness, disability, widowhood, old age or other lack of livelihood in circumstances beyond his control. (2) Motherhood and childhood are entitled to special care and assistance. All children, whether born in or out of wedlock, shall enjoy the same social protection.'

[167] See also ICESCR Art 10(2): 'Special protection should be accorded to mothers during a reasonable period before and after childbirth. During such period working mothers should be accorded paid leave or leave with adequate social security benefits'; Art 11 on the right of everyone to an adequate standard of living for himself and his family, including adequate food, clothing and housing, and to the continuous improvement of living conditions at paragraph 2: 'The States Parties to the present Covenant, recognizing the fundamental right of everyone to be free from hunger, shall take, individually and through international co-operation, the measures, including specific programmes', and Art 12 on the right of everyone to the enjoyment of the highest attainable standard of physical and mental health where steps include as necessary (d) 'The creation of conditions which would assure to all medical service and medical attention in the event of sickness.'

[168] ICESCR Art 2(1); CESCR, General Comment No 19, Right to Social Security (Art 9) UN Doc E/C.12/GC/19, 4 Feb 2008, paras 52–58.

[169] ibid para 10.

[170] 'Social protection remains a charitable undertaking advocated for reasons of efficiency and productivity, and not a matter of right. The empowerment dimension is thus lost, as is the rest of the rights-based framework.' Alston (n 134) para 30.

harness what is often said to be the added-value of human rights as legal rights (human rights-based approaches) and to a lesser degree the added-value of justiciable social rights, here we are interested in how the right to social security, in particular its alignment to the social protection floors, validates the status quo and serves to undermine transformative solutions. The Committee's affirmation of the primary function of social security as a social good and not a tool for economic and financial engineering, and the rights-based approach that elevates rights to claims on power, policy, and resources, have both nonetheless looked past the embedding of the capitalist and indeed neoliberal preconditions that are tied to these outwardly social objectives.

In April 2015 CESCR issued a statement entitled 'Social Protection Floors: An Essential Element of the Right to Social Security and of the Sustainable Development Goals'. A review of the Statement identifies several ways in which the Committee incorporates deep rooted capitalist assumptions that are in important ways anathema to its aims and implants them as preconditions for the realization of human rights. Instead of probing the *terms* under which 'many developing countries have [...] experienced relatively high growth rates', the Committee hitches the social protection agenda to the existence of that growth to argue for 'access to the resources needed to initiate and progressively implement social protection programmes'.[171] The Committee's 'reaffirmation of the redistributive character of social security'[172] to meeting basic needs and furthering equality, left there serves also to mask the social and economic arrangements that allow for inequitable outcomes.[173] Moreover, as noted above, the assumption that redistribution is a categorical good advancing the post-war welfare values of the left ignores how the scheme can in fact take the form of neoliberal welfare: far from ensuring health, education, housing, and social security as decommodified goods and services, the role of the state under this model is to enable market forces to the ends of 'human capital accumulation', ie the creation of consumers.[174] There are other schemes aimed at meeting minimum needs that can be similarly contested.[175]

[171] CESCR, Statement on Social Protection Floors (n 142) para 1.

[172] ibid para 5(b).

[173] See Frasers's definition (and critique) of 'affirmative remedies': 'By affirmative remedies for injustice I mean remedies aimed at correcting inequitable outcomes of social arrangements without disturbing the underlying framework that generates them.' Fraser (n 110) 82.

[174] 'The generally low educational levels and vulnerable health of the poor are seen as an obstacle to prosperity, not least because they prevent them from participating fully in the market.' Lavinas (n 153) 6–7.

[175] Such as the Guaranteed Minimum Income (GMI) provided for in the third Memorandum of Understanding between Greece and its international creditors critiqued by the Greek finance minister as an excuse to drop all other benefits and in fact to minimize redistribution. E Tsakalotas, 'Economic Blues: The Left in Government Times' LSE Public Lecture (London, 10 Nov 2015), http://www.lse.ac.uk/publicEvents/events/2015/11/20151110t2000vHKT.aspx. As critiqued by a variety of academic commentators, while a GMI could provide for the 'minimum', everything else would be left to the market, thereby providing a welfare policy that serves to reinforce, for example, weaker collective bargaining and increasingly 'flexible' labour. So here 'a "guaranteed minimum income" also risks "guaranteeing" the imprint of invisible hand of the freest possible market'. ME Salomon, 'Social Rights as Fiscal Risks and Other Stories from the Dark Heart of Europe' Conference on Sovereign Debt Revisited by Constitutional and International Law, IACL, Athens, 13–14 Nov 2015.

The required 'minimum level of benefits' that gives rise to core obligations with regard to the right to social security is owed, according to the CESCR, to 'all individuals and families'. Just as this may be critically important for people to be able to access goods and services,[176] it is also explicitly modelled on methodological individualism and works against its own attempts and the central need to confront the structural underpinnings of socio-economic injustice.[177] Second, by reading methodological individualism into human rights, they fail to challenge the growth paradigm in any fundamental manner including the contemporary means through which growth is achieved, with all its attendant appropriations. Third, it provides the means through which to reinforce the domination of the state apparatus over citizens, who in so far as they become the claimants of their rights also become the object of state policy and the clients of the state.[178]

The Committee has long emphasized that the Covenant is politically and economically 'neutral', and that its principles are subject to realization within any number of systems be it 'a socialist or a capitalist system, or a mixed, centrally planned, or laissez-faire economy or upon any other particular approach' the only prerequisite being that the interdependence and indivisibility of the two sets of human right are reflected in the system in question.[179] As has been pointed out by Ben Saul, David Kinley and Jacqueline Mowbray, the Committee would seem to reflect this position in its endorsement, on the one hand, of redistribution and state intervention and regulation in the realization of Covenant rights, countering purely free market approaches, and, on the other hand, in its challenges to socialist values, for example by supporting contributory social security schemes (ie social insurance as opposed to non-contributory schemes of social assistance),[180] as well as in its pursuit of redistribution so as to ensure dignity but not to confront inequality more generally.[181] The reflections provided herein on the right to social security and the social protection floors challenge the alleged agnosticism of the Covenant's

[176] CESCR, Statement on Social Protection Floors (n 142) para 8.

[177] For a full account of the structural approach of international human rights law in this area, see De Schutter et al (n 97).

[178] See A Gorz, *Reclaiming Work: Beyond the Wage-Based Society* (Polity 1999) 4. Gorz also writes of this 'bureaucratization of the welfare state' that has 'collective solutions to collective problems and the collective satisfaction of collective needs [...] ruled out' (ibid). In a critique of the celebrated conditional cash transfer programmes in Brazil, Lavinas relatedly highlights what might effectively be seen as conditional rights: 'Rather than recognizing needs, [the new model enabling state] concedes "entitlements", and instead of ensuring equal access to public goods, it offers rewards in exchange for the fulfilment of obligations—the quintessential coinage in this sense being "workfare"'. Lavinas (n 153) 6.

[179] CESCR, General Comment No 3, Art 2(1) on the Nature of States Parties' Obligations' UN Doc E/1991/23 Annex III (1990) para 8.

[180] Saul, Kinley, and Mowbray (n 140) 616.

[181] Salomon (n 82) 2141: 'While the principle of progressive realisation might be said to offer within its terms and logic more than a minimalist doctrine aimed merely at dignity, because it is set instead at a decency standard, to date this interpretation has not been meaningfully developed at the international level. The 'full realization' of all socioeconomic rights still only provides the universally agreed floor below which no-one should fall.' (Findings suggest that there is less income inequality in countries with *high* social expenditure than in countries with lower levels of social expenditure. While this is significant it tells us nothing about how those funds for redistribution were acquired.)

application, situating it instead firmly within capitalism's assumptions of the necessity of capitalist growth, as well as neoliberalism's hallmark of inequality by focusing too much on floors and minimums.[182] Even the Committee's familiar refrain that 'international financial institutions, notably the International Monetary Fund and the World Bank, should take into account the right to social security in their lending policies, credit agreements, [and] structural adjustment programmes'[183] which on one account demands international cooperation and a readjustment by institutions of global governance, on the other hand offers at best 'subordinate reforms', not revolutionary ones.[184] In any case, in linking the right to social security to the social protection floors and now to the SDG target, the need for international cooperation anticipated in the UDHR and subsequently in the Covenant is sidelined, with the social protection floor focus dedicated to national action (which in itself assumes the fiscal space required is made possible by the external actors implicated in domestic policy).[185] Where the SDGs do turn to 'global partnerships for development' we see an unalloyed commitment to the conventional terms of international trade, investment, and finance.

The right to social security and its social protection floors expose a paradox that inhere in human rights today. It is surely not wrong to remark that human rights might have superseded socialism as the main discourse for the critique of capitalism following the end of the cold war,[186] but at one and the same time it has internalized capitalism's assumptions. Freeman suggests that this is reflective of a wider institutional tension within the UN whereby the Organization is both 'committed to human rights, and accepts capitalism as its economic delivery system':[187] the UN, like the ILO, are 'reformist', notes Freeman, in that they accept the legitimacy of capitalism while seeking to reform it.[188] In any case, the key points addressed here are that the interpretation of human rights within an era of global neoliberalism requires an *explicit* awareness of the ways in which capitalism's tenets are embraced and growth is fetishized including as an essential precondition of human betterment and of the forms of social and ecological violence that precede redistributive

[182] On the latter point, see further Moyn: '[H]uman rights at least as canonically established have nothing to say about the principle value of equality that neoliberalism threatens, it seems hard to conclude that they are a useful resource in response.' Moyn (n 84) 151–52. Although the Committee recognizes in principle that what they advocate are 'floors and not ceilings'. CESCR, Statement on Social Protection Floors (n 142) para 10, the general expectation has been to see secured a floor: 'the policy must identify the minimum core content of rights or a social protection floor, as developed by the International Labour Organization, and ensure the protection of this core content at all times'. Letter from the Chairperson of the Committee on Economic, Social and Cultural Rights to States Parties to the Covenant (on austerity measures), 12 May 2012.

[183] CESCR, General Comment No 19 (n 168) para 83.

[184] Gorz (n 178) 7: 'Some of us in the early sixties made a distinction between subordinate and revolutionary reforms. The former predicated on the urgent need to remedy dysfunctions of existing society, the latter on the need to pass beyond existing society towards a different one.'

[185] See Chapter 6 'Global Finance') at 211–224. [186] Freeman (n 32) 25. [187] ibid.

[188] ibid. Chimni argues more forcefully that: 'While the UN still continues to pay obeisance to the global poor, it actively promotes the interests of transnational capital and makes futile appeals to it to serve the cause of international justice.' BS Chimni, 'International Institutions Today: An Imperial Global State in the Making' (2004) 15 EJIL 1, 15.

policies: this approach would offer the first step in the 'neutral' application of socio-economic rights.

3. Capitalist Globalization and the Cosmopolitanism of Human Rights

The SDGs situate social protection systems including social protection floors within the 'national' domain. Likewise, the ILO Social Protection Floor Recommendation 202 from which it emerged provides that 'National social protection floors should be financed by national resources. Members whose economic and fiscal capacities are insufficient to implement the guarantees may seek international cooperation and support that complements their own efforts.' The focus on *national* approaches to confronting poverty is a double-edged sword: it may capture the need for national control, for example forms of economic self-determination and contextual measurements, but it conceals where there is international influence over the manufacturing of socio-economic harms, poverty, and inequality. The demands for 'policy space' that emerged over the past decades as a developing country response to the reach of international trade integration and the erosion of autonomy—and became a live issue also in the realms of international investment and finance[189]—was meant to wrest back the power of developing countries so that they could also be beneficiaries of the global economy. Policy space and 'national ownership' properly understood are not meant merely to leave the solutions to poor (or insolvent) countries while the international structural impediments that delimit those solutions remain firmly in place. In particular ways, the importance given to 'national' adaptation at the expense of global structural issues not only risks undermining the ambition of the SDGs, it leaves national governments to toil at the domestic level while their possibilities are shaped in many ways by the strictures of global capitalism. Notably, it reinforces the position familiar in international economic law that justice is largely to be associated with the internal affairs of states. This is not only too simplistic but thoroughly unjust; in a globalized world where international regulation reaches deep into the domestic systems of states justice has also to occur at the site of international law.[190]

While the Goal on Global Partnerships for Sustainable Development has a target to 'Respect each country's policy space and leadership to establish and implement policies for poverty eradication and sustainable development',[191] a closer look at

[189] This is from the second MoU with Greece and written without deliberate irony: 'In line with the conclusions of the euro-area summit of 26 October 2011, the [Greek] Government will fully cooperate with the Commission, the ECB and the IMF staff teams to strengthen the monitoring of programme implementation, and will provide the staff teams with access to all relevant data and other information in the Greek administration. However the ownership of the programme and all executive responsibilities in the programme implementation remain with the Greek Government.' IMF, Greece: Letter of Intent, Memorandum of Economic and Financial Policies (n 70).

[190] For a full consideration of the implications of this reach for demands of justice see Chapter 2 ('Confronting the Pathologies of International Law').

[191] SDG Target 17.15.

the 2030 Agenda for Sustainable Development sees included the disclaimer: 'while remaining consistent with relevant international rules and commitments'[192] (and it doesn't imply human rights commitments). If national policy space is resisted in so far as it threatens the transnational control by the powerful,[193] 'national ownership' passes the buck for economic and social development to the nation state. Sovereign equality and economic self-determination—bases for national claims—still matter, indeed matter as much as ever, but they are at once a defence against the contrived notions of mutual advantage and universalism, as well as a tool for their misappropriation.

The inequality goal and targets in the SDGs are said to reflect the complementary and transformative structural counterpart to national duties and in particular to the basic needs approach that was criticized in the MDGs precisely for providing social safety nets as a response to an economic model that was and still is increasing inequalities.[194] But at this early stage the transformative nature of SDG 10 and its targets—which aim to reduce inequality within and between countries—is unconvincing first because the target is too vague to be meaningful,[195] and, more importantly, because the SDGs endorse 'solutions' based on the neoliberal global status quo. For example, while empirical findings challenge the suggestion that Bilateral Investment Treaties (BITs) have contributed even to the targeted objective of economic development in the host states,[196] and there are grave concerns about the negative impacts of the foreign investment legal regime on host states and their people,[197] SDG Target 10.b 'Encourages ... foreign direct investment to States where the need is greatest, in particular least developed countries',[198] with the Goal on Global Partnerships for Sustainable Development committed to: 'Adopt and implement investment promotion regimes for least developed countries.'[199] These alleged solutions are in tension with other recent findings, for example that the main force for reduction and compression of inequalities ('convergence') both within and between countries comes from the diffusion of knowledge and *investment* in training and skills.[200] As for trade, the Global Partnerships in the SDGs

[192] Transforming Our World (n 143) paras 21 and 63.

[193] On the resistance of the United States, European Union, and several other developed countries to including a reference to policy space in the SDGs, see R Sengupta, 'Post-2015 Development Agenda: Concluding Negotiations amidst Differences' *Third World Network Info Service on UN Sustainable Development* (26 July 2015), http://www.twn.my/title2/unsd/2015/unsd150714.htm

[194] S Fukuda-Parr, 'The 2030 Agenda and the SDGs—A Course Correction?' Sheffield Political Economy Institute SPERI Blog (30 Sept 2015), http://speri.dept.shef.ac.uk/2015/09/30/the-2030-agenda-and-the-sdgs-a-course-correction

[195] SDG Target 10.4: 'Adopt policies, especially fiscal, wage and social protection policies, and progressively achieve greater equality.'

[196] P Muchlinski, 'Holistic Approaches to Development and International Investment Law: The Role of International Investment Agreements' in J Faundez and C Tan (eds), *International Law, Economic Globalization and Development* (Edward Elgar 2010) 186.

[197] For details, see Chapter 5 ('Foreign Investment').

[198] On the perceived benefits flowing from foreign direct investment, F Macmillan, 'The World Trade Organization and the Turbulent Legacy of International Economic Law-Making in the Long Twentieth Century' in Faundez and Tan (n 196) 170.

[199] SDG Target 17.5.

[200] T Piketty, *Capital in the Twenty-First Century* (Harvard UP 2014) 21.

restate the commitment of the international community to the liberalization of trade as currently practised and thus to 'Promote a universal, rules-based, open, non-discriminatory and equitable multilateral trading system under the World Trade Organization.'[201] But again, findings suggest that countries in the global South that adopted trade liberalization, privatization, and fiscal discipline through the 1990s, even on the basis of the conventional marker, had low economic growth rates both in absolute terms but also relative to other countries that did not follow such reforms or only partially, such as China.[202] The latter part of the SDG key trade Goal dedicated to a 'conclusion of negotiations under its Doha Development Agenda', is far from offering a radical departure from the terms of economic globalization. On a most generous reading, its inclusion is merely to advance the interests of developing countries within the *current* trading order, but, notably, a continued commitment to the Doha Development Round (established back in 2001) was not even reaffirmed at the last WTO Ministerial Conference in Nairobi just three months after the SDGs were adopted.[203] Given how consistent the SDGs are with the current *modus operandi* of the transnational capitalist order, it is at one level surprising that the debate about the inclusion of SDG 10 on addressing inequality was one of the most contentious political battles in the SDG negotiations.[204] Under its predecessor, the MDGs, the UN development goals project might have been characterized, at best, 'as an important humanitarian venture only as long as the various structures of the neoliberal mission are not seriously challenged, nor its beneficiaries displaced'.[205] Beyond the rhetoric of ending poverty and reducing inequality, the SDGs would seem not even to meet that low bar.

International human rights law offers its own cosmopolitan vision that seeks to address extraterritorial violations of socio-economic rights. But history invites reflection. Along with so many other areas of political life, modern international human rights has the territorial state designated as the appropriate entity to be the bearer of duties and in particular a state's *own* citizens—or at best people located within its territory—are deemed the suitable recipients of those legally guaranteed

[201] SDG Target 17.10.

[202] Moore (n 129) 807–08. See also H-J Chang, *Bad Samaritans: The Myth of Free Trade and the Secret History of Capitalism* (Bloomsbury 2008).

[203] SDG Target 17.10. The 10th WTO Ministerial Conference held in Nairobi in December 2015 failed to reaffirm its commitment to the Doha Development Agenda for the first time since its adoption in 2001: 'We recognize that many Members reaffirm the Doha Development Agenda, and the Declarations and Decisions adopted at Doha and at the Ministerial Conferences held since then, and reaffirm their full commitment to conclude the DDA on that basis. Other Members do not reaffirm the Doha mandates, as they believe new approaches are necessary to achieve meaningful outcomes in multilateral negotiations. Members have different views on how to address the negotiations.' Nairobi Ministerial Declaration, WT/MIN(15)/DEC, adopted 19 Dec 2015, para 30. The 'Nairobi package' was adopted at the Ministerial Conference and it contains a series of six ministerial decisions on agriculture, cotton, and issues related to least-developed countries, including a long overdue commitment to abolish export subsidies for farm exports which has distorted agricultural markets for decades at the expense of ensuring the basic needs (and rights) of farmers in the global South.

[204] See Fukuda-Parr (n 194).

[205] ME Salomon, 'Poverty, Privilege and International Law: The Millennium Development Goals and the guise of humanitarianism' (2008) 51 German Yearbook of International Law 39, 71.

rights. Thus, on the one hand, international human rights law developed on the basis of what the territorial state was required to do, or refrain from doing, to its own people. While modern human rights law is celebrated for making the person the subject of international concern and in important ways eroding the principle of non-intervention with the advent of international human rights oversight mechanisms, this focus on what occurs inside a state was in another way regressive of what had come before.

The emergence of the modern independent European state after the peace of Westphalia in 1648 established the principle of state sovereignty by which each prince was free to assert his own will within his territorial domain. The system relied on a form of equality among ('civilized') states whereby each state was to respect the sovereignty of the other allowing each omnipotent state to exercise its full powers within the ambit of its jurisdiction: while what occurred inside a state was of no concern to the international legal order, the legal order also *constrained what a prince could do to the people of another sovereign.*[206] As such, international human rights law marks a significant leap forward on the former parameter by transcending state sovereignty through a system of international oversight that pierces the sovereign veil and affords legal protection to people subjected to abuse of power by their own state. However, on the latter parameter we would do well to see imposed some of those earlier constraints that sought to limit the ability of a state to harm people outside of its borders, and violate their human rights.[207] The Westphalian order was—at least in so far as it regulated life among European nation states—a law of coexistence; it was structured to keep states peacefully apart.[208]

At the heart of the post-1945 world project for peace and social progress sits the aim of international cooperation. While the commitment to territorial privileging shaped international human rights law and its vision of justice, human rights instruments addressing socio-economic rights also codified 'obligations of international cooperation' and the seeds of a truly cosmopolitan human rights legal project. Decades of United Nations consideration and human rights standard-setting in the area of international cooperation have furthered the expectation whereby economic and other policies should be designed in such a way as to avoid causing injury to the interests of other states and to the rights of their people, and, moreover, should actively seek to address existing deprivations.[209]

206 This historical record shows that recognition as sovereign was granted by the Europeans. Of important note in any coverage of order among 'sovereigns' is 'the prior question of how certain states were excluded from the realm of sovereignty in the first place' and how the colonial encounter shaped the doctrine. See further Anghie (n 60) 6.

207 Thanks to Martin Scheinin for this valuable insight on the circumscribed origins of extraterritoriality. (Note: the legal constraints that limited the ability of a state to harm people outside of its borders applied to the people of other European countries.)

208 W Friedmann, *The Changing Structure of International Law* (Columbia UP 1964).

209 See Salomon (n 96); Maastricht Principles (n 97); ME Salomon, 'How to Keep Promises: Making Sense of the Duty among Multiple States to Fulfil Socio-Economic Rights in the World' in A Nollkaemper and D Jacobs (eds), *Distribution of Responsibilities in International Law* (CUP 2014) 366.

Many of the sources are by now familiar. There is the wide-ranging general obligation in the 1945 UN Charter requiring cooperation among member states in the achievement of human rights by all, higher standards of living, and economic and social progress and development, solutions of international economic, social, health, and related problems, and the universal respect for, and observance of, human rights.[210] Notably, the Charter imposes no territorial restriction on the execution of those requirements, instead, the reference to cooperation with the Organization suggests that, under the Charter, the realization of human rights is a duty that states owe to one another in the achievement of common ends.[211] The 1948 Universal Declaration of Human Rights then expressed a revolutionary proposition in Article 28, according to which everyone has a 'right' to a social and international order in which all human rights can be realized. As Stephen Marks points out, if one takes that proposition seriously, then everyone has a right to radical changes in the international political economy and the structures that often inhibit the full enjoyment of human rights.[212]

In a study on the drafting of the UDHR, Asbjorn Eide explains that Rene Cassin, the French delegate at the time, wanted the declaratory text to reflect, at least in an indirect form, *the duty* of states to ensure the enjoyment of economic and social rights.[213] Charles Malik of Lebanon tabled a more ambitious approach. He was of the view that the enjoyment of human rights 'depended not only on the measures which could be taken by states, but on the *restructuring* of the social and international order'.[214] It was the Malik draft that was accepted and that underpins intellectually perhaps the most progressive element of international human rights law.

This approach—the idea of structural change at the global level conducive to the exercise of rights by all—animated the 1986 Declaration on the Right to Development, as we saw in our coverage above. It held that 'effective international cooperation [is] an essential complement to the efforts of developing countries to foster their comprehensive development'.[215] There was the earlier substantiation in

[210] Art 56 of the Charter of the United Nations stipulates that 'All Members pledge themselves to take joint and separate action in co-operation with the Organization for the achievement of the purposes set forth in Article 55', among which purposes Art 55 lists 'universal respect for, and observance of, human rights and fundamental freedoms for all without distinction as to race, sex, language, or religion'.

[211] UN Charter, Arts 1(3) and 1(4).

[212] SP Marks, 'Foreword' in Salomon (n 96) vii, x.

[213] A Eide, 'Article 28' in G Alfredsson and A Eide (eds), *The Universal Declaration of Human Rights: A Common Standard of Achievement* (Martinus Nijhoff 1999) 597, 599.

[214] ibid. Sally-Anne Way's archival work highlights that a 1948 proposal by Malik in which economic, social and cultural rights would require favourable social conditions, resulted in the text 'Everyone has the right to a good social and international order in which the rights and freedoms set out in the Declaration can be fully realized' which later became article 28 of the UDHR. Cassin, for his part, had also proposed a provision that 'Everyone, as a member of society, has the economic, social and cultural rights enumerated below, whose fulfilment should be made possible in every State separately or by international collaboration.' S-A Way, '*Human Rights from the Great Depression to the Great Recession: The United States, 'Western' Liberalism and the Shaping of Economic and Social Rights in International Law*' PhD in progress (London School of Economics and Political Science).

[215] DRD, Art 4(2).

human rights treaties in the language of obligations of 'international assistance and cooperation' as per the International Covenant on Economic, Social and Cultural Rights of 1966 and comparable language later in the Convention on the Right of the Child when it comes to economic, social and cultural rights.[216] Today, the approach taken to international cooperation in the area of socio-economic rights encompasses not only acts and omissions of a state within or beyond its territory that have effects on the enjoyment of human rights outside of that state's territory (extraterritorial obligations more narrowly understood), but also extraterritorial obligations—'of a global character'—to realize human rights universally.[217] The General Assembly's Millennium Declaration provided the principle of a 'shared responsibility for managing worldwide economic and social development'[218] with the 2030 Agenda for Sustainable Development adopted by the General Assembly in 2015 expressing the commitment of the international community of states to 'strengthened global solidarity'.[219]

It is undeniable that obligations of international cooperation aimed at ensuring the exercise of socio-economic rights can be found among the traditional sources of international law and that non-compliance with the obligation can give rise to international responsibility,[220] even if a range of questions as to its implementation are doctrinally inchoate.[221] But the doctrinal and operational underdevelopment of these obligations in the area of socio-economic rights are not to be excused merely as part of the *evolving* promise of international human rights law; more accurately, it is a reflection of the past and current limits of international politics to transform the 'deep global structures' of the political economy.

Obligations of international cooperation to the ends of socio-economic rights and people-centred development is a radical idea and, as mentioned earlier in the context of the right to development, it is precisely its radical prospects that undermines its transformative potential. In the case of socio-economic rights, recognition by states of an obligation of international cooperation is limited and in the case of the right to development the debate has long been so polarized as to be toxic.

216 Convention on the Rights of the Child (1989), entered into force 2 Sept 1990, GA Res A/RES/44/25, annex 44, UN GAOR Supp (No 49) at 167 UN Doc A/44/49 (1989).

217 Maastricht Principles, Principle 8 (n 97).

218 On the principle of a shared responsibility: UN Millennium Declaration (2000) UN Doc A/55/2: Part I, Values and Principles, Art 6, 'Shared responsibility'; see also Report of the UN Secretary-General, 'In Larger Freedom: Towards Development, Security and Human Rights for All' UN Doc A/59/2005; *Report of the UN High-Level Panel on Threats, Challenges and Change, A More Secure World: Our Shared Responsibility* UN Doc A/59/565 (2004).

219 Transforming Our World (n 143) Preamble.

220 See Salomon (n 19); O De Schutter and ME Salomon, 'Economic Policy Conditionality, Socio-Economic Rights and International Legal Responsibility: The Case of Greece 2010–2015', Legal Brief prepared for the Special Committee of the Hellenic Parliament on the Audit of the Greek Debt (15 June 2015), http://www.lse.ac.uk/humanRights/documents/2015/SalomonDeSchutterGreekDebtTruth.pdf; De Schutter et al (n 97).

221 For an exploration of the issues, see the chapters in M Langford, M Scheinin, W van Genugten, and W Vandenhole (eds), *Global Justice, State Duties: The Extra-territorial Scope of Economic, Social and Cultural Rights in International Law* (CUP 2013).

Industrialized states restrict their interpretation of the content of 'international assistance and cooperation' merely to the transfer of financial resources and further argue that it constitutes a moral not legal duty. Through its General Comments and Concluding Observations CESCR undoubtedly recognizes this obligation under the Covenant but we are far from a revolution. That international human rights law is understood as including a law of cooperation doesn't mean that it functions as such. Since international law both governs cooperation and regulates social and economic policy deep within the state, its failure to satisfy human rights requirements on these counts is a telling dereliction.[222]

In its 2008 Statement on the World Food Crisis the Committee invited an important distinction between redistributive and predistributive failures of international law and policy. In the case of the former approach, the Committee remarked that 'The current food crisis represents a failure to meet the obligations to ensure an equitable distribution of world food supplies in relation to need. The food crisis also reflects a failure of national and international policies to ensure physical and economic access to food for all'.[223] Encapsulating a predistributive logic, the Committee called upon states also to 'pay attention to the longer-term structural causes of the crisis and to focus attention on the gravity of the underlying causes of food insecurity, malnutrition and undernutrition, that have persisted for so long'.[224] Here the Committee highlighted, inter alia, agriculture trade rules under the WTO, the need to invest in small-scale agriculture, and in small-scale irrigation and technologies,[225] even if the acknowledgement of structural problems led largely to hortatory recommendations. While there are vital doctrines that advance a progressive extraterritorial agenda and the structural causes of economic violence and not merely its effects,[226] we can recognize how international human rights law has hardly dented the brutality of the international political economy nor reconstituted its underlying logics and practices. As noted in Chapter 1 on the legal rendering of immiseration, the weight of capitalism's logic works against those efforts with the legal mechanisms in the area of international human rights not well-suited to addressing the systemic violations of the global economy. International human rights law is not limited to redistribution, but has not gone so far as to effecting predistribution, and as addressed earlier in the context of social protection floors, at times drives the possibility of predistribution further away.

The cosmopolitanism of international human rights law is failing meaningfully to unsettle the proclivities of global capitalism. Society is subordinated to transnational capitalism and it is true that in many ways human rights thus also operate on the 'margins of globalization'.[227] In part, human rights are alienated because

[222] For a consideration of the animating principles of international law and its implications for justice, see Chapter 2 ('Confronting the Pathologies of International Law') at 53–60.

[223] CESCR, Statement on the World Food Crisis UN Doc E/C.12/2008/1, 20 May 2008, para 9.

[224] ibid para 12. [225] ibid para 13.

[226] For coverage of these doctrines, see De Schutter et al (n 97) 1145ff.

[227] P Gready, 'Reasons to Be Cautious about Evidence and Evaluation: Rights-based Approaches to Development and the Emerging Culture of Evaluation' (2009) 1 Journal of Human Rights Practice 380, 385; see also VK Nagaraj, 'Global Human Rights: For Futures Unlike the Past'

they speak for society and as such have befallen the same fate. In part, their potential is constrained because of the bifurcation of legal regimes into ostensibly economic and non-economic realms, and the continued and direct instrumental use of the former for capitalist expansion and encroachment.[228] Human rights are not the only narrative and practice brought to its knees by globalization;[229] but that they have not uniquely been alienated by globalization is no consolation.

4. Concluding Remarks

Human rights provide a defence against the abuse of political power by the state, just as we rely on that political power to secure human rights. Human rights also provide a defence against abuse of economic power, just as they are circumscribed by that power and in important ways reinforce expressions of it. In the former situation human rights empower the state; in the latter they help sustain neoliberal capitalism.

Paradoxically, the social protection floors celebrated in the SDGs tell us not that we have won an important battle in protecting fundamental socio-economic well-being, but that we have lost. We have lost because we are prepared to settle for preventing or mitigating suffering but not to changing the terms under which that suffering is made possible and reproduced. The social protection floor is redistributive but not predistributive, which are the terms required for a transformative enterprise to take hold. Commentators have suggested that the SDG focus on reducing inequality within and among countries addresses the need for reform of (global) economic governance, offering the much-needed structural accompaniment to the social protection floors commitment.[230] But there is nothing in the SDGs that deviates from international economic law and policy as practised and the very same strategies that have created the immiseration we know today;[231] and there is nothing there that opens up space for real alternatives. The SDG 'solutions' are quite simply those that preserve the

openDemocracy (31 July 2013), http://www.opendemocracy.net/openglobalrights/vijay-nagaraj/global-human-rights-for-futures-unlike-past

[228] As this book explores, there is a long history of transnational capitalist exploitation upon which modern international law is built. On this, Miéville reminds us to avoid placing 'the emphasis [. . .] on the differences between pre- and post-war international law. The continuities are even more important as they trace the dynamic of international legal development.' C Miéville, 'The Commodity-Form Theory of International Law' in Marks (n 28) 123.

[229] As Moyn frames it: 'Human rights look more like a symptom of a much broader syndrome'. Moyn (n 84) 160.

[230] See notably, Fukuda-Parr (n 194).

[231] See Chapter 1 on debunking standard defences as to the benefits of globalization as practised: that the social good is maximized by maximizing the reach and frequency of market transactions; that human well-being is best satisfied by the market and the role of the state is to guarantee the conditions that best allow markets to function; and of course, that the world has never been richer. As Chapter 1 shows, the first two arguments—built on the idea that human need will be best addressed as a by-product of individual greed (profit)—find no empirical support. The third is wholly misleading.

privileged place of transnational capital, with all its attendant assumptions, falsehoods, and harms.

A comparable situation arises with regard to CESCR's celebrated doctrine of prioritizing minimum essential levels of socio-economic rights, support for which has led comfortably to CESCR's endorsement of universal social protection floors. From there we see an endorsement of the mainstream commitment to capitalist growth even if to the ends of national redistribution. The problem we face, however, isn't that human rights are incorrigibly capitalist based on their historical roots, this familiar argument is overstated;[232] even though capitalism looms large in the fabric of international human rights law, human rights law has the potential for being progressive. Instead, human rights can be considered capitalist (and determinate) because they now operate almost fully within the boundaries of what the terms of global capitalist orthodoxy can provide and, in particular, what its intellectual moorings dictate. As addressed herein through the example of social protection floors and the right to social security, regrettably, this is also the case with regard to their most important basic protection: ensuring in the first instance the minimum essential levels of socio-economic rights to anyone who does not have them.

That the Covenant takes for granted capitalism and capitalist production is clear. The Covenant assumes the commodification of social relations, a good example being the ideology of work as a source of rights and the right to an income, including 'the right to an adequate standard of living'.[233] Still the potential of socio-economic rights to guide economic policy and contain market ambitions exists,[234] just as it is true that the full realization of socio-economic rights would challenge existing inequalities and power relations,[235] and well before their full realization. Human rights can be directed at the political project of setting in motion a very different social, economic, and international order but two shifts would need to occur: socio-economic rights would need to be dislodged intellectually from current assumptions that guide their interpretation and application—as their endorsement of methodological individualism above has shown—and a robust redemption of political rights would need to take place. Here, reclaiming political rights constitutive of democracy would be a place to start in addressing economic inequality, since inequality cannot be confronted as long as democracy is captured by vested interests of the minority of the richest capitalists.[236] Human rights don't merely rely on the state for their realization, and they don't only legitimate and reinforce the power of the state: they have also been set up to direct the state. Whether they can direct the state in practice is critical, which relies in the first instance on having a

[232] As Freeman demonstrates, the relationship between the modern concept of human rights and 'bourgeois' theories of property have been exaggerated. Freeman (n 32) 24.

[233] See R Balakrishnan, J Heintz, and D Elson, *Rethinking Economic Policy for Social Justice: The Radical Potential of Human Rights* (Routledge 2016) 1.

[234] See Somers with Curtis (n 1); Salomon and Arnott (n 132).

[235] See Balakrishnan, Heintz, and Elson (n 233).

[236] An important catch 22 is that the incommensurability of democracy and economic inequality requires we address inequality to free up democratic processes but until we free up democracy we will not see inequality addressed.

state apparatus that is not open to capture by private interests and is truly organized to secure values and interests derived of democratic processes.

CESCR avers that 'the Covenant is neutral and its principles cannot accurately be described as being predicated exclusively upon the need for, or the desirability of a socialist or a capitalist system, or a mixed, centrally planned, or laissez-faire economy, or upon any other particular approach'.[237] The Committee thus recognizes that a state party 'may adopt a range of possible policy measures for the implementation of the rights set forth in the Covenant'.[238] CESCR was established in 1987 as neoliberalism ascended and its commitment to 'neutrality' was in part a response to an increasingly pervasive neoliberalism globally as well as an effort to disallow socialism's naturalization of the Covenant as a response.[239] Research has shown that the Covenant rights were wrongly assumed to be borne of socialism (when in fact they were Keynesian), and with the end of the cold war and the fall of communist regimes in Central and Eastern Europe the Covenant's socio-economic rights were seen as the locus where socialist values might continue to be advanced, prompting the defensive need for an articulation of the Committee's 'neutrality'.[240]

But while the Covenant and its elaboration and interpretation by the Committee have been effective in protecting certain people from some socio-economic harms, neither the Covenant nor the Committee's interpretation of it reflects neutrality. It is clear that the Committee seeks to see respected, protected, and fulfilled socio-economic rights, it seeks to defend people against the worst excesses of capitalism, including through advocating for social protection floors. Indeed, it adopts an almost deviant conception of social justice as distribution according to need and not just as the requital of desert.[241] However, the (often tacit) acceptance of the legitimacy of capitalism today, even while seeking to soften its worst tendencies, is to take a position: it is to endorse this capitalism and its world order, whatever attempts are made to protect its victims. So when the Committee affirms that the primary function of the right to social security is as a social good and not a tool for economic and financial engineering,[242] we see an effort at its neutral application just as it both ignores the underlying commitments that reproduce the need for social security and precludes the possibility of alternative (ie: truly neutral) agendas. It can no longer be said that the criticism that emerges from the human rights community is 'non-political', confined to the denunciation of abuses and not the conditions in which those abuses have become possible;[243] any reasonable account of the violations of socio-economic rights today is alive to the intersecting and multi-level forces that produce them, not least those borne of globalization. What we see

[237] CESCR, General Comment No 3 (n 179) para 8.

[238] Optional Protocol to ICESCR adopted 10 Dec 2008, GA Res 63/117 (2008) UN Doc A/RES/63/117, Art 8.4; see also CESCR, General Comment No 3 (n 179) para 8.

[239] Way (n 214). [240] ibid.

[241] See D Miller, *Social Justice* (1976) 338–39, as cited in A Woodiwiss, *Human Rights* (Routledge 2005) 41.

[242] CESCR, General Comment No 19 (n 168) para 10.

[243] Susan Marks on Naomi Klein, S Marks, 'Four Human Rights Myths' (2002) LSE Law, Society and Economy Working Papers 19/2012, 1, 9.

today, and what this chapter has sought to expose, is how the robust doctrinal and practical defence of socio-economic rights—while far from ignorant of context—is nonetheless serving to entrench the tools of injustice that make necessary human rights interventions in the first place. It is true that human rights have not made enough of a difference vis-à-vis neoliberalism[244] although this unsatisfying fact is not unique to human rights;[245] capitalism is a powerful adversary given its proven ability to generate wealth and concentrate power. There is nevertheless an important distinction to be drawn between failing to confront injustice and reinforcing it; the interpretation and application of international human rights law has a foremost function under conditions of economic globalization: to ensure that its terms do not help to reproduce the violent appropriations that sustain globalization. This chapter has sought to highlight the 'help' that is taking place as part of the human rights effort and with what wider implications for a more just world.

Social protection is undoubtedly important on the basis of any standard of justice, but the recent approach to the right to social security as aligned with the ILO and SDG social protection floors buys into a construct that fails to account for and redress the arrangements that keep wealth flowing in particular directions and on the basis of particular forms of alienation, dispossession, and immiseration. Put differently, this practice of social protection addresses the dire living conditions of the most vulnerable, just as it drives the possibility of solutions to widespread alienations further and further away. In writing this chapter it has become clear that human rights have so internalized the status quo that they endorse social protection floors without challenging, at the same time or fully, the fierce means by which they will be provided for. This would include support for a conventional model of economic growth without accounting for its contradictory effects, including that it inevitably creates poverty. Moreover, for the range of reasons addressed herein, international human rights in the area of extraterritorial obligations of international cooperation does not even begin to offset those constructs through demands on the international and institutional order, demands that might open up space for transformation. While it is right to suggest that international human rights law continues to force concessions on capitalism, and indeed itself embodies some one of the most important of those concessions,[246] that is only the start of the story, not the end of it.

The coverage in this chapter fleshes out what Anthony Woodiwiss refers to as the human rights paradox: that 'human rights are intended to protect potential victims by declaring aspects of their lives sacred, but they also contribute to the continuation of the possibility of abuse by protecting some of the activities that gave rise to the same abuse'.[247] To begin the process of overcoming this paradox, it needs to be consistently exposed. Thus along with its mandate to protect the most vulnerable,

[244] Moyn (n 84) 151. Moyn attributes this to the focus on minimums at the expense of inequality.

[245] See, for example, on crisis of the left, J Roos, 'Towards a New Anti-Capitalist Politics' *Roar* (9 Dec 2015), https://roarmag.org/magazine/anti-capitalist-politics-21st-century

[246] For thoughtful considerations, see Freeman (n 32) 25–26; Macpherson (n 16).

[247] Woodiwiss (n 241).

CESCR would endorse social protection floors but it should also state that in doing so it does not necessarily endorse the means by which that redistribution is made possible. The predistributive requirements would then be the subject of a separate and related inquiry into compliance with the Covenant, including its extraterritorial dimensions.

What we have today is the wholesale subordination of the people to the economy and it is under these terms that human rights operate. The aim of human rights need not be a limited one; of limiting the effects of economic and social injustice rather than doing anything about those forms of injustice as such. However, before we probe how human rights can create more just societies, we must first expose the ways in which they are a reflection of those societies and, crucially, how they assist in reproducing the underlying terms of immiseration that will ensure human rights protection is forever necessary.

8
In Lieu of a Conclusion*

International law of the global economy is in a state of disorder. Many international lawyers will find this claim problematic. International law would seem to be functioning well from the standpoint of legal pragmatics. International law as it relates to the global economy has developed a rules-based order and legalized forms of dispute settlement. Continuing the argument, it has moved towards detailed treaties and complex forms of multilateralism in trade and towards a widespread legal regime of bilateral investment agreements with a more recent turn to regional agreements. Though soft law would seem to be the most important form that rules take in global finance, countries tend to comply with these rules by enacting domestic hard law to implement the international soft law. International human rights law, the story goes, offers needed legal assurances for protections of human welfare and the security and choices of the person. Human rights law, the story continues, is a counter-hegemonic regime that works to provide a defence against the harms of economic globalization through the implementation of socio-economic rights and human-centred development.

These claims about the benefits of legality in international economic regulation are fanciful. A more credible picture emerges when we consider who is protected, against what, and those relations that are valued and those that are not.[1] The claims above all require a suspension of a reflective attitude about what international law actually says and does. When it comes to international economic law, it masks power behind a veil of neutrality when it certainly is not neutral in the interests it protects and offends. In the case of international human rights law, there cannot be any 'neutral' application as it is wont to promise as long as it fails to recognize and respond to the ways in which it reinforces neoliberal capitalism and its attendant harms in the delivery of socio-economic rights. International economic law requires us to assume without warrant that because the rules have the status of law or the backing of official authority they must promote the best, indeed only viable, version of 'the good'. They rest on a fallacy that moves towards more treaties with more provisions that are alleged to guarantee human progress. These arguments make the well-known mistake of confusing form with substance. It should

* The title of this chapter is inspired by the title of chapter 6 in BS Chimni, *International Law and World Order* (Sage 1993).

[1] See A Woodiwiss, *Human Rights* (Routledge 2005) xiii–xiv on what lawyers can learn from a sociological reading of law.

The Misery of International Law: Confrontations with Injustice in the Global Economy, John Linarelli, Margot E Salomon, and M Sornarajah.
Published 2018 by Oxford University Press.

be obvious by now that we cannot rest our hopes for justice in international law by denying its accountability to persons whose lives it affects. Socio-economic rights for their part rest on a fallacy that they always operate *against* the alienations and dispossessions engendered by global capitalism. Here the mistake is to confuse substance with form.

Powerful states and other global actors have always shaped international law through conquests for capitalist expansion and international economic law now constitutes and sustains the terms of that expansion. There has never been 'progress' towards something better but an allocation of advantages based on the power of the actors who control the making of the law in any given historical period. The present is no different. The chapters in this book propose that serious pathologies are at work in international law today. International trade may be the subject of a greater number of rules and international agreements than ever in human history, all proffering a rationalization of aggregate welfare, but it is structured along a legacy in which power has been at its very core. The precursor of the contemporary trade agreement—a set of norms or arrangements supporting 'war capitalism'—had the global economy forcibly organized along lines that benefit the rich and powerful at the expense of others who happened to lack the means to counter the force imposed on them. Among the main methods for offsetting that legacy today are trade agreements that recognize the importance of protecting human well-being but only exceptionally. Non-market values are wrongly framed as exceptions to market rules, when in reality they are constitutive of markets. Non-reciprocity exceptions, said to support developing countries, also could be seen as representative of a way of thinking about support for developing countries in the trade law as a (failed) scheme sharing these basic defects. Robust forms of predistribution require we get the core structure of international law right in the first place. Foreign investment has made a similar move from a model based on colonial conquest to investment treaties that were ostensibly designed to balance the interests of the host state and the foreign investor and to secure economic development, but which have been easily shaped by an investor-state arbitration system to promote the interests of powerful corporations with the full force of the law. The result is that the will of domestic communities, the public interest, and democratic control is inappropriately subordinated as a matter of law. Central bankers and the financial elite have constructed the global financial architecture in a way that serves the powerful, creates instability, and produces insecurity particularly for those least able to be bear financial (systemic) risk—people who have nothing to do with the financial practices causing the risk and who often have no stake in any potential gains accumulating from these practices. This legal regime is outright dangerous to a clear majority of persons who benefit very little from it or not at all. The pillar of global finance that deals with sovereign debt and its restructuring reflects a toxic mix of the political capture of the peoples' will by international institutions, domination by creditors, and the absence of accountability for the harms they manufacture. As for socio-economic rights, they overlook the ways in which growth is fetishized including as an essential precondition of human betterment, entrenching the ravages of extreme capitalism in the name of redistribution and foreclosing the possibility of transformative change. In the area of development and extraterritorial obligations, international human rights law has been blocked from making demands on the design of the global economy precisely because of its transformative potential. This latter limitation is itself reflective of political suppression of the most radical elements that human rights law has attempted in order to avoid disturbing the beneficiaries of international economic law and its contract approach. The contract approach provides that justice is a matter for inside the state only and the agreements made outside are subject at most to very basic minimum moral demands; it insinuates that the rules at issue are determined as a matter of bargaining between states regardless of power asymmetries, and it does not require that the interests of the other party or wider public interests are taken into account. The regimes of international economic law, we argue, immiserate many of the recipients of international law, those subject to its dictates but who have no or ineffective influence over its development and no opportunity to pursue alternative routes to human fulfilment. An extreme version of capitalist relations backed by law is the norm with devastating human, economic, social, cultural, and ecological consequences. For all its claims, it is poverty, inequality, and dispossession that are the hallmarks of the global economy under international law.

If we were to reduce the defects of international law that this book deals with into a single concept it would be unaccountability. For international law, the need for accountability is unassailable. International law lacks moral legitimacy without a proper relationship of accountability. International law must be justifiable to those who are subject to it. It should not place persons in positions of economic vulnerability and social and cultural alienation, it should not enrich the few nor allow for domination by those with financial resources. If international economic law is not legitimate, then it does not deserve respect and it can hardly call for compliance with it. If international law fails to make a call for compliance with it on grounds of justice and not simply on alleged incentives, then it is epiphenomenal in its normative implications, naively idealistic in its normative logic, relevant to lawyers in what are often tautological exercises about legal concepts and the meanings of its words but dangerous in its use as a justification for harm.

The unaccountability of international economic law taints the way lawyers reason through it to reach normative prescriptions. Discussions about the content of international law of the global economy often rest on empirically unsubstantiated premises and unwarranted assumptions about the goals to be achieved. This is not about whether one is 'for' or 'against' international trade, foreign investment, or global finance. That is a false choice. The issue is to resolve how, if we are to engage in trade, investment, and finance, that we do so in a manner that is accountable to persons whose lives are affected by international law, often very substantially and negatively. This would also require that there is the possibility not to pursue trade, investment, and finance as we know it; to move beyond a domain consumed by capitalism along with the vision and privileges its neoliberal variant protects. There is a long history of international law that has led us to this point of 'displac[ing] economic justice by the law itself'.[2] Modern international law has continued along this trajectory comfortably separating out the economic from the 'non-economic' realms of institution-building and legal regulation, bringing us to the present, dire condition of the state of the world. And while it is true that international human rights law continues to force concessions on capitalism, and indeed itself embodies some of the most important of those concessions,[3] the deployment of human rights must be considered against the ubiquity of neoliberal globalization under law, and not merely as a discrete, benevolent response to it. This book explores how international law and its regimes of trade, investment, finance, but also human rights are implicated in the construction of misery; how international law is producing, reproducing, and embedding these ills and narrowing the frame of alternatives that might really serve humanity.

This is a book of critique and not of prescription. Prescription cannot be effective and will be prone to wrong answers unless the problems of international law are laid bare. The disorder of international law needs to be exposed if there is to be change for the better. Without exposure through critique, international law will remain an instrument for ideology and power rather than a system of norms and structures that truthfully make the world a better place. With this work we do not hint at great faith, but we can offer one vital message: the possibility of reconstituting the brutal world will depend on whether international law can be made to accommodate that undertaking.

[2] M Somers in Conversation with J Curtis, 'Socially Embedding the Market and the Role of Law' Series on Economics and Law in Conversation, Laboratory for Advanced Research on the Global Economy, Centre for the Study of Human Rights, LSE (Mar 2016), 13, http://www.lse.ac.uk/human-Rights/research/projects/theLab/Economics-and-Law-in-Conversation---Interview-with-Margaret-Somers-FINAL.pdf

[3] For thoughtful considerations, see M Freeman, 'Beyond Capitalism and Socialism' in J Dine and A Fagan (eds), *Human Rights and Capitalism: A Multidisciplinary Perspective on Globalisation* (Edward Elgar 2006) 3; CB Macpherson, *The Rise and Fall of Economic Justice and Other Papers* (OUP 1985).

Select Bibliography

Abi-Saab, G, 'Permanent Sovereignty over Natural Resources' in M Bedjaoui (ed), *International Law: Achievements and Prospects* (UNESCO/Martinus Nijhoff 1991) 600.

Abouharb, MR and Cingranelli, D. *Human Rights and Structural Adjustment* (CUP 2007).

Acemoglu, D and Robinson, JA. *Why Nations Fail: The Origins of Power, Prosperity & Poverty* (Profile 2013).

Acemoglu, D, Robinson, JA, and Verdier, T, 'Can't We All Be More Like Scandinavians? Asymmetric Growth and Institutions in an Interdependent World', National Bureau of Economic Research Working Paper No 18441 (Oct 2012); Massachusetts Institute of Technology Department of Economics Working Paper No 12–22 (Aug 2012).

Addo, H (ed). *Transforming the World Economy: Nine Critical Essays on the New International Economic Order* (United Nations University 1984).

Addo, H. 'Introduction: Pertinent Questions about the NIEO' in H Addo (ed), *Transforming the World Economy: Nine Critical Essays on the New International Economic Order* (United Nations University, 1984) 1.

Adenas, M and Chiu, IH-Y. *The Foundations and Future of Financial Regulation: Governance for Responsibility* (Routledge 2014).

Adler, MD. *Well-Being and Fair Distribution: Beyond Cost–Benefit Analysis* (OUP 2012).

Admati, A and Hellwig, M. 'The Parade of the Bankers' New Clothes: 31 Flawed Claims Debunked' (Dec 2015), http://bankersnewclothes.com/wpcontent/uploads/2016/01/Parade-Continues-2015.pdf.

Admati A and Hellwig, M. *The Banker's New Clothes: What's Wrong with Banking and What to Do About It* (Princeton UP 2013).

Aggarwal, VK and Evenett, SJ. 'US Trade Lobbying Strategy for the 21st Century' Harvard Business Review (5 July 2011).

Agarwala, PN. *The New International Economic Order: An Overview* (Pergamon 1982).

Akbulut, B, Adaman, F, and Madra, YM. 'The Decimation and Displacement of Development Economics' (2015) 46 Development and Change 733.

Akhtar, SI and Jones, VC. *Proposed Transatlantic Trade and Investment Partnership (TTIP): In Brief* (Congressional Research Service 2014).

Akinsanya, A and Davies, A. 'Third World Quest for a New International Economic Order' (1984) 33 International & Comparative Law Quarterly 208.

Alemanno, A. 'The Regulatory Cooperation Chapter of the Transatlantic Trade and Investment Partnership: Institutional Structures and Democratic Consequences' (2015) 18 Journal of International Economic Law 625.

Alexander, G and Penalver, E (eds). *Property and Community* (OUP 2009).

Alexander, G. *Global Debate over Constitutional Property: Lessons from American Takings Jurisprudence* (University of Chicago Press 2001).

Alfaro, L, Kalemli-Ozcan, S, and Volosovych, V. 'Why Doesn't Capital Flow from Rich to Poor Countries? An Empirical Investigation' (2005) 90 Review of Economics & Statistics 347.

Allen, T. 'Liberalism, Social Democracy and the Value of Property' (2010) 59 International & Comparative Law Quarterly 1053.

Allen, T. *The Right to Property in Commonwealth Constitutions* (CUP 2000).

Alston, P. 'Making Space for New Human Rights: The Case of the Right to Development' (1988) 1 Harvard Human Rights Year Book 3.

Alston, P. 'The Myopia of Handmaidens: International Lawyers and Globalization' (1997) 3 European Journal of International Law 435.

Alston, P. 'Resisting the Merger and Acquisition of Human Rights by Trade Law: A Reply to Petersmann' (2002) 13 European Journal of International Law 4 815.

Alston, P. *Report of the Special Rapporteur on Extreme Poverty and Human Rights* UN Doc A/69/297 (11 Aug 2014).

Alvarez, JE. 'A Bit on Custom' (2009) 42 NYU Journal of International Law and Politics 17.

Amin, S. 'Self- Reliance and the New International Economic Order' in H Addo (ed), *Transforming the World Economy: Nine Critical Essays on the New International Economic Order* (United Nations University 1984) 204.

Amin, S. *The Implosion of Capitalism* (Pluto 2014).

Amnesty International. 'This Is What We Die For', Human Rights Abuses in the Democratic Republic of the Congo Power the Global Trade in Cobalt (2016).

Amsdan, AH, Di Caprio, A, and Robinson, JA (eds). *The Role of Elites in Economic Development* (OUP 2012).

Andersen, H. 'Protection of Non-Trade Values in WTO Appellate Body Jurisprudence: Exceptions, Economic Arguments, and Eluding Questions' (2015) 18 Journal of International Economic Law 383.

Anderson, E. *Value in Ethics and Economics* (Harvard UP 1993).

Anderson, GM and Tollison, RD. 'Adam Smith's Analysis of Joint-Stock Companies' (1982) 90 Journal of Political Economy 1237.

Andreou, A. 'Alex Tsipras: Hero, Traitor, Hero, Traitor, Hero' *Byline* (13 July 2015), https://www.byline.com/column/11/article/164

Anghie, A. *Imperialism, Sovereignty and the Making of International Law* (CUP 2004).

Araghi, F. 'Accumulation by Displacement: Global Enclosures, Food Crisis, and the Ecological Contradictions of Capitalism' (2010) 34 Review: Fernand Braudel Center 113.

Araghi, F. 'The End of "Cheap Ecology" and the Crisis of "Long Keynesianism" ' (2010) 45 Economic & Political Weekly 39.

Araghi, F and Karides. M, 'Land Dispossession and Global Crisis: Introduction to the Special Section on Land Rights in the World- System' (2012) 18 Journal of World-Systems Research 1.

Autor, DA, Dorn, D, Hanson, GH, and Song, J. 'Trade Adjustment: Worker Level Evidence (2014) 129 Quarterly Journal of Economics 1799.

Avgouleas, E. *Governance of Global Financial Markets: The Law, the Economics, the Politics* (CUP 2012).

Ayres, I and Gertner, R. 'Filling Gaps in Incomplete Contracts: An Economic Theory of Default Rules' (1989) 99 Yale Law Journal 87.

Backer, LC. 'The Trans-Pacific Partnership: Japan, China, the US, and the Emerging Shape of a New World Trade Regulatory Order' (2014) 13 Washington University Global Studies Law Review 49.

Bairoch, P. *Economics and World History: Myths and Paradoxes* (University of Chicago Press 1993).

Balakrishnan, R, Elson, D, and Patel R. 'Rethinking Macroeconomic Strategies from a Human Rights Perspective' (2010) 53 Development 27.

Balakrishnan, R, Heintz, J, and Elson, D. *Rethinking Economic Policy for Social Justice: The Radical Potential of Human Rights* (Routledge 2016).

Baldwin, RE. 'The Political Economy of Trade Policy' (1989) 3 Journal of Economic Perspectives 119.
Banifitemi, Y. *Precedent in International Investment Law* (Juris 2008).
Bank of England, Financial Stability Report (Nov 2016), http://www.bankofengland.co.uk/publications/Pages/fsr/default.aspx
Barr, MS. 'Who's in Charge of Global Finance?' (2014) 45 Georgetown Journal of International Law 971.
Barry, B. *Justice as Impartiality* (OUP 1995).
Barry, C and Øverland, G. 'Are Trade Subsidies and Tariffs Killing the Global Poor?' (2012) 79 Social Research 865.
Barry, C and Pogge, TW (eds). *Global Institutions and Responsibilities* (Blackwell 2005).
Barry, C and Reddy, SJ. *International Trade and Labor Standards: A Proposal for Linkage* (Columbia UP 2008).
Barth, JR, Caprio, G Jr, and Levine, R. *Rethinking Bank Regulation: Till Angels Govern* (CUP 2008).
Baxi, U. *The Future of Human Rights* (3rd edn, OUP 2008).
Baxi, U. 'India–Europe' in Fassbender, B and Peters, A (eds), *The Oxford Handbook of the History of International Law* (OUP 2012) 744.
Baxter, LG. 'Capture of Financial Regulation: Can We Redirect It Toward the Common Good?' (2011) 21 Cornell Journal of Law and Public Policy 175.
Bean, V and Beauvais, J. 'Global Fifth Amendment' (2003) 78 New York University Law Review 30.
Beckert, S. *Empire of Cotton: A Global History* (Vintage 2015).
Behn, M, Haselmann, R, Kick, T, and Vig, V. 'The Political Economy of Bank Bailouts' (2015) Institute for Monetary and Financial Stability, University of Frankfurt. Working Paper Series 86.
Beitz, CR. *Political Theory and International Relations* (Princeton UP 1979).
Benton, L. *Law and Colonial Cultures* (CUP 2001).
Besson, S and Martí, JL (eds). *Legal Republicanism: National and International Perspectives* (OUP 2009).
Bhala, R, Gantz, DA, Keating, SB, and Simões, BS. 'WTO Case Review 2014' (2015) 32 Arizona Journal of International and Comparative Law 497.
Blackstone, W. *Commentaries on the Laws of England* (University of Chicago Press 2008).
Blake, M. *Justice and Foreign Policy* (OUP 2013).
Blake, M. 'International Law and Global Justice' in Marmor, A (ed), *The Routledge Companion to Philosophy of Law* (Routledge 2012) 335.
Blake, M. 'Coercion and Egalitarian Justice' (2011) 94 The Monist 555.
Blake, M. 'Distributive Justice, State Coercion, and Autonomy' (2001) 30 Philosophy and Public Affairs 257.
Block, F. 'Introduction' in Polanyi, K (ed), *The Great Transformation: The Political and Economic Origins of Our Time* (Beacon Press 2001 edn) xviii.
Blustein, P. 'Behind the Scenes at the IMF on a Fateful Day in the Greek Crisis' Centre for International Governance Innovation (7 July 2015), https://www.cigionline.org/blogs/global-economy/behind-scenes-imf-fateful-day-greek-crisis
Blustein, P. 'The Greek Crisis: Human Errors—And Divine Forgiveness' Centre for International Governance Innovation (20 Feb 2015), https://www.cigionline.org/articles/greek-crisis-human-errors-and-divine-forgiveness
Blyth, M. *Austerity: The History of a Dangerous Idea* (OUP 2013).
Bobbitt, P. *Terror and Consent: The Wars for the Twenty-First Century* (Penguin 2008).

Bobbitt, P. *The Shield of Achilles: War, Peace, and the Course of History* (Knopf 2002).

Bockman, J. 'Socialist Globalization against Capitalist Neocolonialism: The Economic Ideas behind the New International Economic Order' *Humanity* (Spring 2015) 109.

Bohoslavsky, JP. End of Mission Statement. UN Independent Expert on the effects of foreign debt and other related international financial obligations of states on the full enjoyment of all human rights, particularly economic, social, and cultural rights. Mission to Greece (22–26 Apr 2013).

Bohoslavsky, JP. UN Independent Expert on the effects of foreign debt and other related international financial obligations of states on the full enjoyment of all human rights, particularly economic, social, and cultural rights. End of Mission Statement: Greece. *Human Rights Pose Limits to Adjustment—Debt Relief for Inclusive Growth in Greece* (8 Dec 2015).

Bohoslavsky, JP. Report of the UN Independent Expert on the effects of foreign debt and other related international financial obligations of states on the full enjoyment of all human rights, particularly economic, social, and cultural rights: Mission to Greece UN Doc A/HRC/31/60/Add2 (29 Feb 2016).

Bohoslavsky, JP and Goldmann, M. 'An Incremental Approach to Sovereign Debt Restructuring: Sovereign Debt Sustainability as a Principle of International Law' (2016) 41 *Yale Journal of International Law* 13.

Bollyky, TJ. 'Regulatory Coherence in the Trans-Pacific Partnership Talks' in Lim, CL, Elms, D, and Low P (eds), *The Trans-Pacific Partnership: A Quest for a 21st Century Trade Agreement* (CUP 2012) 171.

Bourguignon, F. *The Globalization of Inequality* (Princeton UP 2015).

Bouveret, A. 'An Assessment of the Shadow Banking Sector in Europe' (6 July 2011), http://ssrn.com/abstract=2027007

Bowden, B. 'Civilization and Savagery in the Crucible of War' (2007) 19 Global Change, Peace & Security 3.

Bowden, B. 'The Colonial Origins of International Law: European Expansion and the Classical Standard of Civilization' (2005) 7 Journal of the History of International Law 1.

Bowen, HV. *The Business of Empire: The East India Company* (CUP 2009).

Bradlow, DD. 'Development Decision-Making and the Content of International Development Law' (2004) 27 Boston College International and Comparative Law Review 205.

Brock, G. 'Theories of Global Justice' in Linarelli, J (ed). *Research Handbook on Global Justice and International Economic Law* (Edward Elgar 2013) 1.

Brooks, S, and Lombardi, D. 'Sovereign Debt Restructuring Issues Paper' CIGI Paper No 64 (Apr 2015), https://www.cigionline.org/sites/default/files/cigi_paper_no.64web.pdf

Brownlie, I. 'The Human Right to Development' (Commonwealth Secretariat 1989) 8.

Brummer, C. *Soft Law and the Global Financial System: Rule Making in the 21st Century* (2nd edn, CUP 2015).

Brummer, C. *Minilateralism: How Trade Alliances, Soft Law and Financial Engineering Are Redefining Statecraft* (CUP 2014).

Buchanan, A. 'Rawls's Law of People: Rules for a Vanished Westphalian World' (2000) 111 Ethics 697.

Buchanan, R, Kijo- Bisimba, H and Rittich, K. 'The Evictions at Nyamuma, Tanzania: Structural Constraints and Alternative Pathways in the Struggles Over Land' in White LE and Perelman J (eds), *Stones of Hope: How African Activists Reclaim Human Rights to Challenge Global Poverty* (Stanford UP 2010) 91.

Buckley, RP. 'The Direct Contribution of the International Financial System to Global Poverty' in Schefer, KN (ed), *Poverty in the International Economic Legal System* (CUP 2013) 278.

Bull, H. 'The Importance of Grotius in the Study of International Relations' in Bull, H, Kingsbury, B and Roberts, A (eds), *Hugo Grotius and International Relations* (OUP 1992).

Burns, T. 'The Shadow Banking System as a New Source of Financial Turmoil' in Alexander, K and Dhumale, R (eds), *Research Handbook on International Financial Regulation* (Elgar 2012) 30.

Burrows, O, and Low, K. 'Mapping the UK Financial System' (2015) Q2, 55 Bank of England Bulletin 114.

Bush, O. 'Why Is the UK Banking System So Big and Is That a Problem?' (2014) Q4, 54 Bank of England Quarterly Bulletin 385.

Butt, D. *Rectifying International Injustice: Principles of Compensation and Restitution Between Nations* (OUP 2009).

Byers, M (ed). *The Role of Law in International Politics: Essays in International Relations and International Law* (OUP 2001).

Calomiris, CW, and Haber, SH. *Fragile by Design: The Political Origins of Banking Crises and Scarce Credit* (Princeton UP 2014).

Carmody, C, Garcia, FJ, and Linarelli, J (eds). *Global Justice and International Economic Law: Opportunities and Prospects* (CUP 2012).

Carney, M. 'Inclusive Capitalism: Creating a Sense of the Systemic' Governor of the Bank of England (2014), http:// www.inclusivecapitalism.org;

Carpenter, D and Moss, DA (eds). *Preventing Regulatory Capture: Special Interest Influence and How to Limit It* (CUP 2014).

Cassese, A. *International Law* (OUP 2005).

Cavallar, G. 'Vitoria, Grotius, Pufendorf, Wolff and Vattel: Accomplices of European Colonialism and Exploitation or True Cosmopolitans?' (2008) 10 *Journal of the History of International Law* 181.

Cely, N. 'Balancing Profit and Environmental Sustainability in Ecuador: Lessons Learned from the Chevron Case' (2014) 24 *Duke Environmental Law and Policy Forum* 353.

Chang, H-J. *Kicking Away the Ladder: Development Strategy in Historical Perspective* (Anthem 2002).

Chang, H-J. *Bad Samaritans: The Myth of Free Trade and the Secret History of Capitalism* (Bloomsbury 2008).

Chang, H-J in Conversation with J Curtis, 'History, Law and the Myth of Economic Neutrality' Series on Economics and Law in Conversation, Laboratory for Advanced Research on the Global Economy, Centre for the Study of Human Rights LSE (July 2016), http://www.lse.ac.uk/humanRights/research/projects/theLab/Economics-and-Law-in-Conversation---Interview-with-Ha-Joon-Chang---FINAL.pdf

Chatterjee, P. 'Foreword' (2013) in K Sanyal, *Rethinking Capitalist Development: Primitive Accumulation, Governmentality and Post- Colonial Capitalism* (Routledge 2007).

Chaudhary AS, and R Chappe, 'The Supermanagerial Reich' Los Angeles Review of Books (7 Nov 2016).

Chauffeur, JP. *The Power of Freedom: Uniting Human Rights and Development* (Cato Institute 2009).

Chimni, BS. *International Law and World Order* (Sage 1993).

Chimni, BS. 'The Principle of Permanent Sovereignty over Natural Resources: Toward a Radical Interpretation' (1998) 38(2) Indian Journal of International Law 208.

Chimni, BS. 'Third World Approaches to International Law: A Manifesto' in Anghie, A, Chimni, BS, Mickelson, K, and Okafor O (eds), *The Third World and International Order: Law, Politics and Globalization* (Brill 2003) 47.
Chimni, BS. 'International Institutions Today: An Imperial Global State in the Making' (2004) 15 European Journal of International Law 1.
Chimni, BS. 'The Past, Present and Future of International Law: A Critical Third World Approach' (2007) 8 Melbourne Journal of International Law 499.
Chimni, BS. 'An Outline of a Marxist Course on Public International Law' in S Marks (ed), *International Law on the Left: Re-examining Marxist Legacies* (CUP 2008) 53.
Claessens, S, Underhill, GRD, and Zhang, X. 'The Political Economy of Global Financial Governance: The Costs of Basel II for Poor Countries' (2008) 31 World Economy 313.
Coase, R. 'The Problem of Social Cost' (1960) 3 Journal of Law and Economics 1.
Coates, JC IV. 'Cost–Benefit Analysis of Financial Regulation: Case Studies and Implications' (2015) 124 Yale Law Journal 882.
Coggan, P. *Paper Promises: Money, Debt and the New World Order* (Allen Lane 2011).
Cohen, BJ. 'Phoenix Risen: The Resurrection of Global Finance' (1996) 48 World Politics 268.
Cohen, J and Sabel, C. 'Extra Rempublicam Nulla Justitia? (2006) 34 Philosophy and Public Affairs 147.
Cohen, J. 'Deliberation and Democratic Legitimacy' in Hamlin, A and Pettit, P (eds), *The Good Polity: Normative Analysis of the State* (Blackwell 1989), reprinted in Goodin, RE and Pettit, P (eds), *Contemporary Political Philosophy: An Anthology* (Blackwell 2006).
Copeland, BR and Taylor, MS. *Trade and the Environment: Theory and Evidence* (Princeton UP 2015).
Corten, O and Klein, P (eds). *The Vienna Conventions on the Law of Treaties: A Commentary* (OUP 2011).
Cox, RW. 'Gramsci, Hegemony and International Relations: An Essay in Method' (1983) 12 Millennium: Journal of International Studies 162.
Craig, P and de Búrca, G. *EU Law: Text, Cases, and Materials* (6th edn, OUP 2015).
Cranor, CF. 'Toward a Non-Consequentialist Approach to Acceptable Risks' in Lewens, T (ed), *Risk: Philosophical Perspectives* (Routledge 2007).
Craven, M. 'The Violence of Dispossession: Extraterritoriality and Economic, Social and Cultural Rights' in Baderin MA and McCorquodale R (eds), *Economic, Social and Cultural Rights in Action* (OUP 2007) 71.
Craven, M. 'Between Law and History: The Berlin Conference of 1884–1885 and the Logic of Free Trade' (2015) 3 London Review of International Law 31.
Crawford, J. *Chance, Order, Change: The Course of International Law* (Hague Academy of International Law 2014).
Crawford, J. *Brownlie's Principles of Public International Law* (8th edn, OUP 2012).
Crawford, J (ed). *The Rights of Peoples* (OUP 1988).
Credit Suisse, *Global Wealth Report 2013*, https://publications.credit-suisse.com/tasks/render/file/?fileID=BCDB1364-A105-0560-1332EC9100FF5C83
Crouch, C. *The Strange Non-death of Neoliberalism* (Polity 2011).
Cutler, AC. *Private Power and Global Authority: Transnational Merchant Law in the Global Political Economy* (CUP 2003).
Cutler, AC, 'New Constitutionalism and the Commodity Form of Global Capitalism' in Gill, S and Cutler, AC (eds), *New Constitutionalism and World Order* (CUP 2014) 45.
Dahl, RA. 'The Concept of Power' (1957) 2 Behavioral Science 201.

Dalhuisen, JH. *Dalhuisen on Transnational Comparative, Commercial, Financial and Trade Law* (5th edn, Hart 2013).
Daly, HE. 'Uneconomic Growth and the Illth of Nations: Defining the Optimal Scale of the Macro Economy' Beatty Memorial Lecture (McGill University, 27 Mar 2003), 35 *McGill Reporter* 13 (3 Apr 2003).
Daly, HE. 'A Foreword' in T Jackson (ed), *Prosperity without Growth: Economics for a Finite Planet* (Earthscan 2009) xii.
Daniels, N. *Just Health: Meeting Health Needs Fairly* (CUP 2008).
Daniels, N. *Just Health Care* (CUP 1985).
Darwall, S. *The Second Person Standpoint: Morality, Respect, and Accountability* (Harvard UP 2006).
Darwall, S. *Morality, Authority, and Law: Essays in Second-Personal Ethics* (OUP 2013).
Davidson, N. 'Sketches for a Hamiltonian Vernacular as a Social Function of Property' (2011) 80 Fordham Law Review 1053.
Davis, K, Fisher, A, Kingsbury, B, and SE Merry (eds). *Governance by Indicators: Global Power through Classification and Ranking* (OUP 2012).
De Grauwe, P. 'The ECB Doesn't Learn from Past Mistakes' *Ivory Tower* (16 July 2015), http://escoriallaan.blogspot.be/2015/07/in-2011-at-height-of-sovereign-debt.html
De Schutter, O. *Report of the United Nations Special Rapporteur on the Right to Food: Agribusiness and the Right to Food* UN Doc A/ HRC/13/33 (22 Dec 2009).
De Schutter, O. *Report of the Special Rapporteur on the Right to Food: Large-Scale Land Acquisitions and Leases: A Set of Minimum Principles and Measures to Address the Human Rights Challenge* UN Doc A/HRC/13/33/Add 2 (28 Dec 2009).
De Schutter, O. *The World Trade Organization and the Post-Global Food Crisis Agenda: Putting Food Security First in the International Trade System*. Briefing Note 04 (Nov 2011).
De Schutter, O, Eide, A, Khalfan, A, Orellana, M, Salomon, ME, and Seiderman, I. 'Commentary to the Maastricht Principles on Extraterritorial Obligations of States in the area of Economic, Social and Cultural Rights' (2012) 34 Human Rights Quarterly 1084.
De Schutter, O and Salomon, ME. 'Economic Policy Conditionality, Socio-Economic Rights and International Legal Responsibility: The Case of Greece 2010–2015' Legal Brief prepared for the Special Committee of the Hellenic Parliament on the Audit of the Greek Debt (15 June 2015), http://www.lse.ac.uk/humanRights/documents/2015/SalomonDeSchutterGreekDebtTruth.pdf.
Deakin, S. 'The Contribution of Labour Law to Economic Development and Growth' Centre for Business Research, University of Cambridge Working Paper No 478 (Mar 2016).
Deaton, A. *The Great Escape: Health, Wealth, and the Origins of Inequality* (Princeton UP 2013).
Desierto, DA. *Public Policy in International Economic Law: The ICESCR in Trade, Finance, and Investment* (OUP 2015).
Devereux, S and McGregor, JA. 'Transforming Social Protection: Human Wellbeing and Social Justice' (2014) 26 European Journal of Development Research 296.
Dezalay, Y and Garth, BG. *Dealing in Virtue: International Commercial Arbitration and the Construction of a Transnational Legal Order* (University of Chicago Press 1998).
Dhar, S. 'IMF Macroeconomic Policy Advice in the Financial Crisis Aftermath' (8 Oct 2014) IMF Independent Evaluation Office Background Paper, BP/14/07.
Ding, C. 'Policy and Praxis of Land Acquisition in China' (2007) 24 Land Use Policy 1.
Donnelly, J. 'In Search of the Unicorn: The Jurisprudence and Politics of the Right to Development' (1985) 15 California Western Journal of International Law 473.
Dorsch, M. 'Bailout for Sale? The Vote to Save Wall Street' (2013) 155 Public Choice 211.

Downs, GW and Jones, MA. 'Reputation, Compliance, and International Law (2002) 31 Journal of Legal Studies S94.
Draper, N. *The Price of Emancipation: Slave-Ownership, Compensation and British Society at the End of Slavery* (CUP 2013).
Dreher, A. 'A Public Choice Perspective of IMF and World Bank Lending and Conditionality' (2004) 119 Public Choice 445.
Dumberry, P. *The Formation and Identification of Rules of Customary International Law in International Investment Law* (CUP 2016).
Dunoff, J, and Trachtman, J. 'The Lotus Eaters' (Debate) in Klabbers, J, Peters, A, and Ulfstein, G (eds), *The Constitutionalization of International Law* (OUP 2011) 369.
Dworkin, R. *Sovereign Virtue: The Theory and Practice of Equality* (Harvard UP 2000).
Dworkin, R. *Justice for Hedgehogs* (Harvard UP 2011).
Dworkin, R. 'A New Philosophy for International Law' (2013) 41 Philosophy and Public Affairs 2.
Echols, MA. *Food Safety and the WTO: The Interplay of Culture, Science and Technology* (Kluwer 2001).
Eichengreen, B. *Globalising Capital: A History of the International Monetary System* (2nd edn, Princeton UP 2002).
Eide, A. 'Article 28' in G Alfredsson and A Eide (eds), *The Universal Declaration of Human Rights: A Common Standard of Achievement* (Martinus Nijhoff 1999) 597.
Elson, A. *The Global Financial Crisis in Retrospect* (Palgrave 2017).
Elson, A. *Governing Global Finance: The Evolution and Reform of the International Financial Architecture* (Palgrave 2011).
Emmerij, L, and Jolly, R. UN Intellectual History Project. Briefing Note No 17 (July 2009).
Escobar, A. *Encountering Development: The Making and Unmaking of the Third World* (Princeton UP 1995 with preface to the 2012 edn).
Escobar, A. 'Development, Critiques of' in D'Alisa, G, Demaria, F, and Kallis G (eds), *Degrowth: A Vocabulary for a New Era* (Routledge 2015) 29.
Estlund, D. 'Just and Juster' in Sobel, D, Vallentyne, P, and Wall S (eds). *Oxford Studies in Political Philosophy* Vol 2 (OUP 2016) 9.
Eurodad. *World Bank and IMF Conditionality: A Development Injustice* (Eurodad Report 2009).
European Central Bank, Financial Stability Review (Nov 2016), https://www.ecb.europa.eu/pub/fsr/html/index.en.html
European Parliament Report 2009–14 on the Inquiry on the Role and Operations of the Troika (ECB, Commission, and IMF) with regard to the Euro Area Programme Countries (2013/ 2277 (INI)), A7- 0149/ 2014 (28 Feb 2014).
European Systemic Risk Board, Flagship Report on Macroprudential Policy in the Banking Sector (Mar 2014), https://www.esrb.europa.eu/pub/pdf/other/140303_flagship_report.pdf
EU common position on the UN draft resolution A/69/L.84 on 'Basic Principles on Sovereign Debt Restructuring Processes' Council of the European Union. Cover Note 11705/15 (7 Sept 2016).
Fabrikant, R. 'Production Sharing Contracts in the Indonesian Petroleum Industry' (1975) 16 Harvard International Law Journal 303.
Fakhri, M. 'Food as a Matter of Global Governance' (2015) 11 Journal of International Law and International Relations 68.

Fassbender, B and Peters, A. 'Introduction: Towards a Global History of International Law' in Fassbender, B and Peters, A (eds), *The Oxford Handbook of the History of International Law* (OUP 2012) 2.

Feibelman, A. 'The IMF and Regulation of Cross-Border Capital Flows' (2015) 15 *Chicago Journal of International Law* 409.

Ferguson, N. *The Empire: How Britain Made the Modern World* (Allen Lane 2003).

Ferguson, N and Schularick, M. 'Chimerica and the Global Asset Market Boom' (2007) 10 International Finance 215.

Fidler, DP. 'Revolt Against or from Within the West: TWAIL, the Developing World, and the Future Direction of International Law' (2003) 2 Chinese Journal of International Law 41.

Financial Crisis Inquiry Commission, 'The Financial Crisis Inquiry Report: Final Report of the National Commission on the Causes and Consequences of the Financial and Economic Crisis in the United States' (Jan 2011), https://www.gpo.gov/fdsys/pkg/GPO-FCIC/pdf/GPO-FCIC.pdf

Fine, B. 'Entitlement Failure' 28 Development and Change (1997) 617.

Fish, S. 'Does Philosophy Matter?' New York Times (1 Aug 2011).

Fitzmaurice, A. 'Sovereign Trusteeship and Empire' (2015) 16 Theoretical Inquiries in Law 447.

Fitzmaurice, A. *Sovereignty, Property and Empire, 1500–2000* (CUP 2014).

Fleming, MJ. 'Domestic Financial Policies under Fixed and Floating Exchange Rates' (1962) 9 IMF Staff Papers 369.

Fogel, RW. *Without Consent or Contract: The Rise and Fall of American Slavery* (Norton 1989).

Foreman, A. *A World on Fire: An Epic History of Two Nations Divided* (Penguin 2011).

Forst, R. *The Right to Justification: Elements of a Constructivist Theory of Justice* (Columbia UP 2007).

Frank, AG. 'Rhetoric and Reality of the New International Economic Order' in H Addo (ed), *Transforming the World Economy: Nine Critical Essays on the New International Economic Order* (United Nations University 1984) 165.

Franck, TM. *The Power of Legitimacy Among Nations* (OUP 1990).

Franck, TM. *Fairness in International Law and Institutions* (Clarendon Press 1995)

Freeman, M. 'Beyond Capitalism and Socialism' in Dine, J and Fagan, A (eds), *Human Rights and Capitalism: A Multidisciplinary Perspective on Globalisation* (Edward Elgar 2006) 3.

Friedmann, W. *The Changing Structure of International Law* (Columbia UP 1964).

Fukuda-Parr, S. 'The 2030 Agenda and the SDGs—A Course Correction?' Sheffield Political Economy Institute SPERI Blog (30 Sept 2015), http://speri.dept.shef.ac.uk/2015/09/30/the-2030-agenda-and-the-sdgs-a-course-correction

Gaastra, FS. *The Dutch East India Company: Expansion and Decline* (Walburg Pers 2003).

Galbraith, JK. 'Recession Economics' New York Review of Books (4 Feb 1982).

Gallagher, K. 'Regulating Capital Flows for Development' *G-24 Policy Brief*, No 76 (4 July 2012).

Galston, WA. 'Realism in Political Theory' (2010) 9 European Journal of Political Theory 385.

Garcia, FJ. *Global Justice and International Economic Law: Three Takes* (CUP 2013).

Garciano, L and Lastra, RM. 'Towards a New Architecture for Financial Stability: Seven Principles' in Cottier, T, Jackson, JH, and Lastra, RM (eds), *International Law in Financial Regulation and Monetary Affairs* (OUP 2012) 72.

Gathii, JT. 'Geographical Hegelianism in Territorial Disputes Involving Non-European Land Relations: An Analysis of the Case Concerning Kasikili/Sedudu Island (Botswana/ Namibia)' (2002) 15 Leiden Journal of International Law 581.

Gathii, JT. 'Third World Approaches to International Economic Governance' in Falk, R, Rajagopal, B, and Stevens, J (eds), *International Law and the Third World: Reshaping Justice* (Routledge 2008) 255.

Gawande, K, and Hoekman, B. 'Lobbying and Agricultural Trade Policy in the United States' (2006) 60 International Organization 527.

Ghosh, J. 'From "Development" to "Poverty Alleviation": What Have We Lost?' *Frontline* (4 Sept 2015).

Gianviti, F. 'Economic, Social and Cultural Rights and the International Monetary Fund' in Philip Alston (ed), *Non-State Actors and Human Rights* (OUP 2005) 113.

Gibson, J. *Intellectual Property, Medicine and Health: Current Debates* (Routledge 2017).

Gilabert, P. 'Comparative Assessments of Justice, Political Feasibility, and Ideal Theory' (2012) 15 Ethical Theory and Moral Practice 39.

Gilabert, P. 'Global Justice and Poverty Relief in Nonideal Circumstances' (2008) 34 Social Theory and Practice 411.

Gill, S. 'Market Civilization, New Constitutionalism and World Order' in Gill, S and Cutler, AC (eds), *New Constitutionalism and World* Order (CUP 2014) 29.

Gill, S, and Cutler, AC (eds). *New Constitutionalism and World Order* (CUP 2014).

Gill, S and AC Cutler, 'New Constitutionalism and World Order: General Introduction' in S Gill and AC Cutler (eds), *New Constitutionalism and World* Order (CUP 2014) 6.

Gilman, N. 'The New International Economic Order: A Reintroduction' (2015) 6 Humanity 1.

Goldin, I. 'Divided Nations: Why Global Governance Is Failing and What We Can Do About It' LSE public lecture (20 Mar 2013), http://www.lse.ac.uk/publicEvents/events/ 2013/03/20130320t1830vHKT.aspx

Gong, G. *The Standard of Civilization in International Relations* (OUP 1984).

Gonzalez, CG. 'World Poverty and Food Security' (2015) 3 Penn State University Journal of International Law and International Affairs 56.

Gonzalez, CG. 'Trade Liberalization, Food Security, and the Environment: The Neoliberal Threat to Sustainable Rural Development' (2004) 14 Transnational Law and Contemporary Problems 419.

Gonzalez, CG. 'Institutionalizing Inequality: The WTO, Agriculture and Developing Countries' (2002) 27 Columbia Journal of Environmental Law 433.

Goodin, R. 'Political Ideals and Political Practice' (1995) 25 British Journal of Political Science 37.

Gorton, GB. 'Slapped in the Face by the Invisible Hand: Banking and the Panic of 2007' (9 May 2009), https://ssrn.com/abstract=1401882

Gorz, A, *Reclaiming Work: Beyond the Wage-based Society* (Polity 1999).

Graeber, D. *Debt: The First 5,000 Years* (Melville House 2011).

Gramsci, A. *Selections from the Prison Notebooks*, ed and trans Hoare, Q and Nowell Smith, G (Lawrence & Wishart 1971).

Grant, W. 'The Politics of Agricultural Trade' in Cardwell, M, Grossman, MT, and Rodgers, CP. *Agriculture and International Trade: Law, Policy and the WTO* (CABI 2003) 49.

Gready, P. 'Reasons to Be Cautious about Evidence and Evaluation: Rights-based Approaches to Development and the Emerging Culture of Evaluation' (2009) 1 Journal of Human Rights Practice 380.

Griffiths, J. *Politics of the Judiciary* (Fontana 1997).
Griffin, J. *On Human Rights* (OUP 2008).
Gros Espiell, H. 'Community- Oriented Rights: Introduction' in Bedjaoui, M (ed), *International Law: Achievements and Prospects* (Martinus Nijhoff 1991) 1167.
Grossman, GM and Helpman, E. *Interest Groups and Trade Policy* (Princeton UP 2002).
Grotius, H. *De Jure Praedae Commentaries*, ed and introduction by van Ittersum, MJ (Liberty Fund 2006).
Grotius, H. *De Jure Belli Ac Pacis*, ed and introduction by Tuck, R (Liberty Fund 2005).
Group of Thirty, Enhancing Financial Stability and Resilience: Macroprudential Policy, Tools, and Systems for the Future (Oct 2010), http://group30.org/images/uploads/publications/G30_ EnhancingFinancialStabilityResilience.pdf
Gruber, L. *Ruling the World: Power Politics and the Rise of Supranational Institutions* (Princeton UP 2000).
Gutto, SBO. 'Violation of Human Rights in the Third World: Responsibility of States and TNCs' in Snyder, FE and Sathirathai, S (eds), *Third World Attitudes Toward International Law: An Introduction* (Martinus Nijhoff 1987).
Guzman, AT. 'Reputation and International Law' (2006) 34 Georgia Journal of International and Comparative Law 379.
Guzman, AT. 'A Compliance Based Theory of International Law' (2002) 90 California Law Review 1823.
Guzman, AT. 'Why LDCs Sign Treaties That Hurt Them: Explaining the Popularity of Bilateral Investment Treaties' (1998) 38 Virginia Journal of International Law 639.
Guzman, M, Ocampo, JA, and Stiglitz, JE (eds), *Too Little, Too Late: The Quest to Resolve Sovereign Debt Crises* (Columbia UP 2016).
Guzman, M and Stiglitz, JE. 'Creating a Framework for Sovereign Debt Restructuring that Works' in Guzman, M, Ocampo, JA, and Stiglitz, JE (eds), *Too Little, Too Late: The Quest to Resolve Sovereign Debt Crises* (Columbia UP 2016) 3.
Hacker, JS. *Winner Take All Politics* (Simon & Schuster 2011).
Hacker, JS. 'The Institutional Foundations of Middle-Class Democracy' (2011) Progressive Governance (Oslo).
Hafner-Brown, EM, Victor, DG, and Lupu, Y. 'Political Science Research on International Law: The State of the Field' (2012) 106 American Journal of International Law 47.
Hall, RB and Biersteker, TJ. *The Emergence of Private Authority in Global Governance* (CUP 2010).
Halper, S. *The Beijing Consensus: Legitimising Authoritarianism in Our Time* (reprinted edn, Basic 2012).
Hamdani, K and Ruffing, L. *United Nations Centre on Transnational Corporations: Corporate Conduct and the Public Interest* (Routledge 2015).
Hamlin, A and Stemplowska, Z. 'Theory, Ideal Theory, and the Theory of Ideals' (2012) 10 Political Studies Review 48.
Harrison, J. 'The Case for Investigative Legal Pluralism in the International Economic Law Linkages Debate: A Strategy for Enhancing International Legal Discourse' (2014) 1 London Review of International Law 115.
Hart, J. *The New International Economic Order: Conflict and Cooperation in North–South Relations, 1974–77* (Palgrave Macmillan 1983).
Harvey, D. *The New Imperialism* (OUP 2003).
Harvey, D. *A Brief History of Neoliberalism* (OUP 2007).
Hasenpflug, K and Sauvant, H (eds). *The New International Economic Order: Confrontation or Cooperation Between North and South?* (Wilton House 1977).

Held, D and Young, K. 'The World Crisis: Global Financial Governance: Principles of Reform' LSE Ideas (2009).

Helfer, LR. 'Exiting Treaties' (2005) 91 Virginia Law Review 1579.

Helleiner, E. *States and the Reemergence of Global Finance: From Bretton Woods to the 1990s* (Cornell UP 1994).

Hearing of the Special Committee of the Hellenic Parliament on the Audit of the Greek Debt: Panagiotis Roumeliotis, 15 June 2015. (On file with authors.)

Henckels C. *Proportionality and Deference in Investor-State Arbitration* (CUP 2015).

Hendrix, B. 'Where Should We Expect Social Change in Non-Ideal Theory?' (2013) 41 Political Theory 116.

Henisz, WJ, Zelner, BA, and Guillén, MF. 'International Coercion, Emulation and Policy Diffusion: Market-Oriented Infrastructure Reforms' (2005) 70 American Sociological Review 871.

Hernandez, R. 'The Internationalization of Francisco de Vitoria and Domingo de Soto' (1991) 15 Fordham International Law Journal 1031.

Herndon, T, Ash, M, and Pollin, R. 'Does High Public Debt Consistently Stifle Economic Growth? A Critique of Reinhart and Rogoff' (2014) 38 Cambridge Journal of Economics 257.

Hersch, S. *The Price of Power: Kissinger in the White House* (Summit Books 1983).

Herz, S. 'Rethinking International Financial Institution Immunity' in Bradlow, DD and Hunter, D, *International Financial Institutions and International Law* (Kluwer 2010) 137.

Hickel, J. 'The True Extent of Global Poverty and Hunger: Questioning the Good News Narrative of the Millennium Development Goals' (2016) 37 Third World Quarterly 749.

Hickey, S. 'Relocating Social Protection within a Radical Project of Social Justice' (2014) 26 European Journal of Development Research 322.

Hirshl, R. *Towards Juristocracy: The Origins and Consequences of New Constitutionalism* (Harvard UP 2004).

Ho, DE. 'Compliance and International Soft Law: Why Do Countries Implement the Basle Accord?' (2002) 5 Journal of International Economic Law 647.

Hobbes, T. in MacPherson CB (ed). *Leviathan* (Penguin 1968).

Horn, H, Maggi, G, and Staiger, RW. 'The GATT/WTO as an Incomplete Contract' (2010) 100 American Economic Review 394.

Hossain, K, and Chowdhury, SR (eds). *Permanent Sovereignty Over Natural Recourses in International Law* (St Martin's Press 1995).

Hossein, K (ed). *Legal Aspects of the New International Economic Order* (Francis Pinter 1980).

Hossain, K. *Law and Policy in Petroleum Development: Changing Relations Between Transnationals and States* (Nichols Publishing 1979).

Howse, R, *Climate Mitigation Subsidies and the WTO Legal Framework: A Policy Analysis*, International Institute for Sustainable Development (May 2010).

Howse, R, 'Democracy, Science, and Free Trade: Risk Regulation on Trial at the World Trade Organization' (2000) 98 *Michigan Law Review* 2329.

Howse, R and Langille, J. 'Permitting Pluralism: The Seal Products Dispute and Why the WTO Should Accept Trade Restrictions Justified by Noninstrumental Moral Values' (2012) 37 Yale Journal of International Law 367.

Howse, R. 'Concluding Remarks in Light of International Law' in Esposito, C, Li, Y, and Bohoslavsky, JP (eds), *Sovereign Financing and International Law: The UNCTAD Principles on Responsible Sovereign Lending and Borrowing* (OUP 2013) 385.

Howse, R, Langille, J, and Sykes, K. 'Pluralism in Practice: Moral Legislation and the Law of the WTO After Seal Products' (2015) 48 George Washington International Law Review 81.

Hudec, RE. *Developing Countries in the GATT Legal System* (with an introduction by JM Finger) (CUP 2011).

Hujo, K and Koehler, G. 'Beyond 2015: The Sustainable Development Agenda from Inspiration to Action' Brief 06 (UNRISD Sept 2015).

Humphries, S. *The Theatre of the Rule of Law: Transnational Legal Intervention in Theory and Practice* (CUP 2010).

Hurrell, A. 'International Law and the Changing Constitution of International Society' in Byers, M (ed), *The Role of Law in International Politics: Essays in International Relations and International Law* (OUP 2001) 327.

Hyman, R. 'Markets, Crouch and Neo-liberalism: Praising with Faint Damns?' (2012) 10 Socio-Economic Review 610.

Igan, D and Mishra, P. 'Three's Company: Wall Street, Capitol Hill, and K Street (2014) 57 Journal of Law and Economics 1063.

ILO. *Report of the Social Protection Floor Advisory Group: For a Fair and Inclusive Globalization* (ILO 2011).

Igan, D, Mishra, P, and Tressel, T. 'A Fistful of Dollars: Lobbying and the Financial Crisis' NBER Working Paper No 17076 (May 2011). *IMF Working Paper* 09/287.

IMF. Greece: Letter of Intent, Memorandum of Economic and Financial Policies (15 Mar 2012).

IMF. The IMF's Annual Report 2010: Supporting Balanced Global Recovery, http://www.imf.org/external/pubs/ft/ar/2010/eng/pdf/ar10_eng.pdf

Independent Evaluation Office. *IMF and Social Protection* (IMF Independent Evaluation Office 2017).

Independent Evaluation Office. *The IMF and the Crisis in Greece, Ireland, and Portugal: An Evaluation* (IMF Independent Evaluation Office 2016).

International Monetary Fund, Global Financial Stability Report (Oct 2016), https://www.imf.org/external/pubs/ft/gfsr/2016/02

International Monetary Fund, 'The Fund's Role Regarding Cross-Border Capital Flows' (15 Nov 2010).

Jackson, JH. *The Jurisprudence of the GATT and the WTO: Insights on Treaty Law and Economic Relations* (CUP 2000)

Jakab, Z and Kumhof, M. 'Banks Are Not Intermediaries of Loanable Funds—And Why This Matters' Bank of England Working Paper No 529 (May 2015).

James, A. *Fairness in Practice: A Social Contract for a Global Economy* (OUP 2012).

James, D. 'Investing in Agriculture in Developing Countries: The World Says Yes, But the WTO Says No' *Alternet* (31 Mar 2015), http://www.alternet.org/world/investing-agriculture-developing-countries-whole-world-says-yes-wto-says-no

James, KR. 'The Case for Narrow Banking' (2007), http://www.bcb.gov.br/Pec/seminarios/SemMetInf2007/Port/KevinJames.pdf

Jones, E. 'The Right to Trade: A Mechanism for Revitalising Pro-Development WTO Negotiations?' (2013) 99 Commonwealth Trade Topics.

Jubb, R. 'Tragedies of Non-Ideal Theory' (2012) 11 European Journal of Political Theory 229.

Kadri, A. 'Lab Views, Laboratory for Advanced Research on the Global Economy Interview 3' Centre for the Study of Human Rights LSE (July 2014), http:// www.lse.ac.uk/human-Rights/documents/projects/LABViewsKadri.pdf

Kadri, A. 'The Islamic World and Capitalism: Military Routs, Not Formal Institutions' in Reinert, ES, Ghosh, J, and Kattel R (eds), *Handbook of Alternative Theories of Economic Development* (Edward Elgar 2016) 161.

Kadri, A. 'Development Under Uncertainty in the Arab World' SPEAK OUT at the Laboratory for Advanced Research on the Global Economy, Centre for the Study of Human Rights, LSE (June 2016).

Kahneman, D, and Tversky, A. 'Choices, Values, and Frames' (1984) 34 American Psychologist 341.

Kant, I. 'Toward Perpetual Peace: A Philosophical Project' in *Kant Practical Philosophy* (trans Gregor, M, CUP 1999).

Kay, J. 'Narrow Banking: The Reform of Banking Regulation' (2009), http://www.johnkay.com/wp-content/uploads/2009/12/JK-Narrow-Banking.pdf

Keal, P. '"Just Backward Children:" International Law and the Conquest of Non-European Peoples' (1995) 49 Australian Journal of International Affairs 191.

Kearney, RD and Dalton, RE. 'The Treaty on Treaties' (1970) 64 American Journal of International Law 495.

Keay, J. *The Honourable Company: A History of the English East India Company* (Harper Collins 1993).

Keefe, PR. 'Reversal of Fortune' *New Yorker* (9 Jan 2012).

Kennedy, D. 'Introduction: International Symposium on the International Legal Order' (2003) 16 Leiden Journal of International Law 839.

Kennedy, D. 'The Role of Law in Economic Thought: Essays on the Fetishism of Commodities' (1985) 34 American University Law Review 939.

Kenney, D and Southwick, JD. *The Political Economy of International Trade Law: Essays in Honor of Robert E Hudec* (CUP 2002).

Kennedy, RF. Remarks at the University of Kansas, JFK Presidential Library and Museum (18 Mar 1968), http://www.jfklibrary.org/Research/Research-Aids/Ready-Reference/RFK-Speeches/ Remarks-of-Robert-F-Kennedy-at-the-University-of-Kansas-March-18-1968.aspx

Kentikelenis, A, Stubbs, T, and King, L. 'IMF Conditionality and Development Policy Space 1985– 2014' (2016) Review of International Political Economy 1.

Khalfan, A. 'Accountability Mechanisms' in Langford, M, Scheinin, M, van Genugten, W and Vandenhole, W (eds), *Global Justice, State Duties: The Extra-Territorial Scope of Economic, Social and Cultural Rights in International Law* (CUP 2013).

Khwaja, A, and Mian, A. 'Rent Seeking and Corruption in Financial Markets' (2011) 3 Annual Review of Economics 579.

Kindleberger, CP and Aliber, RZ. *Manias, Panics, and Crashes: A History of Financial Crises* (6th edn, Palgrave 2011).

Kingsbury, B. 'Sovereignty and Inequality' (1998) 9 European Journal of International Law 599.

Kingsbury, B, Krisch, N, and Stewart, RB. 'The Emergence of Global Administrative Law' (2005) 68 Law and Contemporary Problems 15.

Klabbers, J. 'Setting the Scene' in J Klabbers, A Peters, and G Ulfstein (eds), *The Constitutionalization of International Law* (OUP 2011) 1.

Knight, F. 'Memorandum on Banking Reform' Franklin D Roosevelt Presidential Library, Personal File 431 (Mar 1933).

Knox, R. 'Marxism, International Law, and Political Strategy' (2009) 22 Leiden Journal of International Law 413.

Kodres, LE. 'What Is Shadow Banking?' (2013) 50 Finance and Development 42.

Komlik O (on William Vickery, 1998). 'Get Free from the Dogmas of the Apostles of Austerity: Fifteen Fatal Fallacies of Financial Fundamentalism' Economic Sociology and Political Economy (15 Aug 2015), https://economicsociology.org/2015/08/15/get-free-from-the-dogmas-of-the-apostles-of-austerity-fifteen-fatal-fallacies-of-financial-fundamentalism

Kono, DY. 'Optimal Obfuscation: Democracy and Trade Policy Transparency' (2006) 100 American Political Science Review 369.

Koskenniemi, M. *From Apology to Utopia: The Structure of International Legal Argument* (Finnish Lawyers' Publication Co 1989).

Koskenniemi, M. *The Gentle Civilizer of Nations: The Rise and Fall of International Law 1870–1960* (CUP 2001).

Koskenniemi, M. *Epilogue: From Apology to Utopia: The Structure of International Legal Argument* (CUP 2005).

Koskenniemi M et al. Report of the Study Group of the International Law Commission, 'Fragmentation of International Law: Difficulties Arising from the Diversification and Expansion of International Law' International Law Commission, 58th session, General Assembly, A/CN.4/L.682 (13 Apr 2006).

Koskenniemi, M. 'The Politics of International Law—20 Years Later' (2009) 20 European Journal of International Law 7.

Koskenniemi, M. 'What Is International Law For?' in Evans, MD (ed), *International Law* (3rd edn, OUP 2010) 32.

Koskenniemi, M. *The Politics of International Law* (Hart 2011).

Koskenniemi, M. 'What is Critical Research in International Law: Celebrating Structuralism' (2016) 29 Leiden Journal of International Law 727.

Kostovetsky, L. 'Political Capital and Moral Hazard' (2015) 116 Journal of Financial Economics 144.

Krasner, SD. 'International Law and International Relations: Together, Apart, Together? (2000) 1 Chicago Journal of International Law, Article 10.

Krasner, SD. 'Power Structures and Regional Development Banks' (1981) 35 International Organization 303.

Krueger, AO. 'The Political Economy of the Rent-Seeking Society' (1974) 64 American Economic Review 291.

Kukathas, C. 'The Mirage of Global Justice' in Frankel Paul, E, Miller, FD, and Paul, J (eds), *Justice and Global Politics* (CUP 2006).

Kurian, R. 'Lab Views, Laboratory for Advanced Research on the Global Economy Interview 2' Centre for the Study of Human Rights LSE (Mar 2014), http://www.lse.ac.uk/human-Rights/documents/projects/LABViewsKurian.pdf

Lall, R. 'From Failure to Failure: The Politics of International Banking Regulation (2012) 19 Review of International Political Economy 609.

Lamarche, L. 'Unpacking the ILO Social Protection Floor Recommendation from a Women's Rights Perspective' in B Goldblatt and L Lamarche (eds), *Women's Rights to Social Security and Social Protection* (Hart 2014) 65.

Lang, A. 'Trade Agreements, Business and Human Rights: The Case of Export Processing Zones' (Apr 2010) Working Paper No 57.

Lang, A. *World Trade Law After Neoliberalism: Re-imagining the Global Economic Order* (OUP 2011).

Langford, M, Scheinin, M, van Genugten, W, and Vandenhole W (eds). *Global Justice, State Duties: The Extra-Territorial Scope of Economic, Social and Cultural Rights in International Law* (CUP 2013).

Lasswell, HD, and Kaplan, A. *Power and Society: A Framework for Political Inquiry* (Yale UP 1950).
Lastra, RM. 'Systemic Risk and Macro-Prudential Supervision' in Moloney, N, Ferran, E, and Payne, J (eds), *The Oxford Handbook of Financial Regulation* (OUP 2015).
Lastra, RM. 'Do We Need a World Financial Organisation?' (2014) 17 Journal of International Economic Law 787.
Laszlo, E and Kurtzman, J (eds). *Political and Institutional Issues of the New International Economic Order* (Pergamon 1981).
Lavinas, L. '21st Century Welfare' 84 *New Left Review* (Nov–Dec 2013).
Law, DS. Globalization and the Future of Constitutional Rights (2008) 102 Northwestern University Law Review 1277.
Lawson, P. *The East India Company: A History, 1600–1857* (Routledge 1993).
Layard, R. *Happiness: Lessons from a New Science* (Allen Lane 2005)
Lazzarato, M. *Governing by Debt* (JD Jordan tr, semiotext(e) 2013).
Lessig, L. *Republic Lost: 2.0* (rev edn, Twelve 2015).
Lester, S. 'Applying Public Choice Theory to Trade Negotiations and Agreements' draft working paper (10 May 2016), http://law.unimelb.edu.au/__data/assets/pdf_file/0005/1954139/Lester,-Public-Choice.pdf
Levitin, AJ. 'Safe Banking: Finance and Democracy' (2016) 83 University of Chicago Law Review 62.
Lewis, MK. 'The Trans-Pacific Partnership: New Paradigm or Wolf in Sheep's Clothing? (2011) 34 Boston College International and Comparative Law Review 27.
Lim, CL. '"The Law Works Itself Pure"; The Fragmented Disciplines of Global Trade and Monetary Cooperation, and the Chinese Currency Problem' in Lim, CL and Mercurio, B (eds), *International Economic Law after the Global Crisis: A Tale of Fragmented Disciplines* (CUP 2015) 134.
Lim, CL and Mercurio, B (eds). *International Economic Law after the Global Crisis: A Tale of Fragmented Disciplines* (CUP 2015).
Lim, CL. 'The Conventional Morality of Trade' in Carmody, C, Garcia, FJ, and Linarelli, J. *Global Justice and International Economic Law: Opportunities and Prospects* (CUP 2102) 129.
Linarelli, J. 'Analytical Jurisprudence and the Concept of Commercial Law' (2009) 114 Penn State University Law Review 119.
Linarelli, J. 'The Limited Case for Permitting SME Procurement Preferences in the WTO Agreement on Government Procurement' in Arrowsmith, S, and Anderson, RD (eds), *The WTO Regime on Government Procurement: Challenge and Reform* (CUP 2011).
Linarelli, J (ed). *Research Handbook on Global Justice and International Economic Law* (Edward Elgar 2013).
Linarelli, J. 'Concept and Contract in the Future of International Law' (2015) 67 Rutgers University Law Review 61.
Linarelli, J. 'Luck, Justice, and Systemic Financial Risk' (2017) 34 Journal of Applied Philosophy 331.
Lindblom, CE. 'The Market as Prison' (1982) 44 Journal of Politics 324.
Lines, T. *Making Poverty: A History* (Zed Books 2008)
Litan, R. 'The Political Economy of Financial Regulation after the Crisis' in Blinder, AS, Lo, AW, and Solow, RM (eds), *Rethinking the Financial Crisis* (Russell Sage 2012).
Locke, J. *Second Treatise of Government* (Hackett 1980).
Lohmann, L. 'Marketing and Making Carbon Dumps: Commodification, Calculation and Counterfactuals in Climate Change Mitigation' (2005) 14 Science as Culture 203.

Loriaux, S and Herwig, A. 'International Trade, Fairness, and Labour Migration' (2014) 1 Moral Philosophy and Politics 1.

Lowenfeld, AF. *International Economic Law* (2nd edn, OUP 2008).

Lowenfeld, AF. 'The International Monetary System and the Erosion of Sovereignty: Essay in Honor of Cynthia Lichtenstein' (2002) 25 Boston College International and Comparative Law Review 257.

Lovell, J. *Opium Wars: Drugs, Dreams and the Making of China* (Picador 2012).

Lovett, F. *A General Theory of Domination and Justice* (OUP 2010).

Lovett, F. 'What Counts as Arbitrary Power? (2012) 5 Journal of Political Power 137.

Lucas, R. 'Why Doesn't Capital Flow from Rich to Poor Countries?' (1990) 80 American Economic Review 92.

Lysandrou, P and Nesvetailova, A. 'The Role of Shadow Banking Entities in the Financial Crisis: A Disaggregated View' (2015) 22 Review of International Political Economy 257.

Maastricht Principles on Extraterritorial Obligations of States in the Area of Economic, Social and Cultural Rights (2011).

Macklem, P. 'Human Rights in International Law: Three Generations or One?' (2015) 3 London Review of International Law 1.

Macmillan, F. 'The World Trade Organization and the Turbulent Legacy of International Economic Law-Making in the Long Twentieth Century' in Faundez, J and Tan, C (eds), *International Law, Economic Globalization and Development* (Edward Elgar 2010) 170.

Macpherson, CB. *The Rise and Fall of Economic Justice and Other Papers* (OUP 1985).

Magdoff, F. 'Multiple Crises as Symptoms of an Unsustainable System' (2010) 33(2/3) Review: Fernand Braudel Center (Special Issue on Food, Energy, Environment: Crisis of the Modern World System) 103.

Magdoff, F and J Bellamy Foster, 'What Every Environmentalist Needs to Know about Capitalism' (2010) 61 Monthly Review, http://monthlyreview.org/2010/03/01/what-every-environmentalist-needs-to-know-about-capitalism.

Maggi, G and Staiger, RW. 'The Role of Dispute Settlement Procedures in International Trade Agreements' (2011) 126 Quarterly Journal of Economics 475.

Mandelbaum, M. *The Ideas that Conquered the World: Peace, Democracy and Free Markets in the Twenty First Century* (Public Affairs 2002).

Mansfield, ED and Milner, HV. *Votes, Vetoes, and the Political Economy of International Trade Agreements* (Princeton UP 2012).

Mantouvalou, V. 'Are Labour Rights Human Rights?' (2012) 3 *European Labour Law Journal* 151.

Marx, K. *Capital* (new edn, Penguin 1990).

Mason, E. 'Value Pluralism' Zalta, EN (ed), *Stanford Encyclopedia of Philosophy* (summer 2015 edn), http://plato.stanford.edu/archives/sum2015/entries/value-pluralism

Marks, S. 'Naming Global Administrative Law' (2005) 37 New York University Journal of International Law and Politics 995.

Marks, S. 'Exploitation as an International Legal Concept' in Marks, S (ed), *International Law on the Left: Re-examining Marxist Legacies* (CUP 2008) 281.

Marks, S. 'Human Rights and the Bottom Billion' (2009) 1 European Human Rights Law 37.

Marks, S. 'Human Rights and Root Causes' 74 Modern Law Review 1 (2011) 57.

Marks, S. 'Four Human Rights Myths' LSE Law, Society and Economy Working Papers 10/2012, 1.

Marks, SP. 'Emerging Human Rights: A New Generation for the 1980s?' (1981) 33 Rutgers Law Review 435.

Mattli, W and Woods, N (eds). *The Politics of Global Regulation* (Princeton UP 2009).

Maupin, J. 'MFN-based Jurisdiction in Investor-State Arbitration: Is There Any Hope for a Consistent Approach?' (2011) 14 *Journal of International Economic Law* 157.

Maurer, N. *The Empire Trap: The Rise and Fall of US Intervention to Protect American Property Overseas* (Princeton UP 2013).

Mazzucato, M. *The Entrepreneurial State: Debunking Public v Private Sector Myths* (Anthem 2015).

McCarty, N, Poole, KT, and Rosenthal, H. *Political Bubbles: Financial Crises and the Failure of American Democracy* (Princeton UP 2012).

McCarty, N, Poole, KT, Romer, T, and Rosenthal, H. 'Political Fortunes: On Finance and its Regulation' (2010) 139 Daedulus 61.

McCrudden, C. *Buying Social Justice: Equality, Government Procurement and Legal Change* (OUP 2007).

McKinsey Global Institute, *Debt and Deleveraging: The Global Credit Bubble and Its Economic Consequences* (July 2011).

McKinsey Global Institute. *Debt and Deleveraging: Uneven Progress on the Path to Growth* (Jan 2012).

McKinsey Global Institute. *Debt and (Not Much) Deleveraging* (Feb 2015).

McKinsey Global Institute. *Financial Globalization: Retreat or Reset?* (Mar 2013).

McLachlan, C, Shore, L, and Weineger, M. *International Investment Arbitration: Substantive Principles* (OUP 2008).

Meltzer, JP. 'From the Trans-Pacific Partnership to a Free Trade Agreement of the Asia-Pacific?' (5 May 2015), http://www.brookings.edu/blogs/future-development/posts/2015/05/05-tpp-trade-meltzer

Mercuro, N and Medema, SG. *Economics and the Law: From Posner to Postmodernism and Beyond* (2nd edn, Princeton UP 2006).

Merry, SE. 'Measuring the World: Indicators, Human Rights and Global Governance' (2011) 52 Current Anthropology 83.

Mian, A, and Sufi, A. *House of Debt* (University of Chicago Press 2014).

Mian, A, Sufi, A, and Trebbi, F. 'The Political Economy of the Subprime Mortgage Credit Expansion' (2013) 8 Quarterly Journal of Political Science 373.

Mian, A, Sufi, A, and Trebbi, F. 'The Political Economy of the US Mortgage Default Crisis' (2010) 100 American Economic Review 1967.

Michaels, R and Pauwelyn, J. 'Conflict of Norms or Conflicts of Law? Different Techniques in the Fragmentation of Public International Law' in Broude, T, and Shany, Y (eds), *Multi-Source Equivalent Norms in International Law* (Hart 2010) 19.

Miéville, C. 'The Commodity-Form Theory of International Law' in Marks, S (ed), *International Law on the Left: Re-examining Marxist Legacies* (CUP 2008) 92.

Milanovic, B. *Global Inequality: A New Approach for the Age of Globalization* (Harvard U Press 2016).

Milanovic, B. 'Global Income Inequality' in Ehrenpreis, D (ed), *The Challenge of Inequality* (UN Development Programme, International Poverty Centre 2007).

Miller, RW. *Globalizing Justice: The Ethics of Poverty and Power* (OUP 2010).

Mills, CW. '"Ideal Theory" as Ideology' (2005) 20 Hyapatia 165.

Moyn, S. 'A Powerless Companion: Human Rights in the Age of Neoliberalism' (2014) 77(4) Law and Contemporary Problems 147.

Mody, A. 'Saving the IMF' *Project Syndicate* (9 Apr 2016), https://www.project-syndicate.org/onpoint/saving-the-imf-by-ashoka-mody-2016-04

Mody, A. 'Wolfgang Schauble, Debt Relief and the Future of the Eurozone' Bruegel Blog (6 Aug 2015), http://bruegel.org/2015/08/wolfgang-schauble-debt-relief-and-the-future-of-the-eurozone

Mooney, CW Jr. 'A Framework for a Formal Sovereign Debt Restructuring Mechanism: The KISS Principle (Keep It Simple, Stupid) and Other Guiding Principles' (2015) 37 Michigan Journal of International Law 57.

Moore, HL. 'Global Prosperity and Sustainable Development Goals' (2015) 27 Journal of International Development 801.

Mouyal, LM. *International Investment Law and the Right to Regulate: A Human Rights Perspective* (Routledge 2016).

Muchlinski, P. 'Holistic Approaches to Development and International Investment Law: The Role of International Investment Agreements' in Faundez, J and Tan, C (eds), *International Law, Economic Globalization and Development* (Edward Elgar 2010) 186.

Mundell, R. 'Capital Mobility and Stabilization Policy under Fixed and Flexible Exchange Rates' (1963) 29 Canadian Journal of Economic and Political Science 475.

Nagaraj, VK. 'Global Human Rights: For Futures Unlike the Past' openDemocracy (31 July 2013), http://www.opendemocracy.net/openglobalrights/vijay-nagaraj/global-human-rights-for-futures-unlike-past

Nagel, T. 'The Problem of Global Justice' (2005) 33 Philosophy and Public Affairs 113.

Nardin, T. 'International Ethics and International Law' (1992) 18 Review of International Studies 19.

Nardin, T. *Law, Morality and the Relations of States* (Princeton UP 1983).

Nawaz, T. *New International Economic Order: A Bibliography* (Greenwood Press 1980).

Neff, SC. *Justice Among Nations: A History of International Law* (Harvard UP 2014).

Nel, P. 'The Rise and Fall of BITs', www.otago.ac.nz/politics/otago061036.pdf

Ngai, P and Chan, J. 'Global Capital, the State, and Chinese Workers: The Foxconn Experience' (2012) 38 Modern China 383.

Nixon, R. *Slow Violence and the Environmentalism of the Poor* (Harvard UP 2011).

Norberg, J. 'American and European Protectionism is Killing Poor Countries and Their People' (25 Aug 2003), http://www.cato.org/publications/commentary/american-european-protectionism-is-killing-poor-countries-their-people

Nozick, R. 'Coercion' in Morganbesser, S, Suppes, P, and White M (eds), *Philosophy, Science, and Method: Essays in Honour of Ernst Nagel* (St Martin's Press 1969) 440.

Nussbaum, MC. 'Perfectionist Liberalism and Political Liberalism' (2011) 39 Philosophy and Public Affairs 3.

Oberg, M. 'The Legal Effects of Resolutions of the UN Security Council and the General Assembly' (2005) 16 European Journal of International Law 880.

Obstfeld, M. 'Trilemmas and Trade-offs: Living with Financial Globalisation' BIS Working Papers No 480 (Jan 2015).

Obstfeld, M, and Taylor, AM. *Global Capital Markets: Integration, Crisis, and Growth* (CUP 2005).

Obstfeld, M and Taylor, AM. 'Globalization and Capital Markets' in Bordo, MD, Taylor, AM, and Williamson JG (eds), *Globalization in Historical Perspective* (University of Chicago Press 2003) 121.

Ocampo, JA. 'The Case for Regulating Cross-Border Capital Flows' International Monetary Fund Macro Conference, https://ideas.repec.org/h/mtp/chapts/026201761x-16.html

Oldham, J. *English Common Law in the Age of Mansfield* (University of North Carolina Press 2004).

Oldham, J. 'New Light on Mansfield and Slavery' (1988) 27 Journal of British Studies 45.

O'Neill, O. 'Abstraction, Idealization and Ideology in Ethics' (1987) 20 Royal Institute of Philosophy Series 55.

Orakhelashvili, A. 'The 19th-Century Life of International Law' in Orakhelashvili, A (ed), *Research Handbook on the Theory and History of International Law* (Edward Elgar 2011) 441.

Orford, A. 'Beyond Harmonization: Trade, Human Rights and the Economy of Sacrifice' (2005) 18 Leiden Journal of International Law 179.

Orford, A. 'Food Security, Free Trade, and the Battle for the State' (2015) 11 Journal of International Law and International Relations 1.

Outlanders, M. 'Why Is the German Homeownership Rate So Low?' (2009) 24 Housing Studies 355.

Overseas Development Institute Briefing Paper. *The Global Financial Crisis: Poverty and Social Protection* (Aug 2009).

Oxfam. 'Wealth: Having It All and Wanting More' Oxfam Issue Briefing (Jan 2015), https://www.oxfam.org/sites/www.oxfam.org/files/file_attachments/ib-wealth-having-all-wanting-more-190115-en.pdf

Özsu, U. 'In the Interests of Mankind as a Whole: Mohammed Bedjaoui's New International Economic Order' (2015) Humanity 129.

Pagden, A. *The Burdens of Empire: 1539 to the Present* (CUP 2015).

Pagnattaro, MA. 'Labor Rights are Human Rights: Direct Action is Critical in Supply Chains and Trade Policy' (2013) 10 South Carolina Journal of International Law and Business 1.

Pahuja, S. *Decolonising International Law: Development, Economic Growth and the Politics of Universality* (CUP 2011).

Partnoy, F and Skeel, D Jr. 'The Promise and Perils of Credit Derivatives' (2007) 75 University of Cincinnati Law Review 1019.

Pashukanis, EB. *Law and Marxism: A General Theory* (1929, Ink Links trans 1978).

Pashukanis, EB. 'International Law' in Beirne, P and Sharlet, R (eds), *Pashukanis: Selected Writings on Marxism and Law* (trans Maggs PB, Academic Press 1980) 168.

Patnaik, P. 'The Accumulation Process in the Period of Globalisation' (2008) 43 Economic & Political Weekly 108.

Patnaik, P. 'A Left Approach to Development' (2010) 45 Economic & Political Weekly 33.

Peel, J. *Science and Risk Regulation in International Law* (CUP 2010).

Peerenbom, R. *China's Long March Towards the Rule of Law* (CUP 2007).

Pettit, P. *Republicanism* (OUP 1997).

Phillips, M. 'Reflections on the Transition from Ideal to Non-Ideal Theory' (1985) 19 Nous 551.

Pierce, JR, and Schott, PK. 'The Surprisingly Swift Decline of US Manufacturing Employment' (Apr 2015 draft), http://faculty.som.yale.edu/peterschott/files/research/papers/pierce_schott_pntr_512.pdf.

Piketty, T. *Capital in the Twenty-First Century* (trans Goldhammer, A, Harvard UP 2014).

Piketty, T. *Chronicles on Our Troubled Times* (trans Ackerman, S, Viking 2016).

Pils, E. 'Voice, Reflexivity and Say: Governing Access to and Control of Land in China' in De Schutter, O and Pistor, K (eds), *Governing Access to Essential Resources* (Columbia UP 2015) 127.

Pistor, K. 'A Legal Theory of Finance' (2013) 41 Journal of Comparative Economics 315.

Plato. 'The Republic' in Cooper, JM (ed), *Plato, Complete Works* (Hackett 1997).

Pogge, TW. 'Cosmopolitanism and Sovereignty' (1992) 103 Ethics 48.

Pogge, TW and Reddy, SG. 'How Not to Count the Poor' (29 Oct 2005), https://ssrn.com/abstract=893159

Pogge, TW. 'Growth and Inequality: Understanding Recent Trends and Political Choices' (2008) 55(1) Dissent 66.
Pogge, TW. *World Poverty and Human Rights* (2nd edn, Polity 2008).
Polanyi, K. *The Great Transformation: The Political and Economic Origins of Our Time* (Beacon 1944).
Porras, IM. 'European Origins, the Doctrine of Provident Function of Commerce, and International Law's Embrace of Economic Growth' (2013) 107 ASIL Proceedings 374.
Porras, IM. 'Constructing Sovereignty in the East Indian Seas: Property, Sovereignty, Commerce and War' (2006) 31 Brooklyn Journal of International Law 741.
Posner, EA. 'How Do Bank Regulators Determine Capital Adequacy Requirements?' (2015) 82 University of Chicago Law Review 1853.
Postema, GJ. *Legal Philosophy in the Twentieth Century: The Common Law World, Vol 11* (Springer 2011).
Poulsen, Skovgaard LN. *Bounded Rationality and Economic Diplomacy: The Politics of Investment Treaties in Developing Countries* (CUP 2014).
Pozsar, Z, Adrian, T, Ashcraft, A, and Boesky, H. 'Shadow Banking' (2013) 19 Economic Policy Review, http://ssrn.com/abstract=2378449
Prasad, ES, Rogoff, K, Wei, SJ, and Kose, MA. *Effects of Financial Globalization on Developing Countries Some Empirical Evidence* (IMF 2003).
Prashad, V. *The Poorer Nations: A Possible History of the Global South* (Verso 2014).
Puig, S. 'Social Capital in the Arbitration Market' (2014) 25 European Journal of International Law 387.
Purvis, N. 'Critical Legal Studies in International Law' (1991) 32 Harvard International Law Journal 81.
Raikka, J. 'The Feasibility Condition in Political Theory' (1998) 6 Journal of Political Philosophy 27.
Rajagopal, B. *International Law from Below: Development, Social Movements and Third World Resistance* (CUP 2003).
Rajan, RG. *Fault Lines: How Hidden Fractures Still Threaten the Global Economy* (Princeton UP 2010).
Ramirez, SA. 'Taking Economic Human Rights Seriously after the Debt Crisis' (2011) 42 Loyola University Chicago Law Journal 713.
Rasmussen, KB. *Foreign Economic Policy 1973–1976* (US GPO 2009).
Ratner, SR. *The Thin Justice of International Law: A Moral Reckoning of the Law of Nations* (OUP 2015).
Rawls, J. *Lectures on the History of Political Philosophy* (Harvard UP 2007).
Rawls, J. *Political Liberalism* (2nd edn, Columbia UP 2005).
Rawls, J. *The Law of Peoples* (Harvard UP 2001).
Rawls, J. *A Theory of Justice* (rev edn, Harvard UP 1999).
Raz, J. *The Authority of Law* (2nd edn, OUP 2009).
Reich, R. *Saving Capitalism: For the Many, Not the Few* (Icon 2016).
Reid, E. *Balancing Human Rights, Environmental Protection and International Trade: Lessons from the EU Experience* (Hart 2014).
Reinhart, CM and Rogoff, KS. *This Time Is Different: Eight Centuries of Financial Follies* (Princeton UP 2009).
Reinisch, A and Wurm, J. 'International Financial Institutions before National Courts' in Bradlow, DD and Hunter, D (eds), *International Financial Institutions and International Law* (Kluwer 2010) 103.
Ricks, M. *The Money Problem* (University of Chicago Press 2016).

Rigod, B. *Optimal Regulation and the Law of International Trade: The Interface between the Right to Regulate and WTO Law* (CUP 2015).

Risse, M. *On Global Justice* (Princeton UP 2015).

Rittich, K. 'The Future of Law and Development: Second-Generation Reforms and the Incorporation of the Social' in Trubek DM and Santos, A (eds), *The New Law and Economic Development: A Critical Appraisal* (CUP 2006) 203.

Rittich, K. 'Governing by Measuring: The Millennium Development Goals in Global Governance' in Buchanan, R and Zumbansen, P (eds), *Law in Transition: Human Rights, Development and Transitional Justice* (Hart 2014) 165.

Robeyns, I. 'Ideal Theory in Theory and Practice' (2008) 34 Social Theory and Practice 341.

Robins, N. *The Corporation That Changed the World: How the East India Company Shaped the Modern Multinational* (2nd edn, Pluto 2012).

Rodgers, G, Lee, E, Swepston, L, and Van Daele, J. *The International Labour Organization and the Quest for Social Justice, 1919–2009* (Cornell UP/ILO 2009).

Rodrik, D. *The Globalization Paradox* (OUP 2012).

Rodrik, D. 'The Globalization Dilemma and the Way Out' (2012) 47 Indian Journal of Industrial Economics 393.

Rodrik, D and Subramanian, A. 'Why Did Financial Globalization Disappoint?' (2009) 56 *IMF Staff Papers* 112.

Rolland, SE. *Development at the WTO* (OUP 2012).

Roos, J. 'Towards a New Anti-Capitalist Politics' *Roar Magazine*, https://roarmag.org/magazine/anti- capitalist-politics-21st-century

Roth, BR. 'Marxian Insights for the Human Rights Project' in Marks S (ed), *International Law on the Left: Re-examining Marxist Legacies* (CUP 2008) 220.

Rothkop, D. *Power Inc.: The Epic Rivalry between Government and Big Business* (Farrar 2013).

Rowden, R. *The Deadly Ideas of Neoliberalism: How the IMF Has Undermined Public Health and the Fight against AIDS* (Zed 2009).

Ruckert, A. 'Towards an Inclusive-Neoliberal Regime of Development: From the Washington Consensus to the Post-Washington Consensus' (2006) 39 Labour, Capital and Society 36.

Ruggie, JG. 'International Regimes, Transactions, and Change: Embedded Liberalism in the Postwar Economic Order' (1982) 36 International Organization 379.

Ruggie, JG. Report of the UN Special Representative of the Secretary-General, Guiding Principles on Business and Human Rights: Implementing the United Nations 'Protect, Respect and Remedy' Framework (A/HRC/17/31) (2011).

Ruggie, JG. 'The Past as Prologue? A Moment of Truth for UN Business and Human Rights Treaty' IHBR Commentary, Kennedy School of Government, Harvard University (July 2014).

Saad-Filho, A. 'Social Policy for Neoliberalism: The Bolsa Familia Programme in Brazil' (2015) 46 Development and Change 1227.

Sacerdoti, G. 'New International Economic Order (NIEO)' *Max Planck Encyclopaedia of Public International Law* (June 2014).

Sachs, JD. 'Developing Country Debt' in Feldstein, M (ed), *International Economic Cooperation* (University of Chicago Press 1988).

Saenz, C. 'Republicanism: An Unattractive Version of Liberalism' (2008) 7 Ethics 267.

Sagafi-Nejad, T. *The United Nations and Transnational Corporations: From Code of Conduct to Global Compact* (Indiana UP 2008).

Salomon, ME. *Global Responsibility for Human Rights: World Poverty and the Development of International Law* (OUP 2007).

Salomon, ME. 'Poverty, Privilege and International Law: The Millennium Development Goals and the Guise of Humanitarianism' (2008) 51 *German Yearbook of International Law* 39.

Salomon, ME. 'Why Should It Matter That Others Have More: Poverty, Inequality and the Potential of International Human Rights Law' (2011) 5 *Review of International Studies* 2137.

Salomon, ME. 'The Future of Human Rights' (2012) (Special Issue on International Law, Human Rights and the Global Economy: Innovations and Expectations for the 21st Century, Guest editor Salomon, ME) 4 Global Policy 455.

Salomon, ME. 'Deprivation, Causation and the Law of International Cooperation' in Langford, M, Scheinin, M, van Genugten, W, and Vandenhole W (eds), *Global Justice, State Duties: The Extra-Territorial Scope of Economic, Social and Cultural Rights in International Law* (CUP 2013).

Salomon, ME. 'From NIEO to Now and the Unfinishable Story of Economic Justice' (2013) 62 International and Comparative Law Quarterly 31.

Salomon, ME. 'How to Keep Promises: Making Sense of the Duty among Multiple States to Fulfil Socio- Economic Rights in the World' in Nollkaemper, A and Jacobs, D (eds), *Distribution of Responsibilities in International Law* (CUP 2014) 366.

Salomon, ME, 'You Say You Want a Revolution: Challenges of Market Primacy for the Human Rights Project' in Vandenhole, W (ed), *Challenging Territoriality in International Human Rights Law: Building Blocks for a Plural and Diverse Duty-Bearer Regime* (Routledge 2015) 188.

Salomon, ME and Arnott C. 'Better Development Decision-Making: Applying International Human Rights Law to Neoclassical Economics' (2014) 32 Nordic Journal of Human Rights 44.

Salomon, ME. 'Of Austerity, Human Rights and International Institutions' (2015) 21 European Law Journal 521.

Samuels, A. 'The Epicenter of American Equality' *The Atlantic* (23 Sept 2016).

Sandel, M. *What Money Can't Buy: The Moral Limits of Markets* (Penguin 2013).

Sands, P, and Klein, P. *Bowett's Law of International Institutions* (5th edn, Sweet & Maxwell 2001).

Sarfaty, GA. 'Why Culture Matters in International Institutions: The Marginality of Human Rights at the World Bank' (2009) 103 American Journal of International Law 647.

Sassen, S. *Territory, Authority, Rights: From Medieval to Global Assemblages* (Princeton UP 2006).

Saul, B, Kinley, D, and Mowbray, J. *The International Covenant on Economic, Social and Cultural Rights: Commentary, Cases and Materials* (OUP 2014).

Sauvant, KP. 'Negotiations of the United Nations Code of Conduct on Transnational Corporations: Experiences and Lessons Learned' (2015) 16 Journal of World Investment and Trade 11.

Sauvant, KP and Sachs, LE (eds). *The Effect of Treaties on Foreign Direct Investment: Bilateral Investment Treaties, Double Taxation Treaties, and Investment Flows* (OUP 2009).

Scanlon, TM. *What We Owe to Each Other* (Harvard UP 1998).

Schachter, O. 'The Evolving International Law of Development' (1976) 15 Columbia Journal of Transnational Law 1.

Schachter, O. 'The Invisible College of International Lawyers' (1977) 72 Northwestern Law Review 217.

Schill, S. *The Multilateralization of International Investment Law* (CUP 2009).

Schill, S (ed). *International Investment Law and Comparative Public Law* (OUP 2010).

Schill, S, and Bray, H. 'Good Faith Limitations on Protected Investments and Corporate Restructuring' in Mitchell, AD, Sornarajah, M, and Voon, T (eds), *Good Faith and International Economic Law* (OUP 2015).

Schneiderman, D. *Constitutionalizing Economic Globalization: Investment Rules and Democracy's Promise* (CUP 2008).

Schneiderman, D. *Resisting Economic Globalization* (Palgrave, 2013).

Schneiderman, D. 'How to Govern Differently: Neo-liberalism, New Constitutionalism and International Investment Law' in Gill, S and Cutler, AC (eds), *New Constitutionalism and World* Order (CUP 2014) 165.

Schreuer, C. 'Fair and Equitable Treatment in Arbitral Practice' (2005) 6 Journal of World Investment and Trade 357.

Schrijver, N. *Sovereignty over Natural Resources: Balancing Rights and Duties* (CUP 1997).

Schuh, GE. 'Developing Country Interests in WTO Agricultural Economic Policy' in Kenney, D and Southwick, JD (eds), *The Political Economy of International Trade Law: Essays in Honor of Robert E Hudec* (CUP 2002) 435.

Schularick, M. 'A Tale of Two Globalisations: Capital Flows from Rich to Poor in Two Eras of Global Finance' (2006) 11 International Journal of Finance and Economics 339.

Schularick, M. 'The End of Financial Globalisation 3.0' *Economists' Voice* (Jan 2010).

Schularick, M and Steger, TM. 'Financial Integration, Investment, and Economic Growth: Evidence from Two Eras of Financial Globalisation' (2010) 92 Review of Economics and Statistics 756.

Schwarcz, S. 'Systemic Risk' (2008) 97 Georgetown Law Journal 193.

Scott, H. 'Regulating Systemic Risk through the Reform of Capital Regulation' in Cottier, T, Jackson, JH, and Lastra, RM. *International Law in Financial Regulation and Monetary Affairs* (OUP 2012) 222.

Sell, SK. *Private Power, Public Law: The Globalisation of Intellectual Property Rights* (CUP 2003).

Sen, A. *The Idea of Justice* (Penguin 2010).

Sen, A. *Development as Freedom* (Anchor 1999).

Sengupta, A. UN Independent Expert on the Right to Development, 4th Report UN Doc E/CN.4/2002/WG.18/2, 20 Dec 2001.

Shea, D. *The Calvo Clause: A Problem of Inter-American and International Law and Diplomacy* (University of Minnesota Press 1955).

Shell, GR. 'Trade Legalism and International Relations Theory: An Analysis of the World Trade Organization' (1995) 44 Duke Law Journal 829.

Sher, G. *Approximate Justice: Studies in Ideal Theory* (Rowman & Littlefield 1997).

Simmons, AJ, 'Ideal and Nonideal Theory' (2010) 38 Philosophy and Public Affairs 5.

Simmons, B, Dobbin, F, and Garrett, G (eds). *The Global Diffusion of Markets and Democracy* (CUP 2007).

Simmons, BA. 'The Legalization of International Monetary Affairs' (2000) 54 International Organization 573.

Slaughter, AM. *A New World Order* (Princeton UP 2004).

Sloane, B. *United Nations General Assembly Resolutions in Our Changing World* (Transnational 1991).

Slobodian, Q. 'Ordoglobalism: The Invention of International Economic Law', Scales of Economy Conference, University of Sydney (July 2016), https://www.academia.edu/28283843/Ordoglobalism_The_Invention_of_International_Economic_Law.

Smith, EF. 'From Concessions to Service Contracts' (1992) 27 Tulsa Law Journal 493.

Somers, M in Conversation with Curtis, J 'Socially Embedding the Market and the Role of Law' Series on Economics and Law in Conversation, Laboratory for Advanced Research on the Global Economy, LSE (Mar 2016).

Sornarajah, M. 'Power and Justice in International Law' (1997) 1 Singapore Journal of International and Comparative Law 28.

Sornarajah, M. 'A Law for Need or a Law for Greed? Restoring the Lost Law in the International Law on Foreign Investment' (2006) 6 International Environmental Agreements: Politics, Law and Economics 329.

Sornarajah, M. 'The Return of the NIEO and the Retreat of Neoliberalism in International Law' in Bhuiyan, S, Sands, P, and Schrijver, N (eds), *International Law and Developing Countries: Essays in Honour of Kamal Hossein* (Brill 2013) 32.

Sornarajah, M. *Resistance and Change in the International Law on Foreign Investment* (CUP 2015).

Sornarajah, M. 'On Fighting for Global Justice: The Role of the Third World International Lawyer' (2016) 37 Third World Quarterly 197.

Sornarajah, M. *International Law on Foreign Investment* (4th edn, CUP 2017).

Sparks, SA. 'The Quest for Policy Space in a New Generation of International Investment Agreements' (2010) 13 Journal of International Economic Law 1037.

Spence, J. *The Search for Modern China* (Norton 2013).

Stark, BJ. 'What's Left? A Review of "International Law on the Left" by Susan Marks' (2010) 42 George Washington International Law Review 191.

Stein, JV. 'Do Treaties Constrain or Screen? Selection Bias and Treaty Compliance' (2005) 99 American Political Science Review 611.

Steinberg, R, and Zasloff, JM. 'Power and International Law' (2006) 100 American Journal of International Law 64.

Stemplowska, Z. 'What's Ideal about Ideal Theory?' (2008) 34 Social Theory and Practice 319.

Stiglitz, JE. 'Foreword' in Polanyi, K (ed), *The Great Transformation: The Political and Economic Origins of our Time* (Beacon Press 2001 edn) vii.

Stiglitz, JE. *The Roaring Nineties: A New History of the World's Most Prosperous Decade* (Norton 2003).

Stiglitz, JE. 'The Global Crisis, Social Protection and Jobs' (2009) 148 International Labour Review 1.

Stiglitz, JE, Sen, A, and Fitoussi, J-P. *Mismeasuring Our Lives: Why GDP Doesn't Add Up* (New Press 2010).

Stiglitz, JE. *The Price of Inequality* (Princeton UP 2013).

Stiglitz, JE. *The Great Divide* (Allen Lane 2015).

Stiglitz, JE and Charlton, A. 'The Right to Trade: A Report for the Commonwealth Secretariat on Aid for Trade' (Aug 2012).

Streeck, W. 'The Crisis of Democratic Capitalism' (2011) 71 New Left Review 5.

Streeck, W. *Buying Time: The Delayed Crisis of Democratic Capitalism* (trans Camiller, P, Verso 2014).

Streeck, W. *How Will Capitalism End?: Essays on a Failing System* (Verso 2016).

Stuckler, D and Basu, S. *The Body Economic: Eight Experiments in Economic Recovery from Iceland to Greece* (Penguin 2013).

Sumner, DA. 'Picking on the Poor: How US Agricultural Policy Hurts the Developing World' *American Boondoggle: Fixing the 2012 Farm Bill* (American Enterprise Institute 2012).

Swift, A. 'The Value of Philosophy in Nonideal Circumstances' (2008) 34 Social Theory and Practice 363.

Tamanaha, BZ. 'Understanding Legal Pluralism: Past to Present, Local to Global' (2008) 30 Sydney Law Review 378.
Tan, C. 'Mandating Rights and Limiting Mission Creep: Holding the World Bank and the International Monetary Fund Accountable for Human Rights Violations' (2008) 2 *Human Rights and International Legal Discourse* 1.
Tepperman, J. 'Brazil's Anti-Poverty Breakthrough: The Surprising Success of Bolsa Família' (Jan–Feb 2016) 95 Foreign Affairs 34.
The Impact of the Crisis on Fundamental Rights across the Member States of the EU, Study for the LIBE Committee Directorate-General for Internal Policies (2015).
The Preliminary Report of the Hellenic Parliament on the Audit of the Greek Debt (2015), http://cadtm.org/IMG/pdf/Report.pdf
Thomas, A. *Republic of Equals: Predistribution and Property-Owning Democracy* (OUP 2017).
Thomas C. 'Where Is the Third World Now?' (1999) 25 *Review of International Studies* 225.
Tienhaara, K. *The Expropriation of Environmental Governance: Protecting Foreign Investors at the Expense of Public Policy* (CUP 2009).
Titi, C. *The Right to Regulate in International Investment Law* (Nomos/Hart 2014).
Tolokonnikova, N and Žižek, S. *Comradely Greetings: The Prison Letters of Nadya and Slavoj* (Verso 2014).
Tomasi, J. *Free Market Fairness* (Princeton UP 2012).
Trachtman, JP. 'Legal Aspects of a Poverty Agenda at the WTO: Trade Law and "Global Apartheid"' (2003) 6 Journal of International Economic Law 3.
Trachtman, JP. *The International Economic Law Revolution and the Right to Regulate* (Cameron May 2005).
Trachtman, JP. *The Economic Structure of International Law* (Harvard UP 2008).
Trachtman, JP. 'Developing Countries, the Doha Round, Preferences, and the Right to Regulate' in Thomas, C and Trachtman, JP (eds), *Developing Countries in the WTO Legal System* (OUP 2009).
Trachtman, JP. *The Future of International Law: Global Government* (CUP 2013).
Trebilcock, MJ, Howse, R, and Eliason, A. *The Regulation of International Trade* (4th edn, Routledge 2013).
Trebilcock, MJ and Mota Prado, M. *Advanced Introduction to Law and Development* (Edward Elgar 2014).
Trebilcock, MJ and Pue, K. 'The Puzzle of Agricultural Exceptionalism in International Trade Policy' (2015) 18 Journal of International Economic Law 233.
Tuck, R. *The Rights of War and Peace: Political Thought and the International Order from Grotius to Kant* (OUP 2001).
Tucker, P. 'Regimes for Handling Bank Failures: Redrawing the Banking Social Contract' British Bankers' Association Annual International Conference (30 June 2009).
Tucker, P. 'Macroprudential Policy at the Bank of England' *Quarterly Bulletin* 2013 Q3, http://www.bankofengland.co.uk/publications/Documents/quarterlybulletin/2013/qb130301.pdf
Tullock, G. 'The Welfare Costs of Tariffs, Monopolies, and Theft' (1967) 5 Western Economic Journal 224.
Turner, A. *Between Debt and the Devil: Money, Credit, and Fixing Global Finance* (Princeton UP 2016).
Tushnet, M. 'The Inevitable Globalization of Constitutional Law' (2009) 49 Virginia Journal of International Law 985.
UN Food and Agriculture Organization. *The Future of Food Agriculture: Trends and Challenges* (FAO 2017).

UN OHCHR. Background Paper, 'Promoting a Rights-based Approach to Economic, Stabilization, Recovery and Growth' (OHCHR 2013).
UN. Report of the High-Level Panel on Threats, Challenges and Change. A More Secure World: Our Shared Responsibility UN Doc A/59/565 (2004).
UN. Report of the High-Level Task Force on the Implementation of the Right to Development UN Doc A/HRC/15/WG.2/TF/2/Add 1, 6th session (25 Mar 2010).
UN. Report of the Secretary-General. In Larger Freedom: Towards Development, Security and Human Rights for All UN Doc A/59/2005.
UNDP. Human Development Report 2005: International Cooperation at a Crossroads: Aid, Trade and Security in an Unequal World (UNDP 2005).
Valentini, L. 'On the Apparent Paradox of Ideal Theory' (2009) 17 Journal of Political Philosophy 332.
Van Harten, G. 'Five Justifications for Investment Treaties: A Critical Discussion' (2010) 2 Trade Law and Development 19.
Van der Walt, AJ. *Constitutional Property Clauses: A Comparative Analysis* (Kluwer 1999).
Varoufakis, Y. 'Commentary to the 3rd Memorandum of Understanding between the European Commission Acting on Behalf of the European Stability Mechanism and the Hellenic Republic and the Bank of Greece' (11 Aug 2015).
Varoufakis Y. *And The Weak Suffer What They Must?: Europe, Austerity and the Threat to Global Stability* (Vintage 2016).
Varoufakis, Y. *Adults in the Room: My Battle with Europe's Deep Establishment* (Bodley Head 2017).
Vascianne, S. 'The Fair and Equitable Standard in International Investment Law and Practice' (1999) 70 British Yearbook of International Law 99.
Ville, F de, Orbie, J, and Van den Putte, L. TTIP and Labour Standards. European Parliament, Directorate-General for Internal Policies, IP/A/EMPL/2015-07 (June 2016).
Vinuales, J. *Foreign Investment and the Environment in International Law* (CUP 2012).
Viterbo, A. *International Economic Law and Monetary Measures: Limitations to States' Sovereignty and Dispute Settlement* (Edward Elgar 2012).
Vitoria, F de. *De Indis* (1532).
Vogel, D and Swinnen, JFM. *Transatlantic Regulatory Cooperation: The Shifting Roles of the EU, the US and California* (Edward Elgar 2011).
Wade, RH. 'What Strategies Are Viable for Developing Countries Today: The World Trade Organization and the Shrinking of "Development Space"' (2003) 10 Review of International Political Economy 621.
Wade, RH, and Wolf M [debate]. 'Are Global Poverty and Inequality Getting Worse?' in Held, D and McGrew, A (eds), *The Global Transformations Reader* (2nd edn Polity 2003) 441.
Wade, RH. 'Income Inequality: Should We Worry About Global Trends?' (2011) 23 European Journal of Development Research 513.
Wade, RH. 'Capitalism and Democracy at Cross-Purposes' (2013) 28 New Zealand Sociology 208.
Waibel, M (ed). *The Backlash against Investment Arbitration* (Kluwer 2010).
Walde, TM. 'Transnational Investment in the Natural Resources Industries' (1979) 11 Law and Policy in International Business 691.
Waldron, J. 'Superseding Historic Injustice' (1992) 103 Ethics 4.
Waldron, J. 'International Law: A "Relatively Small and Unimportant" Part of Jurisprudence?' in Duarte D'Almeida, L, Edwards, J, and Dolcetti, A (eds), *Reading HLA Hart's 'The Concept of Law'* (Hart 2013) 209.

Walter, A. 'Emerging Countries and Basel III: Why Is Engagement Still Low?' Centre for International Governance Innovation, New Thinking and the New G20 Series, Paper No 4 (13 Mar 2015).

Walzer, M. *Spheres of Justice: A Defense of Pluralism and Equality* (Basic 1984).

Weber, RH. 'Does Financial Law Suffer from a Systemic Failure? A Study of the Fragmentation of Legal Sources' in Lim, CL and Mercurio, B (eds), *International Economic Law after the Global Crisis: A Tale of Fragmented Disciplines* (CUP 2015) 35.

Way, S-A. *Human Rights from the Great Depression to the Great Recession: The United States, 'Western' Liberalism and the Shaping of Economic and Social Rights in International Law.* PhD in progress (London School of Economics and Political Science, 2018).

Weeks, JF. *Economics of the 1%* (Anthem Press 2014).

Weller, M and Hohmann, J (eds). *The UN Declaration on the Rights of Indigenous Peoples: A Commentary* (OUP 2017).

Wenar, L. *Blood Oil: Tyrants, Violence, and the Rules That Run the World* (OUP 2016).

Wertheimer, A. *Coercion* (Princeton UP 2014).

Wiens, D. 'Prescribing Institutions without Ideal Theory' (2012) 20 Journal of Political Philosophy 45.

Williams, B. *In the Beginning Was the Deed: Realism and Moralism in Political Argument* (Princeton UP 2005).

Williams, E. *Capitalism and Slavery* (André Deutsch 1944).

Williams, RA. *The American Indian in Western Legal Thought. The Discourses of Conquest* (OUP 1990).

Williamson, J. 'A Short History of the Washington Consensus 1' in Serra, N and Stiglitz, JE (eds), *The Washington Consensus Reconsidered* (OUP 2008) 14.

Wills, JJ. The World Turned Upside Down? A Critical Enquiry into the Counter-Hegemonic Potential of Socioeconomic Rights Praxis in Global Civil Society. PhD thesis, School of Law, University of Leicester (Jan 2014). (*Contesting World Order: Socioeconomic Rights and Global Justice Movements* (CUP 2017)).

Wise, TA. 'Feeding the World: The Ultimate First World Conceit' *Triple Crisis* (18 July 2015), http://triplecrisis.com/feeding-the-world-the-ultimate-first-world-conceit

Wolff, J and de-Shalit, A. *Disadvantage* (OUP 2013).

Woodiwiss, A. *Human Rights* (Routledge 2005).

Wouters, J and Odermatt, J. 'Are All International Organizations Created Equal?' (2012) 9 International Organizations Law Review 8.

Yancy, G and Mills, C. 'Lost in Rawlsland' *New York Times* (16 Nov 2014).

Yen, TH. *The Interpretation of Investment Treaties* (Brill 2014).

Young, IM. *Responsibility for Justice* (OUP 2011).

Young, IM. 'Responsibility and Global Justice: A Social Connection Model' (2006) 23 Social Philosophy and Policy 102.

Young, K. 'Empirical Examination of Transnational Lobbying Over the Basel Committee on Banking Supervision' (2012) 19 Review of International Political Economy 1

Ypi, Y. 'On the Confusion between Ideal and Non-ideal in Recent Debates in Global Justice (2010) 58 Political Studies 536

Zaretsky, R. 'What Would Thucydides Say About the Crisis in Greece?' *New York Times* (1 July 2015).

Zimmer, MJ. 'Inequality, Individualized Risk, and Insecurity' (2013) Wisconsin Law Review 1.

Zimmerman, CD. *A Contemporary Concept of Monetary Sovereignty* (OUP 2013).
Zimmerman, CD. 'The Concept of Monetary Sovereignty Revisited' (2013) 24 European Journal of International Law 797.
Zucman, G. *The Hidden Wealth of Nations: The Scourge of Tax Havens* (University of Chicago Press 2015).

Index

The manufacturer's authorised representative in the EU for product safety is Oxford University Press España S.A. of El Parque Empresarial San Fernando de Henares, Avenida de Castilla, 2 - 28830 Madrid (www.oup.es/en or product.safety@oup.com). OUP España S.A. also acts as importer into Spain of products made by the manufacturer.
Printed and bound by CPI Group (UK) Ltd, Croydon, CR0 4YY
14/09/2026
02216306-0008